A PROLOGUE TO REVOLUTION

The Political Career of George Grenville (1712-1770)

Allen S. Johnson

University Press of America, Inc.
Lanham • New York • London

Copyright © 1997 by
University Press of America,® Inc.
4720 Boston Way
Lanham, Maryland 20706

3 Henrietta Street
London, WC2E 8LU England

Library of Congress Cataloging-in-Publication Data

Johnson, Allen S.
A prologue to revolution : the political career of George Grenville
(1712-1770) / Allen S. Johnson.
p. cm.
Includes bibliographical references and index.
1. Grenville, George, 1712-1770. 2. United States--History--
Revolution, 1775-1783--Causes. 3. Great Britain--Politics and
government--1727-1760. 4. Great Britain--Politics and government--
1760-1789. 5. Prime ministers--Great Britain--Biography. I. Title.
Da50l-G73J64 1996   941.07'092--dc21   96-44589 CIP

ISBN 0-7618-0600-8 (pbk: alk. ppr.)

For Leigh, Amy, Cindy and Vince

TABLE OF CONTENTS

LIST OF ILLUSTRATIONS

PREFACE

Whenever historians have sat down to apportion the blame for the American Revolution, a major share has usually been laid upon the shoulders of George Grenville (1712-1770), who was King George III's First Minister from 1763 to 1765. Grenville has also been designated one of the evil geniuses of the attack on English liberty of the press which centered about John Wilkes. A large selection of his papers was published in 1853, but for a century and a third no historian undertook his biography or even a detailed study of his political career. Only one has appeared to this date, that by Phillip Lawson published by Oxford University Press in 1984. This paucity of attention to what is an important historical character may be difficult to explain—unless, as has sometimes been asserted, a biographer must be in full sympathy with his subject. Perhaps no historian has felt he could be in full sympathy with Grenville. But the historian may sympathize without either praising or condoning; one may recognize shortcomings without loss of interest or liking.

This study makes no pretense to being a biography; it is intended solely as the history of a career in politics. None of the family life or personal history of Grenville has been included except what was felt to have a direct bearing on the political story. Military affairs, foreign affairs, and even the general political scene have been subordinated to the central narrative, which concentrates only on those aspects of politics in which Grenville was immediately concerned. Some of the main ideas of the study are summed up in the Conclusion.

Two matters of mechanics seem to require explanation. In quoting from manuscript material, the original spelling has been retained without the use of *sic* except in cases of obvious slips of the pen. I have followed the example of most writers and editors of papers of the period in revising the punctuation of some passages to conform with modern usage. This has seemed particularly necessary in many cases in order to make the sense of a passage clear when it is quoted out of context. A brief description of the manuscripts collections used will be found in the bibliography. Dates before September 2, 1752, when the British Empire adopted the Gregorian calendar, have been set down in the Old Style; all after September 14, 1752 are in the New Style, except that in every case the beginning of the year is assigned to January 1.

I wish to express my appreciation to at least a few of those to whom I owe obligations. To the National Trust and the Right Honourable Earl of Egremont I owe thanks for permission to use the prints of portraits of George Grenville by Sir Joshua Reynolds and the second Earl of Egremont by William Hoare. The National Portrait Gallery gave its permission to use photographs of portraits of Earl Temple, the Earl of Bute, the Duke of Newcastle, King George III, and the Marquis of Rockingham. The North Carolina Museum of Art gave permission to use the portrait of William Pitt by William Hoare.

A grant from the Commonwealth Study Center at Duke University enabled me to do much of the initial research for this book in England. A Knapp Foundation grant helped finance a summer at the Huntington Library in the Stowe MSS. and North Carolina Wesleyan College granted me sabbaticals during which I completed the research in England and the final rewriting. To the staffs of the North Carolina Wesleyan College Library and the Duke University Library I owe a great debt, and to the staffs of the other libraries in which I have worked: the British Library, the Public Record Office, the Institute of Historical Research of the University of London, the Sheffield Public Library, the Henry L. Huntington Library of San Marino, California, and the William L. Clements Library at the University of Michigan, Ann Arbor.

Thanks are also due to those who gave permission to examine and use privately held manuscript materials: to the Right Honourable the Earl Fitzwilliam and the trustees of the Wentworth-Woodhouse Muniments for permission to examine the manuscripts of Charles, second Marquis of Rockingham, and of Edmund Burke; to the late Sir Lewis Namier for permission to use transcripts of manuscripts in his possession; to the late Sir John Murray for permission to use the extensive collection of manuscripts of George Grenville and the Grenville family in his possession, and for his gracious hospitality and interest during the course of that examination; and to the trustees of the British Library and of the Public Record Office for permission to use the voluminous manuscript sources in those repositories.

A special note of thanks should go to Dr. Robert Zipf, pathologist of Nash General Hospital, Rocky Mount, N.C., for his help in interpreting Grenville's autopsy and his cause of death. The staff of Walker-Ross printers of Rocky Mount, particularly Mrs. Jill Williams, was enormously helpful in preparing copy for the press. And without the constant encouragement of my wife, Leigh, and her enthusiastic and unfailing assistance as copyist and research assistant in most of the manuscript collections used, this study would likely never have been completed.

Allen S. Johnson
Rocky Mount, N.C.
15 August 1996

The Right Honorable George Grenville

CHAPTER I

THE FORMATIVE YEARS, 1712-1741

From Marble Arch, the way out of London lies along highway A40 through Middlesex and into Buckinghamshire. Just past Beaconsfield, the road ascends sharply into the Chiltern Hills. Southwest to northeast they march across the southern reaches of the counties of Oxford, Buckingham, Hereford, and Bedford. The ancient, worn range hedges a broad valley below—a sea of green swells, broken occasionally by a lonely, towering hill. From the crest of the ridge, the swells cascade down into the valley of the River Thame—or the vale of Aylesbury, as it is also called—and roll away north and west on the other side. To the right, on the far horizon beyond Aylesbury town, looms a low range of hills, dim in the distance. And in the north, beyond the rim of the sky, more low hills reach down from Northamptonshire. Between these ranges lies a stretch of green, fertile land, rippling with grain, lush with pasture, and punctuated with patches of woodland. Two towns, Buckingham in the north and Aylesbury in the south, serve the commercial needs of the valley. And here and there, tucked away among spacious parks of woods and lakes, are the country estates of a rural aristocracy, now fast disappearing, which once controlled a world-wide empire.

In the opening years of the eighteenth century, this area stretching from the River Thame to the northwestern boundary of the county was the political dominion of two Buckinghamshire families. In the north, three miles beyond Buckingham town, the Temple family had its seat at Stowe, already becoming one of the showplaces among English country houses. Fourteen miles to the south, the estate at Wotton, at the very edge of the county, near Thame in Oxfordshire, was the home of the Grenvilles.

Of the two families, the Temples were the wealthier and more influential. It had long held the patronage of the borough of Buckingham; for three-quarters of a century before the birth of George Grenville in 1712, Temples had sat for Buckingham in the House of Commons. Sir Peter Temple sat for the borough in the last two parliaments of Charles II, and thereafter each succeeding generation of Temples sent its representatives to St. Stephen's Chapel.[1]

1

Temples traced their ancestry from Robert Temple of Temple Hall in the reign of Henry III.2 Peter Temple founded the seat at Stowe in the reign of Edward II. For over four hundred years, Temples had held, developed, and expanded the spacious estates.3 A younger branch was descended from John, the younger son of Peter Temple in the time of Edward VI. It had already produced Sir John Temple (1600-1677), Master of the Rolls under Charles I and governor of Ireland under Cromwell, as well as Sir William Temple (1628-1699), the statesman, diplomat, and author. From this Irish line would come also Henry John Temple, Viscount Palmerston, the nineteenth century Prime Minister.4

The elder line at Stowe, meanwhile, gained some lesser prominence. Thomas Temple was returned for Andover in 1588, and sat in several of Elizabeth's parliaments. Under James I he gained sufficient notice from the Crown to be knighted in 1603 and made baronet in 1611.5 It does not appear, however, that the Stowe line gained office under the Crown or distinguished itself particularly on the national scene before the latter half of the seventeenth century. It was then that Sir Richard Temple, the grandfather of George Grenville, took his seat in the Commons for Buckingham in the Restoration Parliament. Returned for all the parliaments of Charles II, James II, and William III, he soon became recognized as one of the leading members of the House. Charles II took special note of his prominence in the agitation over the Popish Plot and the debates on the Exclusion Bill. He appointed Sir Richard First Commissioner of the Customs, and Temple held the office until 1694.6

When Sir Richard Temple died in 1697, he was succeeded in his baronetcy and in his constituency by his eldest son, Richard, who was elected for Buckingham in his father's place. The new Sir Richard Temple was twenty-two years old in 1697, a bluff, hearty soldier with little education. At the age of sixteen he had obtained an ensigncy in Prince George's regiment of foot; in spite of his youth, his rise in the army was rapid. He served under Marlborough in Ireland and the Netherlands during the War of the League of Augsburg. A colonel at the beginning of the War of the Spanish Succession in 1701, he was made brigadier in 1706, major-general in 1708, and lieutenant-general in 1710. At the same time, he continued to serve in Parliament. During the first election of Queen Anne's reign, he was with the army on the Continent; and since the family interests in Buckingham were not properly attended to, he lost his seat to Roger Price of Westbury, another Buckinghamshire worthy. But shortly after his return to England, one of the county seats fell vacant and he was elected to it in November, 1704. In 1706 he regained his seat for the borough.7 Thus by 1712, when our narrative begins, Sir Richard Temple had gained a position of prominence in military and political affairs in the realm.

The Grenvilles of Wotton-Underwood were neither as wealthy nor as influential as the Temples of Stowe, but nonetheless they were the dominant family in the southwestern corner of the county. The Vale of Aylesbury, lying along the Thame west of Aylesbury town, had long been the bailiwick of the squires of Wotton Hall. Nestled among woods and lakes on the western edge of the county just south of Akeman Street (the ancient Roman road stretching from Aylesbury to Bicester), Wotton Hall was one of the finest manor houses in Buckinghamshire, though not to be compared with the mansion at Stowe. The Grenvilles were a solid, well-to-do family of the county squirearchy.

Tradition, probably unfounded, held that the Grenville claim to the Wotton estate went back to the time of William the Conqueror. Certainly the family was one of the oldest in the county. Grenvilles are recorded as tenants of the manor by the reign of Henry III, and there is evidence that members of the family were resident in the parish long before that.8 Lineal descent they claimed from Richard de Grenville, witness to a land grant in 1213, and through a collateral line from another Richard de Grenville, one of the knights who came to England with William the Conqueror. Gerard de Grenville, who died in 1164, held three knight's fees of Walter Giffard, second Earl of Buckingham and Longville; apparently one of these was the Wotton manor. If this is true, he was the first of the Grenville line to receive the estate as a fief.9

From this time forward, Grenvilles were among the gentry of the county. Eustace Grenville, for instance, was listed by the Commissioners of 1433 among the gentlemen of Buckinghamshire.10 By the seventeenth century, Grenvilles were holding the most important offices in county political circles, as when Richard Grenville, who succeeded to the Wotton estate in 1618, was pricked sheriff in 1636 and 1642 and elected Knight of Buckinghamshire in 1654, 1656, and 1658. Likewise his son Richard became High Sheriff of the county in 1671.11

Yet such prominence as the Grenvilles gained was strictly on the county level. It was an achievement of considerable moment, therefore, when in 1710 the last-mentioned Richard Grenville negotiated a marriage between his eldest son, Richard (1678-1727), and Hester Temple, the sister and co-heir of Sir Richard Temple of Stowe. Sir Richard, as we have seen, was by this time a member of parliament, a lieutenant-general, and one of the wealthiest men in England. Marriage alliance was one of the

principal means of family advancement. Sir Richard had no children; by
this marriage he was attempting to preserve and advance the family prestige and wealth which he had effectively built up. Thus were united two
of the most influential families of Buckinghamshire; united, their fortunes were to expand far beyond what either had ever attained separately.

ii.

It is not possible to obtain more than the briefest glimpse of the life of
Richard and Hester Grenville during the early years of their marriage.
Almost no correspondence or records of this period were preserved
among the masses of papers later stored at Stowe. Perhaps such materials were never considered of sufficient importance to transfer to the family seat in later generations, and so they perished in the fire that consumed
Wotton House in October, 1820. It is possible that there were never many
materials anyway. Richard Grenville was not a particularly literate or
communicative man. Such letters of his as have survived reveal rather
pedestrian interests, uncertain grammar and spelling, and bluff, not to say
crude, attitudes.[12] In this, of course, he was not unlike the great majority
of eighteenth-century English squires. The intellectual force of the family was Hester, who developed into a real political matriarch as her sons
grew up and entered politics. But likewise almost none of her early
papers have survived.

In September, 1711, Hester presented Richard with his first child, a
son, who in the family tradition was given the name Richard. Apparently
the birth at Wotton was attended with some complications. The child was
large, with "a fist wch in a little time will be big enough to knock one
down," and as the rest of him seemed "proportionable," Grenville won-
dered to his sister, Lady Conway, "how he got out."[13] Apparently the
fevers which followed the delivery were sufficiently disturbing to
Grenville or to his physician that when a second pregnancy neared term
he rented a house in London and moved the whole family to be near more
expert medical attention.[14] So on October 14, 1712, a second son was
born in the parish of St. Martin's, Westminster. When he was baptised on
November 11 in the church on the site where St. Martin's-in-the-Fields
now stands on Trafalgar Square, he was given the name George, a name
which many of his Grenville ancestors had borne.[15]

We should take particular note of the fact that there were only a few
days more than a year's difference in the ages of the first two Grenville
children, and that they were both male. The fact goes far to explain many

of the psychological characteristics of the two, and especially of George. From his earliest years, he was always faced with the competition of the older, larger, more developed brother. Dick was close enough to the same age for George to have to compete with him, but enough older always to have an edge during the psychological formative years. Dick developed the serenity, or perhaps arrogance is a better word, of the older brother; George, the inferiority feelings, always having to prove himself, never being able to be content with his victories or to accept responsibility for his defeats.

Six other children followed during the next eight years, four of whom were to live and take places of prominence on the political scene. James, the third son, was born three years after George. Like many middle children of large families, he developed a calm, sweet disposition. "Jemmy," as the family always called him, was the favorite—the charming, spoiled child who knew how to wheedle and cozen. Of all the brothers, he only would be able to claim the credit, if it was a credit, of never having quarreled with their brother-in-law, William Pitt. But likewise he lacked the drive and the firmness of purpose and attention to detail which enabled the older brothers to fight their way to the top of the political "greasy pole," as Benjamin Disraeli was later to describe it. "Jemmy" would always be in the political shadow of one or another of his brothers.

Henry, the fourth son, was born two years after James in 1717. As ambitious as Dick and George, and perhaps as capable, he had the reputation, borne out in such correspondence as has survived, of vanity and pompousness, even deviousness. The family saw to it that "Harry" got a seat in Parliament, as he sat with his brothers in St. Stephen's Chapel during their heyday in the Tenth and Eleventh Parliaments.[16] But he made his name in a rather humdrum career outside England, first as a popular governor of Barbados, 1746-56, and then as Ambassador to Constantinople, 1761-1765. On his return to England in 1765, he held office briefly as a Commissioner of Customs. But perhaps his most brilliant accomplishment was his marriage to the beautiful heiress, Peggy Banks, in 1757.[17]

The career of the fifth son, Thomas, born in 1719, seemed to promise great success either in politics or the navy—or perhaps both. He was elected to the Commons for Bridport in Dorset, December 12, 1746, at a time when the family was gaining recognition as influential men in the ministry. But less than five months later, on May 3, 1747, as Captain of H. M. S. *Defiance,* he was killed in action off Cape Finisterre in Spain. The disaster put an end to what would likely have been a brilliant naval career. "Tommy" was already captain of a ship of the line at age 27; a popular officer of spirit, temper, and judgment, it seems likely that he would have gone far in either the navy or politics. Commanding officers are not generally sparing of encomiums when writing epitaphs for their fallen captains, but nonetheless it was significant that Admiral Lord Anson described Thomas Grenville to the Duke of Bedford, First Lord of the Admiralty, as "by much the cleverest officer I ever saw."[18]

By far the favorite child of the family, however, was the sixth and youngest, a girl born in 1720 and named Hester after her mother. "Hetty" was the apple of the eye of all of her brothers; she would remain so even when family quarrels rent the brothers in bitter controversy. Her marriage to William Pitt in 1754 was to seal an already strong political bond between Pitt and the Grenvilles and to have a profound influence on the political history of the century.

The principal concern of our study, however, is George, the second son. Almost nothing can be learned from the family papers about George's childhood until he entered Eton College in the early 1720's. Grenville, however, wrote a "narrative" during the 1760's in which he briefly described his childhood. Sir Richard Temple loved his sister Hester and took a lively interest in her children, having none of his own. He had his estate entailed on her and her children, "whom he took care of from their childhood, and almost educated as his own...."[19] One imagines that George and his brothers and sister spent their time not only at Wotton but also among the halls and terraces at Stowe.

The Stowe which George Grenville doubtless first visited in early childhood was hardly the magnificent estate which became the envy of all England and half of Europe in the latter eighteenth century. The house itself was a large, handsome late-seventeenth-century building, built by George's grandfather and still quite new. But it was much smaller than the imposing 916-foot-long facade which the house attained at the hands of George's brother, Richard, when he succeeded to the estate as second Earl Temple. And the gardens, which were to be called by the time of Temple's death in 1779 "the noblest and best planned" in all England,[20] were merely terraces on the south side. The "marsh" which lay beyond was to become a lake, "a noble piece of water," by the 1740's.[21]

When George Grenville was born, however, his uncle was on active service as lieutenant-general under the Duke of Marlborough on the Continent. Only in April, 1713, when the war was being concluded and Marlborough's political fortunes had changed, did Temple return to Stowe upon being dismissed from his command. With the accession of the Hanoverians in 1714, his command was restored, with the general's pay which could finance building; and in 1715 he married an heiress, Anne Halsey, which gave him real opportunity for improvements. Charles Bridgeman, a brilliant landscape designer, was engaged to lay out the lake and extensive gardens, and Sir John Vanbrugh, a fellow member of the Kit-Cat Club with Temple, found time apart from designing Marlborough's Blenheim Palace to create many graceful buildings for the gardens.[22]

Meanwhile the political fortunes of Temple also soared following the Hanoverian Succession. In 1713 he had not only lost his command; he had been defeated for reelection to Parliament for the town of Buckingham. Apparently influence was applied against him from the Court. Temple and his colleague, Sir Edmund Denton, appealed the election to the House of Commons, but as the body was controlled by the Tories the result was a foregone conclusion.[23] Such reversals of fortune were themselves reversed, however, when in 1714 the weathercock of politics turned the other way. At the accession of George I, Marlborough and Temple with him were immediately taken into favor. Sir Richard Temple became Baron Cobham of Cobham in Kent, took his seat in the House of Lords, and was sent as plenipotentiary to the court of Emperor Charles VI to announce the accession of George I. Two years later, although there is no record of any political activity on his part, he was made a member of the Privy Council.[24]

These new triumphs were shared with his sisters. The marriage to Anne Halsey produced no children. When the title of Viscount Cobham was conferred on him in 1718, it was provided that, in the event he remained childless, the title should descend to his younger sister, Hester Grenville. In the unlikely event that she died childless, it would then go to his older sister, Christian, the wife of Sir Thomas Lyttelton, Bart., of Hagley in Worcestershire.[25]

George's father also benefitted from Cobham's growing influence. When the seat for Wendover in southern Buckinghamshire fell vacant in the early part of 1715, Richard Grenville was elected and took his seat in the Commons on March 17, 1715. In 1721 he was returned for Cobham's bailiwick of Buckingham, three miles from Stowe, and he continued to represent that borough until his death in 1727.[26]

iii.

While these events were taking place, young Dick and George Grenville had been enrolled in Eton College; the year 1725 found them in the fourth form.27 At this time Eton shared with Westminster and Winchester Schools the almost exclusive function of training and educating those sons of the nobility and gentry who were not tutored at home or by private instructors. Eton was a school of politics as well as of academic studies, all the more effective in that its students were drawn from families of almost all shades of political opinion. Among the faculty, Dr. Henry Godolphin, the Provost, was a younger brother of the great politician of Queen Anne's reign and a personification of the school's aristocratic dignity and connections. The headmaster, Henry Bland, as a close friend of Sir Robert Walpole, who at this time was at the height of his power, frequently contributed pamphlets in support of Walpole's ministry. The very atmosphere at Eton was surcharged with the politics of the day.

The formal education which the boys received, however, had rather degenerated since Tudor or Stuart times. Whereas earlier monarchs and statesmen were versed in modern languages and had studied history and statescraft both in theory and practice, eighteenth century young gentlemen occupied their time almost completely with the Greek and Latin classics. Such topics as mathematics, geography, and spelling, which form the backbone of the modern child's curriculum, were relegated to half-holidays, when they were taught by the inferior masters. Likewise training in modern languages was limited to holidays. And the study of history, that best preparation for politics, seems to have been almost entirely neglected at the public schools, as was science. Only the oppedans, senior students who boarded in town rather than living in the college residences, received any systematic training in modern languages or history.28

The collegers, those who lived in the residence halls, did not live an easy life. Hazing and bullying by the older boys made life miserable for the youngsters. In the classroom, discipline was maintained by the threat and frequent execution of brutal canings. But those who were able to survive were bonded as friends for life. Young George was among many boys with whom he would later be associated on the political scene. His three younger brothers were at Eton; they entered sometime between 1725 and 1728. His cousin George Lyttelton, the eldest son of his aunt Christian, was in the sixth, or highest form, in 1725.

More important were those he might not have known at home or at Stowe. For a few years he was a schoolmate of William Pitt, his future political associate and brother-in-law. Tunstall represents Pitt at this time as a shy, lonely figure, possibly already afflicted with the gout which would plague him all his adult life. The future "great commoner," he asserts, was already showing signs of a peculiar genius. Perhaps. But the evidence for these assertions is problematical, since Pitt's early papers are as sketchy as Grenville's. One suspects that he was speculating about the boy from his knowledge of the man.[29] But since Pitt was four years older than Grenville, it seems unlikely that they would have been intimately acquainted.

There were other boys of his own age, however, with whom he would be intimately associated in his later career. A year younger than he was John Stuart, who in 1723 at the age of ten had succeeded to the Scottish earldom of Bute. No man other than Grenville's own brothers and Pitt was to have such a profound influence on Grenville's career as this Scot. Another friend, also already an earl at this early age, was William Villiers, Lord Jersey. Although he was never to cut a great figure on the political scene, Jersey was to remain one of Grenville's most intimate friends throughout his life. And among the still younger boys, whom Grenville doubtless knew, were his future political associates Sir Francis Dashwood and Charles Pratt, later Lord Camden, and such authors and poets as Thomas Gray and Horace Walpole.[30]

If Tunstall was perhaps speculating about Pitt as an Eton scholar, it seems almost without question that Jesse was doing so when he wrote about Grenville at the same stage. As a student, he asserts, George was neither indolent nor dull. Indeed he was keen in perception and diligent almost to the point of drudgery. Lacking somewhat in imagination, he was nevertheless apt in comprehending and retaining materials and in pursuing to logical conclusions. The other boys, however, thought him uninteresting, Jesse asserts; he cared little for sports and mirth and was seldom one to contribute original ideas. In any argument, he was always likely to take the traditional side of the question.[31] If Jesse had any documentation for these descriptions, he did not reveal it and it has since vanished. The portrait he paints seems valid enough as speculation about what the stubborn, conservative, inflexible politician of the 1760's may have been like as a child. But contemporary testimony and surviving correspondence are so sparse as not to support or contradict.

Whatever he was like personally as an Eton scholar, George enjoyed Eton, attained positions of leadership there, and was sad to leave. About May, 1728, he was promoted to the sixth form, and before he left in November, 1729, he attained, as he put it, "the honour of being second oppedant of the greatest school in England."[32]

Meanwhile, in February, 1726, the senior Richard Grenville died. No record has survived to indicate how the death of his father affected

George or any other member of the family. Grenville wrote many years later, however, that his uncle, Lord Cobham, took all the Grenville children under his wing at that point. He educated them "almost...as his own." Dick was sent abroad to finish his education, probably with a tutor on the grand tour of the Continent, while George and his brothers completed their studies at Eton.[33]

iv.

George was, of course, a younger son, without prospect of fortune. On his father's death, George was left an annuity of £3,000, which at four per cent per annum yielded him an income of £120, hardly a princely sum. When he finished Eton, he was faced with the choosing of a profession. Dick could take the grand tour and return to learn the business of managing the estate at Wotton, with the prospect increasingly likely that he would inherit Stowe as well when Cobham died.[34] George would have to earn his living. The respectable choices for a young man of the aristocracy were not many: the clergy, law, medicine, the army, the navy, and the government service. For a time he seems to have hesitated between the Church and the bar. When he left Eton November 25, 1729, it was to enroll in Christ Church college, Oxford. Presumably he intended to enter the Church; few young men went to Oxford or Cambridge for any other purpose. "I left Eton for good and all the day before yesterday," he wrote to Dick, who was still abroad. "All my brothers, tho' a little concerned at my leaving 'em, yet are very well. I shall go to Christ Church shortly."[35]

In this letter to his older brother there were both the pride and the apprehension of the boy off to the university for the first time. The apprehension was well-founded. From the first, Grenville did not like Oxford. Part of the trouble was the adjustment to the change from Eton. He had had "the honour of being second oppedant" at Eton, he complained to Dick in early December, and now his place was "changed to be the last of the University, and to see many that I have commanded at Eaton my superiors here."[36] But almost every college freshman has experienced such feelings, at least in some degree. The reasons for his dissatisfaction must have run deeper. The indolence and licentious conduct which had so offended the Wesley brothers at Christ Church a few years earlier could have been part of the cause,[37] but the likelihood seems remote. He was never one to be much offended by the conduct of his fellows. It seems more likely that he felt misdirected in the theological curriculum, since there is no evidence that he ever felt any vocation to the Church.

Spending the Christmas recess at Wotton only aggravated his discontent. Writing to Dick of the impending meeting of Parliament on January 13, he lamented that about that time he would have to "change this pleasant habitation for the most unpleasant one in Europe. I need not tell you after this description that I mean Oxford."38

Whether after this early experience Grenville ever entertained ideas of taking his degree at Oxford is not clear, but he did stay long enough to matriculate as a degree candidate in Christ Church, February 6, 1730.39 Even before he returned from Wotton after Christmas, however, he had determined that he would not stay at Oxford long. "This is the last time" to return there, he wrote; "when I change next it will be to the Temple, and as my continuance there is likely to be of some duration I must and will make it agreeable—whether it is or no."40

In November, 1729, about the time that he went up to Oxford, he had also been admitted to the Inner Temple.41 Sometime in the spring of 1730, he abandoned Oxford and turned his whole attention to the study of law. Writing an autobiographical sketch many years later, he made no mention of his ever having been to Oxford. His decision to study law, he stated then, was based on Lord Cobham's advice.42 Apparently he was happy in his studies at the Inner Temple, for the complaining letters ceased. Not only was he temperamentally suited for the law, there was evident need for a lawyer in the family. Few families were more litigious than the Temple-Grenvilles!43

For the next several years, George divided his time almost entirely between the Inner Temple and Stowe.44 Obviously most of his time was spent at the inn of court. No evidence appears which might indicate with whom he read at the Inner Temple or in what areas of law he specialized. For six years he remained at the Temple. Then the Bench Table, or executive council of the inn of court, petitioned Parliament on November 18, 1735, that he be called to the bar. The petition was approved on November 22 following, and Grenville became a full-fledged barrister.45

The real importance of his becoming a barrister can only be conjectured. It is not certain that Grenville ever pursued the practice of law for a living, or indeed that he ever appeared in court or before the bar of the Parliament to represent a client. It is certain, however, that from this time forward he conducted the legal business of the family. In May, 1736, he took chambers in Sir Robert Sawyer's buildings at the Inner Temple "for his own life,"46 which may indicate the intention to practice law. Apparently he spent a large amount of his time there, for most of his letters to his family during the latter 1730's were dated from the Inner

Temple.[47] Much of the correspondence between Dick and George during this period concerned the legal and business affairs of the family, which George had his hands full managing. At one point George suggested to Dick that he breed his second son to the law in order to take some of the work off his shoulders.[48] There is no mention anywhere in the surviving correspondence that he had any other clients.

If he ever did actually practice law for a livelihood, he probably did so no longer than until 1744, when public office and a salary gave him some financial security. Soon thereafter he gave up his chambers in the Temple.[49] By the time he went out of office in 1755, Cobham's death had provided him with a comfortable living.

Family relations throughout the period when George was acquiring his education in the 1720's and 1730's were close and intimate, and they remained so for a long period of time after he entered the House of Commons in 1741. George and Dick were particularly close. They corresponded frequently and regularly during the years Dick spent on the Continent from 1727 to 1732. The letters which passed between them on family business during the latter 1730's are always full of protestations of the greatest affection and regard. When George fell ill with a respiratory infection, perhaps chronic tuberculosis, in the fall of 1736, Dick expressed his concern to Anna Chamber, who at that point was about to become his wife: "My brother, who continues in a very bad way, set out for Bath on Thursday. I love him dearly, but I am so much obliged to you that I will not say a word more upon that head."[50]

But family relations among the Grenville-Temples meant more than merely personal affections by this time; there were important political relations as well. Since 1733, Lord Cobham had been in opposition to Sir Robert Walpole's ministry, and he was recruiting his nephews to carry on his fight in the House of Commons. Cobham's "cubs" were soon to make their mark in national politics as the "Boy Patriots." Before turning to that story, however, we must pause to consider the national political scene in which it was taking place.

NOTES

CHAPTER I

[1] *Arthur Collins, Peerage of England: Genealogical, Biographical, and Historical,* 9 vols., London, 1812, II, 412; T. H. B. Oldfield, *The Representative History of Great Britain and Ireland,* 6 vols., London, 1816, III, 52-57.

[2] John Burke, *Peerage, Baronetage, and Knightage,* London, 1949, p. 1965.

[3] Collins, *Peerage,* II, 410.

[4] John Langton Sanford and Meredith Townshend, *The Great Governing Families of England,* 2 vols., Edinburgh and London, 1865, II, 8.

[5] *Members of Parliament,* a return to two orders of the House of Commons, dated 4 May 1876 and 9 March 1877, 2 parts, London, 1878-1891, I, 424; Collins, *Peerage,* II, 413-414.

[6] *Members of Parliament,* I, 540, 546, 552, 557, 564, 572; Collins, *Peerage,* II, 411; Joseph Haydn, *The Book of Dignities,* London, 1894, pp. 273-274.

[7] Edward Irving Carlyle, "Richard Temple," *The Dictionary of National Biography,* edited by Sir Leslie Stephen and Sir Sidney Lee, 22 vols., London, 1917 ff., XIX, 518. (Hereafter cited as D. N. B.)

[8] George Lipscomb, *The History and Antiquities of the County of Buckingham,* 4 vols., London, 1847, I, 286; Collins, *Peerage,* II, 390.

[9] Collins, *Peerage,* II, 391; *The Victoria History of the County of Buckingham,* 4 vols., London, 1905-1927, IV, 130. (Hereafter cited as *V. C. H., Bucks.*)

[10] *V. C. H., Bucks,* IV, 131.

[11] Collins, *Peerage,* II, 409-410. The office of sheriff by the late seventeenth century was one more to be avoided than sought by those with serious political ambitions. It was burdensome and expensive; no one holding the office could stand for Parliament; and while the honor was significant, the power of the office was negligible. Consequently the office became, as in this case, one dealt out to younger men eager to work their way into the graces of the powerful. See John Harold Plumb, *Sir Robert Walpole,* 2 vols., Cambridge, 1956-61, I, 47.

[12] The mass of the family papers are now deposited in the Henry B. Huntington Library in San Marino, California. Hereinafter referred to as Stowe MSS.

[13] Richard Grenville to Lady Conway, September 27, 1711, Stowe MSS., box 11.

[14] Richard Grenville to his mother at Wotton, September 23, 1712, Stowe MSS, box 11. It was quite typical of Richard to report to his mother that baby Dick's "waters pass'd but little" during the journey, "tho once every one in the coach rec'd some little damage but myself."

[15] Collins, *Peerage,* II, 415; Lipscomb, *Buckingham,* I, 600. The church in

which George Grenville was baptised was not that designed by James Gibbs which stands today on the northeast corner of Trafalgar Square. That building was begun ten years later in 1722.

[16] *Members of Parliament,* II, 133, 137.

[17] *The Grenville Papers,* edited by William James Smith, 4 vols., London, 1852-1853, I, xvii. Margaret Banks was the sister of John Hogkinson Banks and a celebrated beauty of the time. Apparently the couple were engaged for a long time, for in 1745 George Grenville speaks of Harry's going down to the country "with his love Peggy." Grenville to Thomas Grenville, December 8, 1745, *Grenville Papers,* I, 47.

[18] *Members of Parliament,* II, 87; *Grenville Papers,* I, 62 n.

[19] Grenville's narrative, *Grenville Papers,* I, 422-423.

[20] H. Meister, quoted in R. Bayne-Powell, *Travellers in Eighteenth Century England,* London, 1951, p. 149; Lewis M. Wiggin, *The Faction of Cousins,* Yale, 1958, p. 53.

[21] W. Gilpin, *A Dialogue upon the Gardens...at Stowe,* Buckingham, 1748, p. 4., quoted in Wiggin, *Faction of Cousins,* p. 53; Laurence Whistler, Michael Gibbon, and George Clarke, *Stowe: A Guide to the Gardens,* n.d., 1968, p. 5.

[22] Whistler *et al., Stowe,* pp. 5-7. After Vanbrugh's death in 1726, James Gibbs, William Kent, and Giacomo Leoni added their contributions to the house and gardens in the 1720's and 1730's.

[23] V. C. H., *Bucks,* IV, 547; Oldfield, *Representative History,* III, 95.

[24] Carlyle, "Richard Temple," *D. N. B.,* XIX, 518.

[25] George Edward Cokayne, *The Complete Peerage of England, Scotland, Ireland, Great Britain, and the United Kingdom,* new edition, 13 vols., London, 1910-1953, III, 341.

[26] *Members of Parliament,* II, 37, 50.

[27] *Eton College Lists, 1678-1790,* edited by Richard Arthur Austen-Leigh, Eton, 1907, pp. 20-25. The exact date on which the Grenville boys were entered at Eton, or whether they were entered together or separately, cannot be determined. The lists of students at the college are very sketchy. Only two lists are extant which bear their names, one dated 1725 and one, 1728. The latest one prior to the 1725 list is dated 1718. Likewise there is no evidence to indicate whether either or both were tutored at home before entering Eton. Thus the most that can be deduced is that the two oldest brothers were entered at Eton between 1718 and 1725.

[28] Basil Williams, *The Life of William Pitt, Earl of Chatham,* 2 vols. London, 1914, I, 31-32; Basil Williams, *The Whig Supremacy, 1714-1760,* 2nd. ed., Oxford, 1962, pp. 139-140; Plumb, *Walpole,* I.

[29] *Eton Lists,* pp. 19-28; Brian Tunstall, *William Pitt, Earl of Chatham,*

London, 1938, p. 23.

[30] *Eton Lists,* pp. 19-28. The information on Lord Jersey is drawn from several letters between Grenville and Jersey in the Grenville manuscripts in the possession of Sir John Murray, London. The collection will hereafter be referred to as Murray MSS .

[31] J. Heneage Jesse, *Memoirs of Celebrated Etonians,* 2 vols., London, 1875, I. 230.

[32] George Grenville to Richard Grenville, c. December, 1729, Murray MSS.

[33] Grenville's narrative, *Grenville Papers,* I, 422-423; Cobham to Richard Grenville, January 9, 1736, Murray MSS.: "...as to the money paid for you abroad, I will not suffer it to be brought in with the particulars of your debts."

[34] The decision to settle his estates on Richard was not taken by Cobham until 1737, when Richard married Anna Chamber: "Lord Cobham and my mother...were desirous that he should marry, and to enable him to do it to the highest advantage, Lord Cobham publicly declared that he would settle his whole estate upon him, which he accordingly did, upon his marriage." Grenville's narrative, *Grenville Papers,* I, 423.

[35] November 27, 1729, Murray MSS.

[36] George Grenville to Richard Grenville, n.d. (early December, 1729), Murray MSS.

[37] John Wesley was at Oxford when Grenville arrived, having returned to teach in November, 1729, after two years of assisting his father in his Epworth parish in Lincolnshire. There is no evidence, however, that he and Grenville had any contact during the latter's brief stay.

[38] George Grenville to Richard Grenville, n.d. (late December, 1729), Murray MSS.

[39] *Alumni Oxonienses,* 1715-1886, 3 vols., London, 1888, II, 562.

[40] George Grenville to Richard Grenville, n.d. (late December, 1729), Murray MSS.

[41] *A Calendar of the Inner Temple Records,* 5 vols., London, 1896-1936, IV, 209.

[42] Grenville's narrative, *Grenville Papers,* I, 423.

[43] For example, on June 5, 1733, Richard Grenville noted payment of £1,896.10.0 for "law expenses in London." Richard Grenville's account book, Stowe MSS., p. 64.

[44] Grenville's narrative, *Grenville Papers,* I, 423.

[45] *Inner Temple Records,* IV, 310. The admission register of Lincoln's Inn, another of the inns of court, shows that on February 21, 1734, "George Grenville, son of Richard Grenville of Wotton, Bucks, Esq.," was admitted to that society. This was, of course, during the period of his last preparation for the

bar. Perhaps he read with some particular barrister in some subject. The documents, however, are silent. *The Records of the Honourable Society of Lincoln's Inn,* London, 1896, 2 vols., I, 408.

[46] *Inner Temple Records,* IV, 317. Richard kept careful account of all George spent above the interest on his £3,000 annuity, and advanced him £380 to purchase chambers in 1736. Richard Grenville's Account Book, p. 301, Stowe MSS.

[47] Murray MSS.; Stowe MSS.

[48] December 8, 1738, Stowe MSS., box 8. This was in the years immediately after Dick's marriage, before it became obvious that he would have no sons. His only child, a daughter, Elizabeth, was born September 1, 1738, and died July 14, 1742.

[49] *Inner Temple Records,* IV, 488.

[50] n.d. (November, 1736), Murray MSS. The illness lasted on into the spring and George did not recover fully until he had spent the summer of 1742 on the Continent for his health. See below, pp. 40-41.

CHAPTER II

POLITICS AND POLITICIANS, 1721-1770

i.

It is now nearly three quarters of a century since Sir Lewis B. Namier published his epochal interpretations of eighteenth-century British politics.[1] In that span, many historians have followed his lead in reinterpreting the political history of the century between the Glorious Revolution and the French Revolution.[2] It would be presumptuous of this writer to re-work the ground they have tilled so well. Let it suffice only to outline four major areas in which the career of George Grenville was to have impact.

British politics in the mid-eighteenth century revolved around 1) the varying loyalties and aspirations of the members of the ruling class; 2) the Crown and its constitutional position, the nature of the Parliament, and the manner in which king, ministers, and Parliament interacted; 3) the primitive machinery of political organization; and 4) the by no means primitive modes of manipulating public opinion.

"The history of the institutions of any people," wrote W. T. Laprade in 1926, "is concerned primarily with the ruling class that gave shape to the institutions."[3] Thus the history of eighteenth-century British politics is concerned almost exclusively with the ruling class, the aggregation of landed and moneyed families which controlled the sources of power. The landed gentry were preoccupied, as ever, with building families and estates of as great wealth and permanence as possible. Among the families, the ancient processes continually operated: marriage, purchase, litigation, inheritance; rise, amalgamation, decay. As in any age, men seldom felt secure. True, republicanism moldered in Cromwell's grave. The Church, with a few concessions to the dissenters, had apparently been made secure against Rome by the Revolution and the Act of Settlement. Loyalty to the Crown required little courage and involved little risk. Yet it was by no means certain until well after the Rebellion of 1745 that the Hanoverian regime would not be overturned. The return of the Stuarts

17

would have stranded the bulk of the ruling class, who had had no choice but to identify their fortunes with the German dynasty. Likewise, war, economic changes, death, or political miscalculation might ruin the painstaking work of generations in putting together a family estate.

The lust for money with which to buy land or improve it; the desire for prestige, power, and patronage; the wish to do one's duty for the state all directed the member of the ruling class to politics. The Crown (and its ministers) was the fountainhead of honor. By it titles, offices, and honors were dispensed to the politically useful. The ruling class, of course, thus monopolized the chief places in the government, the Church, and the army and navy. Service to the state called for compensation. But in return for their honors and privileges, the members of the ruling class—or at least the more conscientious and able among them—worked diligently at the jobs of administration and leadership. Privilege entailed leadership, and fortunately there were many who did not shirk the responsibility. The young Duke of Portland in 1767 was displeased with his brother's obsession with hunting, which led him to withdraw from public affairs. "Since I have been able to exercise my reason," wrote the Duke, "I never could persuade myself that men were born only for themselves. I have always been bred to think that Society has its claims upon them, & that those claims were in general proportioned to the degrees of their fortunes, their situation, & their abilities."[4]

The key to politics and place lay in the eighteenth-century relationship of king, ministers, and Parliament. The seventeenth century had demonstrated the indispensability of the Parliament. In the closing years of that century, the country was ruled by a king who was absent most of the time on the Continent, fighting in a world war which made unprecedented financial demands on the English nation. Interested less in contesting for power with the Parliament than in keeping it in such a humor as would yield the necessary and incessant appropriations, he allowed the Parliament to consolidate the position it had taken in its struggles with the earlier Stuarts. By the time George Grenville learned his politics, therefore, there was no question of other sources of funds for the Crown than Parliamentary grants. The consequence was that the king had to seek Parliamentary acquiescence in many major decisions of policy. And the consequence of that fact, in turn, was that the king had to seek servants who could manage the Parliament.

Hence it was natural—nay, imperative—that the king should draw his advisers from among the members of the Parliament. For the men who controlled and directed blocks of votes in the House of Commons—and hence the men who could manage the Commons—were to be found either in that House or in the Lords. The peers held a major proportion both of the offices and of the power in public affairs. They were the heads of the great families, the owners of the properties and the dispensers of the patronage by which many of the lower House were selected. Their sons, relatives, friends, and proteges were sent by them to sit in the Commons. By their patriarchal and financial authority, they directed their clans there. They were, moreover, the natural advisers of the Crown; they filled many councils and performed many duties simply by virtue of their status as peers. In addition, many of them were shrewd political manipulators or learned counsellors. By the time George Grenville appeared on the political scene, the Duke of Newcastle had already established himself as a master of political management. During Grenville's career, others fully as skillful appeared: his brother, Earl Temple; his political opponent and then associate, the Marquis of Rockingham;5 as well as such wise and experienced counsellors as the Earls of Hardwicke and Mansfield.6

Although the House of Lords was the main seat of control and influence, the House of Commons was the main seat of action. Its roots spread more extensively through the ruling class than did those of the Lords. It clutched the money bags. It could make the greater noise in a crisis, and could engross more of the public attention. Indeed, nothing of moment could be done without it. Properly organized and aroused, it could make or crush any ministry. The king therefore always sought to have in his ministry someone who could manipulate, manage, and lead that body. It is significant that during most of the century the First Minister was a member of the Commons.

Managing the Parliament was not the only problem faced by the King's ministers; they also had to manage the king. The problem was not simple, for personally the Georges were difficult. Each in his own way presented problems which few ministers were able to solve satisfactorily. Violent, morose, isolated by language barriers, insane—whatever might be the problem or peculiarity, the king still had to be got along with and managed if the business of the nation was to go on. Each minister handled the problem of personality in a different way, but each had to handle it.

Complicating the problem of personality, furthermore, was that of nationality. The Georges were Germans, and the first two never forgot the fact. Their dominions in Hanover, indeed, were the first concern of George I and George II, to which affairs British came no better than second. The preference given to Hanover was obvious to any observer of

British politics, and it was often the subject of bitter debates in the Parliament. One might oppose measures favoring Hanover on the conviction that British interests were being sacrificed to Hanoverian. But even without conviction, the Hanoverian issue could be ridden for the sake of opposition. For men already determined to oppose, it was a ready-made weapon to use against the king's ministers.

ii.

It was the theory of the king that he was free to name his servants, although as we have seen he prudently chose some who could ease his relations with the Parliament. When peculiar circumstances or bankruptcy of leadership among those he preferred forced him to name office-holders he disliked, the king sullenly bided his time until he could dismiss them.[7] Few politicians wished to be in opposition to those the king favored; that way lay lean times. If one "forced the closet," he held office tenuously. Furthermore, by reason of the loyalties which clustered around the throne and the patronage of the Crown, the king always controlled the largest single block of votes in either House. To attempt to carry on the business of the country without the favor of the king and the support of his personal following in the Parliament was a trying and precarious experiment. Those politicians who found themselves so neglected that they resorted to the desperation of opposition usually rallied in nondescript groups around the heir to the throne, who was always in opposition to the king but always held very sound reversionary prospects,

Government never lost an election—or perhaps *selection* would be a better word, since the majority of seats were not contested. But controlling members' votes after they had taken their seats was another matter. There was no political organization resembling the modern party system; there were only small groups and factions acting in concert with each other for brief periods on particular questions. Many might be the rationalizations, but the fundamental questions which could most move the factions to common action were two: how to get into office? how to stay in?

Among the little groups, there was continual flux, rearranging, coalescing, disrupting, in the manner of French political parties (but without their dogmatism and without any "political principles"). There has been little study of the mechanics of concert in this situation. Groups and leaders had to meet together to arrange alliances and policies, but there were few generally accepted modes of convention and liaison. The coffee houses, for political purposes, were turning more and more into clubs,[8] but none of them in this period could be designated as the site of a political high command such as existed in Shaftesbury's Green Ribbon Club of Charles II's reign or in the later Carleton Club in the younger Pitt's time. More tangible were the special meetings at taverns to produce agreement among large numbers of members of the House of Commons. Several hundred of them organized the opposition to Sir Robert Walpole in February, 1742, in two or three meetings at the Fountain Tavern.[9] In the spring of 1769, the followers of Rockingham and Grenville in the House of Commons met at the Thatched House Tavern to conclude an alliance of opposition against Grafton's ministry.[10]

Such mass meetings, however, were rare. More frequent were the political dinners of the factional chiefs, at which policy would be laid out. The orders could then be sent out to lieutenants. For example, Lord Hardwicke wrote of an opposition meeting in the spring of 1763: "I am to dine today at Devonshire House at what, I suppose, will be called a political dinner—Mr. Pitt, the Duke of Newcastle, Marquess of Rockingham and Lord Temple...."[11] Grenville and the other principal leaders in his ministry evidently made a practice of regular political dinners:

> We broke up at the Duke of Bedford's on Thursday with fixing our dinner for Thursday next (wrote Halifax to Grenville). The Thursday before we dined with Sandwich, and the Thursday before that the dinner was at my house. Next Thursday therefore is your turn; of which I thought proper to give you a hint, as you have such a multiplicity of other matters in your thoughts.[12]

The leaders, of course, also met informally on the circuits of visits to the great country houses—Woburn, Claremont, Stowe—, at the various entertainments in London during the town season, and at the races and the assizes. Sometimes the incessant meetings in town[13] would be varied by what amounted to a convention at such a political institution as Stowe or Claremont, or perhaps at a favorite gathering place, such as Bath. Thus in May, 1764, the Newcastle forces gathered at Claremont to plan a comprehensive strategy of opposition to the Grenville ministry. In the autumn of 1765, to turn the tables, Grenville, Bedford, Sandwich, and the other members of the former Grenville administration convened at Bath to concert opposition against the government of Rockingham and the Newcastle faction.[14] Almost any gathering, of course, could serve as a point of contact and liaison. In preparation for Walpole's last Parliament, in addition to the great conferences in town, "cabals" were "held at all the Horse Races in the Country"; every "Village Assembly" became a "Council of Malcontents."[15]

Finally, the families and their retainers and hangers-on formed groups in themselves. Recruited and deployed by the heads of the clans, family groups were among the most dependable types of factions on which to build political alliances. "Connexion," indeed, was the standard ladder by which to climb in the eighteenth century.[16]

It was only at the end of Grenville's career that some really advanced techniques of organization began to be employed. The excitement of the Middlesex election affair and the agitation for various reforms of Parliament bred organizations such as the "Society for the Support of the Bill of Rights" and other radical groups, highly organized and centrally directed. Finally by 1780 the organizers of the Yorkshire Association had learned the technique of corresponding societies (perhaps from America?) and the national convention.

iii.

So the mechanics of political organization slowly evolved in the eighteenth century. Not slowly at all, the politicians seized on the tools for manufacturing—or perhaps merely shaping and expressing—what is hopefully called public opinion. The principal object here, and in the making of political alignments, was to control the votes of the members of Parliament. Thus most of the noise raised by propagandists and agitators in the eighteenth century was aimed at influencing the ruling class in its convention, the Parliament.

Many roads might be taken to that end. One of the most obvious and most effective was the printed word, disseminated in the form of pamphlets, newspapers, and periodicals. Written either by the politicians themselves or by hired hacks, the printed pieces aimed at intensifying and mobilizing as many as possible of the latent prejudices and loyalties felt by the people behind some leader or some immediate program of action. The audience addressed was much larger than the number of those who read. News, often given the proper slant by skillfully worded paragraphs in the newspapers, travelled quickly among the rabble by word of mouth. And pamphlets, newspapers, and magazines were not consumed solely by the members of the ruling class. The coffee house still served as a place where many could hear the pieces read and discussed by those literate and articulate persons who were able to do so—and perhaps paid to do so. Every paper or pamphlet passed through numerous hands and was heard by numerous ears. Perhaps the *Craftsman* which Pulteney and Bolingbroke produced or Temple's *North Briton* received the sort of reception among country gentlemen which Robert Harley's *Examiner* had received at Scarborough in an earlier reign. The parish parson, it was reported, received the paper on Sunday,

> and after evening service the parson usually invites a good number of friends to his house, where he first reads over the paper, and then comments upon the text; and all the week after carries it about with him to read to such of his parishioners as are weak in the faith, and have not had the eyes of their understanding opened; so that it is not doubted but he will in time make as many converts to the true interest of the State, as he ever did to the Church.[17]

True, all those who heard were not members of the Parliament or electors of members; the great majority were not. But when the appeals to popular prejudices and loyalties sifted down among the populace by word of mouth, they prepared the ground for possible mobilization of the masses in case of crisis. Caution was necessary. "Oral appeals were not made to crowds. There was no adequate police. A crowd became a mob. The social cement could not stand the strain. The safety of life and property was involved." Yet with the ground properly prepared, factions in opposition might dare to use mobs when they were properly manipulated. Leaders might maintain and direct "agents to guide the mob..., to give it drink and thus increase the noise, to find it effigies to burn, to furnish cries to make the points desired, if possible perchance to get it safely broken up." Once roused, mobs could get out of the control even of those who raised them. They were dangerous weapons, feared almost as much by those who aroused them as by those against whom they were aroused. Yet they were often tremendously effective; they could howl and frighten, wreck and stone, until ministers would sometimes back out of measures unwelcome to their opponents. Occasionally a minister might even be frightened out of office. Thus mobs, however dangerous, were always a temptation to use as a weapon by those in opposition.

Parliaments, therefore, often sat amid a clamor raised inside and outside the Houses. Sometimes ministers tried to raise a noise to counter the opposition, but it was always more difficult to defend than to criticize. The successful leader had to sense when it would be prudent to give way before the clamor and when it could be safely defied.[18]

Another mode of influencing the opinions of the ruling class and the Parliament was the use of addresses and petitions to the king and the Parliament. The expedient was frequently resorted to both by the government and by the factions in opposition. Addresses to the king, usually prepared at headquarters and given the proper propaganda slant, would be sent out to the universities, corporations, and groups about the country likely to be favorable to the programs envisioned. The recipients in turn would dutifully copy the addresses and send them back—and of course, they usually found their way into print. In 1765-1766, Lord Rockingham met with representatives of the London merchants trading with North America and drew up a petition to Parliament for redress of colonial grievances concerning the Stamp Act. Sent out to all the commercial and manufacturing towns of Great Britain, it returned in a flood of petitions designed to influence the opinion of the sitting Parliament. In 1769-1770, again, the opposition leaders drew up a petition to the king for dissolution of the Parliament and then sought signatures to it in the counties and boroughs as a part of their campaign against the ministers.[19]

Many of the devices and techniques used to influence the opinions and shape the prejudices of the ruling class and the Parliament evolved or were perfected during George Grenville's political career. But many had reached a high state of perfection by the time he appeared on the political scene in 1741. The decade of the 1730's was a fertile period of experiment and experience, for during that decade the opposition to Sir Robert Walpole swelled to flood tide.

It is an axiom in politics that the longer a leader exercises power, the more enemies he will make. By 1741, Walpole had held the central power in the British government for twenty-one years, in the course of which time he had made many enemies. And as the number of his enemies increased, the strength of the opposition to his government increased accordingly. Because it was as a member of that opposition that George Grenville entered upon his political career, it is necessary to survey briefly the manner in which the opposition developed and how George Grenville was swept into it.

iv.

Walpole had never been entirely without opposition in his conduct of the government; from the time of his accession to power in 1720-1721 there had been a significant rumble of discontent and dissent not only in the country at large and in the Parliament, but even to an extent in his ministry. For several years, however, it was almost completely ineffective, due largely to a lack of co-operation among various opposing elements. Many men under the Georges were always ready to oppose any ministry the king might employ, but they were not so ready to act in concert with others. More significant, however, was a lack of able leadership. As a result, by 1722 the opposition began a decline; by 1725 it was scattered and completely ineffective, while at the same time Walpole reached the height of his success in controlling not only the country, the ministry, and the Parliament, but the king as well.[20]

Two events occurred in 1725, however, which furnished the opposition with leadership capable of uniting the disordered elements into an articulate body. The first was the final, open break between Sir Robert Walpole and his lieutenant, William Pulteney.[21] A mature politician, an energetic and effective debater, Pulteney had been one of Walpole's staunchest and most reliable supporters in his rise to power before 1720. Once the summit was reached, however, Walpole was largely able to dispense with his aid; he was too independent, too ambitious, too able for Walpole to dominate in high office. Consequently, Pulteney was not given positions in the government which he felt his services and abilities warranted. Resentment festered slowly, with several disagreements occurring between 1721 and 1725, but in the latter year an open break on the floor of the Commons resulted in Pulteney's dismissal from his office of Cofferer. Thereafter, he entered into regular opposition to the ministry and set about to organize the elements already in opposition into an effective body.[22]

In these efforts he received aid from Henry St. John, Viscount Bolingbroke,[23] who in 1725 returned to England from France. An outstanding statesman during the reign of Anne, he had fled to France shortly after the accession of George I from fear of imprisonment as a Jacobite. The charges circulated against him were largely unfounded, but his flight was taken as an admission of guilt. His enemies quickly had him attainted for high treason, whereupon his peerage and his possessions were forfeited.[24] By 1723, however, he had obtained a removal of the attainder, though he was still deprived of his peerage. Thus, though debarred from the House of Lords, he was ready in 1725 to join with Pulteney in opposition to Walpole, one of the authors of his disgrace, and to work behind the political scenes in the organization of an effective party of opposition to the ministry.[25]

About them these two drew several of the leaders of the various disunited elements in both Houses of Parliament. In the Commons, the early leaders were William Pulteney, the ablest debater of the group, his cousin Daniel Pulteney, and Sir William Wyndham, a friend of Bolingbroke's whom his contemporaries characterized as a "Hanoverian Tory." In the Lords, the chief opposition leader was John, Lord Carteret,[26] considered by many as one of the ablest men in the realm. An experienced statesman, he was in addition an accomplished scholar in the classics and in modern languages. Though he would engage in spirited opposition, it was without a trace of rancour or vindictiveness.

By December, 1726, this tight little group had begun publishing a periodical which they called the *Craftsman,* a weekly propaganda sheet conducted by Nicholas Amhurst and contributed to by Bolingbroke, Pulteney, and others of the group. With skillful management, it proved one of the opposition's most powerful weapons.[27]

One principle was almost a certainty under the Georges: the Prince of Wales would be in opposition to the Court. George, Prince of Wales, was no exception in 1725, and the new opposition came naturally to rally around him. For the two years until his accession to the throne in 1727, he served the new opposition as a nominal head and leader. Immediately upon ascending the throne, however, he abandoned the opposition completely and gave Walpole his whole support. Shortly thereafter, when his eldest son, Frederick, followed the pattern his father had set, the opposition quickly acclaimed him as its nominal leader.

Much has been written to the effect that political opposition was regarded in the eighteenth century as approaching unconstitutionality, and that therefore the opposition gathered around the heir to the throne to escape that calumny. John Owen[28] has pointed out, however, that even though this political fiction was paid lip service by both administration and opposition, it had little or no impact on practical politics. Certainly "Poor Fred" was no effective political leader. Such leadership and coherence as the opposition had must be supplied from within.

For nearly a decade into the new reign, the movement had little success. Walpole was masterful at keeping his opponents divided and off balance and the House of Commons pliant and quiescent. Indeed, in 1731 there were rumors that the *Craftsman* might give up its crusade against the "sole minister" altogether. In 1733, however, Walpole made a misstep which gave them renewed opportunity, The introduction of the Excise Bill enabled Pulteney, Carteret and their friends to put together the nucleus of a really powerful party.

The measure was not in itself unsound. The financial aspects were well considered, and Walpole thought the move good politics as well. But it was a novel idea; there were naturally some protests, as against any new tax. The *Craftsman* seized the issue to launch a propaganda tirade. Probably much to their surprise, the populace got greatly exercised at the idea of prying tax collectors invading private homes and "arbitrary government" tyrannizing the people. Likely Walpole could have carried the measure through Parliament anyway, but he thought it prudent, considering the storm of protest, to withdraw it from consideration without a floor fight.

Although it was not long before the surface of politics was calm again, the Excise experience shook the Walpole ministry. As late as February of the following year, influential ministers such as the Duke of Dorset and Lords Wilmington and Harrington were thinking of resigning their offices owing to "the King's coldness to those who in Parliament voted against Sir Robert Walpole's schemes and to a personal hatred of Sir Robert."29

The major cause of this discontent within the ministry was the way Walpole and the king reacted to opposition to the Excise Bill by their Parliamentary supporters. Walpole himself informed Lord Scarborough, when he went to resign his post as Master of the Horse, that "surrendering his office would prove very prejudicial to his majesty's affairs;" the populace was stirred up, particularly about the removal of army officers who had supported the opposition against the Excise Bill.30 One of those army officers was Richard Temple, Viscount Cobham.

Until 1733, Cobham had been nearly apolitical in the House of Lords. He had voted regularly and uncomplainingly for all of Walpole's measures. But for some reason (the documents are silent) he joined in the protest against the Excise Bill.31 His reward was summary dismissal from his post as colonel of the King's Own Regiment of Horse. His resentment was swift and fierce; the opposition received a new, enthusiastic member.

Cobham now became a recruiting officer of rising young talent for the opposition. Such was his desire that Walpole should not go unpunished for his incivility that he began strenuously to organize his young relatives and friends into an effective voice in the Commons, where they could engage Walpole in debate. Dick Grenville, just home from the grand tour in the fall of 1732, was a likely recruit as head of the Grenville clan. In the general election of 1734, he was elected to the Commons for Cobham's borough of Buckingham.32 Meanwhile, his cousin by marriage, Thomas Pitt, who had married a daughter of Cobham's sister

Christian, was returned for both his family borough of Old Sarum and for that of Okehampton. Old Sarum was accordingly given to his younger brother, William Pitt, who was at this time a cornet in Cobham's former regiment of horse.[33]

The following year another nephew joined the ranks of Cobham's recruits. George Lyttelton, who was already prominent in the service of the Prince of Wales as one of the Prince's equerries, gave the "cousin-hood" a liaison with the nominal leader of the opposition, for Lyttelton was the Prince's "chief favorite," with whom he advised "in all his affairs."[34]

These four young men formed the nucleus of an energetic group which came to be called the "Boy Patriots" or "Cobham's Cubs." Lyttelton and Pitt quickly assumed the lead. Little noise was made during the first session of the Parliament in 1735, but in 1736 more fire was shown. Pitt, the tall, slim cornet of horse with the long neck and great aquiline nose, chose to deliver his maiden speech in the House in a spectacular manner. The occasion was an address of congratulation to the king on the marriage of the Prince of Wales. Pitt seized the occasion to deliver an ironic eulogy on George II's domestic and patriotic virtues and on the Prince's dutiful behavior which thoroughly delighted opposition ranks. That he was dismissed from his cornetcy for his pains made little difference; he was soon recognized as one of the rising orators in the House, and the chastening but left him freer to engage in his attacks upon the government.[35]

Yet the opposition made little real progress. A new periodical, *Common Sense,* took the field beside the *Craftsman* early in 1737, but it too lacked fire. A really controversial issue was needed. It was found in the disputes over the commercial rivalry with Spain. The Spanish had never been able to manage their own slave trade with their colonies, but they had nevertheless always resented England's undertaking to conduct it for them. True, the *Asiento* of the Treaty of Utrecht had granted England this right, but that made it none the less irritating. When to this legal trade the British added a considerable smuggling trade with Spain's American possessions, there naturally followed reprisals against British shipping—reprisals which often overstepped the bounds of mere search and seizure of contraband goods. Many and violent were the protests of British sea captains against the outrages of the Spanish *guardas costas*.

Walpole and his ministry made genuine and sincere efforts to settle the differences with Spain. Negotiations with the Spanish government proceeded almost to a solution, with both sides evidencing an earnest desire for a settlement and making real concessions to such an end. Their efforts were overruled, however, chiefly by the action of the Parliamentary opposition.

The Patriot papers seized upon the issue of Spanish depredations to launch a stormy campaign against the Spanish. Public resentment was soon fanned into such a clamor for war that Walpole was intimidated into embarking upon a war which he had consistently opposed and which there were ample prospects of avoiding.[36] His natural but evident reluctance, moreover, was attacked in a violent harrangue by Pitt, and in the division which followed, Walpole's majority in the Commons was only twenty-eight.[37]

As the nation observed the apathetic manner in which Walpole conducted the war, his majorities in both Houses of Parliament became slimmer and slimmer during 1739 and 1740. In February, 1741, the opposition forced an outright test of strength. Led by Samuel Sandys in the Commons and by Carteret in the Lords, they introduced motions for removal of Walpole from Office. The ministry was able to muster majorities in both Houses, but the margins were slender and the action close. In the Commons, only the defection of William Shippen and his Jacobites provided the margin of victory.

The bear was at bay, however, and the dogs returned to the attack with unabated vigor. When the Eighth Parliament of Great Britain was dissolved in April, 1741, the opposition bent every effort to find greater support in the Ninth. Cobham and the "Boy Patriots" canvassed their political domains for new seats. Dick Grenville held one of the family's seats for Buckingham borough. For some time, however, he had been managing the Grenville estates, enclosing lands, consolidating holdings by purchase, and making himself known widely in the county. The "cousinhood" decided that he could win one of the seats for Buckinghamshire, and the election machinery was set in motion. The expense was not inconsiderable, even though Temple-Grenville influence was dominant. Voters had to be entertained at taverns all over the county, at a cost of £128/01/0; money, over four hundred pounds, was "left in the several towns" for the use of supporters; £62/12/0 was spent on various jobs on election day; and £235/06/03 was laid out for "wine, Brandy, shrub, & strong beer... before and at the election...." Dick reckoned his total expenses at £926/06/09.[38]

Meanwhile, the seat for the borough of Buckingham was available for another member of the family. The choice fell, naturally, on the second brother, George. His election was unopposed, and there were only thirteen members of the corporation. Nonetheless, there were expenses. Among the Stowe MSS., in the handwriting of one of the estate clerks, appears "an account of money paid for the election of Geo. Grenville at the town of Buck^m , 1740/1." The members of the corporation were treated to a grand dinner, at the expense of £14/12/06, more than a pound per person! There were May poles to erect (£0/10/06), "musicians of all sorts at 2/6^d each" (£1/0/0), half a hogshead of ale for the thirsty (£2/0/0), five guineas "paid to Mr. Garrett the Bailiff for the Poor," and various cryptic expenses, such as the five guineas paid to "Price the under sheriff for a very extraordinary expedition." Altogether, Dick Grenville noted expenses of £58/12/07 for his brother's election.[39]

Likewise getting elected was time-consuming, even without opposition. The new candidate had to present himself to the electors. George left the home of Lady Suffolk to go to his election on April 26,[40] and the return from the poll was not made until May 4.[41]

Heretofore George's main task had been to handle the legal affairs of the family. He had worked closely with Dick in the purchases and enclosures of the preceding half decade. Occasionally he gave political advice of a legal nature, as when he answered a question of Dick's as to how far his parliamentary privilege protected him.[42] Now he was to be involved directly in the political activities of the family and of the opposition. His Aunt Christian ventured that it was "a bold stroke indeed for so young a lawyer to begin with being against the Crown, as George G. Has done. I wish he may come off with applause, but must blame his friends for putting him on so hazardous a point." William Murray, she feared, would be more than a match for him in legal debate.[43] The solicitous aunt, however, had misplaced her concern. George was not risking his legal career; he had discovered his real vocation: politics

NOTES

CHAPTER II

[1] *The Structure of Politics at the Accession of George III,* 2 vols., London, 1929, and *England in the Age of the American Revolution,* London, 1930.

[2] Especially notable has been the work of D. G. Barnes, John Brooke, Sir Herbert Butterfield, John Owen, J. H. Plumb, Sir Richard Pares, Charles Ritcheson, and Robert Walcott.

[3] William Thomas Laprade, *British History for American Students,* New York, 1926, p. 4.

[4] Portland to Lord Edward Bentinck, February 28, 1767, quoted in A. S. Turberville, *A History of Welbeck Abbey and its Owners,* 2 vols., London, 1938-1939, II, 68.

[5] Charles Watson-Wentworth, second Marquis of Rockingham (1730-1782). Richard Grenville succeeded his mother as second Earl Temple in 1752 (see below, Chapter IV).

[6] Philip Yorke, first Earl of Hardwicke (1690-1764), and William Murray, first Earl of Mansfield (1705-1793).

[7] For examples in 1746 and 1756, see below, Chapters IV, V.

[8] William Thomas Laprade, *Public Opinion and Politics in Eighteenth Century England to the Fall of Walpole,* New York, 1936, p. 280.

[9] Laprade, *Public Opinion and Politics,* pp. 432-434.

[10] See below, Chapter XVI.

[11] To Royston, March 8, 1763, Philip Yorke, *The Life and Correspondence of Philip Yorke, Earl of Hardwicke, Lord High Chancellor of Great Britain,* 3 vols., Cambridge, 1913.

[12] February 16, 1765, Murray MSS.

[13] See, for example, an account of a meeting of the Newcastle forces, Devonshire to Hardwicke, June 14, 1757, Yorke, *Hardwicke,* II, 400.

[14] See below, Chapters X, XIV; Chesterfield to Huntingdon, Stanhope, November 13, 28, 1765, Bonamy Dobree, editor, *The Letters of Philip Dormer Stanhope, Fourth Earl of Chesterfield,* 6 vols., London, 1932, VI, 2678, 2685-2686.

[15] Laprade, *Public Opinion and Politics,* pp. 427-428.

[16] For a detailed treatment of the "family connexion" interpretation of eighteenth-century politics, see Namier, *England in the Age of the American Revolution and Structure of Politics,* Namier and John Brooke, *The History of Parliament: The Commons,* London, 1964, 3 vols., and Robert Walcott, Jr., *English Politics in the Early Eighteenth Century,* Cambridge, Mass., 1956. One

suspects that the picture of semi-permanent family cliques which Namier, Brooke, and Walcott paint to replace the exploded idea of "Whig" and "Tory" parties still goes too far toward over-simplifying the situation. Only a minute examination of the factions in their continual state of flux reveals the true nature of the political alignments of the period.

[17] Durden to Harley, December 5, 1710, Historical Manuscripts Commission, *The Manuscripts of his Grace the Duke of Portland,* 10 vols., London, 1892-1931, IV, 641.

[18] Laprade, *Public Opinion and Politics,* pp. 12-15.

[19] See below, Chapters XIII, XVI.

[20] Charles Bechdolt Realey, *The Early Opposition to Sir Robert Walpole, 1720-1727,* Philadelphia, 1931, pp. 153-155.

[21] Afterwards created Earl of Bath (1684-1764).

[22] Realey, *Early Opposition to Walpole,* pp. 165-166; *The Historical Register,* 25 vols., London, 1714-1738, X (1725), chronological diary, p. 26.

[23] 1678-1751.

[24] *Historical Register,* II (1715), chronological diary, p. 52; Laprade, *Public Opinion and Politics,* pp. 169, 174-175.

[25] Philip Henry Stanhope, fifth Earl Stanhope, *History of England from the Peace of Utrecht to the Peace of Versailles, 1713-1783,* 7 vols., London, 1853, II, 71-73; Basil Williams, *The Whig Supremacy, 1714-1760,* Oxford, 1939, p. 194.

[26] Afterwards Earl Granville (1690-1763).

[27] Williams, *Pitt,* I, 51, 98-99; Williams, *Whig Supremacy,* pp. 194-195.

[28] John Beresford Owen, *The Rise of the Pelhams,* London, 1957, pp. 62-86.

[29] Historical Manuscripts Commission, *Diary of the First Earl of Egmont (Viscount Percival),* 3 vols., London, 1920-1923, II, 33.

[30] H. M. C., *Egmont Diary,* II, 34.

[31] For speculation on Cobham's motives, see Wiggin, *Faction of Cousins,* p. 2.

[32] *Members of Parliament,* II, 72.

[33] *Members of Parliament,* II, 74; Williams, *Pitt,* I, 41.

[34] Note by Lyttelton, n.d., Robert Phillimore, *Memoirs and Correspondence of George,* Lord Lyttelton, 2 vols., London, 1845, I, 145.

[35] *Parliamentary History,* IX, 1221-1223; Williams, *Pitt,* 65-67.

[36] Harold W. V. Temperley, "The Causes of the War of Jenkins' Ear, 1739," *Transactions of the Royal Historical Society,* Third Series, III (1909), 197-236.

[37] Coxe, *Robert Walpole,* III, 519; *Parliamentary History,* X 729-786 1243-1279.

[38] Stowe MSS., miscellaneous election accounts.

[39] Richard Grenville's account book, p. 114; miscellaneous election accounts, Stowe MSS.

[40] Lady Suffolk to G. Berkeley, April 25, 1741, Lewis Melville, *Lady Suffolk and her Circle,* London, 1924, p. 261.

[41] *Members of Parliament,* II, 85.

[42] George Grenville to Richard Grenville, December 14, 1738, Stowe MSS, box 8: "As to your parliamentary question I scarce dare venture an opinion as you say disputes have arisen about it & I am very ignorant of it. We allways say yt ye Parlt make their own privileges what they will but ye law knows of none but the safety of their persons; nevertheless I will tell you how I understand it. You are privileged from suits during ye sitting only; at other times ye justice of the nation is not stopp'd but I take it any violence done to a member of Parliament either in his person servants or estate unless it is in consequence of some legal process or proceeding is esteemed a breach of privilege tho' it be committed during the recess of Parliament...."

[43] Christian Lyttelton to Charles Lyttelton, n. d., Maud Wyndham, *Chronicles of the Eighteenth Century,* 2 vols., London, 1924, I, 97.

Thomas Pelham-Holles, 1st Duke of Newcastle

CHAPTER III

THE BOY PATRIOTS, 1741-1744

i.

George Grenville joined his brothers and cousins in the House of Commons at a time when the wave of opposition to Sir Robert Walpole was reaching its crest and was preparing to break and engulf the First Minister. Grenville was caught up in this wave in December, 1741, through little initiative of his own. For the next three years, the Grenville clan was to continue in opposition to the King's ministers. Although his efforts were not to be the most effective or spectacular, no one among the Cobham set would be more enthusiastic or energetic than George Grenville.

The election had been a success for the opposition, but no one could say how much of a success. The Prince of Wales, "Poor Fred," had done well in Cornwall with the aid of the Pitts. Twenty-seven of the forty-four seats for the well-represented county would be held by the opposition, while notable shifts also occurred in Dorsetshire and Scotland. And as it turned out, George was not the only new Grenville in the house. His cousin George Lyttelton was elected not only for Oakhampton but also for Old Sarum, the pocket borough of the Pitts. The latter seat was thus at the disposal of the cousinhood, and Jemmy as the third son was the natural choice. Meanwhile the Tory contingent had held its own, though there would be some challenges of their elections when the Parliament met. Although they kept to themselves on the back benches and refused to act on a common plan with the rest of the opposition, they could be counted upon to vote against the administration. With few losses and numerous additions to the opposition, Walpole's majority had almost disappeared.[1] Hopeful supporters of the ministry reckoned their majority at sixteen, but George Bubb Doddington,[2] a recent convert to the opposition, wrote that "if we take the proper measures, sixteen and nothing is the same thing."[3] Such "proper measures" the opposition was not long in getting under way.

Yet when the excitement of the election campaign was over in May, there was a long lull in political activity until the Parliament met in December. "The politics of the age are entirely suspended," wrote Horace Walpole, Sir Robert's son, at the end of June; "nothing is mentioned; but this bottling them up, will make them fly out with the greater violence the moment Parliament meets."[4] If political discussion was absent (an assertion very difficult to credit), the opposition press was not silent. The *Craftsman* and *Common Sense,* joined by a new tri-weekly, the *Champion,* discharged broadside after broadside against the "sole minister." They did not lack for ammunition. They rang all the changes on the old charge that Walpole's position with the King was unconstitutional.

The conduct of the war continued to be an object of attack, and now not only the Spanish conflict but the whole Continental situation could be played upon to his disadvantage.

Walpole's direction of the war against Spain caused criticism enough, but in 1740 the war became involved in a greater conflict. In that year both Emperor Charles VI and King Frederick William of Prussia died. Young Frederick II treated the Pragmatic Sanction, by which the rulers of Europe had guaranteed the succession and possessions of Maria Theresa as Charles VI's rightful heir, as a mere scrap of paper. Throwing his excellent Prussian army into the Hapsburg province of Silesia, he precipitated Europe into a general war.

When France joined Prussia, in accordance with her ancient anti-Hapsburg tradition, Britain found herself forced into a new war while the old was yet undecided. However much Walpole wished to avoid the entanglement, the forces against him were too great. The flagrant nature of Frederick's attack, the treaty obligations which had been incurred under the Pragmatic Sanction, and the emotional appeal of the beautiful young Queen in distress forced the Minister to renew British pledges of support by agreeing to a subsidy of 300,000 pounds and sending 12,000 troops to the Continent.

As autumn progressed, news of reversals abroad continually lowered Walpole's popularity. In October came the news of the failure of the attack at Cartegena on the Spanish main, shortly followed by a report of another failure in Cuba. To these were added the heavy losses in shipping owing to the Spanish war. All of these the populace readily ascribed to the Minister's favoritism in selecting officers or to his insufficient preparations. Finally came a decisive blow to Walpole's credit in the announcement of the neutrality of Hanover. Even before the new Parliament assembled, observers could see that the end for the beleaguered Minister could not be far away.

The balance between the ministry and the opposition was decided by the results of the trials of election petitions at the opening of the session. On December 22, two ministerial supporters were unseated for Westminster by a majority of four. The division was a hand writing on the wall. Walpole set about feverishly during the Christmas recess to regain support, but his fate had already been decided.5 When the opposition carried a Berwick election petition, January 19, without even a division, there could no longer be any doubt.

For a few more agonized days and weeks Sir Robert continued to cling to the wreck of his power. On January 21 the opposition brought him to a supreme personal test. Pulteney introduced his famous motion calling for papers relating to the war to be referred to a secret committee. Involving as it did several charges against the conduct of the war and numerous personal invectives against the minister, the motion was crucial. Within living memory, the Tower and even the scaffold had awaited disgraced ministers. By dint of tremendous exertion, Sir Robert was able to defeat the measure by three votes, 253 to 250.6

George Grenville chose the debate on this motion as the occasion for his maiden speech in the Commons. No transcript of the speech exists, but it is certain that it was a worthy effort, for Horace Walpole, naturally a strong supporter of his father's ministry, mentions it among "several glorious speeches on both sides."7 Although he would never be a brilliant orator—thunder and lightning were the province of his brother-in-law— Grenville was early showing his ability as a debater.

As the session progressed, the tide ran ever stronger against the minister. The end came on February 2, 1742, when a question on a Chippenham election petition was carried against the ministry by the margin of sixteen votes, 241 against 225. The opposition had made it evident that Walpole could no longer control the Commons; he prepared to retire. After accepting a peerage, February 9, as Earl of Orford, he resigned on the eleventh the offices he had held for twenty-one years.8

ii.

From the point of view of Grenville and the Cobham faction the victory was hollow. To their disgust, Walpole's colleagues succeeded in pulling the teeth of the opposition by luring away a few of its leaders. Carteret took the seals as Secretary of State for the Northern Department and Sandys became Chancellor of the Exchequer. Pulteney, declining to take office, took a seat at the Cabinet Council and the promise of a peerage instead. The rest of the opposition was left out in the cold. Lord Wilmington, Walpole's Lord President, immediately succeeded to the Treasury, while the Duke of Newcastle[10] kept the seals for the Southern Department, which he had held since 1724.

The "Boy Patriots," meanwhile, were sullen and disgruntled. Cobham, it is true, regained the command of a regiment and was named to the Privy Council, but he had expected a much larger share of power. More dissatisfied were his "cubs." Pitt and Lyttelton, while holding positions in the household of the Prince of Wales, had nevertheless desired office in the ministry. The three Grenvilles were excluded from any office whatever.

The chief agent in this adroit settlement was the Duke of Newcastle, who had been secretly intriguing with Pulteney and Carteret while the Parliamentary clash was in full career. His aims were to divide the opposition, to insure his own position, and to provide a safe retreat for the defeated First Minister. In all three objectives he succeeded handsomely, for the teeth of the opposition had been effectively drawn.[11]

Although the resentment of the "Boy Patriots" over this slight was bitter and deep, it did not during that session take the form of organized opposition. George Grenville, indeed, would have been unable to bear the strain of further struggles such as those which resulted in Walpole's overthrow. For several years he had been in delicate health, and the exertions of the debates during January and February had sapped his remaining strength. Lord Cornbury,[12] a friend in the opposition, wrote the following August reproaching him for his excessive zeal in the cause of the cousinhood. "I do not know," he counselled, "that any party is worth killing oneself for." He admitted that such a family group was for the young politician "what, whether one will or no, one must finally act for," but he advised moderation. "If I know you," he said, "your zeal is not according to knowledge with respect to your own constitution."[13]

When Grenville received this letter he was in France on the way to the Riviera. Things were too serious merely for the Bath waters! In October Dick reported gloomy prospects. He had just received, he wrote "a very bad account of poor George. I hope however that his state is not quite so desperate as they fear, for we hear from his travelling companion that he was extremely mended at Avignon, and intended soon to set out for Aix."[14] He was soon on the mend. The family's anxiety was relieved when Hetty received a letter from George himself in Aix-en-Provence reporting that he was "considerably better."[15] His aunt, Lady Cobham, effused at the news.

I was extremely glad to hear by the last letters that you really find your-self much better. I hope to God you will continue mending and that when you return you will be fat and strong. I approve and so dos *(sic)* my lord of your going to Italy. What can you do better? It will be warmer and a bet-ter climate for your complaint and divert you more than where you are.... I would not have you write yourself because I think it is bad for your health, but soon be a great man & get yourself a secretary.... Hetty is very well. We all love and wish you better health, Dear George. Be careful of yourself & take care your beds on the road are well aired as you travel. God bless you, my dear George. I am affectionately yours

A Cobham[16]

Whether George heeded this solicitous advice is unrecorded, or even whether he actually went on to Italy. His health continued to mend, how-ever. By early December he was able to return to England and soon to London. Apparently the Mediterranean sun and the clear air of the Riviera had a magical effect on his illness. It was many years—until the closing days of his life—before his health was seriously endangered again.

iii.

In England the Cobham set, continually professing their concern for Grenville's health,[17] meanwhile had found a new "tyrant" to slay in Lord Carteret. Almost as soon as he entered office in February, 1742, Carteret became as much the "sole minister" as Walpole had ever been. Engaging in personality, frank and jovial in manner, he had the particular advantage of having a fluent command of German and considerable acquaintance with Continental politics. George II was charmed and flattered; he had always put German before English interests. Carteret almost immediate-ly became the King's favorite.

Walpole as Prime Minister had loathed the war and its diplomacy; Carteret revelled in it. He and George III planned a campaign against Paris. Sixteen thousand Hanoverian troops in British pay, 16,000 British soldiers, 6,000 Hessians, and a Dutch army were to march on the French capital. The Dutch, however, were extremely cautious in committing their troops, and the whole force sat inactive around Ghent for nearly a year.

The opportunities of opposition in this situation were too obvious to miss, and the "Cobham Cubs" did not miss them. As soon as the second session of the Ninth Parliament assembled in November, 1742, they made common cause with Shippen and his Jacobite brethren in opposition. From the first day, the new opposition opened a violent fire on Carteret, Hanover, and in an only slightly more restrained manner, the King. Dick, keeping George posted on events in St. Stephen's while his brother recuperated in France, reported the situation on November 22. Lord Cobham and Lord Gower[18] had signalled the advent of renewed opposition by refusing to attend the Cabinet Council. "We have had very warm work in the House of Commons the first day upon the Address," wrote Dick. "Pitt spoke like ten thousand angels; your humble servant was so inflamed at their indecency that he could not contain, but talked a good while with his usual modesty. Jemmy, too, was all on fire, but could not get a place." The prospects for the opposition were bright. On the address it had divided 150 against 259, but members reckoned themselves at two hundred. And the ministry too recognized their strength. "It is inconceivable how colloguing and flattering all the ministers are to all of us," Dick reported, "notwithstanding our impertinence. We shall have a glorious day about the 16,000," he predicted. "We shall then see who are Hanoverians, and who Englishmen."[19]

When that "glorious day" arrived on December 10, George had returned to England and to St. Stephen's, his health and his energies restored. In his letter of November 22, Dick had relayed his doctor's permission to return. George had already pledged himself that, in view of his health, he would submit himself entirely to Dick's judgment in the matter of opposition. There would be many opportunities open; both sides were clamoring for support. If he were to refuse guidance to George, Dick ventured, there would be many in the Commons who would undertake it "the moment they see you enter St. Stephen's Chapel."[20]

The debates on the Hanoverian troops were not so glorious as Dick had anticipated. George Grenville spoke late in the debate, reiterating arguments already advanced against deploying troops in Flanders and hiring Hanoverians, and deploring the "animosities between our sovereign and our fellow subjects." Yet "such animosities must inevitably arise," he asserted, "from this detestable preference of the troops of Hanover." Apparently, however, there were more "Hanoverians" than "Englishmen" in the Commons; the ministry carried the measure by a majority of sixty-seven, 260 against 193.[21]

The minority had fallen only seven short of Dick's estimate of two hundred, but the ministry had rallied greater strength than had been expected. Thus defeated, the opposition went no further in its challenge against continuing the Hanoverian troops in British pay. Rather it concentrated its fire during the ensuing year upon the moneys levied for troops which had already been raised.[22] But while opposition in the Commons was quiescent, the purposes for which the "Boy Patriots" had undertaken opposition were being advanced by other developments. Relations within the ministry were working in favor of the admission of the "cubs" to office.

iv.

Since the formation of the new ministry, there had been dissension within the governmental ranks. Carteret, secure in the favor of George II, snubbed and despised his fellow ministers, displaying toward them "an obstinate and offensive silence" and often leaving them "in entire ignorance...both with respect to the operations of the war, and the sources from whence they arose."[23] Such behavior could only be resented, and it was not long before Sandys and several members of the old Walpole administration had formed a coalition against Carteret within the ministry. Though all the ministers supported Carteret's measures and foreign policy in the Parliament, they were dividing more and more into rival factions .

A test of strength came between the two groups when Lord Wilmington died, July 2, 1743, thus leaving vacant the key post of First Lord of the Treasury. During the period of Wilmington's declining health, Carteret had persuaded Pulteney, now Earl of Bath, to declare himself a candidate for the position. Pulteney as an ally in the important post of the Treasury would, of course, strengthen Carteret's position immeasurably in the Cabinet Council. But at the same time, the opposing faction of the ministry, supported by Walpole, now Lord Orford, a confidential adviser to the King, put forward Henry Pelham, the younger brother of the Duke of Newcastle. The King, becoming convinced that the support of the Pelhams would be necessary to counteract the unpopularity of the Hanoverian ventures, had Carteret notify Pelham of his appointment, August 16, 1743.[24]

Soon after the appointment, Lord Orford advised Pelham as to how to get control of the government over Carteret and his supporters. "Your strength," he suggested, "must be formed of your own friends, the old corps, and recruits from the Cobham squadron, who should be persuaded now Bath is beaten, it makes room for them, if they will not crowd the door when the house is on fire, that nobody can go in or out."[25] Had such a coalition been undertaken at this time, it appears likely that George

Grenville would have come into office over a year earlier than he did. No such alignment was to be accomplished for some time, however, even though the Pelhams and the Cobhamites were in a manner united in their disapproval of Carteret's policies. The Cobhamites, aware of this coincidence of opinion, were hoping that the Pelhams might accept overtures for a coalition on terms dictated by the cousinhood. But such overtures the Pelhams would not hear of.

While the ministry was breaking into factions, rifts were also occurring in the ranks of the Patriots. Pitt, Lyttelton, and Chesterfield[26] had disagreed with Lord Cobham over Carteret's foreign policy. While they agreed in opposing his Hanoverian measures, they nevertheless recommended a vigorous prosecution of the war by British troops. Cobham continued to oppose the sending of troops abroad. The Grenville brothers were put in a ticklish situation, for whatever their views on the issue might be they were not really free. Cobham was not only their political patron; he was the head of the family and the source of much of their future prestige. The Grenvilles, therefore, continued at this point to support their uncle against Pitt and Lyttelton.[27] Yet, with such divisions within the government and without, it was difficult to discover whether Cobham was leading them forward or backward. The whole political scene was in such a state of disarray that Orford exclaimed: "There are so many inconsistencies arise in every view, that order can arise out of nothing but confusion."[28]

In the latter part of November, the rivalry between Carteret and the Pelhams reached a crisis in the Cabinet Council. A difference arose over a convention with Austria, and with the aid of their friend Hardwicke, the Lord Chancellor,[29] the Pelhams were able to prevail over Carteret in the Cabinet Council by a majority of five to four.[30]

v.

Meanwhile the Cobhamites were changing their approach. By the time the third session of the Ninth Parliament met in December, 1743, they had come to realize that the Pelhams could not take them into the government except under stipulations while Carteret was in office. Thus in the new session they fell with renewed virulence upon that minister and his Hanoverian measures in order to widen the breach in the ministry and hasten his fall. The better to oppose, the Patriots divested themselves of all connections with the government. Lord Cobham notified Newcastle of his resignation from his colonelcy, and Lord Gower resigned his office of

Privy Seal.31

The opposition was exceptionally vehement in its attacks from the first of the session. In several of the battles in the Commons, since Pitt and Lyttelton still refused to oppose measures dealing with the sending of British troops abroad, George Grenville led the way for the Cobham forces. In the debate on the address of thanks to the King's speech, he turned his venom on the Hanoverians, declaring that the British would "never rest until the electoral are separated from the regal dominions."32 On December 15, however, he made a false step. Against the advice of Pitt and without his support, Grenville introduced a motion that "in consideration of the exhausted and impoverished state of this kingdom, by the great and unequal expense it has hitherto been burthened with," the King be petitioned that no alliance be entered into by Great Britain without consulting the States General of Holland. The step proved ill-advised, for it was immediately ripped apart by William Murray,33 now Solicitor-General, and the consequent defeat on the division by 209 votes against only 132 served to increase the disunity of the opposition.34

Yet Grenville continued to lead the way when the Commons assembled after the Christmas holidays. On January 11, 1744, he introduced a motion against the use of British troops abroad. Pitt had agreed in a caucus of the cousinhood that he would not oppose the measure,35 but both he and Lyttelton steadfastly refused to say a word in its favor. The ministry defeated it without an effort, 277-165.36 And so the session continued, with Grenville leading the way for the opposition and with Pitt and Lyttelton sitting in stony silence. At times the opposition rallied respectable numbers of votes, but never so many as to cause the ministers anxiety.37

Meanwhile the attack in the Lords was meeting with more success. The opposition there launched a fierce attack upon the Treaty of Worms, intended further to lower the popularity of Carteret. The treaty, concluded in September, 1743, called among other things for a subsidy to Sardinia by Great Britain in the amount of £200,000 annually. The fierceness of the attack and the animosity displayed toward Hanover and Carteret almost made the Pelhams demand the dismissal of Carteret and accede to the overtures of the Cobhamites. Orford, however, advised them to await a more favorable opportunity.38

On February 15, however, there came an announcement which largely put an end to opposition. On that date the King informed the Parliament that he had received "undoubted intelligence" that a French fleet was preparing to invade England in the interest of the Pretender. With only slight opposition—Grenville made a bitter speech against the suspension of the Habeas Corpus act[39]—the government acted promptly to safeguard the country against the supposed threat. But throughout the crisis Grenville insisted that France intended "to terrify, not to invade us."[40]

There came no opportunity to return to Carteret and the Hanoverian issue during that session, for the King prorogued the Parliament before the threat of invasion had completely passed. The opposition was thus deprived of further opportunity to promote Carteret's dismissal through Parliamentary opposition. The chance to force the closet was gone glimmering.

vi.

Yet as events transpired, both objectives—Carteret's dismissal and the opportunity to enter the ministry with the Pelhams—were achieved before the next meeting of the Parliament, which was set for November 27, 1744. The war, under Carteret's direction, was going badly; in the same measure, the minister's reputation was falling at home. In May, 1744, Frederick II broke his agreements of neutrality with Maria Theresa and re-entered the war against Austria, which was almost drained of troops. At the same time, France finally declared war upon Austria and Great Britain, whom she had been fighting for three years. The pressure on her Alsatian frontier relieved by Frederick's re-entry, France now threw an army of 80,000 men into the Netherlands, menacing the British there with vastly superior forces.[41] Carteret's entire policy had broken down.

Under such circumstances, the Pelhams and their allies in the Cabinet Council, Hardwicke and Harrington,[42] finally decided that they could no longer endure Carteret's direction of foreign affairs, even though he still retained the favor of the King. Accordingly, they presented a memorandum to the King, November 1, 1744, in effect giving him the alternative of dismissing either Carteret or them.[43] George II had to choose between his favorite and his inclinations for Hanover on the one hand and the Pelhams and control of the House of Commons on the other.

While the King deliberated, Carteret, now Earl Granville,[44] appealed to the opposition for support. Through the Prince of Wales, he made overtures to the Cobhamites and their associates, promising wide admissions to office among their group and a dissolution of Parliament in order that more support might be gained.[45] In his overtures, however, he found himself anticipated by the Pelhams. Newcastle hinted at the idea of approaching the opposition in a letter to Hardwicke, November 3,[46] and the Lord Chancellor was not long in putting the idea into effect. He immediately approached Chesterfield, who relayed the offer of negotiation to the opposition groups.

There was a desire among almost all the members of the opposition to coalesce with the Pelhams and to facilitate the removal of Carteret. They could not agree among themselves as to whether they should make stipulations as to policies or simply accede to those of the Pelhams. Some of the leaders, principally Bedford,[47] Chesterfield, and Pitt, wished office without any regard to changes of policy. Cobham and most of his nephews, on the other hand, called for such measures as a repeal of the Septennial Act, the introduction of an effective place-bill in the Commons, and a new foreign policy. To settle the matter, a committee of nine leaders of the opposition[48] was selected, and it was decided that the whole opposition would abide by the vote of the majority of the committee.

Pitt's position among the Cobham set was demonstrated in the vote, for he and Lyttelton joined Bedford and Chesterfield against their patron in favor of coalescing without stipulation. The rifts in the cousinhood were widening, and Pitt was supplanting Cobham as the leader of the group. Cobham nevertheless acceded to the decision, after Newcastle eased the matter by promising that Hanoverian interests should be subordinated to English in foreign policy and that Cobham should have a share in the distribution of offices.[49]

Thus the overtures of the Pelhams were accepted and those of Lord Granville refused by the opposition. Thwarted by the Patriots, Granville now solicited the support of Orford, but that veteran politician realized the situation and gave him no encouragement. When George II asked Orford's advice, he replied that it would be best to comply with the wishes of the majority of the Cabinet Council, and the King reluctantly followed his advice. On November 23, he notified Hardwicke that Granville should resign.[50] The following day "the Earl of Granville, late Lord Carteret, was turned out of his office of Secretary of State, sore against the King's will, and Lord Harrington kissed hands for the seals in his room."[51]

Negotiations were now set under way for a "broad bottom" ministry. With some judicious shifting of offices, several of the leaders of the opposition were accommodated with places. Chesterfield, the agent for the negotiation in conjunction with Cobham, received the post of Lord Lieutenant of Ireland and was appointed Ambassador to the Hague.

Bedford was placed at the head of the Admiralty, and several of the other peers secured posts, with Gower regaining the Privy Seal. Lord Cobham declined to take any office, but put in his claim for his nephew, George Grenville, who was offered a seat at the Board of Admiralty.[52]

Grenville then shocked his uncle by announcing that he could not accept the office, even though he had been striving toward it ever since he had entered the Parliament. His reason was apparently a fear of dividing the cousinhood even further, for Pitt had been denied office. Newcastle had promised Cobham that Pitt should have the post of Secretary at War, but the King stood in the way. George II objected strongly to admitting any of those who had been violent in their opposition to his foreign measures, and Pitt was among the major offenders in this respect. Chesterfield had led the attack against Hanover in the Lords, and as a result the Pelhams had virtually forced the King to grant him his appointments. "I command you to trouble me no more with such nonsense," "the King cried upon granting this concession. "Although I have been forced to part with those I liked, I will never be induced to take into my service those who are disagreeable to me."[53] In the face of such peremptory commands, the Pelhams dared not press Pitt's nomination.

And with Pitt excluded, Grenville foresaw that the young firebrand would break even further from his uncle if he accepted office. He therefore declared that so long as Pitt was excluded he could not accept office, "the only reasons for which were my friendship for Mr. Pitt, and my apprehension of family uneasiness."[54] Cobham, however, was persistent in pressing his nephew to accept. Perhaps he feared that Pitt was gaining too much of an influence over George. Dick, too, advised him to accept, as did Pitt himself. Finally, when Cobham "complained bitterly" to Grenville's mother and "engaged her likewise" to press him, he gave in and kissed hands for the office on December 27, 1744.[55]

For three years Grenville had spent his time, his energy, and even his health in supporting the interests of the Cobhamites in the Commons, and now his efforts were rewarded with political office. Ambition, ability, and hard work were involved. So too were circumstances and particularly the support of the "cousinhood." Grenville hesitated to step upon the first rung; thereafter, he would climb eagerly.

NOTES

CHAPTER III

[1] *Members of Parliament,* II, 93; *Commons Journals,* XXIV, 18-19, 85, 89-92. On the Tories and their participation in opposition, see Owen, *Rise of the Pelhams,* pp. 73-75.

[2] Afterwards Baron of Melcombe-Regis (1691-1762).

[3] To the Duke of Argyle, July 3, 1741, Coxe, *Robert Walpole,* III, 577.

[4] Walpole, *Letters,* I, 109.

[5] *Parliamentary History,* XII, 326; Coxe, *Robert Walpole,* I, 691-692.

[6] *Parliamentary History,* XII, 332-373; Coxe, *Robert Walpole,* I, 693-694.

[7] To Sir Horace Mann, January 22, 1742, *The Letters of Horace Walpole, Fourth Earl of Orford,* edited by Mrs. Paget Toynbee, 16 vols., London, 1903-1905, I, 165.

[8] Coxe, *Robert Walpole,* I, 695.

[9] The term "Cabinet Council" is used in the documents of the time to denominate an inner council of responsible ministers in the government. At no time was it a formal body with a fixed membership. Men with and without office might be called to it. Nor was its membership uniform within any one administration. The men called varied with the type of question under consideration. For instance, Pitt's Cabinet Council on war measures often included John, Lord Ligonier (1678-1770), the Lieutenant-General of the Ordnance, whose office was not of ministerial rank. Grenville, when faced with important legal questions, often called in Lord Chief Justice Mansfield, who held no governmental office.

[10] Thomas Pelham-Holles, first Duke of Newcastle (1693-1768).

[11] Coxe, *Robert Walpole,* I, 698-706; *Parl. Hist.,* XII, 409-411; William Coxe, *Memoirs of the Administration of the Right Honourable Henry Pelham,* 2 vols., London, 1829, I, 30-31.

[12] Henry Hyde, Viscount Cornbury, eldest son of Henry, fourth Earl of Clarendon. He died before his father, May, 1753.

[13] August 3, 1742, *Grenville Papers,* I, 5.

[14] Richard Grenville to Lady Denbigh, October 21, 1742, Historical Manuscripts Commission, *Report on the Manuscripts of the Earl of Denbigh,* part V, London, 1911, p. 238.

[15] Lady Cobham to Lady Denbigh, n. d. (late October, 1742), H. M. C., *Denbigh MSS.,* p. 238.

[16] To George Grenville, October 26, 1742, Stowe MSS., box 17.

[17] See letters to Grenville from Cornbury, Pitt, Lyttelton, Murray, and Richard Grenville, August-November, 1742, *Grenville Papers,* I, 1-20.

[18] John Leveson Gower, second Baron Gower (1694-1754), who had been one of the leaders in the Lords in the later opposition to Walpole.

[19] Richard Grenville to George Grenville, November 22, 1742, *Grenville Papers,* I, 19- 20.

[20] *Grenville Papers,* I, 18.

[21] *Parl. Hist.,* XII, 1051-1053.

[22] *Parl. Hist.,* XIII, 1-44; Coxe, *Pelham,* I, 57.

[23] Williams, *Pitt,* I, 99.

[24] Coxe, *Pelham,* I, 59, 81-85; H. M. C., *Egmont Diary,* III, 273.

[25] Orford to Pelham, August 25, 1743, Coxe, *Pelham,* I, 92.

[26] Philip Dormer Stanhope, fourth Earl of Chesterfield (1694-1773), who had been one of the members of the opposition in the Lords since his dismissal from his place at court during the disputes over the Excise Bill.

[27] Grenville's narrative, *Grenville Papers,* I, 423.

[28] Orford to Pelham, September 18, 1743, Coxe, *Pelham,* I, 101.

[29] Philip Yorke, first Earl of Hardwicke (1690-1764).

[30] H. M. C., *Egmont Diary* (November 27, 1743), III, 276-277.

[31] Coxe, *Pelham,* I, 112-113.

[32] *Parl. Hist.,* XIII, 144.

[33] A former associate of Grenville's among the "Boy Patriots" until he accepted office in November, 1742. Afterwards Earl of Mansfield and Lord Chief Justice of the King's Bench (1705-1793).

[34] *Parl. Hist.,* XIII, 384-388; Coxe, *Pelham,* I, 122-124.

[35] Grenville's narrative, *Grenville Papers,* I, 423.

[36] *Parl. Hist.,* XIII, 389-462.

[37] *Parl. Hist.,* XIII, 401-407, 463, 504; Coxe, *Pelham,* I, 127, 129.

[38] Coxe, *Pelham,* I, 76-133; *Parl. Hist.,* XIII, 504-505; Philip Yorke, *The Life and Correspondence of Philip Yorke, Earl of Hardwicke, Lord High Chancellor of Great Britain,* 3 vols., London, 1913, I, 323-325.

[39] Walpole to Mann, March 1, 1744, Toynbee, *Walpole's Letters,* II, 10.

[40] *Parl. Hist.,* XII, 641-645, 672, 675; Coxe, *Pelham,* I, 142-146, 152.

[41] Stanhope, *History,* III, 181-182; Yorke, *Hardwicke,* I, 333-334.

[42] William Stanhope, first Earl of Harrington (1683-1756). He had been Secretary of State under Walpole and Lord President of the Council since Walpole's fall.

[43] "Copy of a paper presented to the King," November 1, 1744, Coxe, *Pelham,* I, 177-185.

[44] Carteret had come into the title of Earl of Granville on the death of his mother, October 18, 1744.

[45] Coxe, *Pelham,* I, 188.

[46] Coxe, *Pelham,* I, 186.

[47] John Russell, fourth Duke of Bedford (1710-1770), was one of the younger lords in the opposition and was regarded as one of the "Boy Patriots," though not strictly of Cobham's group.

[48] Led by Bedford, Chesterfield, Gower, Cobham, Pitt, & Lyttelton.

[49] Richard Glover, *Memoirs of a Celebrated Literary and Political Character,* London, 1813, pp. 26-27.

[50] Yorke's parliamentary journal, *Parl. Hist.,* XIII, 975-93; Coxe, *Pelham,* I, 189-190.

[51] H. M. C., *Egmont's Diary* (November 24, 1744), III, 303.

[52] Glover, *Memoirs,* pp. 25-27.

[53] Stone to Hardwicke, December 6, 1744, Coxe, *Pelham,* I, 197.

[54] Grenville's narrative, *Grenville Papers,* I, 424.

[55] Grenville's narrative, *Grenville Papers,* I, 423-424; Haydn, *Book of Dignities,* p. 178 .

William Pitt, 1st Earl of Chatham

CHAPTER IV

GRENVILLE AND PITT, 1744-1755

The next eleven years, from December, 1744, to November, 1755, were years of great advancement for the Grenville family and the Cobham cousinhood. They were years of intimacy as well. The Grenvilles and their associates were still young men, struggling up the lower rungs of the political ladder. They did not yet know the corrosive effect which political competition would have upon their intimate relationship as they approached and reached the summit of power. While there was room for all, the cousins were united in their headlong climb. Among those climbers, George Grenville was not the hindmost.

It is always difficult to separate and analyze the influences which enable a man to rise to the top in the political world. So many and so varied are the forces which change the individual in politics into the public figure that one despairs of weighing the importance of any one. Nevertheless, the fact that George Grenville during the years from 1744 to 1755 came more and more to be recognized as a major figure on the political scene may be attributed to at least three general factors. First, his ability, his training, his untiring industry and attention to detail, and his assiduous application to the duties of his offices brought recognition and promotion. Secondly, the inheritance of great wealth and prestige upon the deaths of Lord Cobham and Hester Grenville gave the Grenville brothers an ever-increasing influence in the political and social world. Thirdly, and perhaps most important, George Grenville was a member of the ambitious and energetic group of "Boy Patriots" and an intimate friend, both politically and personally, of the most spectacular young man in the House of Commons, William Pitt.

During those eleven years, Pitt and the Grenvilles were united under the Pelham administration. The only dissonance was a contest for leadership between Pitt and Lord Cobham, who was more and more thrust into the background in the councils of the cousinhood until his death in 1749. Pitt and George Grenville were on the most intimate terms. Pitt, indeed informed Grenville on one occasion: "Your friendship will ever be deemed by me the first of public honors and private comforts."[1] That the future "great commoner" could at this time sign himself "unalterably and affectionately yours" was to have a profound effect on Grenville's political advancement, for that attachment was political as well as personal.

During the first months of his tenure of office in the Admiralty, Grenville was involved, as were most of the other ministers, in agitation to bring Pitt into office. Although the Pelhams had hesitated to mention Pitt's name to the King in December, 1744, they recognized that if affairs in the Commons were to run smoothly the tongue of the young firebrand would have to be stilled with office. One of the terms of the settlement with Cobham and the Cubs was a promise that the Pelhams would take the first favorable opportunity to persuade the King to accept Pitt as Secretary at War. The ministers fully intended to comply; the time, however, did not seem propitious. The King was disgruntled and indignant over the manner in which he had been forced to part with Granville and to admit men to his government who had outdone themselves in opposition to him and his minister. That indignation was in no manner decreased by the remonstrances of the remaining ministers that they did not enjoy the full confidence of the sovereign.[2] It seemed, indeed, as though George II was merely awaiting a favorable opportunity to dismiss his ministers altogether. Certainly it was no time to broach to the King such a subject as Pitt's candidacy for the position of Secretary at War; such a step might provide that very opportunity!

It soon began to seem, nevertheless, that the step would have to be taken regardless of the King's disposition toward his ministers. The situation in the Commons demanded it, for the ministers, largely because of the incompleteness of the settlement with the Patriots, were still having difficulties in managing the House. "Their coalition," wrote Horace Walpole soon after the new session opened in Westminster, "goes on as one should expect; they have the name of having effected it; and the Opposition is no longer mentioned: yet there is not a half-witted prater in the House but can divide with every new minister on his side...whenever he pleases. They actually do every day bring in popular bills, and on the first tinkling of the brass all the new bees swarm back to the Tory side of the House."[3]

At the same time, Pitt was demonstrating to the Pelhams not only how dangerous he could be in opposition—with those abilities they were already unhappily familiar—but also how valuable a supporter he could be to the government when he chose to fight on its side. On January 23, 1745, he gave striking proof of his potential value to the ministry by appearing from his sick bed to support the government in a bitter debate on army estimates for Flanders. Philip Yorke reported that "Mr. Pitt's fulminating eloquence silenced all opposition," and the measure passed the House with only a single negative vote.[4] Throughout the year 1745, however, the orator was fully as ready to oppose the ministers as to support them. Whether he supported or opposed, he could count on the backing of the Grenville brothers. Dick and George, even though George was in office, rallied loyally to whatever call Pitt sounded; when he sounded attack, they attacked.[5] Their sallies were often telling and always sharp, even if sometimes Pitt found little support other than "his words, and his haughtiness, and his Lytteltons, and his Grenvilles."[6] It was becoming increasingly evident to the ministers that if all was to go smoothly in the Commons, Pitt must be brought into office.

On repeated occasions, therefore, Newcastle and Pelham approached the King on behalf of Pitt. George II remained adamant. At length the Pelhams pushed matters too far. George II, displeased with his ministers' refusal to submit to Dutch demands for greater support in the continental war and indignant at being controlled by those he disliked, brought affairs to a crisis by announcing that he had accepted Lord Bath's[7] advice and would refuse to grant Pitt's nomination. Thereupon the whole Cabinet Council trooped into the King's closet on February 10 and 11 and gave up their seals of office. Pitt, in the face of such strong royal opposition, gave up his pretensions to the Secretaryship at War, but the ministers were insistent that he be admitted to office.

Rather than submit to dictation by the Pelhams, George II turned for aid to Bath and to his favorite, Granville, asking them to form a new ministry. The result of their efforts does much to illuminate the place to which ministerial dependence on a majority in the Commons had progressed. Since 1724, Newcastle had been tightening his grasp on the control of the lower house through the extensive use not only of the governmental patronage but of his own vast fortune as well. Since 1724, also, no one had attempted to undertake the conduct of the Commons without the Duke's support. Now Bath and Granville set about to form a ministry without him. They soon realized the hopelessness of the task. Not only could they secure no adequate support in the Commons; they could find only two men who were willing to embark upon ministerial office without such support. Within the short space of forty hours, they reported again to the King and resigned their commission.[8]

George II was thus vividly brought to realize his weakness in the hands of the Pelhams and the House of Commons. The old ministers were

called upon to resume their employments, and the King reluctantly submitted to their advice with regard to Pitt. Cobham, speaking for the cousinhood before the cabinet crisis, had expressed himself as "very desirous
to come into" the Pelham ministry and "to bring in *his boys.*" In addition
to the stipulation that Pitt be made Secretary at War, he had requested a
position of £1,000 a year for Jemmy Grenville, who as yet had no independent income.9 Newcastle and Pelham now complied with both
requests, though in deference to the King's wishes Pitt agreed to take
another office than Secretary at War. Instead he was given the profitable
post of joint vice-treasurer of Ireland. Jemmy was given a vacant seat at
the Board of Trade.10

The Grenville clan was thus provided with the necessary employments, and for the time they were satisfied. Within the space of a few
months, Thomas Winnington, the Paymaster of the Forces, died, and Pitt
was appointed to succeed him in that extremely lucrative position. From
that time on, Pitt and the Grenvilles "took the strongest part with the
Administration." As Newcastle observed, there seemed "to be the best
disposition in the old and new friends to make one strong, solid, and irre-
sistible corps, which, I think, will succeed."12

ii.

It was comfortable to rest within the ministerial fold after the long
years in the wilderness of opposition, but there were still elements of disquiet. The contest for leadership of the Patriot group was raging between
Pitt and Cobham, and Pitt seemed to be winning. Cobham, old and ill,
could not match futures with Pitt; the Grenvilles were naturally inclined
to follow the star of the greatest brilliance and promise. And Cobham as
naturally was resentful. The stipulations he made to Newcastle for Pitt
and Jemmy in February, 1746, were the last he was to make for the cousinhood. In taking "the strongest part with the Administration," Pitt and
George had to reverse their conduct against both the Pelhams and
Walpole. Pitt did so with so unembarrassed a countenance that Cobham,
with whom he had acted so long in opposition, was highly incensed. Pitt,
wrote Glover,

> co-operated with the Pelhams in every point, and brought himself to a level
> with the Earl of Bath in the public disesteem, not more by his votes than
> by his hot and unguarded expressions in Parliament; the most indecent of
> which was a needless encomium on the late Sir Robert Walpole, reproach-

ing himself for his opposition to him, and professing a veneration for his ashes.[13]

"This," Grenville recorded, "gave the last blow to all intercourse between Lord Cobham and him."[14]

The break placed the Grenvilles in a precarious position. Their uncle, of course, had the disposition of his vast fortune solely at his discretion, and he had so many nephews! Dick particularly stood to lose by antagonizing his uncle. He was torn between two poles: on the one hand stood Pitt, whom as a friend he loved and admired; on the other stood Cobham, whom as an uncle he may have loved and whose estates without a doubt he desired. Quite possibly the reason that Dick did not press claims to office when George and Jemmy entered the ministry was that he feared to antagonize his uncle by seeming to adhere too closely to his young rival.[15] George, too, was cautious. Wishing to support Pitt, and yet being "determined to preserve every mark of duty and attachment to my uncle, to whom I was so much indebted,"[16] he resolved to give as little offense as possible by keeping his mouth shut. When debates on crucial issues came, such as that of April 10, 1746, on taking 18,000 Hanoverians into British pay, he gave his vote with the government along with Pitt, Lyttelton, Dick, and Jemmy, but "Pitt was the only one of this *ominous* band that opened his mouth." Dick, indeed, was treading on dangerous ground. Two years before, wrote Walpole, he "had declared in the House that he would seal it with his blood that he never would give his vote for a Hanoverian. Don't you shudder at such perjury?"[17]

Even though his friends supported with silence, Pitt was spectacular enough to make up the lack. Newcastle congratulated himself upon gaining him to the ministerial side. In the debate on the Hanoverian troops, "Mr. Pitt spoke so well that the Premier told me he had the dignity of Sir William Wyndham, the wit of Mr. Pulteney, and the knowledge and judgment of Sir Robert Walpole," related the Duke; "in short, he said all that was right for the King, kind and respectful to the *old corps,* and resolute and contemptuous of the Tory opposition."[18] With his new leader already in such high esteem with the Pelhams, Grenville could have little doubt that he had chosen to follow the fortunes of the right man.

Meanwhile he took care to confine himself strictly to his duties in the Admiralty except on questions on which he could be certain that Pitt and Cobham would not disagree. Jemmy was less cautious. When Pitt became Paymaster, he consented to take the position of deputy Paymaster under him. This step "greatly irritated Lord Cobham, and was the occasion of a mark of offense" against Jemmy "in Lord Cobham's will."[19] The bitter old man was making the split in the family group irreparable.

iii.

On the Admiralty board, George applied himself earnestly to the work of the navy. Among his papers appears one of the exercises he set himself, presumably at this time: a reign-by-reign summary of the development of British naval strength.[20] Dick, perhaps only half in jest, suggested that he use his post to promote the family fortunes. "Provide a most excellent station for poor Tom," he wrote George shortly after he took office; "that if the public be not benefitted by your administration, your family at least may, which is so far at least doing good, and is about as much as is expected from any placeman's hands."[21]

Actually George had handled Tommy's legal affairs in his naval career ever since he entered the navy. In April, 1743, for instance, Tommy took a French ship at sea and asked his brother's legal advice on getting it condemned and sold. The French ship was carrying Spanish goods from Vera Cruz, and was taken in Portuguese waters, which made for complications. George gave his advice; he volunteered to "make the attorney general give us his opinion on the matter." Henry was pressed into service to act as Tommy's agent. He figured "the agency at 5 per cent is 7 or £8,000" if the ship sold, as they estimated, for £180,000.[22]

When he became a Lord of the Admiralty, therefore, George naturally took an active interest in his brother's career. He wrote greeting him as "your brother seaman, for such I now am," and informed him that he had had him given an independent Mediterranean command. "By all the information I can get," he wrote, "this is the most advantageous station in our power at present, & I find it is what is most desired by the officers." The reason for an independent command was "that if you meet with anything worth keeping it may be all your own as you will not be part of the Squadron nor under the command of any admiral."[23] The following year he tried to use his influence with the Duke of Bedford, First Lord of the Admiralty, to have Tommy transferred to the command of a larger ship, but the vessel was already put under Admiral Lord Anson's command, unknown to George, and the maneuver failed.[24]

With his ability and industry and with his influential friends, George confidently expected to be promoted quickly from the Admiralty to some more prestigious position. Yet when two vacancies occurred on the Treasury Board in July, 1746, he was overlooked. The positions were given to H. B. Legge,[25] who had come to the Admiralty after Grenville, and to Hugh Campbell, who had not been in office. At this, George displayed the haughty pride which characterized the whole family. This was preferment over his head. Dismissing any thought that the appointments might have been based on merit, he forthwith applied to Pelham to resign his office because of the slight. The Prime Minister, doubtless realizing that if George's resignation were accepted, Pitt's and the whole cousinhood's would soon follow, was profuse with excuses and promises. If Grenville would remain at his post, he pledged, the next promotion out of the Admiralty would be his. Accordingly, when another vacancy occurred at the Treasury Board in June, 1747, Grenville received the promotion "without any further difficulty or application."[26]

A position as a Lord of the Treasury was not the only gain in prestige which the Grenville clan made in June, 1747. They also demonstrated their increasing stature in politics in the general election of 1747, which took place for Buckingham in that month. In their concentration on the national political scene, the Grenvilles had not been able to disregard the grass-roots of their power. Local prestige entailed local responsibilities. For much of the summer of 1744, for example, George was occupied with putting through measures for a turnpike in northern Buckinghamshire. Such patronage paid dividends; George could complain that there were "almost as many difficulties and as much opposition to mending our ways here as to reforming our manners in town," but he knew that he was building not only the roads but his own fortune.[26] The election proved the extent to which the Grenvilles' prestige had advanced in Buckingham.

Heretofore, the Temples and Grenvilles had shared the seats for Buckingham with the Denton family by agreement. Each election saw one Temple or Grenville and one Denton take his seat in the Commons for the borough. In 1747, however, the Grenvilles felt themselves strong enough to oust the Dentons from their seat and claim it for themselves. They had strengthened their position among the borough's thirteen electors when one of their number, Carter, died in November, 1742. "There was the devil to pay there about the choice of a burgess," reported Dick. One of the Dentons' supporters, Read, had "struck for the government of the Corporation." Dick was forced to journey down from London at the beginning of the session to take care of the matter, but the Denton interests had been defeated.[27]

Thus both Dick and George announced themselves as candidates for the borough's seats in 1747. Dick reported the situation to Pitt in exuberant terms:

> Our election comes on tomorrow, and I am sanguine enough, even without
> spa water, not to be under the least apprehension. The state of the account
> betwixt the opposition and me stands as follows: 700 £ a vote offered by
> my antagonist (Denton), not one six-penny piece offered, promised, or
> given by me, and not a convert made against me. Is it not an honour to rep-
> resent such a corporation?[28]

Three days later, he was even more enthusiastic:

> My cares are over! Victory, the most compleat that ever was, has attend-
> ed us at Buckingham....We polled each of us ten, the great Denton four and
> his inimitable friend and apothecary, Crap Reede, bestowed his second
> vote on the parson of the parrish....[29]

The Grenvilles, indeed, were becoming recognized both as local
potentates and as influential men with the ministry. By 1747, George was
in a position to obtain ministerial favors for his friends in the Commons
and thus to increase the prestige and following of the family in that
House. For example, James Oswald, member for a Scottish borough,
solicited George's favor in obtaining advancement in the navy for one of
his supporters at home. The naval officer's father, he said, was "one of my
best friends in the borough and was of the greatest service to me all last
election."[30] And there were also favors to be done at home. One friend in
1748 requested him to bring pressure on the local Buckinghamshire tax
assessor, Dancer, not to lay a window tax on the local school, and in 1749
one of his supporters in Buckingham needed "a few franks."[31]

Such prestige, however, was not without its unpleasant aspects. As has
been suggested before, it is axiomatic in politics that power breeds enemies as well as more power. The Grenvilles were certainly not without
their enemies, either in Buckinghamshire or in Westminster. In the winter of 1747-1748, their enemies brought a test of power upon the
Grenvilles. Hitherto, the county assizes had been held at Buckingham in
the summer and Aylesbury in the winter, but in 1747, since the jail was at
Aylesbury, anti-Grenville interests in the county managed to have the
summer assizes also held in Aylesbury. This the Grenvilles considered a
challenge to their interests in north Buckinghamshire. The assizes were a
symbol of their prominence in that section of the county. The meeting of
the assizes, of course, was an important political and social event, a peri-

od of business activity for local shops and innkeepers, a time for talking politics and making the necessary contacts between the members of the corporation and the controlling family. To lose the assizes would make it appear that the Grenvilles were losing influence not only with the ministry but even in their own bailiwick. Thus it was necessary for the family to gird its loins and fight the matter out in the Commons.[32]

When on February 19, 1748, Dick as head of the clan introduced a bill in the Commons for returning the summer assizes to Buckingham, it was a signal for anti-Grenville interests in the Commons to rally to the support of Aylesbury. There followed a scathing attack by the enemies of the Grenvilles not only upon the bill, which was described as "the arrantest job that ever was brought into Parliament," but also upon the honor, the reputation, and even the patriotism of the Grenville family. In this crisis Pitt rose to the defense of his friends. He called the gentlemen to order in his haughtiest strain, ably defending the bill and repaying with ample interest the tauntings and invectives which had been thrust at his associates. The final passage of the bill by a comfortable majority was testimony not only to the weight of the family in the House, but also to the effectiveness of the combination of Pitt and the Grenvilles.[33]

iv.

In the following year, the family's prestige was still further increased. On September 13, 1749, Lord Cobham died at Stowe, and the title of Viscountess Cobham and the Temple estates passed, according to the jointure of 1718, to Lady Hester Temple Grenville. Cobham's death meant little to the outside world of politics. He had been superseded in his faction by Pitt and since 1746 had declined "to take any public part whatsoever."[34] To the Grenville brothers, however, it meant many things. The boys at last were free to follow politics as they chose without fear of what their wealthy uncle might think of their policies and what he might do in consequence. What the brothers felt personally toward their uncle one can only conjecture. Of the brothers, almost the only one capable of very deep feelings was George. The proud Dick, the irresponsible Jemmy, the vain Harry were probably little affected. George likely experienced genuine grief; he had been closer to his uncle and more open and frank with him. He was not one to let his emotions control him, however, nor was he given to looking back. And he too had his political freedom.

Economic independence, too, came with Cobham's death. George's caution not to offend his uncle by his political behavior paid its dividends.

Cobham's will entailed the Temple estates on George and his heirs male after Dick, and, more important for the immediate future, it gave him a legacy of five thousand pounds.[35] With such a provision, George could maintain an establishment of his own of modest proportions. He was no longer dependent upon his salary when in office or upon his family when out. Always hereafter he took care to live strictly within the income of his patrimony. He "early accustomed himself to a strict appropriation of his income and an exact economy in its expenditure as the only sure ground on which to build a reputation for public and private integrity, and to support a dignified independence." Whatever emoluments he gained from public service he was scrupulous in saving for the fortune of his children. "The being in or out," he is reported to have said, "makes no difference in my establishment or manner of life. The only difference is, that my children's fortunes would be increased by my being in,... and that is being as little dependent upon office as any man who was not born to a great estate can possibly be."[35]

The prestige of a title also came to the Grenville family. George and his brothers were now entitled to use "Honorable" before their names and were recognized as among the wealthiest families of the realm. With such recognition, however, the Grenvilles were not satisfied. Scarcely was Cobham in the ground[36] when Dick set about having his mother created a countess, with descent of the title, of course, to her heirs male. George was engaged to persuade their mother, who "in general" gave her approval. She was careful to say, however, that she did not desire it for herself; she stated "she would be sorry anybody should think her desirous of any step of this kind in any other light than as the properest means of transfering it to her children."[37] With such sentiments the Grenville children had no quarrel!

Dick wanted the title Buckingham if it could be had. "I do not find my affairs in a state to part with 700 1. or 800 1. more for the difference of writing *Temple* as a title instead of a name."[38] George accordingly took the matter to Newcastle, who "expressed his desire to do anything to oblige" the Grenvilles.[39] Since the title of Buckingham was already bestowed and the family did not like Newcastle's suggestion of Earl Cobham, they finally decided on the title which Dick felt he could not afford: Temple. By the patent issued on October 18, 1749, Vicountess Cobham became Countess Temple of Stowe, with Dick assuming the courtesy title of Viscount Cobham as heir to the earldom.[40]

v.

Inheritance was one means of acquiring prestige, influence, and wealth. Political activity was another. A third, no less effective, was marriage. The immediate reason for Lord Cobham's settling his fortune on Dick, it will be remembered, was to enable him to marry well.[41] Wealth attracted wealth. Though Dick's marriage seems to have been a love match as well as a marriage of convenience,[42] he obtained a sizeable fortune with his bride in 1737.

George had no such wealth to attract a bride. His legacy of £3,000 from his father's will earned him a mere £160 a year.[43] Otherwise he was dependent on his salary as a public official and whatever he earned at law.

Nonetheless, it appeared for a while that George had prospects of acquiring a considerable estate by marriage. At least since early 1744, he had been on terms of close friendship if not intimacy with Elizabeth Wyndham, the daughter of Cobham's old political associate, statesman of Queen Anne's reign, and leader of the Tories in the House of Commons since the Hanoverian succession, Sir William Wyndham.[44] For many years Elizabeth had been a close friend and confidante of George's sister, Hester, with whom she carried on a regular correspondence.[45] No letters between George and Elizabeth during this period have survived. We can only follow the romance at a distance. When they became engaged is uncertain. By 1746 she was frequently in his company, as may be seen from her correspondence with Hester. On September 25, 1746, for instance, she described to her friend an occasion on which she and George were caught in a rainstorm while going visiting and were thoroughly drenched.[46]

Certainly they were engaged for several years before the death of the Duke of Somerset, Elizabeth's maternal grandfather, in December, 1748. It was widely known in society that they were waiting for his death to marry in the hope of a large legacy. Elizabeth was his favorite grandchild. She visited him frequently in his lingering last illness, and he was accustomed to give her a Christmas present of a hundred pounds every year. But the Duke did not approve of her marriage to a younger son of a new family. Although he settled the largest part of his estate on her older brother, Sir Charles Wyndham, he left her only an annuity equal to his annual Christmas gift. Society was scandalized. It was "just such a legacy," scoffed Horace Walpole, "as you would give to a housekeeper to prevent her going into service again." Betty commented that she had "counted more on the grandfather's vanity than on his heart," but she laid the slight to his vanity having been "wounded" by news of the impending marriage.[47] That meant that the couple had to be satisfied with their own resources: George's £3,000, the £10,000 left Elizabeth by her father's will, and the Duke's £100 a year.[48]

If they were disappointed, they were not daunted. George and Elizabeth resolved to marry immediately. The vows were spoken on May 16, 1749.[49] George did not get the great fortune he had hoped for, but he gained a bride who was rich in many other ways. The daughter of Sir William Wyndham and Katherine Seymour, she had been brought up in a family which teemed with politics. Without doubt she could be an understanding and intelligent helpmate to an aspiring politician. Her personality charmed the whole political world. She had a slight stammer, which moved Lord Bolingbroke on one occasion to regret "that one who talked so well should have any difficulty in speaking." The French Ambassador paid her the higher compliment of observing that he enjoyed her company because of "les jolies choses qu'elle me fait dire." As a young woman she had a reputation for her beauty, but smallpox left her scarred. She seems not to have minded the loss of her beauty any more than her stammer. "I have never heard of anyone who regretted her beauty less," wrote Lady Blandford.[50]

There seems little foundation for Lord John Russell's supposition that she was "a strong-minded, probably ambitious woman, and was believed to exercise great influence over her husband's political conduct."[51] Her letters to Grenville and such contemporary comment as appears reveal her, indeed, as an intelligent and sympathetic companion, but show nothing of a dominating character. Rather she was a devoted wife and mother, intent almost solely (except when acting occasionally as amanuensis to George or when involved in the social affairs of the county or the Court) in caring for the family while Grenville was occupied with matters of state. She was encouraging, perhaps, but not domineering. There is no evidence, furthermore, that they ever in their married life were on other than terms of great love and affection. The trials of Elizabeth's almost continual ill health seemed only to make them stronger. Their letters to one another were always headed "my dearest life" or "my dearest love."[52] In an age notorious for its philandering, when several of Grenville's associates in politics were members of the infamous Hell Fire Club at Medmenham Abbey and other such societies, Grenville remained throughout his married life a devoted husband and family man.

Marriage, of course, brought other connections than those with the bride herself; her brothers were also to play an important role in

Grenville's life. The Grenville clan had been closely associated with Sir William Wyndham until his death in 1740; the families were close friends. Now Sir Charles Wyndham became one of the considerable men of wealth in the country and a political power as well. From the Duke of Somerset he inherited the estate of Petworth, worth fourteen thousand pounds a year, and control of borough interests in the Commons. Then in 1750 his uncle, the last Duke of Somerset of the elder line, left him another vast estate, the Earldom of Egremont, and more borough interests. Grenville's connection with Egremont in politics was to grow ever closer until their triumvirate ministry with the Earl of Halifax was ended by Egremont's death in August, 1763.53

With the younger brother, Percy Wydham-O'Brien, Grenville was to remain on always friendly terms personally and politically until the end of his own life. Though a younger son, Percy was also well provided for, having inherited in 1741 the estates of his uncle, Henry O'Brien, Earl Thomond, the husband of his mother's sister. In 1756 he also obtained the extinct title of his uncle as well, being created Earl Thomond in the Irish peerage. A member of the Commons until his death in 1744 (Irish peers, of course, did not sit in the House of Lords at Westminster, and so were eligible to sit in the Commons), Thomond was to hold various minor ministerial and household positions from 1755 to the end of Grenville's administration in 1765.56 From the beginning of Grenville's prominence in political life until his death, Thomond was his faithful supporter and friend, though their relationship was not as close as that between Grenville and Egremont. Perhaps the loyalty of Thomond was influenced in part by his obligations to Grenville, for during the latter part of his political life he was in debt to George for ten thousand pounds.57

His brothers-in-law, indeed, were to prove valuable connections to Grenville. Not only did they give him added stature and prestige in the political world, they would be his only reliance among his kinsmen when the final decision came to break with his own blood brothers and seek advancement on his own.

vi.

The split which was to rend the Grenville family possibly had its beginnings in George Grenville's mind at about this period, for he afterwards wrote that it was during 1749 that he first began to notice an "indifference, coldness, and slight" on Pitt's part toward his "every wish and opinion."58 It was George's nature to resent anything which might be regarded as a slight. The Grenvilles, particularly George and Dick, were coming to look upon themselves as the equal of anyone in the realm. The acquisition of wealth, a title, and political office had not made them modest. Pitt they regarded with admiration, esteem, even love, but nevertheless they looked upon him, somewhat as the old Duke of Somerset had regarded George, as a younger son of a "new" family, without "weight," without fortune. Pitt was a kind of political foundling whom Cobham had discovered. He had no "connexions" other than those provided by the Grenvilles, who were soon to become his brothers-in-law. Indeed, at the height of Pitt's career, George and Dick would look upon him as only one of their triumvirate. George was not irritated with his conduct. Pitt was already one of the recognized leaders of the country, eagerly cultivated and patronized by the Pelhams and sharing in their councils. The Grenvilles, nevertheless, felt that Pitt should still consult their wishes and opinions in matters of policy in return for their support and patronage. When the Paymaster proceeded to act independently of the brothers, George felt slighted, even though Pitt continued to give him the strongest evidences of his friendship. Particularly galling was Pitt's opposition, early in 1749, to a proviso supported by Grenville and Lyttelton on a bill for punishing mutiny and desertion. George felt that Pitt had "treated with slight the conscientious opinions of those who had voted for it."[59]

Another slight quickly followed from another quarter. In May, 1749, Bubb Dodington resigned his position as Treasurer of the Navy. Pelham had promised Grenville, in view of his resentment of Legge's preferment above him in 1746, that Legge would not be promoted from the Treasury before him. Nevertheless on May 3 Legge received the appointment to fill Dodington's vacant office.[60] Pelham and Newcastle apparently felt that it would be politic to promote Legge even in spite of the promise to Grenville. Of Grenville's loyalty to them they felt certain, regardless of the disappointment; Legge, on the other hand, was courting the new faction in the ministry headed up by the Dukes of Bedford and Cumberland.[61] The Pelhams feared that if his cupidity were not satisfied with this lucrative office, their own power in the ministry would be diminished.[62] With regard to Grenville, they calculated correctly. He was severely disappointed and resentful of the breach of promise, but he neither made protest nor revolted. He merely nursed his grievances and continued giving, as he expressed it, "what support I was able to those who never gave any to me."[63]

Grenville thus continued at the Treasury for five more years, or until the spring of 1754. The seven years spent at the Board were excellent training in governmental finance. With his training and his natural bent for detailed work, Grenville took to the study of finance eagerly and seriously. By the time he was promoted from the Treasury he could lay just claim to considerable experience in public finance.

vii.

During the time he served on the Treasury Board, on October 7, 1752, Countess Temple died. She left a letter for Dick, dated June 25, 1750, which is the most revealing of all the materials by her hand which have survived. The particular disagreements to which she refers cannot be identified, but the attitudes are significant. A copy went to both Dick and George, and a note in Elizabeth's hand observes that it was delivered to George "after her death by Lady Hester Grenville."

When this comes to you I shall be no more: but remember my child that what I am now agoing to write is the last and dyeing injunction of a fond parent to a beloved son: and would be the request of my last moments were I sure I should be able to see or speak to you. I chuse therefore this way to conjure you by all the tyes between us: by all the unwearied care I have from the first moment of your being taken of your self and affairs: by all the good I have ever done you: and by all I have suffered and foregone in the accomplishment of that good: and all the sorrows I have of late days gone through: that you would settle your own estate in case you have no sons: on George and his sons in the first place: on Jemmy and his in the next: and on Harry and his in the last: and that no consideration may ever engage you to lessen in the person of George or any of your brothers the estates that for your sakes I have takeing *(sic)* much joy as well as much pains to join together: and reflect that the two strong points of the greatest part of my life has bin to make you all happy by union and affection to one another: and by your fortunes being considerable: and that every interest and pleasure of my own has altogether giveing *(sic)* way to those motives: and now I think from your knowledge of me tis unnecessary for me to declare (but yet in justice to all my children I will do so) and that in the most solemn manner too: that what I have said is wholly owing to the suggestions of my own heart & mind without the least intimation desire or knowledge of any mortal: and is indeed but the repetition of what you know I have constantly said upon the same subject: and which for a long time you seem'd so fully as well as kindly to agree with me in: that I

looked upon myself more secure of your fulfilling my wishes from the
manner you treated of it in: than if you had engaged your self by many
promises: who or what has bin the cause of your holding a more doubtfull
language of late: I am far from desiring to enter upon: I will content myself
only with doing justice to yr brother George: by most solemnly protesting
and that from many years experience too: that I believe never man acted
more worthyly and kinder than he has done by you in all respects: particularly in those matters in which my brother Cobham my self and you have
been concerned: those affairs you know I must be mistress of and do as
solemnly averr: that the greatest misunderstanding I can ever remember to
have had with him proceeded from his too strongly defending you: and
endeavoring to make me think and act differently than I was inclined to:
and thought I had reason for....64

There is no record of how the death of their mother affected the
Grenvilles. She had been a strong-minded, active force in their lives. One
can only guess from their subsequent characters how they may have felt.
Dick was cold and reserved, Jemmy rather irresponsible, Harry self-cen-
tered, George sensitive but quick to resent a slight. Only Hetty seems to
have been natural and outgoing in her personal relations. But whatever he
felt, Dick (or Lord Temple, as he now became) put his mother's injunc-
tions into force. The family estates were entailed on George in the lack of
heirs of his own body. Temple took up residence at Stowe, and began
rebuilding the house on a grand scale, decorating the grounds with temples, arches, columns, and classical pavillions, and entertaining magnifi-
cently the nobility and even royalty of Britain and Europe. Meanwhile,
according to his mother's wishes, he leased the Wotton estate to George.
Hetty was to have two rooms at Wotton, again according to her mother's
instructions, until her marriage to William Pitt in 1754. These last instructions of Countess Temple were obeyed by her heir even when the brothers were bitter political enemies and refused to speak to one another.

The new Earl Temple was one of the richest men in England. His
cousin George Lyttelton doubtless exaggerated when he wrote that Dick
would "now be the richest man in England, so you may expect to see new
beauties at Stowe."65 Nonetheless his wealth was enough to command
the respect of the whole political world and the services of many political hangers-on.

viii.

Thus the Grenvilles took their place among the first families in the realm. Never modest, they were coming to regard power and influence as their due. In March, 1754, when Prime Minister Henry Pelham died, they confidently expected that the reorganization of the ministry would result in promotions for them. Probably few were surprised when Newcastle himself assumed his brother's place at the head of the Treasury, but there was speculation on all sides about who would become Secretary of State and leader of the Commons. The men most frequently mentioned were Pitt and Henry Fox.[66] Pitt showed some of the haughtiness for which he and the Grenvilles would become proverbial. He would not ask Newcastle for the position, as Fox had immediately done.[67] He apparently did not consider it necessary. In his letters to Lyttelton and the Grenvilles, he was already apportioning offices on the assumption that he would be Secretary of State. George, he suggested, should be Chancellor of the Exchequer.[68] Considering Grenville's experience in the Treasury, the appointment would perhaps have been appropriate. But it was not to be. Pitt learned later in the day that Fox was to have the Chancellorship of the Exchequer, "notwithstanding any reluctance to yield it in the ministers." George, however, should surely have the post of Secretary at War.[69] Four days later the situation was still in a state of flux, but Pitt had "no doubt that George Grenville's turn must come."[70]

It soon became evident, however, that Pitt's own turn was not going to come. Fox was offered the seals of Secretary of State, but he turned them down when he learned that he would be almost powerless in the office. He would have neither the management of the patronage in the Commons nor any hand in the arrangements for the imminent general election. Newcastle reserved that province wholly to himself; the borough mongering which he had directed so long as Secretary of State he would now direct as First Lord of the Treasury. The seals, on Fox's refusal, were given to one of the drudges among the governmental ranks, Sir Thomas Robinson, while Legge became Chancellor of the Exchequer. Once again Legge had been promoted ahead of Grenville.

It was assumed by most men, as it certainly was by Pitt, that he had been excluded from high office by the personal enmity of the King. Nonetheless, he wrote to Newcastle on behalf of his friends. In a long, flattering letter, he observed to the Duke that there could be "no shadow of difficulty in Mr. Grenville being made Treasurer of the Navy."[71] With Legge already taken care of in the Exchequer, the Duke recognized the validity of Grenville's claim to the lucrative office, and the request was granted.[72] On April 4, 1754, George Grenville kissed the King's hands for the office of Treasurer of the Navy.[73]

ix.

The same month brought on the general election of 1754. Owing to their increased stature in the country, the Grenvilles had no occasion to seek electioneering opportunities; their services and support were eagerly sought. In Buckingham, of course, there was no difficulty. Temple retained his firm hold on the electors of the borough. George and Jemmy, who had taken the elder brother's place for the borough when Dick went to the Lords, were returned as a matter of course. The Grenvilles, however, could not limit their activities to their own bailiwick. From Thomas Potter, the son of the former Archbishop of Canterbury and a friend of the Grenvilles, there came an appeal for help at Aylesbury. George took it upon himself to use the family influence with the Aylesbury electors, and Potter acknowledged his debt. Grenville had "a right to be informed of the result," he wrote; "out of 60 free and incorruptable voters 55 have absolutely promised me and their influence will oblige a majority of the rest to accept from me the same which any other candidate shall offer."[74] Again, Potter wanted Temple to "lay his commands" on one of his Aylesbury electors to intercede with a certain Quaker of whom Potter was unsure.[75]

Appeals also came from outside Buckinghamshire. Temple was involved in an election in Oxfordshire, where his candidates were defeated only to be reinstated in petition to the Commons.[76] George lent his aid to his cousin, Temple West, in gaining the seat which Jemmy had vacated for the Dorsetshire borough of Bridport. Corbyn Morris, a customs official in Edinbough,[77] undertook the task of managing the details of West's election, promising that he would "sacredly obey" all of Grenville's directions. He would write to the burgesses and the necessary London connections, and as soon as Grenville got him leave from his duties he would come down to Dorset to direct the election.[78] If some of the Grenville's candidates failed of election—as did Temple West at Bridport—that was no disgrace. Even the Duke of Newcastle was not successful in all his attempts at election management.

Perhaps most significant in the election were the attempts of the Grenvilles to help a young protégé, John Wilkes, in wresting a seat for the

Northumberland borough of Berwick-upon-Tweed from the powerful Delaval family. Wilkes, the twenty-seven-year-old son of a city malt distiller who had married the daughter of an Aylesbury gentleman, had been introduced to Temple by Potter. Squint-eyed and ugly, he was nevertheless possessed of a charming wit, a facile pen, and no conscience whatsoever. Temple was attracted to him, and he became a great favorite with the Grenvilles. They had apparently intended that he stand for Aylesbury, as had the ministry,[79] but those plans fell through. Wilkes thereupon undertook to contest Berwick, perhaps, as Almon asserts, on Temple's instigation.[80]

Grenville, who had already used his influence to get Wilkes appointed Sheriff of Buckinghamshire,[81] now contributed an open letter to the Berwick burgesses in his support.[82] But even with an expenditure of perhaps four thousand pounds and the support of the ministry,[83] Wilkes was defeated. The interests of the Delavals were too strong. In spite of vigorous support from Pitt when Wilkes petitioned the election in the Commons, John Delaval's election was sustained.[84]

The aid to Wilkes in 1754 was significant for the Grenvilles not so much in the outcome of the election as in the relationships which were made and strengthened. Wilkes came more and more to be an intimate of Temple and Grenville, and men began to say also that Wilkes was "a friend it seems of Pitt's."[85] John Wilkes, indeed, was destined to play a key role in the political careers of Pitt, Temple, and Grenville.

x.

The opening of the new parliament in November, 1754, saw the Grenville clan strengthened in its family influence by the actual addition of William Pitt, for on November 16, 1754, Pitt married Hetty Grenville. Unfortunately, neither Pitt nor the Grenvilles would let the marriage stand in the way of political quarrels when they came to disagree in politics in later years. For the present, however, the Grenville "brotherhood," as Hetty called it, was cemented even more firmly by the marriage. Grenville, overcoming his resentment of Pitt's conduct toward him, had done everything in his power to foster the union,[86] and doubtless Temple and the other brothers had also.

Pitt, however, was not so ready in November, 1754, to "take the strongest part with the government" as he had done since 1746. Both he and Fox were much offended by Newcastle's disposition of the office of Secretary of State the preceding spring. By the time the new Parliament assembled, the two orators had come to an agreement to unite in opposing the Newcastle administration. In this effort, moreover, Pitt had the support of his new brother-in-law, George Grenville. Though they had been strained earlier, the ties between them had been strengthened by the marriage, and they were to hold fast for several more years. The ties between Pitt and Fox, on the other hand, did not even last out the session. For the space of a few short weeks the two took every opportunity to make Sir Thomas Robinson look ridiculous in his conduct of the Commons, and the combination of their talents was more than a match for the inexperienced Secretary of State. In January, however, Newcastle came to Robinson's rescue. He opened new negotiations with Fox which resulted in his appointment as a Cabinet Councillor and his agreement to support Robinson in the Commons. Although Fox still expressed a desire to continue relations with Pitt, the latter decided to put an end to the intercourse. He and Grenville, though both in office, remained in opposition to the administration.[87]

The break with Fox, however, cast Pitt and Grenville adrift. Fox in reality had the lead in the Commons, and Pitt rather hinted than declared opposition.[88] This was the signal for the appearance on the stage of John, Earl of Bute. Since his Eton days with Grenville, Bute had married the daughter of the fabulously wealthy Wortley Montague, retired to the Island of Bute for years of solitary study and country life, and at last emerged into London society, where he was introduced to the court of the Princess Dowager of Wales at Leicester House. Quickly he became one of the favorite advisers of the Princess and was made tutor to young George, Prince of Wales. As always, the Prince was the center of a group of politicians out of office who looked to his accession as the means of gaining place in the government, and Bute quickly put himself at its head. Thus by the spring of 1755 Lord Bute was one of the principal agents of the Princess in the Leicester House faction. Upon Pitt's break with Fox, Bute advised the Princess to sound him on the prospects of his joining Leicester House in opposition. Pitt's reply was an immediate affirmative. Grenville, indeed, had been seriously considering the idea the summer before.[89] When Bute and Pitt had held two interviews, a secret meeting was arranged at Grenville's house in Upper Brooke Street between Pitt and the Princess.[90] The upshot of the negotiation was a complete treaty of accord between the cousinhood and the Leicester House faction, in which Pitt agreed to govern himself "as they directed him."[91] Thereupon the cousinhood openly avowed the connection and were distinguished by marks of favor from the Princess "in the most public manner."[92] These were Grenville's first political contacts with Bute, to whom he was later to attach himself to the total disruption of the "brotherhood" in politics. That family faction, indeed, had already begun to crumble. Lyttelton had for some time been displeased with the opposition of Pitt and Grenville to the ministry of which they were all a part. Walpole thought he was afraid for his place:

> Sir George Lyttelton, who could not reconcile his content with Mr. Pitt's discontents, has been very ill with the *cousinhood*. In the grief of his heart he thought of resigning his place, but, *somehow or other* stumbled upon a negotiation for introducing the Duke of Bedford into the ministry again, to balance the loss of Mr. Pitt.

Having consulted Newcastle on the matter, he "carried away *carte blanche*" to Bedford, who "bounded like a rocket, frightened away poor Sir George, and sent for Mr. Pitt to notify the overture. Pitt and the Grenvilles are outrageous; the Duke of Newcastle disclaims his ambassador, and everybody laughs." In short, the Grenville clan quickly repudiated Lyttelton; Temple gave him the nickname of "apostolic nuncio." "Think how I prick up my ears," cried Walpole, "...to hear a Lyttelton vent his grievances against a Pitt and Grenvilles."[93]

Pitt and the Grenvilles still continued to oppose when the Parliament met again in November, 1755. In the debates on the address of thanks they were among a numerous party who offered battle to the ministry of which they themselves were a part. Grenville's speech, said Walpole, was "very fine and much beyond himself, and very pathetic;" Pitt spoke "beyond what ever was."[94] Men began to wonder what was to come of this "opposition in administration." "The expectation of the world is suspended," wrote Walpole three days after the Parliament met, "to see whether these gentlemen will resign or be dismissed; perhaps neither; perhaps they may continue in place and opposition; perhaps they may continue in place and not oppose."[95] The suspense, however, did not last long. Before a week was out Newcastle had made his decision; both Pitt and Grenville received notices that the King had "no further occasion" for their services.[96]

That same day Grenville received a letter of congratulation from his friend Lord Bute. The Princess's favorite painted for his "worthy friend" a rosy picture of the situation and of Grenville's future with the Leicester House opposition. "'Tis glorious," he said, "to suffer in such a cause and with such companions; in times like these, the post of honour is a private station. I own from my heart I congratulate you, and I am proud to call a man of your distinguished character my friend; for well may this be the prelude only to what your merit loudly calls for."[97]

For twelve years while he had been in office, Grenville had been influenced and almost dominated by his relationship with William Pitt. For several years yet those relations were to continue. But there were elements of discontent which bade fair to disturb the alliance after 1755. Even in 1749, Grenville had felt that Pitt had not been fair to him, but there had been nowhere else he could turn. He had had no choice but to give his support to those who never gave any to him. By 1755 a new star was appearing on the horizon in the person of Lord Bute. The cousinhood might have a bright future in prospect with the Newcastle ministry, but who could say what would come when the old George II died and young Prince George took his place? Even if Newcastle and the cousinhood remained in favor, Pitt and Temple, not Grenville, would hold the leadership and find greatest advancement. Grenville was shrewd enough to see that the tutor and favorite of young George would be a good friend to cultivate. The influence of this singular man, which Grenville was already beginning to feel, was to open a new phase in his political fortunes.

NOTES

CHAPTER IV

[1] Pitt to Grenville, October 29, 1746, *Grenville Papers,* I, 52.

[2] William Coxe, *Memoirs of Lord Horatio Walpole,* 2 vols., London, 1820, II, 99, 127-128.

[3] Walpole to Mann, February 1, 1745, Toynbee, *Walpole's Letters,* II, 73-74.

[4] Yorke's Parliamentary Journal, *Parl. Hist.,* XIII, 1056; Walpole to Mann, February 1, 1745, Toynbee, *Walpoles Letters,* II, 74.

[5] Grenville's narrative, *Grenville Papers,* I, 424.

[6] Walpole to Mann, November 22, 1745, Toynbee, *Walpole's Letters,* II, 154.

[7] William Pulteney had been created Earl of Bath, July 14, 1742.

[8] Sir James Grey to Sir Thomas Robinson, March 26, 1746, Coxe, *Pelham,* I, 290-292.

[9] Dick, of course, had the Grenville family estates to support him.

[10] Newcastle to Chesterfield, February 18, 1746, Coxe, *Pelham,* I, 292-296.

[11] Haydn, *Book of Dignities,* p. 244; Grenville's narrative, *Grenville Papers,* I, 424.

[12] Newcastle to Chesterfield, February 18, 1746, Coxe, *Pelham* I, 296.

[13] Glover, *Memoirs,* p. 33.

[14] Grenville's narrative, *Grenville Papers,* I, 424.

[15] Wiggin, *Faction of Cousins,* pp. 168-169.

[16] Grenville's narrative, *Grenville Papers,* I, 425.

[17] Walpole to Mann, April 15, 1746, Toynbee, *Walpole's Letters,* II, 185.

[18] Newcastle to Cumberland, April 17, 1746, Coxe, *Pelham,* I, 306.

[19] Grenville's narrative, *Grenville Papers,* I, 424-425.

[20] Stowe MSS., Box 100.

[21] Richard Grenville to George Grenville, January 8, 1745, *Grenville Papers,* I, 34.

[22] Thomas Grenville to George Grenville, February 28, 1743, *Grenville Papers,* I, 20-24; George Grenville to Thomas Grenville, April 6, 1743, Stowe MSS., Box 8; Henry Grenville to Thomas Grenville, March 29, 1743, Stowe MSS., Box 10.

[23] George Grenville to Thomas Grenville, January 24, 1745, Stowe MSS., Box 8.

[24] George Grenville to Thomas Grenville, Bedford House, January 28, 1746; February 5, 1746; to Anson, April 5, 1746, Stowe MSS., Box 8.

[25] Henry Bilson Legge (1708-1764), fourth son of the Earl of Dartmouth.

[26] Grenville's Narrative, *Grenville Papers,* I, 425-426.

[27] George Grenville to Thomas Grenville, June 10, 1744, *Grenville Papers,* 1, 26.

[28] Richard Grenville to George Grenville, November 22, 1742, *Grenville Papers,* I, 19.

[29] Richard Grenville to Pitt, June 25, 1747, Chatham Manuscripts, Public Record Office 30/8, 61, f. 3. (Hereafter cited as Chatham MSS. The numeral preceding the folio number refers to the bundle number.)

[30] Richard Grenville to Pitt, June 28, 1747, Chatham MSS., 61, f. 5.

[31] Oswald to Grenville, August 5, 1747, Murray MSS. More correspondence on patronage is in Stowe MSS., Box 100.

[32] W. Halstead to Grenville, July 26, 1748, Stowe MSS., Box 99; C. Price to Grenville, November 6, 1749, Stowe MSS., Box 98.

[33] Tunstall, *Pitt,* pp. 91-92; Wiggin, *Faction of Cousins,* pp. 124-125.

[34] *Parl. Hist.,* XIV, 202-246.

[35] Grenville's Narrative, *Grenville Papers,* I, 425.

[36] Elizabeth Grenville to Hester Grenville, n. d. (September, 1749), Chatham MSS., 34, ff. 115-116.

[37] William Knox, *Extra Official State Papers,* 2 vols., London, 1789, II, 35-36.

[38] Richard Grenville to Hester Grenville, September 17, 1749, Chatham MSS., 62, f. 7: "We think of burying Lord Cobham this evening or tomorrow."

[39] George Grenville to Richard Grenville, September 24, 1749, *Grenville Papers,* I, 80.

[40] Richard Grenville to George Grenville, September 28, 1749, *Grenville Papers,* I, 81.

[41] George Grenville to Richard Grenville, September 28, 1749, *Grenville Papers,* I, 62.

[42] See *Grenville Papers,* I, 82-91.

[43] See above, p. 10.

[44] His letters to Anna Chamber before their marriage can only be styled ardently amorous. Murray MSS.

[45] Richard Grenville's account book, p. 153, Stowe MSS. Dick paid him a semi-annual £80 on Lady Day (March 25) and Michaelmas (September 29), English quarter days for reckoning rents and accounts. Lord Temple continued to make these semi-annual payments to Grenville's bankers, Coutts & Co., for the rest of Grenville's life, even during the years when they were political opponents and not on speaking terms. Personal Accounts T3NN3, 1733-1763, Stowe MSS.

[46] George Grenville to Thomas Grenville, June 10, 1744, *Grenville Papers,* I, 26; ElizabethWyndham to Hester Grenville, September 8, 1746, Chatham MSS., 34, f. 63.

[47] Chatham MSS., 34.

[48] Chatham MSS., 34, f. 78.

[49] Wyndham, *Family History,* pp. 117-122; Walpole to Mann, December 15, 1748, Toynbee, *Walpole's Letters,* II, 352.

[50] Even so, Grenville managed to live off his investments. Years later he told Lord Camelford that from the first office he ever held till he became minister he had made it an invariable rule to add the year's salary to his capital, contenting himself with carrying the interest the succeeding year into his expenses. "His prudence," observed Camelford, "rather bordered on parsimony." Fortescue MSS. at Boconnoc, quoted by Sir Lewis Namier in Namier and Brooke, *Commons,* II, 539.

[51] Walpole to Montague, May 18, 1749, Toynbee, *Walpole's Letters,* II, 384.

[52] Wyndham, *Family History,* pp. 107-108.

[53] *Correspondence of John, Fourth Duke of Bedford,* edited by Lord John Russell, 3 vols., London, 1842-1846, III, 324 n.

[54] Almost all of the surviving correspondence between them is now in the Murray MSS.

[55] See below, Chapter VII.

[56] G. E. C., *Complete Peerage,* XII, 713. Irish peers, of course, were permitted to sit in the Commons during the eighteenth century.

[57] Thomond to Grenville, July 4, 1748, April 8, 1759, July 30, 1770, Murray MSS.

[58] Grenville's Narrative, *Grenville Papers,* I, 426.

[59] Grenville's Narrative, *Grenville Papers,* I, 426-427.

[60] Haydn, *Book of Dignities,* p. 256.

[61] Henry Frederick, Duke of Cumberland (1721-1765), younger brother of Frederick, Prince of Wales.

[62] Hardwicke to Yorke, March 2, 1749, Yorke, *Hardwicke,* II, 86; Legge to Bedford, November 9, 1749, *Bedford Correspondence,* I, 580.

[63] Grenville's Narrative, *Grenville Papers,* I, 427.

[64] Stowe MSS., Box 10.

[65] Lyttelton to Miller, October, 1752, *An Eighteenth Century Correspondence,* edited by Lillian Dickens and Mary Stanton, London, 1910, pp. 193-194.

[66] Afterward Baron Holland (1705-1774).

[67] Coxe, *Lord Walpole,* II, 348; Walpole to Mann, March 7, 1754, Toynbee, *Walpole's Letters,* III, 216-218.

[68] Pitt to Lyttelton and the Grenvilles, March 7, 1754, *Grenville Papers,* I, 107.

[69] Pitt to Temple, March 7, 1754, *Grenville Papers,* I, 111.

[70] Pitt to Temple, March 11, 1754, *Grenville Papers,* I, 114.

[71] Coxe, *Pelham,* II, 308-309.

[72] Pitt to Newcastle, March 24, 1754, Newcastle MSS, British Library Additional Manuscripts 32734, f. 322. (Hereafter cited as Add. MSS.)

[73] Newcastle to Pitt, April 2, 1754, *The Correspondence of William Pitt, Earl of Chatham,* edited by William Stanhope Taylor and John Henry Pringle, 4 vols., London, 1838-1840, I, 98.

[74] Haydn, *Book of Dignities,* p. 256.

[75] Potter to Grenville, December 21, 1753, Murray MSS.

[76] Potter to Grenville, January 11, 1754, *Grenville Papers,* I, 102-103.

[77] Wiggin, *Faction of Cousins,* p. 153-154.

[78] Morris was to become Commissioner of the Customs under Grenville's administration and to hold the post until 1778, a year before his death.

[79] Morris to Grenville, August 28, 1753, Murray MSS.

[80] Memo by Newcastle, March 16, 1754, Newcastle MSS., Add. MSS. 32995, ff. 65, 75.

[81] John Almon, *The Correspondence of the Late John Wilkes, with his Friends,* 5 vols., London, 1805, I, 27.

[82] Potter to Grenville, January 11, 1754, *Grenville Papers,* I, 102; Potter to Wilkes, January 15, 1754, Wilkes MSS., Add. MSS. 30867, f. 95.

[83] Grenville to Wilkes, April 12, 1754, Wilkes MSS., Add. MSS. 30877, f. 1.

[84] Newcastle to the King, April 24, 1754, Newcastle MSS., Add. MSS 32755, f. 176.

[85] Fox to Hartington, November 26, 1754, James Waldegrave, first Earl Waldegrave, *Memoirs from 1754 to 1758,* London, 1821, pp. 147-148.

[86] Fox to Hartington, November 26, 1765, Waldegrave, *Memoirs,* p. 147.

[87] Grenville's Narrative, *Grenville Papers,* I, 431.

[88] Coxe, *Lord Walpole,* II, 364; Grenville's narrative, *Grenville Papers,* I, 432.

[89] Chesterfield to Dayrolles, February 4, 1755, Dobree, *Chesterfield's Letters,* V, 2135.

[90] James Wallace to Grenville, July 9, 1754, Murray MSS.

[91] Edmond, Lord Fitzmaurice, *Life of William, Earl of Shelburne,* 2 vols., London, 1875-1876, I, 70; Grenville's narrative, *Grenville Papers,* I, 432-433.

[92] Waldegrave, *Memoirs,* p. 39.

[93] Grenville's narrative, *Grenville Papers,* I, 433.

[94] Walpole to Bentley, December 13, 1754, Toynbee, *Walpole's Letters,* III, 271-272.

[95] Walpole to Conway, November 15, 1755, Toynbee, *Walpole's Letters,* III, 367.

[96] Walpole to Mann, November 16, 1755, Toynbee, *Walpole's Letters,* III, 371.

[97] Holderness to Grenville, November 20, 1755, *Grenville Papers,* I, 148.

[98] Bute to Grenville, November 20, 1755, *Grenville Papers,* I, 149.

CHAPTER V

GRENVILLE AND BUTE, 1755-1762

The first years of the Grenville cousinhood in office were years of great progress and success for the young politicians, but they were also years of increasing disagreement and lack of confidence among them. There was still an outward appearance of unity; in the next six years the cousinhood was to attain the very pinnacle of British politics, and it was to reach it as a family group. Yet there were ominous signs of disagreement and even disunion in 1755. Lyttelton had already broken with his cousins by the winter of 1754, and grievances were being nurtured less overtly in other breasts. In 1749 and in 1754 George Grenville had been slighted by Pitt, as he saw matters; there would be occasions for further resentments in the coming period. The political situation did not altogether promote unity. If the increasing competitiveness of politics as the young men advanced toward the summit called for family cohesion, it engendered friction and jealousies as well. Nearing the pinnacle, there was less and less room. They jostled as often as they aided one another in their climb. It is no wonder that the brotherhood crumbled at the height of its power; the wonder would have been had it held together.

Ever since 1749, as we have seen, Grenville had nursed a resentment of Pitt's patronizing attitude toward him, without outward complaint. His allegiance to his brother-in-law remained firm enough to nerve him to opposition and to sustain him in his dismissal in 1755. The years from 1755 to 1762, however, saw a change of political allegiance. Gradually he came to forsake his brother-in-law, at the height of his power, for his friend, who promised to become the new power in the nation. In finally adhering to Bute, Grenville sacrificed the connections which had brought him into politics and helped him up the political ladder, for Pitt and his brothers abandoned him both politically and socially. The change of allegiance was gradual, of course, although a definite breaking point came in the fall of 1761. Thereafter, Grenville continued his quest for political power by making himself indispensable in Bute's domination of the political scene.

Two members of the old Cobham group joined the government which carried on after the dismissal of Pitt and Grenville in November, 1755. Lyttelton, "misled to clamber over the ruins of his old friends," accepted the post of Chancellor of the Exchequer, while Bubb Dodington succeeded to Grenville's vacant place as Treasurer of the Navy, thus being "marked out for perdition" by the Grenville clan.[1] Already determined upon opposition, Pitt and Grenville were stirred to even greater efforts by this apostasy. The session which followed their dismissal showed no signs of animosity between them. The brothers, along with Henry Legge, who was dismissed at the same time from the Exchequer, began a violent campaign of opposition in the Commons. The chief objects of their fulminations were the treaties which the ministry had concluded with Hesse in July and with Russia in September. The treaties, which provided for the hiring of foreign troops at a cost of £800,000,[2] were made in preparation for the war which was inevitably approaching with France over colonial difficulties in America and India. Preparation was obviously necessary. Yet Grenville and Pitt maintained that such subsidies were unwarranted in time of peace. The move was opposition simply for the sake of opposition. Meanwhile, in the Lords Temple began an attack by asking for the papers relating to the treaties and by belaboring the Lord Chancellor for his part in their negotiation. He too had little grounds for action and found little support. A motion of censure was lost by a count of 85 to 12.[3]

The brothers were soon to have surer grounds for complaint. Though no war had been declared (nor would it be until May 18, 1756), fighting was already taking place between the French and British and was going against the British. Moreover, there was a widespread panic in England over the possibility of a French invasion.[4] As the news of Braddock's defeat in America and of other reversals arrived, the new opposition took up a mighty cry against the administration. Soon after the King prorogued the Parliament on May 27, 1756, the culmination of the series of reversals came with the news of the capture of Minorca by the French. The people, already aroused, were now spurred into rage against the ministers.

Newcastle was further plagued in May by the news that Austria had signed a treaty of alliance with France. In September, Frederick II of Prussia invaded Saxony and precipitated the feared general war, and news arrived of the capture of Oswego.[5] The war was going wrong on all sides! Pitt, meanwhile, was knocking loudly at the door. During the session past he had outdone himself in the Commons, and though his efforts were seldom constructive, his criticism of the conduct of the war had caught the public fancy. In their storming of the closet, Pitt and the Grenvilles had popular support, even though they lacked "weight" in the Commons, Under such pressure from home and abroad, the ministry soon began to crumble; on October 15 came the first ominous crack, as Fox announced his intention to resign.[6]

The ministers now faced the necessity of taking Pitt again into the government. With the support of Leicester House and his strong public backing, he could not be ignored. Accordingly, Newcastle informed the King that Pitt was necessary to his councils, and George II "peevishly" gave his approval for the opening of negotiations with the opposition firebrand.[7] Pitt had no intention, however, of merely joining Newcastle's administration; he intended to form his own with himself and the Grenville clan at its head. When he conferred with Hardwicke, the ambassador of the government, on October 19, Pitt insisted that Newcastle retire from the ministry, since it was under his direction of affairs that the military reversals had taken place. The King refused the terms peremptorily. Pitt, however was not to be put off so easily. He took a "more private channel to the King," using the good offices of Lady Yarmouth, the royal mistress, and despite George II's protest that "she does not meddle and she shall not meddle,"[8] the appeal had the desired effect. On October 26 Newcastle and Hardwicke resigned. The King, after first calling upon Fox to form a ministry, was forced by Pitt's contemptuous refusal to join a coalition with his rival to accede to the popular idol's demands. By Pitt's desire and with Bute's support, the formation of a ministry was entrusted formally to the Duke of Devonshire.[9] Pitt was given the seals of the Southern Department with the chief power in the ministry, and the Grenvilles received their rewards. Temple became First Lord of the Admiralty, and Jemmy took a seat at the Treasury. Pitt called for a promotion for George Grenville to his own former office of Paymaster of the Forces.[10]

In the awarding of the Paymastership, however, complications arose. Pitt had refused to enter a coalition with Fox, but if things were to go smoothly in the Commons he could not afford to ignore his rival in the distribution of offices. And Fox had his eye upon the lucrative Paymastership as the price of his support in the Commons. Pitt wanted Grenville to have the office and tried to dissuade Fox, telling him it would be "too like Mr. Pelham in the year 1742" for Fox to have the office and that he had "better let G. Grenville have it, and be Treasurer of the Navy."[11] For some time the matter was left unsettled. When the list of the ministry was made out by Devonshire, Grenville and Fox were listed jointly for the offices of Paymaster and Treasurer of the Navy. Fox, however, was not to be put off. He refused to enter the ministry without the Paymastership, and Pitt, thinking himself sure of his brother-in-law's support, sacrificed Grenville to strengthen his ministry by including his dangerous rival. Within a few days, Grenville learned that Fox was to be Paymaster and that he was to remain in his old position as Treasurer of the Navy.12

The old wound in Grenville's breast was reopened. The resentment toward Pitt had almost healed, but by this slight it was renewed and increased. The slight might not have hurt so much had Pitt been diplomatic about it. Grenville had told his brother-in-law that he would look "with the greatest pleasure upon every party formed with you." If Pitt had taken the trouble of explaining to Grenville the necessity which had dictated Fox's preferment and had assured him of his continued good wishes, the matter might have been forgotten. Pitt, however, never mastered the art of handling men; on this as on many another occasion he erred by maintaining a lofty superiority. Grenville learned of Fox's appointment not from the new First Minister but from Temple and Jemmy, "nor did Mr. Pitt, however extraordinary it may appear, ever speak to [him] again upon this subject."14 To one of Grenville's temperament, the slight was unforgivable. Far more galling than the loss of the higher office was Pitt's supercilious behavior. From this time forward the brothers-in-law grew more and more distant.

ii.

The tenure of office of the new ministry was short. Kissing hands for its offices on December 4, 1756, it lasted only until the early days of April, 1757. The King still distrusted Pitt and had a personal antipathy to Temple, and the ministers had only a small following in the Parliament. Chesterfield opined that Pitt had almost as many enemies as the King of Prussia.15 And perhaps the ministers were their own worst enemies, for when Temple openly opposed the address of thanks in the Lords on the issue of Hanoverian troops and shortly thereafter behaved insolently to the King in his closet, George II declared that he would rather give up his throne than endure Temple another month.16

It was obvious by mid-March that the ministry could not continue as it was constituted. The King was more than ready to be rid of the Grenville crew upon the first excuse which offered. It came with the formation of an "army of observation" and with the appointment of the Duke of

Cumberland to head it at the insistence of Frederick II. Coached by Fox, Cumberland refused to head the force to the Continent unless Pitt ceased to be minister.[17] The King quickly complied, and on April 5 and 6 Temple and Pitt were dismissed. George and Jemmy Grenville immediately resigned.[18]

There followed nearly three months of ministerial anarchy before any solution could be found for setting up a new government. Neither Pitt nor Newcastle was willing to yield the chief place in a coalition ministry, and neither had the strength to form a government alone. Pitt had great popular support and an eloquent appeal on the floor of the Commons, but he lacked the parliamentary following and control which Newcastle had. Yet Pitt's stubbornness finally won out; Newcastle at last consented to take only the nominal headship in the Treasury rather than to disrupt the country further. In June the new ministry was formed, with George and Jemmy again taking their former places. To placate the King's resentment, Temple was given the Privy Seal, while Lord Anson replaced him in the Admiralty.[19]

At one point in the negotiations Pitt put George Grenville forward for Chancellor of the Exchequer, perhaps in an attempt to make up for having sacrificed him the previous fall. But Newcastle was firm in opposing the move, and Grenville, "finding that the coalition was impeded by what was demanded for him, desired to waive the Exchequer."[20]

Thus the ministry was formed which was to prosecute the war that carried Great Britain to the highest pinnacle of world prominence she had ever known. And much to his regret and resentment, George Grenville was outside the fold of the Cabinet Council. The Treasurership of the Navy had "never been esteemed a ministerial employment."[21]

With a unanimity born of necessity, the ministers left off their rivalries and intrigues and concentrated upon the successful prosecution of the war. Grenville no less than the members of the Cabinet Council contributed his efforts. The gouty "great commoner," as Pitt was coming to be called, was often unable to attend the Commons during important business because of ill health. The conduct of the House then devolved upon Grenville and, to a lesser extent, upon Legge. But even while he directed affairs in the Commons, Grenville was drawing apart not only from Pitt but also from the other members of the family, whom he considered privy to Pitt's slights to him. He saw his brothers frequently enough, of course, but if one may judge from his correspondence as well as from the "narrative" he composed in 1762, his relations with them became more and more formal and perfunctory. He had his own family and in-laws, his own fields to supervise and cows to tend, his own set of friends. He might still transact the family business, as when he invested some of his own and Temple's money in the naval funds,[22] but relations were cool. Temple never spent £33.12.0. on watches for George's boys as he did for Jemmy's.[23] The ties with the family were loosening.

With his connection with Leicester House, his growing resentment of Pitt, his weakening ties with his family, and his strong ambition, it was natural that when a new and promising element appeared in the ministry from the Leicester House "party" Grenville would ally himself with it. The opportunity presented itself soon after George II died, October 25, 1760. The young George III soon offered the office of Secretary of State to his friend and counsellor, Lord Bute. The favorite had the political sagacity to decline such a revolutionary step,[24] but he continued to cultivate the King's favor and remained alert for a more cautious opening to gather additional strength. He was quickly appointed a member of the Privy Council, and thereafter he was consulted on all matters of important policy.

Though Bute had never held ministerial office, he was hardly a political novice. His had been one of the guiding hands in negotiating for the coalition between Pitt and Newcastle in May and June, 1757.[25] In fact, Bute had been able to exert a considerable influence all during Pitt's administrations, both because of his connection with the "great commoner" at Leicester House and because of his position with regard to the young Prince of Wales. During the first years of their association, Bute and Pitt had been on the most intimate terms. Bute addressed Pitt in his letters to him as "My Dearest friend" and signed himself "your most affectionate friend."[26] By the time Bute entered the Cabinet Council, however, his criticism of Pitt's measures in prosecuting the war and particularly of his continental subsidies had occasioned quarrels between them and had reduced the salutations in their correspondence to an icy "Dear Sir" or to nothing at all.[27]

Between the two former friends and present antagonists stood the Duke of Newcastle, the nominal head of the ministry. It was he who brought the King's favorite into the government and persuaded Pitt to accept him. The old Duke felt that he could not continue in the ministry without including both the rival elements. Bute, meanwhile, consented to enter with Pitt only because Newcastle refused to go on without the "great commoner." Even then he drew a promise from Newcastle that the latter would support him against Pitt in the event of difficulties between them.[28]

It was thus among three factions of a very disjointed coalition that George Grenville was forced to choose upon the accession of George III: Pitt, with his popular support and that of the rest of the Grenville family; Newcastle, with his parliamentary support; and Bute, with the support of the King. Newcastle might be easily dismissed, for in spite of his power Grenville had no real ties with the Duke and saw little promise in him for the future. Between Pitt and Bute he hesitated. On Pitt's side was the argument of their long friendship, their family connection, and the fact that Temple and Jemmy stood solidly with the "great commoner." Yet there were still the rankling resentments of 1754 and 1756, which Pitt had done little to assuage. Pitt had not given him his full deserts. Even if Pitt continued to hold power, Temple would be his lieutenant, not George, for Temple was the head of the family and had the influence and wealth. Bute, on the other hand, had as yet no lieutenants, and his seemed the rising star of the political heavens. Grenville could see in the favorite the likely coming power in the new reign.

Unlike Pitt, Grenville had not broken his allegiance to Leicester House. His old friendship with Bute had been strengthened by his placing his friend Charles Jenkinson in Bute's service as his private secretary.[29] Indeed, even after Bute had broken with Pitt he could write to Grenville signing himself "ever, dear George, with the greatest regard and most sincere friendship, yours,"[30] The choice was difficult, but coalition with Bute certainly offered promise!

By December, 1760, Grenville had made at least a tentative decision in favor of Bute and against Pitt. In that month he openly opposed Pitt's bill for a tax on ale and beer. Men began to wonder "what can be the meaning of this appearing difference between George Grenville and Mr. Pitt?" Newcastle heard that Grenville "might make some opposition," but Pitt "seemed not to believe" the reports.[31] Nevertheless, the fact of a coalition between Grenville and the favorite was confirmed in the following February, when Bute had Grenville appointed a member of the ministry.[32] The position was actually one rather of honor than of power, and it did not carry with it the right to attend the meetings of the Cabinet Council.[33] Bute made arrangements, however, for his personal secretary, Jenkinson, to keep Grenville informed of all the important transactions in the inner Cabinet.[34] Meanwhile the favorite himself assumed the seals for the Northern Department, March 25, 1761, replacing the Earl of Holderness, who received a pension from the King.[35]

During the shakeup which attended Bute's replacing Holderness, the Eleventh Parliament rose, and with the announcement of the retirement from the Speakership of Sir Arthur Onslow, who had served in that capacity since 1728, Grenville saw a solution to the dilemma of choosing between his family and the favorite. This "most neutral place in the government" would have suited his capacities and temperament admirably. With his intricate knowledge of parliamentary procedures, gained through study and experience, and with his passion for logical precision and detail, Grenville would have made a worthy successor to Onslow, who was justly regarded as one of the most able Speakers ever to occupy the chair. Grenville looked upon the Speakership as "the highest honour that could have befallen me, and a safe retreat from those storms and that uneasiness to which all other public situations, and more expecially at this juncture, are unavoidably exposed."[36]

iii.

His path was to lead another way. Already events were preparing which were to force Grenville's final decision between Pitt and Bute. The war with France was entering upon its final stages. Early in 1761 the Duc de Choiseul announced the readiness of the French to treat for peace. In addition to calling a conference at Augsburg, he sent a special negotiator, de Bussy, to London to begin direct negotiations. The ministers in London, however, were not agreed among themselves on the idea of making peace. Newcastle, to be sure, desired peace almost at any price. From the vantage point of the Treasury, he saw the unheard-of debt which the war was piling upon England's shoulders, and he turned away in dismay. Pitt, on the other hand, had never been one to assess his war measures in terms of their cost. While Newcastle managed the finances, he dictated the strategy, which redounded to his own glory as well as the nation's. He wished the war to continue until a peace could be achieved equally glorious by his own standards. Bute, like Newcastle, wished immediate peace, but not peace at any price. He wished Pitt out of the Cabinet Council, however, for Pitt controlled and even dictated policy. Therefore he encouraged Newcastle in his desire for immediate peace, and the Duke played into his hands. By mid-April, 1761, Newcastle in his desire for peace was thinking Pitt's war policies impracticable, and was open in his opposition to them.[37] Bute, on the other hand, continued deferential to Pitt. When Egremont applied to the favorite with the request that he "be employed at the future congress" to settle the peace terms, Bute wrote to Pitt asking his opinion on the matter.[38] It did little harm to make that gesture; he could depend upon the King's appointing his nominee in any case. Egremont was soon selected as minister plenipotentiary to Augsburg.39

But in spite of such deference, Pitt and Temple were not long in recognizing that Bute wished them out of the ministry. By June Temple was complaining to his leader that "nothing can be more impertinent or ridiculous than Bute's language."40 They must have seen, moreover, that by the summer of 1761 both George Grenville and his brother-in-law, Egremont, were in Bute's camp.41 To Pitt's invitation to him, asserting that his presence at the Privy Council on July 8 was "highly necessary,"42 Grenville replied thus coldly: "Dear Sir—I am much obliged to you for the favor of your letter and for your attention in pointing out to me so strongly the propriety of my attendance.... I am ever your affectionate friend and brother."43 Temple apparently sensed the coldness between Pitt and Grenville,44 but it probably worried him little, since he and even Grenville thought that the younger brother would soon be in the Speaker's chair and out of the active political arena.

Yet in September the questions at issue among the ministers were brought to a crisis which forced Grenville to abandon his ideas of the Speakership. In August France had concluded a treaty with Spain which provided for a close alliance between the two countries in defense and commerce and for a Spanish declaration of war against Great Britain should hostilities last until May 1, 1762. Though the details of the treaty were kept secret, the fact of its existence and some information concerning its contents became known to Pitt, who on September 17 broke off the negotiations with France.45 The following day in Cabinet Council he demanded an immediate declaration of war against Spain. Here Bute and Newcastle had their chance, and when the question was put to a vote Pitt found himself supported only by Temple among the councillors. The other ministers advised that before war was declared one more attempt should be made in Madrid to preserve peace. Pitt, however, was adamant in his demands, in spite of the solicitations of Bute and his group.46 It was decided on September 21 that any action against Spain would be postponed until the receipt of further dispatches from Paris.47

Meanwhile, Bute and Newcastle were considering what would be the issue if they continued to oppose Pitt's Spanish war. It began to appear that only two alternatives were open to them. Either they would have to acquiesce in immediate war against Spain or they would have to carry on without Pitt, who would probably resign. Newcastle doubted that the popular idol would go so far, but if Pitt did quit the Duke resolved to consult and act with Bute. He "could see no better scheme," he professed, "than that of George Grenville's being Secretary of State." Bute suggested Chancellor of the Exchequer, but Newcastle disagreed. To take Pitt's lead in the Commons, Grenville would need authority in the ministry; as Secretary "he would have the Bank and authority of Minister in the House of Commons, which is not the case of a Chancellor of the Exchequer, where there is a First Lord, who is not quite a cypher."[48]

By September 26 it began to appear that Newcastle and Bute would have to carry on without Pitt whether the "great commoner" resigned or not. George III, reported Newcastle, was "every day more offended with Mr. Pitt, and plainly wants to get rid of him in all events." Newcastle believed the King would have to dismiss Pitt if he did not resign; with Pitt in the ministry, war with Spain or not, things "must go on very awkwardly," for if they took up Pitt's Spanish war they would have to abandon his German one.[49] Thus on September 26, Bute, Newcastle, and Devonshire met to plan a new administration. The chief place to fill, of course, was Pitt's. It would be difficult to find a man who could replace Pitt as both Secretary of State and leader of the Commons. Grenville's name was first suggested, but Bute quickly rejected it. Grenville "had not a manner of speaking which would do against Mr. Pitt." Fox was considered, but was rejected because Newcastle felt that his reputation as a treacherous politician would scarcely support him as a replacement for the most popular man in England. Bedford also was considered for Secretary of State, but Bute thought him too much a follower of Newcastle and a threat to his own supremacy in the ministry.[50] No decision was reached on the matter, but it seemed, in spite of their initial rejection, that the office would go to Grenville almost by default!

The crisis came on October 2, when the Cabinet Council met to decide for peace or war with Spain. Pitt and Temple again found themselves overwhelmingly opposed on the issue of a declaration of war, whereupon the "great commoner" calmly announced his intention to resign, since he could not "continue a Minister of the King's without the direction of his affairs." Temple, not so calm but fully as determined, followed immediately with an announcement of his own intention to resign.[51]

iv.

While these events were taking place in London, Grenville had retired to Wotton. Bute had told him on September 25 that the outlook was doubtful but not serious enough to detain him in town. Now the crisis had come; on October 2 after the meeting of the Cabinet Council he wrote

Grenville that he knew "whenever (the King's) service demands your presence, you will not lose a minute in coming here." He desired to see "dear George" at dinner the following day.52 It was two o'clock in the morning when Bute's messenger delivered the letter at the door at Wotton. By four o'clock, Grenville's carriage was lumbering over the frosty Buckinghamshire hills toward London.

Grenville had ample time to think as the carriage jolted along. The decision of his career had arrived! Now was the time when he would have to decide once and for all between Pitt and Bute. So long as all had been within the ministry, the choice had involved only personal friendships and allegiances. Now it was a question of his career. Temple had his estates and his fortune. Pitt had made his name, and was receiving legacies from patriotic citizens right and left. But Grenville had as yet neither fortune nor fame, and it appeared unlikely that he would ever gain either if he went out of office with his brothers. He would lose even the salary which he now drew. And who could say whether, if he abandoned Bute, he would ever again have this opportunity for advancement? Bute now had the King's ear, and it was extremely unlikely that he would soon allow it to be shared again by Pitt and Temple.

The path of prestige and political fortune seemed definitely to lie with Bute, but the price was high, perhaps too high. If Pitt and Temple went into opposition, they would likely treat Grenville as they had treated Lyttelton when he abandoned them for place in 1754.53 It would be poor recompense to gain prestige in an administration under Bute at the expense of alienating his family. Elizabeth's brothers, Egremont and Thomond, were in Bute's camp, but he dreaded to break ties with his own brothers and with Hetty, who was a long-time friend of Elizabeth. If only some way might be found to retain both the family ties and those with Bute!

Such must have been the thoughts which coursed through Grenville's mind as the horses raced down the highway between Amersham and Chalfont. Suddenly a coach loomed out of the morning mists, and Temple was beside him on his way from London. Grenville stopped the chaises and clambered into his brother's to discuss the situation with him. The atmosphere was tense; Temple had come down from town at this early hour to avoid talking with anyone about his resignation. Grenville outlined his case. He was willing to "withdraw" if Pitt and Temple thought it necessary, he said, but it did not appear to him that he stood "in the same case" as they, not having been involved in the struggle in the Cabinet Council. Temple agreed. The measure of resignation, he said, "simply regarded Mr. Pitt and himself;... he did not see another person in the kingdom who ought to resign for the same cause." He advised his brother to continue on to London and "do whatever he thought best for himself," repeating that he saw no reason for anyone else's resigning.[54] The problem of the family ties, it seemed, was solved.

Bute and Newcastle, meanwhile, continued to argue over the choice of a successor to Pitt. Newcastle was determined "never to agree" to Grenville's having the Exchequer, and wished him in Pitt's place instead. "The moment Mr. Grenville is Chancellor of the Exchequer," he had told Hardwicke, "it is to him, and to him only, to whom the King will apply; and it is he, who will have singly the King's confidence.... I should not pass one easy moment in the Treasury after that was done."[55] Grenville was Bute's man, and Newcastle would have no competition from him in the Treasury. Hardwicke thought he should have no office in the ministry, but should be allowed to follow his own inclination and become Speaker of the Commons. Both Newcastle and Bute disagreed. The favorite, indeed, counted Grenville his only reliable ally in the ministry. "If he remains Speaker," he wrote Newcastle, "...I see no system whatever proper for this dangerous minute."[56]

Newcastle continued to insist that Grenville be given the seals. "Mr. Grenville's rank, knowledge, and ability would, when Secretary of State, enable him to take upon him the conduct of the House of Commons," he maintained. "And the Duke of Newcastle is persuaded that all his Majesty's principal servants in Parliament would not only entirely cooperate with him, but would give their utmost assistance to Mr. Grenville to enable him to carry on his Majesty's business with success."[57] If Bute was to have his lieutenant in the ministry, it would have to be as Secretary of State and leader of the Commons, despite his "manner of speaking." When Grenville arrived in town on October 3, Bute "opened to him the King's intention of giving the seals to him."[58]

Now, however, it was Grenville's turn to balk. Still thinking of maintaining close relations with Pitt and Temple, he announced that delicacy prevented his accepting the positions which his brother-in-law had so recently resigned. Rather he wished to be allowed to "go into the Chair" and avoid giving offense to his brothers. Despite the insistence of Bute, Egremont, and the King, Grenville remained adamant. Some other solution had to be sought. The King's influence was brought to bear to persuade Grenville to undertake the conduct of the Commons. He was given "the fullest assurances of the King's support of him through all difficulties," and was told that "his honour was the King's honour, and his disgrace would be the King's disgrace." To Grenville's plea to be allowed to become Speaker, the King replied that he must undertake the Commons "to resist Mr. Fox's power."[59] Finally Grenville consented to take the conduct of the Commons provided that it were separated from the seals, which he could in no case accept. On October 7, Bute offered the office of Secretary of State to Egremont, while Grenville took the leadership and remained at his post as Treasurer of the Navy. The Cabinet Council was to be restricted to four: Newcastle, Bute, Egremont, and Grenville.[60]

v.

Having eaten his cake, Grenville found to his chagrin that he no longer had it. Apparently Pitt gave his approval of Grenville's taking the leadership; at least Grenville took it only after discussing the matter with Pitt on October 6.[61] But Temple was different. Grenville's merely remaining in his subordinate office as Treasurer of the Navy would probably not have been offensive to him. One surmises this was what Temple had in mind when he advised his brother to remain in office. But Grenville's accepting a position in the very Cabinet Council from which his brothers had just resigned and his taking up Pitt's scepter in the commons was too bold an effrontery for Temple. When Grenville called on him soon after, Temple refused to allow him admittance and sent word that he never wished to see his face again. Jemmy knew which side his bread was buttered on; he admitted Grenville when he called, but was "so rude and offensive" to his brother that he left immediately.[62] Temple even talked of putting George off the Wotton estate and giving it to Jemmy, who had gone out of office with him.[63] Such threats were mere bluster, it proved, but they nevertheless spelled a disruption of Grenville's family relations. His delicacy in refusing the seals had been in vain. Now there was a distinct possibility that Temple would carry Pitt into active opposition and that Pitt's fulminating oratory would be employed against him in the Commons. Grenville began to have serious qualms about the security of his position.

His fears were further roused on October 11 by the likelihood of a lack of support in the Cabinet Council. Bute, Newcastle, and Grenville met to discuss the choice of a Speaker. Newcastle had suggested on October 7 that Sir George Savile be given the post.[64] Grenville "put an absolute negative" on Saville and "was very positive and determined for Mr. Morton," whom he felt he could trust more implicitly.[65] Newcastle was fully as strong against Morton. He asserted that he was a tory and a "very low, inconsiderable man,"[66] but what he probably had in mind was that he could be controlled by Bute. Thereupon Bute complained to Newcastle that if "his friend Mr. G. Grenville was to be put into the most difficult station and to be mortified, hurt, and not supported; and this because I (Newcastle) had put a negative upon Mr. Morton...he would advise him to return to the chair."[67] The new leader of the Commons was already becoming a real problem to the other ministers, and the session had not even opened!

After a conversation with Newcastle on October 13, Bute sent Gilbert Elliott[68] to Grenville with a letter. Grenville was to read it and allow Elliott to return it to Bute, since it contained several remarks disparaging to Newcastle. After Elliott had left, Grenville dictated to Elizabeth a summary of the letter. Bute assured him that Newcastle would no longer oppose their plans. When the peace was made, the Duke would resign whenever called upon. Until that time there was no harm in letting the "crazy old man...tide over a year or two more of his political life," since Bute had now "no reason to find fault with his behavior."[69]

Bute was troubled at Grenville's state of mind. He saw, he said, "all the symptoms of a mind extremely agitated turning every incident in the blackest light and viewing with an eye of despondency every part of your intended situation." Grenville, he assured, would have the full support of George III. "Your eyes will see and from you I shall hear the transactions of each day. Part of your duty will be to report to the King the conduct of these gentlemen. The King will be informed. That is sufficient. For when you know him better you will find a firmness extremely calculated to support his own authority delegated by him to others." Grenville would also have Bute's own support in conducting the Commons; "...from the minute you are there, your honour my honour, your disgrace, my disgrace is his (the King's), to all intents and purposes...."[70]

Still Grenville was not entirely satisfied. Support in the closet and in the Cabinet Council would not help much in the House of Commons against Pitt. He would do the best he could, he told Hardwicke, but he must be supported. Hardwicke was particularly struck with his concern over Henry Fox's attitude. Grenville seemed to fear Fox almost as much as Pitt and wanted no competition from him.[71] As usual, Fox had his price; in return for his following Grenville's direction in the Commons, he demanded a peerage for his wife. Again Bute pulled the strings. On October 15 the order was given to "yield to Mr. Fox," and another of Grenville's hurdles was cleared. In view of Grenville's fear of Fox's too active support "lest his superior abilities eclipse him," Fox agreed "to act, speak, or not to speak, when, and as my Lord Bute will advise."72

Support was now assured on all sides. Hardwicke even reported that "everybody in town" had agreed to Grenville's management of the Commons.73 Yet Grenville was still extremely uneasy. Newcastle had let him know that his control of the patronage in leading the Commons was to be restricted rather severely.74 The old Duke was keeping the purse strings firmly in his own hands. Moreover, Grenville was disturbed about his relations with his family. Bute told Hardwicke that Grenville had "teaz'd him out of his life" from worry over the rupture with his brothers. Temple's refusing to receive him or "see his face more" preyed especially on his mind. He began to feel that he had deserted his family.75 He even began to consider backing out of his position before he antagonized his brothers beyond reconciliation.

Newcastle and Bute were much alarmed at the prospect of Grenville's breaking up the ministry which had been formed. For nearly two weeks Grenville kept them on edge with his "uncertainty and balancing." Bute was so exasperated by October 29 that he went to the King and told him he was ready to give the matter over. Newcastle had "two most long and tedious conversations" with Grenville and felt that he had "contributed a little to quiet him." Yet Grenville still feared Fox and bemoaned the loss of his family and connections. "What a figure shall I make!" he cried. "Mr. Fox has superior parliamentary talent to me. Mr. Fox has a great number of friends in the House of Commons attached strongly to him. Mr. Fox has great connections, I have none. I have no friends; I am now unhappily separated from my own family."76 All Newcastle's assurances were of no avail; Grenville was still afraid of both his family and Fox. Finally, Bute persuaded him to undertake his part in the ministry and desert his family for good by promising that "Mr. Fox, who is ready to assist him, and do anything, *shall do nothing at all*."77 Thus the situation was finally resolved. Grenville took the sole conduct of the Commons and turned his back resolutely on the chasm between himself and his brothers. He had engaged wholly in the service of the King and the favorite. George III expressed himself well satisfied "to find Mr. Greenville *(sic)* so proper in his way of thinking."78

One more problem of support remained, however; the government's majority in the Commons was not completely in line. On the evening of November 1, the principal supporters of the ministry met to hear the draft of the King's speech and the address of thanks which were to open the new parliament on November 3. Charles Townshend,79 the Secretary of War, was "discontented with the precedence given to George

Grenville"[80] and raised an objection that the militia was not mentioned in the address, engaging in a rather heated altercation with Grenville. The militia was one of Pitt's favorite talking points; Townshend's conduct suggested to Grenville that he was thinking of joining forces with Pitt in opposition. Again Grenville was fearful. The King urged Bute to see to Townshend's conduct, "for if George is not supported in this first instance he cannot go on with that comfort I should wish every man in my service."[81] The following evening, Townshend recanted all he had said and begged Grenville's forgiveness. The new leader haughtily accepted his apology.[82] The parliamentary support was secure for the battle with Pitt.

vi.

While the ministers were thus jockeying for position, Pitt's fortunes also had been varying. Immediately following his resignation, Grenville mentioned to Bute "what he apprehended to be the distressed state" of Pitt's private finances and as much as possible forwarded Lord Bute's disposition to recommend to the King to give him a mark of favour."[83] Bute immediately took up the idea as a device for discrediting the "great commoner." He wrote "by the King's command" to offer Pitt his choice of being Governor-General of Canada or Chancellor of the Duchy with a salary of £5,000. The royal impatience to show the world the "high opinion" he had of Pitt's merit was a delicate invention of Bute's. Actually the favorite wished it to appear that Pitt had been bribed to retire from office.[84] Pitt was too astute to take anything so direct, but the peerage for Hester and the £3,000 pension he accepted for himself had almost the same effect. When the details of the peerage and the annuity were announced in the Gazette on October 10, the effect was precisely what Bute had desired, particularly since Bute took the unusual step of announcing the full details of the pension.[85] The immediate impression was that the disinterested "great commoner" had been bought out of his office.

The public clamor was immediate and violent. Pitt's effigy was burned in the City, his stronghold of popularity, and the new Lady Chatham was reviled as Lady Cheat'em. Even one as familiar with the political world as Horace Walpole was carried away by the clamor. "I am in such a passion," he wrote, "I cannot tell you what I am angry about—why, about Virtue and Mr. Pitt; two errant cheats, gipsies!"[86]

Had matters remained in this state, Pitt's resentment might have flared into violent opposition in the Commons, realizing Grenville's worst fears.

Counter-attacks, however, brought him back his popularity before the session opened. On October 15 an open letter from Pitt to his friend William Beckford, one of the West Indian merchants in the City, explained his full conduct in resigning and in accepting the peerage and pension. The move proved as effective a maneuver as that of Bute. "Mr. Pitt's most extraordinary and unwarrantable letter," wrote Newcastle, "has had a most extraordinary and unanswerable effect, and has brought back to him his mad noisy city friends, who were for a time displeased with him."[87]

Newcastle feared that the return of Pitt's popularity and the vote of thanks he received from the Common Council of the City would make him even more dangerous in opposition,[88] and his fears were increased when on November 9 the London mobs turned a dinner for the King and Queen at the Guildhall into a triumphal ovation for Pitt and Temple.[89] The fears were unwarranted, however. Neither Pitt nor Temple was ready to oppose the ministers with any spirit when the session opened. True, Temple had objections to the address when it was read and made some remarks on court favor, attempting to draw out Bute, but he was much more temperate than had been expected.[90] Pitt was even conciliatory when he rose to justify his conduct on the Spanish war and to urge the continuance of his measures in the American and Continental campaigns. Though he did show some heat when baited by Richard Rigby and Grenville, he refused to enter into a personal battle with his brother-in-law.[91]

The real struggle came not in the Parliament but within the ministry itself, between Newcastle on the one hand and Bute and Grenville on the other, as early as October 23—before any final settlement was defined. On that date Bute, Newcastle, Hardwicke, Grenville, and Egremont met to decide on issues in the Spanish dispute. Bute, meanwhile, without consulting Newcastle, had already declared to Wall, the Spanish minister, that England was ready to settle her disputes amicably with Spain on condition that Madrid declare that there was no clause in the treaty with France of an offensive nature toward Great Britain. In view of the known terms, this was an obvious impossibility for Wall, and Newcastle therefore considered the message as unnecessarily provocative to Spain. Bute, having opposed a declaration of war to get rid of Pitt, did not scruple now to provoke the war he had opposed. Upon a vote, Newcastle and Hardwicke were overruled by Bute, Grenville, and Egremont, and the message to Wall was sustained.[92] Pitt in such a position had resigned, but Newcastle only protested that the policy would lead to war and clung doggedly to the Treasury.

The stand taken toward Spain by the ministers led to a motion in the Commons on December 11 that the papers relating to the negotiations be laid before the House. Grenville and Pitt measured their swords against each other in the debate. Such a motion, argued Grenville, was "of the most dangerous consequence." To call for papers "whilst a negotiation was depending...would tend to loosen all confidence from foreign powers." Pitt spoke artfully and ably in favor of the motion, but it was rejected without a division.[93]

While affairs with Spain now proceeded rapidly toward a declaration of war by England on January 4, 1762, another cause for contention among the ministers arose in the question of the German war. Newcastle, Bute, and Grenville were all agreed that Pitt's measures of meeting the enemy in all quarters of the globe were impractical and were costing more than the fiscal structure of the country was able to stand. All three wished to "contract" the war. Contention arose, however, over the manner and the place for such contraction. Newcastle, whose experience extended back to the wars in which Marlborough had won such glories on the Continent and who had served two kings whose primary interests centered largely in Germany, favored a concentration on the land war which Frederick II was conducting in Germany. Bute and Grenville, the younger men, were greatly impressed by the resounding victories in the colonies and on the high seas. They spoke of Newcastle's German war as a "foreign system" employing "foreign ideas" and were in favor of abandoning Frederick II altogether.[94]

All such considerations were contingent, of course, upon the continuation of the war itself; Newcastle was in favor of immediate peace, even on the most modest terms. "If we think to outwar Mr. Pitt," he said, "we shall find ourselves greatly disappointed. But if our real view is peace... by that only shall we gain the better of Mr. Pitt and serve the publick."[95] His aim was to get "a good peace as soon as we can."[96] In these views also Newcastle found himself opposed by Bute and Grenville, who, as we have seen, overruled him in sending a provocative note to Spain. Grenville informed the Duke that "he was for the war wherever France was vulnerable, and for supporting the King's engagements so long as it was practicable."[97]

The two questions of war or peace and the continuation of the German war became the objects of a contention which was to last until Newcastle left office in May, 1762. When news came in mid-November that war with Spain seemed imminent, Newcastle promised the King "every kind of harmony with George Grenville."98 Personal contentions would not subdue his patriotism. Yet the war with Spain brought the issue of the German war into sharper focus, and the quarrel continued. There was a likelihood that Spain would invade Portugal, and Bute had pledged that England would come to the aid of her ancient ally. Under these circumstances troops would have to be withdrawn from Germany. Bute informed Newcastle that the German war would have to be abandoned.99

The measure was facilitated by the death of the Tsarina Elizabeth, Frederick II's enemy, in January, 1762, and her replacement by Tsar Peter III, who was an almost fanatical admirer of the Prussian monarch. Peter immediately abandoned the war against his idol, and Frederick was free to concentrate his energies in other directions. This relieving of the pressure on Frederick provided a good excuse for discontinuing the unpopular Prussian subsidy, the treaty for which was just expiring. Grenville had found himself obliged to defend the payment against a torrent of criticism in the Commons; his only grounds were those of treaty obligations.100 He was more than willing to be relieved of the duty of defending a measure that was so troublesome. Yet Bute had already agreed to renew the subsidy before the news of the Tsarina's death arrived.101 It would be simple enough to withdraw English troops from Germany, but could the favorite go back on his agreement to help Frederick financially? After much wavering and hesitation, Bute decided that he could. On April 12 he informed Newcastle of his decision, and on April 30 Bute, Grenville, and their faction outvoted Newcastle, Hardwicke, and Devonshire in Cabinet Council, making final the refusal of the payment.102

vii.

In the Parliament, meanwhile, the session went smoothly. Grenville was cautious in his direction of affairs lest he antagonize Pitt in his measures. Indeed, at the beginning of the session he was careful to make "no declarations of what might hereafter be measures, so as to give anybody a handle for fixing him down to any particular system."103 His caution was wise, for time brought the ministers to follow the broad policy laid down by Pitt and gave the "great commoner" little grounds for attack. Probably Pitt would have left off opposition altogether had it not been for Temple's urging him on. The debates on the address which reopened the session after Christmas were "not worth coming for.... Mr. Pitt spoke, it seemed as if because he had promised Lord Temple, and said little else than that he was very lame." Temple in the Lords spoke "ill and angrily," but it seemed as though he was merely looking for something to complain about.104 Business in the Commons went on with an ease beyond Grenville's fondest expectations .

But with the arrival of mid-April, 1762, Newcastle and Grenville became involved in a personal dispute. Ever since Pitt's resignation, Newcastle had felt his influence in the ministry declining. At the end of December, 1761, he was complaining that Bute, Grenville, and Egremont settled all matters of importance between them. "My advice or opinion are scarce ever asked, but *never* taken," he complained. "Was ever any man in my station or infinitely less treated with so much slight and contempt?" he cried to Hardwicke. "*I will not* go on."105 Go on he did, however, but not without harboring an ever-increasing jealousy of the prerogatives of the Treasury. When in April Grenville opposed Newcastle's plan to grant the Prussian subsidy, the Duke felt it was an interference in the affairs of the Treasury. Grenville had based his opposition on the contention that if Great Britain increased the national debt by another twenty million pounds with the subsidy, it would make any further military or naval expenditures impossible for the following year.106 "I am not sure," wrote Newcastle, "that his view may not be to force me out, and to set himself at the head of the Treasury."107 Hardwicke felt that Grenville's thrust was not "meant as an attack upon the Treasury, but all aimed at the *German War.*"108 It is difficult to imagine, however, that the ambitious Grenville did not harbor just such intentions as Newcastle suggested.

The telling proof of Grenville's intentions in Newcastle's eyes came when the Duke proposed to the Cabinet Council to raise two million pounds for the prosecution of the war. Grenville "opposed it with the utmost warmth,"109 and not only argued his point in the Cabinet but went even to the King to contend that one million would be sufficient.110 Finally Newcastle began to think of resigning; Grenville and Bute could have suggested the idea to him long before! "Every day convinces me that I grow more insignificant," he moaned. "My remaining in the Treasury to be baited and perhaps overruled by Mr. Grenville would be of no service to the publick and very disagreeable to myself."111

Newcastle said on May 2 that he would "endeavour to steer as clear as possible of making a personal point between Mr. Grenville and myself,"112 but the issue of the two million pounds had already become precisely that. "I will never be overruled by Mr. Grenville in a point *singly* relating to the Treasury," he declared, "Mr. Grenville and I cannot *jointly* have the conduct of the Treasury."113 The King also became convinced that Grenville was "weak enough to think he may succeed the Duke of N- and therefore wishes to have him out of office."114

The quarrel was brought to a head when Newcastle discovered that Samuel Martin, the Secretary to the Treasury, was supplying Grenville and Bute with Treasury papers even before the First Lord himself saw them. "This lays me under great difficulties," he told Devonshire. "Whatever shall be done, my present resolution is...to let the King know that *that* has passed in the course of this affair which makes it impracticable for me to continue long in the Treasury."115 Bute and Grenville piled one more straw on the camel's back. The next day after Newcastle's discovery, Martin relayed their order to the Treasury clerks to draw up an account of what savings there would be if the troops were withdrawn from Germany. Newcastle then made up his mind to resign, though he acquiesced in Grenville's suggestion that he remain in office until after the parliament was prorogued in order "to avoid everything that could give any disturbance or raise a flame just at the end of the session."116

Bute and Grenville now began to make arrangements for the formation of a new ministry. Bute intended that, while he himself took the Treasury, Grenville should become Chancellor of the Exchequer, but Grenville refused to concur.117 George III thought Grenville's conduct "extraordinary, when he wished last year to have been the Duke of Newcastle's Chancellor of the Exchequer." "He is very far out if he thinks himself capable of a post where either decision or activity are necessary," said the King, remembering Grenville's hesitation and balancing the preceding fall; "for I never yet met with a man more doubtful or dillitory. We must not let slip what we had lately in our eye, the placing him in the Admiralty. There he could be easily spurr'd on, and would be out of the way."118

Bute, however, put a higher estimate on Grenville's usefulness. The qualms about his family relations were over now. Bute considered altering his plans to concede to Grenville's wishes. "I have been forced to make an unpleasant arrangement where I am immediately concerned," he told Grenville, "on your mind revolting against what I had ever looked upon as fixed."119 Apparently Bute intended to give Grenville the Treasury and either remain as Secretary of State or give up office altogether. This George III would not hear of. He told his favorite that "either the thought of his not accepting the Treasury or of his retiring chill my blood." The King had the solution. If a suitable Chancellor of the Exchequer could not be found, simply select "an honest quiet man" and go elsewhere for advice in financial matters.120 A "quieter" man in financial ability could hardly have been found than Sir Francis Dashwood, whom Bute finally selected for the Exchequer.

Still the problem remained of what office Grenville should have. The King thought that he might be "uneasy at holding the same employment he has possessed for these nine years."[121] One can scarcely imagine a greater understatement! If Grenville were not given some promotion in office, it was probable that he would seek reconciliation with his brothers in the opposition. There was, of course, Bute's vacant place as Secretary of State. But it seemed that Grenville was to be slighted in any instance, for when the favorite mentioned this idea to the King, it was vigorously opposed. George III objected to having brothers, Grenville and Egremont, as both Secretaries of State. He complained of "the impropriety of it," though it was obvious that the real reason was a fear that the brothers, holding such important positions, might gain an ascendancy over Bute and force him out. The King suggested rather that Egremont be transferred to the Lord Lieutenancy of Ireland. Bute professed to "laugh at the King's notion of impropriety," but doubtless he too saw the danger of the brothers becoming recalcitrant. He approached Egremont, but that lord firmly refused to give up the seals for a subordinate position. Bute had to persuade the King that the acceptance of the brothers was an absolute necessity.[122] When the interview was over, he informed Grenville that he had succeeded. "I have kept my word," he said; "this affair is quite over, and I entreat you to think no more about it."[123]

Four days later, Newcastle formally resigned his office, and the ministerial shuffle began. On May 28, Bute kissed hands for the position of First Lord of the Treasury, and on the following day George Grenville became Secretary of State for the Northern Department.[124] The ministerial offices were settled. Yet one problem still remained. If Grenville was to remain leader of the Commons, as Bute designed, he had of necessity to be a member of the House. The change of offices necessitated his reelection for Buckingham. He applied to Temple for permission to stand for the borough. Had Temple been inclined to be vindictive, he might have caused considerable difficulty for his estranged brother. He replied, however, that he left Grenville at liberty to do as he chose; he would recommend no one to run against him. Grenville thus applied to the High Bailiff of the borough for election.[125] The bailiff replied that since Temple had "signified to us that his Lordship will not interest himself one way or the other upon this vacancy," they would oblige him with reelection, having chosen him so often in the past "at his lordship's desire."[126]

With his accepting the Secretaryship of State, the final stamp was put upon Grenville's break with his brothers and his adherence to Bute. By making himself indispensable to Bute, he had risen this far toward power. The circumstances of politics during the next year were to make him independent of the favorite and yet indispensable to the Crown.

NOTES

CHAPTER V

[1] Glover, *Memoirs,* p. 50.

[2] Yorke, *Hardwicke,* II, 259; Walpole to Montague, December 20, 1755, Toynbee, *Walpole's Letters,* III, 366-367.

[3] Rigby to Bedford, December 4, 1755, *Bedford Correspondence,* II, 176; *Parl. Hist.,* XV, 529-531, 659-662.

[4] Stanhope, *History,* IV, 62, 72. On the beginnIngs of the war consult Sir Julian S. Corbett, *England in the Seven Years' War,* 2 vols., London, 1918, I, 10-138.

[5] Stanhope, *History,* IV, 76, 79-80.

[6] Rigby to Bedford, October 15, 1756, *Bedford Correspondence,* II, 201; Horace Walpole, *Memoirs of the Last Ten Years of the Reign of King George the Second,* 2 vols., London, 1822, II, 250.

[7] Newcastle to Yorke, October 15, 1756, Yorke, *Hardwicke,* II, 323.

[8] Hardwicke to Joseph Yorke, October 31, 1756, Yorke, *Hardwicke,* II, 331-332.

[9] William Cavendish, fourth Duke of Devonshire (1720-1764), who had succeeded to the title upon the death of his father in 1755.

[10] Walpole, *George II,* II, 93.

[11] Fox to Sackville, November 4, 1756, H.M.C., *Stopford-Sackville MSS.,* I, 51.

[12] Grenville's narrative, *Grenville Papers,* I, 438.

[13] Grenville to Pitt, August 26, 1756, Chatham MSS., 34, f. 17.

[14] Grenville's narrative, *Grenville Papers,* I, 438.

[15] Chesterfield to Philip Stanhope, January 12, 1757, Dobree, *Chesterfield's Letters,* V, 2217.

[16] Rigby to Bedford, March 3, 1757, *Bedford Correspondence,* II, 239; Glover, *Memoirs,* pp. 108-109; Walpole, *George II,* II, 197-198.

[17] Chesterfield to Dayrolles, April 26, 1757, Dobree, *Chesterfield's Letters,* V, 2223-2224; Walpole, *George II,* II, 196-198.

[18] Temple to Grenville, April 8, 1757; Grenville to Holderness, April 9, 1757, *Grenville Papers,* I, 192-194.

[19] Hardwicke to Anson, June 18, 1757, Yorke, *Hardwicke,* II, 404.

[20] Walpole, *George II,* II, 211; Glover, *Memoirs,* pp. 143-144.

[21] Waldegrave, *Memoirs,* pp. 105-106.

[22] Legge to Grenville, May 8, 1758, Murray MSS.

[23] Temple's personal account book, Stowe MSS., p. 232.

[24] Bute to Newcastle, March 6, 1761, Newcastle MSS., Add. MSS. 32919, f. 485.

[25] Newcastle to Chesterfield, May 7, 1757, Newcastle MSS., Add. MSS. 32871, f. 39.

[26] See Chatham MSS. and *Pitt Correspondence,* I, 223-224, 240-241, 301.

[27] See *Pitt Correspondence,* I, 323, 475; Thad Riker, *Henry Fox, First Lord Holland,* 2 vols., Oxford, 1911, II, 165-169.

[28] Namier, *England,* p. 331.

[29] See above, Chapter II.

[30] Bute to Grenville, December 13, 1758, Murray MSS.

[31] Hardwicke to Royston, December 17, 1760, Hardwicke MSS., Add MSS. 35352, f. 157. Newcastle thought Bute intended to give Grenville the Exchequer and put "some friend of his at the head of the Treasury." Newcastle to Devonshire, December 19, 1760, Newcastle MSS., Add. MSS. 32916, f. 207.

[32] Bute to Grenville, February 11, 1761, *Grenville Papers,* I, 339.

[33] See Denys A. Winstanley, "George III and his First Cabinet," *English Historical Review,* XVII (October, 1902), 680.

[34] Jenkinson to Grenville, March 24, 26, 1761, *Grenville Papers,* I, 359-361.

[35] Robert D'Arcy, fourth Earl of Holderness (1718 -1778).

[36] Grenville to Prowse, October 14, 1761, *Grenville Papers,* I, 438.

[37] Newcastle to Hardwicke, April 17, 1761, George Harris, *Life of Lord Hardwicke,* 3 vols., London, 1847, III, 243.

[38] Bute to Pitt, April 14, 1761, *Pitt Correspondence,* II, 114-116.

[39] Bute to Egremont, April 24, 1761, Egremont Manuscripts, Public Record Office, Bundle 29.

[40] Temple to Pitt, June 20, 1761, Chatham MSS., 61, f. 62.

[41] For Grenville's association with Bute see letters from Bute and Jenkinson in *Grenville Papers,* Murray MSS., and Ninetta S. Jucker, *The Jenkinson Papers, 1760-1766,* London, 1949. For Egremont's connection see Egremont to Grenville, August 6, 1761, *Grenville Papers,* I, 383-384, and Bute to Grenville, July 16, 1761, Murray MSS.

[42] Pitt to Grenville, July 2, 1761, *Grenville Papers,* I, 374-375.

[43] July 6, 1761, Chatham MSS., 34, f. 27.

[44] See Richard Lyttelton to Grenville, June 23, 1761, Murray MSS.

[45] Stanhope, *History,* IV, 230-239 .

[46] Newcastle to Hardwicke, September 20, 1761, Yorke, *Hardwicke,* III, 323.

[47] Newcastle to Hardwicke, September 21, 1761, Yorke, *Hardwicke,* III, 325.

[48] Newcastle to Mansfield, September 20, 1761, Newcastle MSS., Add. MSS. 32929, ff. 2-3.

[49] Newcastle to Hardwicke, September 26, 1761, Newcastle MSS., Add.

MSS 32928, ff. 362-363.

[50] Newcastle to Hardwicke, September 26, 1761, Newcastle MSS., Add. MSS. 32928, ff. 362-365.

[51] Minutes of the Cabinet Council, October 2, 1761, Newcastle MSS., Add. MSS. 32929, ff. 18-23; Jenkinson to Grenville, October 2, 1761, *Grenville Papers*, I, 391.

[52] *Grenville Papers*, I, 388, 392-393.

[53] See above, Chapter IV.

[54] Grenville's narrative, *Grenville Papers*, I, 409-411.

[55] Newcastle to Hardwicke, September 26, 1761, Newcastle MSS., Add MSS. 32928, ff. 364-365.

[56] Bute to Newcastle, October 6, 1761, Newcastle MSS., Add. MSS. 32929, f. 74.

[57] Minute by Newcastle, October 3, 1761, Newcastle MSS., Add. MSS. 32929, f. 48.

[58] Grenville's narrative, *Grenville Papers*, I, 411.

[59] Grenville's narrative, *Grenville Papers*, I, 411-412, 452.

[60] Bute to Newcastle, October 6, 1761, Newcastle MSS., Add. MSS. 32929, f. 76. Grenville claims that Egremont was given the seals at his suggestion. Grenville's narrative, *Grenville Papers*, I, 411. He had Thomond made Cofferer of the Household. Newcastle to Bedford, October 30, 1761, *Bedford Correspondence*, III, 67.

[61] Bute to Newcastle, October 6, 1761, Newcastle MSS., Add. MSS. 32929, f. 74.

[62] Grenville's narrative, *Grenville Papers*, I, 411, 414.

[63] Horace Walpole, *Memoirs of the Reign of King George the Third*, 4 vols., London, 1845, I, 84.

[64] Newcastle to Grenville, October 7, 1761, *Grenville Papers*, I, 393- 394.

[65] John Morton, at this time M. P. for Abingdon.

[66] Newcastle to Devonshire, October 14, 1761, Newcastle MSS., Add. MSS. 32929, f. 252.

[67] Newcastle to Hardwicke, October 13, 1761, Hardwicke MSS.; Add. MSS. 35421, ff. 112-113.

[68] (1722-1777), member for Selkirkshire and one of Bute's personal adherents. At this point he held the lucrative but politically powerless position of Treasurer of the Chamber.

[69] Heads of Bute's letter to Grenville, October 13, 1761, *Grenville Papers*, I, 395-396. The original of Bute's letter is preserved in the Bute MSS.

[70] Bute to Grenville, October 13, 1761, Bute MSS., quoted in Namier and Brooke, *Commons*, II, 538. Namier feels it significant that in his summary

Grenville omitted that he would report to Bute as well as to the King, but this seems unwarranted. It was obvious that Grenville would report to the head of the ministry; Grenville was impressed that he would report directly to the King also. See Namier and Brooke, *Commons, II,* 538- 539.

[71] Hardwicke to Newcastle, October 15, 1761, Newcastle MSS., Add. MSS. 32929, f. 332.

[72] Newcastle to Devonshire, October 14, 15, 1761, Newcastle MSS., Add. MSS. 32929, ff. 255, 258; Newcastle to Hardwicke, October 28, 1761, Yorke, *Hardwicke,* III, 336.

[73] Hardwicke to Charles Yorke, October 10, 1761, Yorke, *Hardwicke,* III, 330-331.

[74] Minute by Newcastle, October 10, 1761, Newcastle MSS., Add. MSS. 32929, ff. 152-154.

[75] Hardwicke to Newcastle, October 17, 1761, Newcastle MSS., Add. MSS 32929, f. 364.

[76] Newcastle to Devonshire, October 31, 1761, Newcastle MSS., Add. MSS. 32930, ff. 225-226.

[77] Newcastle to Devonshire, October 31, 1761, Newcastle MSS., Add. MSS. 32930, f. 227.

[78] George III to Bute, n. d., Romney Sedgwick, *Letters from George III to Lord Bute, 1756-1766,* London, 1939, p. 66.

[79] Younger brother of George, Viscount Townshend, and grandson of the statesman of the reign of George I (1725-1767). On Grenville's role in the drafting of the speech, see Newcastle to Devonshire, October 31, 1761, Yorke, *Hardwicke,* 336-337.

[80] Walpole to Mann, December 12, 1761 Toynbee, *Walpole's Letters,* V, 152.

[81] George III to Bute, November 5, 1761, Sedgwick, *Letters,* pp. 66-6l

[82] Walpole, *George III,* I, 87-88.

[83] Grenville's narrative, *Grenville Papers,* I, 412-413.

[84] Bute to Pitt, October 6 1761, *Pitt Correspondence,* II, 146-148.

[85] Newcastle to Hardwicke and Devonshire, October 9, 1761 Newcastle MSS., Add. MSS. 32929, ff . 141-143.

[86] Walpole to the Countess of Aylesbury, October 10, 1761, Toynbee, *Walpole's Letters,* V, 131. See also letters to Mann, Montague, Conway, October 10-12, 1761, pp. 128-135.

[87] Newcastle to Bedford, October 20, 1761, Newcastle MSS., Add. MSS. 32930, f. 176.

[88] Newcastle to Hardwicke, October 23, 1761 (two letters), Newcastle MSS., Add. MSS. 32929, ff. 470, 472.

[89] Nuthall to Lady Chatham, November 12, 1761, *Pitt Correspondence,* II,

166-168.

90 Walpole, *George III,* I, 87-88.

91 Milbank to Rockingham, December 10, 1761, George Thomas Keppel, Earl of Albemarle, *Memoirs of the Marquis of Rockingham and his Contemporaries,* 2 vols., London, 1852, I, 73-80.

92 Newcastle to Hardwicke, October 21, 1761; Hardwicke to Newcastle, October 23, 1761; Newcastle to Hardwicke, October 23, 1761; Newcastle to Hardwicke, October 24, 1761, Newcastle MSS., Add. MSS. 32929, ff. 421, 470, 472; 32930, f. 8.

93 Minute on proceedings of the Commons by James West, December 11 1761, Newcastle MSS., Add. MSS. 32932, f. 141.

94 Bute to Grenville, October 13, 1761, *Grenville Papers,* I, 396; Milbank to Rockingham, December 12, 1761, *Rockingham Memoirs,* I, 76.

95 Memorandum by Newcastle, October 11, 1761, Newcastle MSS., Add. MSS. 32929, f. 190.

96 Newcastle to Devonshire, October 15, 1761, Newcastle MSS., Add. MSS. 32929, ff. 258-259.

97 Newcastle to Hardwicke, October 18, 1761, Hardwicke MSS., Add. MSS. 35421, f. 124.

98 George III to Bute, November 18, 1761, Sedgwick, *Letters,* p. 70.

99 Newcastle to Devonshire, December 26, 1761; memorandum by Newcastle, December 31, 1761; memorandum by Newcastle, January 2, 1762, Newcastle MSS., Add. MSS. 32932, ff. 363, 419; 32933, f. 34.

100 Walpole, *George III,* I, 101-104.

101 Bute to Michell, January 1, 1762, Newcastle MSS., Add. MSS. 32933, f. 106.

102 Newcastle to Hardwicke, April 13, 1762, Newcastle MSS., Add. MSS. 32937, ff. 85-91; Newcastle to Rockingham, May 4, 172, Rockingham Manuscripts, Sheffield City Library, 2, f. 2.

103 Sackville to Irwin, November 16, 1761, H. M. C., *Stopford-Sackville MSS.,* I, 87.

104 Fox to Ilchester, January 20, 1762, Giles Stephen Holland Fox-Strangeways, sixth Earl of Ilchester, *Henry Fox, First Lord Holland, His Family and Relations,* 2 vols., London, 1920, I, 161.

105 Newcastle to Hardwicke, December 26, 30, 1761, Newcastle MSS., Add. MSS. 32932, ff. 363, 408.

106 Newcastle to Devonshire, April 13, 1762, Newcastle MSS., Add. MSS. 32937, f. 85.

107 To Hardwicke, April 10, 1762, *Rockingham Memoirs,* I, 106.

108 Hardwicke to Newcastle, April 10, 17621 Newcastle MSS., Add. MSS.

32937, f. 17.

[109] Newcastle to Devonshire, April 8, 1762, Newcastle MSS., Add, MSS. 32936, f. 340.

[110] Grenville's narrative, *Grenville Papers,* I, 449.

[111] To Devonshire, April 13, 1762, Newcastle MSS., Add. MSS. 32937, ff. 92-93.

[112] To Hardwicke, Hardwicke MSS., Add. MSS. 35421, f. 251.

[113] To Hardwicke, April 17, 30, 1762, Newcastle MSS., Add. MSS. 32937, ff. 183, 450.

[114] George III to Bute, May 6, 1762, Sedgwick, *Letters,* p. 100.

[115] May 5, 1762, Newcastle MSS., Add. MSS. 32938, ff. 67-68.

[116] Newcastle to Devonshire, May 6, 1762, Newcastle MSS., Add. MSS. 32938, f. 85.

[117] Rigby to Fox, May 20, 1762, Giles Stephen Holland Fox-Strangeways, sixth Earl of Ilchester, *Letters to Henry Fox, Lord Holland,* London, 1915, p. 151.

[118] George III to Bute, n. d. (c. May 15-17, two letters), Sedgewick, *Letters,* 104-105.

[119] Bute to Grenville, May 22, 1762, *Grenville Papers,* I, 446.

[120] George III to Bute, n. d., Sedgwick, *Letters,* p. 109.

[121] George III to Bute, n. d. (c. May 17, 1762), Sedgwick, Letters, p. 105.

[122] Bute to Grenville, May 22, 1762, "near one," *Grenville Papers,* I, 447.

[123] Bute to Grenville, May 22, 1762, "four," *Grenville Papers,* I, 448.

[124] Haydn, *Dignities,* pp. 157, 224.

[125] May 28, 1762, *Grenville Papers,* I, 453.

[126] May 30, 1762, Stowe MSS., loose papers.

John Stuart, 3rd Earl of Bute

Charles Wyndham, 2nd Earl of Egremont

CHAPTER VI

THE BUTE MINISTRY, 1762-1763

The situation which faced the new Bute ministry at its formation appeared particularly favorable. Militarily, little could be desired. In almost every quarter of the globe, Britain and her allies were meeting with success, and greater successes were in prospect for the coming summer months. Within the ministry there was an unwonted harmony. Pitt, Temple, and Newcastle were gone, and in their places sat Grenville and Egremont, loyal followers of Bute. Grenville's stubbornness disappeared once he had ensconced himself as one of his Majesty's Principal Secretaries of State. In the Parliament, there seemed little to fear. Pitt appeared disinclined to active opposition, and Temple, though angry and disgruntled at both Bute and Grenville, was no Pitt in the Lords. Newcastle's grip on the Commons was not what it had been in the previous reign. In the general election of 1761, Bute and the King had largely taken from him the dispensation of the government's patronage. Members who sat now for "treasury boroughs" owed their allegiance not to Newcastle but to the King and his minister.

Yet the situation was not so rosy for the ministers as it might have appeared at first glance. Bute realized what Newcastle's resignation meant to the Duke and to the coterie of "old whig" lords around him. Almost since the Hanoverian succession they had held predominant places in the King's government. Their control of the ministry and particularly of the Treasury they had looked upon as something belonging to the fixed order of nature. With Newcastle's virtual dismissal, their world came tumbling down about them. The Duke concluded at the time of his resignation that "many of my friends will be turn'd out."[1] It was simply in the nature of things that the group would fight back. Although there was no likelihood that they would band together in organized opposition to all ministerial measures—ideas of "loyal opposition" existed only in the most rudimentary form at this date—Bute could nevertheless depend upon scattered opposition by individuals and by groups to any measure they did not approve. And since he and Newcastle had disagreed violently on measures within the ministry, Bute anticipated opposition equally violent, if sporadic, in the Parliament.

One medium through which Bute expected opposition to be expressed was an opposition press, in the style of the old *Craftsman* of Walpole's day. One such paper already existed, a weekly called the *Monitor,* which was backed by the wealthy and powerful Beckford West Indian interests in the City. Since its founding in 1755, it had been a consistent supporter of Pitt, both in office and out. While Pitt declined to press opposition in the Commons, the *Monitor* and its conductors, Arthur Beardmore and John Entick, carried it on through the press.[2] Realizing that the tempo of propaganda warfare would quicken greatly with Newcastle's resignation, Bute hastened to establish his own weekly propaganda sheet. His measures would not go undefended in the public forum! Entitled the *Briton* and conducted by Dr. Tobias Smollett, the paper made its first appearance on the very day that Bute took office.[3] The *Monitor* had a challenger.

This was the signal for the appearance on the national stage of John Wilkes, the Grenvilles' Buckinghamshire protégé. Wilkes was an ambitious young man, and though undisturbed by principles, he had been apparently much perplexed by the split in the family of his patrons. He was much indebted to Temple and Grenville and had been on the best of terms with both. When the split arrived in the winter of 1761-62 he had had to choose between Temple's wealth and Grenville's political favor. At first he chose the latter, making an offer of his service to Bute in February, 1762.[4] The favorite, however, did not appreciate Wilkes' capabilities and spurned his services. He could hardly have made a move he would regret more. Wilkes naturally turned then to Temple, who was happy to receive him. When the *Briton* appeared, Temple quickly engaged Wilkes to conduct a weekly in opposition to Bute's. In derision of both the favorite and his propaganda organ, they named it the *North Briton.*

The intention of Temple and Wilkes was to play upon two prejuduces to which the English people would respond: a distrust of the influence of the Princess Dowager of Wales, who was of German descent, and a hatred of all Scotsmen, and hence perforce of Bute. Yet in attacking Bute as a Scotsman, they had to create something of a fiction. Bute indeed was born in Scotland of the royal house of Stuart, which would hardly endear him to the rabidly anti-Jacobite English populace, but he was scarcely a Scotsman's Scotsman. Having married a Yorkshire heiress, having lived for many years in London as tutor and advisor at Leicester House, and having won the favor of the most English king England had had in two centuries, he did not completely qualify as the arch-prototype of the north Briton. Nevertheless, Temple and Wilkes chose this fiction as their means of attack, and they developed it with telling effect. They did not scruple to endanger the reconciliation of two generations since the union. The prejudices against the Scots and the distrust of the Princess were combined and mutually reinforced by the continuing of implications already made in the *Monitor* (reputedly by Wilkes) that there was an improper relationship between the Princess and Bute.5

The first *North Briton,* perhaps the production of both Temple and Wilkes, made its appearance on June 5, 1762. It pretended to be written by an overly enthusiastic Scot, using this medium to call attention to the Scottish "infiltration" into the prominent places in the ministry. The paper, violent and scurrilous, took an immediate hold on the public fancy. Temple supplied information and advice as well as copy for Wilkes and his colleague, Charles Churchill, although he sometimes urged more caution than Wilkes wished to employ.6 "My father," commented Horace Walpole, "was not more abused after twenty years than Lord Bute is in twenty days."7 Pitt was openly critical of the lengths to which the North Briton was going. He "expressed himself warmly" to Temple "against all kinds of political writing, as productive of great mischief."8

As was the practice of the time, Wilkes and Temple kept their authorship of the papers as close a secret as they could. In their letters to each other they disclaimed all knowledge of the identity of the author and veiled communications in the most indirect allusions.9 Their caution was well advised, for the ministers were naturally incensed by the unscrupulous attack. Grenville as Secretary of State undertook to discover who were its authors. The papers themselves, of course, were published anonimously, but the printer was known. Grenville had him cited before him, and after having loaded him with "the most opprobrious terms" informed him "that unless he would give up the rascally author he should feel the weight of his anger and authority." The printer excused himself on a point of honor, but the Secretary persisted. He must give up the author that Grenville might "treat the rascal as he deserved," or he would instantly commit him to prison. Hesitating to the last moment, the printer at last cried just as his warrant was making out, "Rather than go to prison I will confess, as I was not enjoined secrecy. The author of it is Earl Temple."10

Any ideas of treating the "rascal as he deserved" must have flown as Grenville learned that his brother was the author of the objectionable pieces. Aside from family connections, it would have been unwise, to say the least, to attempt legal action against the known lieutenant of the popular "great commoner." The ministers let the idea of retaliation rest. Not so Temple! In the sixth number of the paper he struck back at Grenville with a stinging indictment of his brother's desertion of his family. The pretended Scot gloated over the acquisition of a "gentleman whom...we have entirely secured and detached from his friends (and *di boni*, what friends!) and family, to whom he has such infinite obligations.... This is not in itself a wonderful acquisition," the north Briton hastened to say;

> but I consider it as the first-fruits of our labours among the great families of the English nobility.... This gentleman has already spurned all obligations, and has broke through whatever would have engaged every other man, for he has sacrificed every social and friendly tie to cement with us. His intense zeal (a symptom frequent among renegadoes) has been demonstrated on many occasions; and in a great assembly, if he has failed to persuade, he has never failed to weary out his adversary, and to sink him in a deadly lassitude, perhaps a lethargy.[11]

Probably it was about this time, after Grenville's examination of their printer, that Temple instructed Wilkes to take the precaution of sending back to him all materials and letters which Temple had sent him.[12] How long Temple continued to contribute directly to the sheet is a matter of conjecture. One imagines that after about mid-August he left the actual writing to Wilkes and Churchill, for after the tenth number, which appeared on August 7, 1762, they left off the pretense of being a Scot and arraigned Bute openly from an Englishman's point of view. The Scot device suited Temple's devious nature, but Wilkes wished to be more open and direct. As the fall progressed, Wilkes and Churchill continued the personal attacks on the ministers, but they inveighed as well against the conduct of the peace negotiations which were under way.

ii

In spite of the favorable situation of British arms when he took the Treasury, Bute's first wish was to put an end to the war as quickly as possible. His purpose was two-fold. He wished first, as had Newcastle, to relieve the country of the expense of a war which had nearly doubled the national debt. In addition, he wished peace in order to be able to consolidate the King's ministry on a firm peace-time footing. In the late spring, therefore, while the news of victories poured in, the First Minister reopened negotiations for peace with France through the minister of neutral Sardinia, the Count de Viry. On June 4 the latter forwarded letters from Choiseul stating the terms which the French would accept for peace. Among other things, the French court refused to cede St. Lucia to British demands in exchange for Martinique, which British forces had captured early in the spring. Such was the anxiety of the King and his favorite for peace that they were ready to give up this British demand and accede to the French terms in order to obtain an immediate settlement. George III expressed his hopes that the peace was "as good as sign'd" and urged his minister "for God's sake keep firm tomorrow in Council, and this country will be drawn out of its difficultys."13

The King, however, did not reckon with the Cabinet Council. When Bute presented the French terms and George III's proposal of acceptance, he found himself opposed by Grenville and the whole Cabinet Council except Bedford, who like Bute was eager for peace on the most modest terms. Egremont termed the French proposals unreasonable and captious, and Grenville, Melcombe, and Mansfield, the other councillors, backed him in his refusal to acquiesce in Bute's ideas.14 Bute was forced to authorize the sending of despatches to Versailles demanding the surrender of St. Lucia.

Though he expressed no reasons for his sudden opposition to his chosen leader, an explanation for Grenville's actions readily presents itself. As manager of the Commons, it would be Grenville's responsibility to defend the peace that was being arranged when it was presented to that body. Pitt had quit the ministry rather than give concessions to Britain's enemies. If this concession were given up to France, Grenville could expect to have to defend it before the Commons against Pitt's bitter invective. When he learned, within a day or so, who was behind the vicious attacks of the *North Briton,* his determination to avoid unnecessary concessions must have been redoubled. To be a party to the needless giving away of a valuable conquest would be one of the surest ways to expose himself to the broadsides of Pitt in the Commons and of Temple in the press. Egremont had supported Grenville in the Cabinet Council, but secretly he sided with Bute and the King. When the letter demanding the cession of St. Lucia was turned over to Viry, Bute and Egremont privately hinted that if France were to agree to all the other articles, Britain would withdraw her demand for St. Lucia. Egremont, however, wished to keep the fact of his cooperation with Bute a secret from his brother-in-law. He asked the King to command him to give Viry the message in order to "prevent Greenville's knowing it to be his own thought."15 As the weeks passed before the French replied, Egremont still schemed behind

Grenville's back. George III could not keep him five minutes in the closet, "so fearful is he that Greenville should have any suspicion."16

At length a letter arrived from Choiseul on July 24 giving French approval to all the British articles except the surrender of St. Lucia. This was precisely what Bute had desired. It was accompanied, however, by a letter from Grimaldi, the Spanish Ambassador at Versailles, containing terms for peace between Spain and England which even Bute regarded as totally inadequate. The first minister then decided, again with the concurrence of Egremont and the King, to press for a separate peace with France.17 In this move he was opposed by the whole Cabinet Council, with Grenville again at their head. "How grating must it be to Lord Bute," wrote Fox, "...to find his Cabinet Councillors...differ from him in Council without declaring their minds to him first in private."18

Grenville won his point; Bute proposed to the Cabinet Council that Bedford be sent to Versailles to negotiate preliminary terms of peace with both France and Spain. The King's consent was given to the terms demanded by France, but in return France was required to persuade Spain to be a party to the treaty. In the event that Spain could not be persuaded, the French were to pledge themselves not to aid Spain in the war with Britain. To this all the Cabinet Councillors agreed.19 Yet to gain this point Grenville had agreed to surrender St. Lucia, and on that point Bute had triumphed. The favorite wrote to Egremont after the council as if Grenville no longer counted as a minister. "I mean by Ministers your Lordship and myself," he said. Nevertheless, he was ready to forget "Mr. Grenville's dissenting from me in word, look, and manner through the whole examination of the preliminaries. However unpleasant, I forget it."20 Indeed, Bute was forced to forget it and carry on, for he saw nowhere else to turn. He had even turned to Newcastle for support to regain control of his Cabinet Council from Grenville. The old Duke's answer was an inflexible "no."21 Bute and Egremont might concert policies between them, but Grenville still retained his influence in the Cabinet Council.

More struggles lay ahead. On September 4 Bedford received his commission from the King as plenipotentiary, and on the sixth he left for Paris to begin negotiations with France and Spain.22 As the negotiations proceeded, Grenville won Egremont over to his own side in the ministerial struggle. Between them they prevailed upon Bute to curtail Bedford's plenipotentiary powers by requiring that the preliminary terms be submitted to the King for approval before they were considered binding. This was an obvious attempt to take the negotiations out of the hands of

Bedford, with whose pacifist sentiments they were well acquainted, and place them under the surveillance of the Cabinet Council. There Grenville would be able to see that the terms were kept high. Bute assured Bedford, however, that the measure was intended merely to relieve him of the sole blame should the peace be unpopular.[23] Richard Rigby, a lieutenant of Bedford's, felt that Grenville and Egremont had prevailed upon Bute against his will. Grenville, he said, was "frightened out of his wits" at the prospect of a peace which conceded too much. Egremont was governed by Grenville "like a child." Rigby deplored to his leader "the cursed situation in which these two rascally Secretaries of State are disposed to plunge their master, your grace, and their *friend,* the Minister."[24]

Nor was this the only interference by Grenville and Egremont in the negotiations at Versailles. On the day that Rigby wrote, September 29, news arrived in England that British forces had captured the Spanish stronghold of Havana. Grenville had insisted even before the news arrived that the expedition would succeed and that some compensation should be demanded for it.[25] Now he was doubly insistent. To let so valuable a prize be returned without compensation was clearly to invite trouble from Pitt and the opposition. Even though the preliminaries were almost settled in Versailles, the whole Cabinet Council agreed that compensation for Havana must be required. But how much? Bute was willing to accept Florida as sufficient, while Grenville and Egremont, to leave no opportunity for the opposition, favored insisting upon both Florida and Puerto Rico at least.[26] Bute feared that to press too many new demands might disrupt the negotiations; he remained firm in spite of being outnumbered in the Cabinet Council. Grenville and Egremont declared that they would sign no treaty which did not give adequate compensation for Havana.[27]

The Cabinet Council had reached an impasse. The King summoned the two secretaries to his closet and lectured them sternly "upon their scruples,"[28] but neither would move an inch from his position. George III then decided that he must have a new ministry. He told Bute, October 2, that if the favorite could suggest no other plan by the following morning he was willing to call in Newcastle and Fox to replace Grenville and Egremont as the Secretaries of State. The two, he felt, "by mutual jealousies will be less formidable than were but one of the two parties to take office."[29] Thus was the favorite's hand to be strengthened.

Meanwhile the meeting of the Cabinet Council scheduled for October 4 was postponed until the King and Bute could arrange their support. Grenville suggested that the question be settled by calling Devonshire,

Newcastle, and Hardwicke to the Cabinet Council to break the deadlock. This Bute rejected "with some seeming contempt." Not one of them would come, he said; besides, he had no right to summon Newcastle and Hardwicke, since they were not in the King's service.[30] Newcastle approved of the idea of attending Cabinet Council without office if he could have the "disposition of employments," meaning the patronage, but Hardwicke considered Grenville's proposal "a very absurd one."[31] Devonshire, however, still held office as Lord Chamberlain. Grenville insisted that if he was to defend this peace at least one more minister should share the responsibility for accepting it. This much the King granted, and Devonshire was invited to attend.

That Duke, however, was a member of "an association" which had been formed against Bute early in the summer, consisting of Cumberland, Newcastle, Hardwicke, Pitt, Devonshire, and Richmond.[32] Bute had learned of the association in June.[33] It was thus no surprise to the minister to learn that Devonshire refused to attend Cabinet Council at the King's invitation. He was not sufficiently abreast of the situation to be of service, he said, and he hoped the King would excuse him from "attending at a Council where it is impossible to give any opinion in the uninformed situation I am in."[34] His wish that the King should understand his position was of no avail; George III took the refusal as a personal affront not only from Devonshire but also from Newcastle, Cumberland, and Richmond. He quickly changed his plans with regard to Newcastle and set about to invite Fox and Charles Townshend into his government instead. The House of Commons might be managed, he said, "without these proud Dukes."[35] When he discussed the matter with Grenville, the Secretary could only "sigh and groan," but he admitted that the ministry would have to be "widened."[36]

On October 6, therefore, George III summoned Fox and informed him that Grenville was, in Fox's words, "half unable, half unwilling" to continue in his capacity as manager of the Commons. When he offered the Paymaster the leadership of the Commons and Grenville's office as Secretary of State, Fox declined to take both. He would undertake the leadership, he said, but he could not accept the burden of the seals. George III "with difficulty" agreed to his refusing the seals, and arrangements were made for Fox's becoming Cabinet Councillor and "his Majesty's Minister in the Commons."[37] This accession of strength, however, was not enough for Bute. He still did not have sufficient strength in the Cabinet Council to gain an ascendency over Grenville. And as Secretary of State Grenville was still in an excellent position to obstruct

Bute's making of the peace on his own terms. Accordingly, another change in the ministry was arranged. On October 9, Grenville was informed that he was required to resign his position as Secretary of State, which was to be given to Lord Halifax, and that he was to replace the latter in the Admiralty. Only the day before, Bute had assured him that "no negotiation was on foot." Grenville's ire was up. He "entered his protest very strongly" both against the calling in of Fox and against his own demotion. It seemed almost a betrayal on the part of the King after George had persuaded Grenville the year before to give up his dream of the Speakership in order to "resist Mr. Fox's power." Not only did Grenville importune Bute; he carried his complaints even to the throne. The only consolation he received there was George III's cynical comment: "We must call in bad men to govern.bad men!"38

Yet the forced exchange was not all gall. Bute considerably lessened its bitterness when he talked to Grenville on October 11. The peace was his object, not triumph over Grenville. The exchange did not arise from any personal resentment on his part. He gave Grenville the definite impression, indeed, that he intended to resign as soon as the peace was secured and through the parliament. Moreover, sweet music to Grenville's ears, he had "always wished to see me (Grenville) at the head of the Treasury."39 Such an admission was tantamount to an outright promise and Grenville needed nothing else. He professed himself content and said he would give whatever assistance was desired in the Commons.40

In reality, the arrangement was not bad. Grenville still retained his seat in the Cabinet Council, and he had the prospect of succession to the Treasury. What was more, he was relieved of the anxieties which the responsibility of guiding the peace through parliament would entail; he need not defend or even support the concessions which Bute made. The favorite doubtless felt compelled to leave Grenville the major part of his power lest he renounce his allegiance and go back to Pitt and Temple, weakening the ministry and strengthening the opposition. But in spite of concessions, Grenville was still bitter about his loss of prestige—and loss of salary. Newcastle summed the matter up when he wrote that it was hard to believe "that they would venture to use Mr. Grenville so ill as to take him from an employment of the first rank and confidence of...8 or 9,000£ per annum to put him at the head of the Admiralty with barely £2,500."41 It was a bitter pill, and Grenville did not swallow it easily. As late as the following January, the King expressed his anxiety to Bute over Grenville's sullen resentment. He was, said the King, "at war with every man, because he will not forgive the change of his office."[42]

Despite this element of discord, affairs in the Cabinet Council progressed much more smoothly after the addition of Fox and Halifax to offset Grenville and Egremont. Having secured his supremacy by this adroit political stroke, Bute was able to push through more moderate demands for compensation for Havana, and the negotiations for peace pushed rapidly toward a conclusion. Yet the new harmony, or at least facility, in ministerial relations was offset by other problems, for by now the clamor against the peace-making in the opposition press was raising popular discontent of serious proportions.

iii.

The propaganda war which had begun when Bute took the Treasury turned at the end of the summer from one of personalities to one of attack and defense of ministerial measures and particularly of efforts toward negotiating the peace. To combat the *Monitor* and the *North Briton,* a new administration paper called the *Auditor* took its place beside the *Briton* in the public forum. Both were woefully out-generalled by Temple and his associates. Like Pitt, the English people in the main were intoxicated with victories and wished to wring the greatest concessions possible from France and Spain. When the ministers gave up point after point in quest of a quick peace, it was no difficult task for propagandists as skillful as Temple and Wilkes to raise the public ire against the government. The *Briton* and the *Auditor* found themselves up against an impossible task. Toward the end of September, the "clamour" against the peace-making had reached a steady roar. Temple, in the midst of the clamor, was "all flax, tow, pitch, and combustibles."[43] When the news of the capture of Havana arrived, compensation was "what *all* the world" cried out for. Grenville and Egremont would "get great credit and reputation," ventured Newcastle, if they brought the ministry to demand "proper satisfaction." Such was the state of the public mind that "the ministers will be tore in peices *(sic)* if they don't insist upon it."[44]

Not all this public excitement was owing to the efforts of the opposition press, of course. The papers merely fanned the flames of a popular grievance. To the ministers, however, the papers were an outward and visible cause. The attempt to outfight them on their own ground was obviously proving futile, but there might be other ways of silencing violent opposition. The *Monitor* and the *North Briton* in their enthusiasm had not stopped at the line of outright libel against the principal ministers of the

King. If some way could be discovered of proving the authorship of the sheets, the ministers could silence them by simple legal prosecution. As the time came for the preliminary terms of peace to be presented to the parliament, the desirability of silencing the opposition press became more and more apparent. The opportunity came when Jonathan Scott, a former editor of the *Monitor,* was persuaded to give testimony that Beardmore and Entick were its editors. On November 6, Halifax as Secretary of State issued identical warrants for the arrest of Beardmore and Entick. Each was cited as "the author, or one concerned in the writing, of several weekly very seditious papers, entitled the *Monitor* or *British Freeholder.*" In accordance with these and other warrants, Beardmore, Entick, and the printers and publishers of the *Monitor* were taken into custody during the week which followed, together with all their books and papers.45

The arrests at first had the desired effect. By November 13, Temple was writing to Wilkes in a very dejected tone. "Is all pitiful submission," he asked, "or is there a spark of real spirit and virtue left in this country." Lest Wilkes try to show too much spark, however, Temple begged him to "weigh" his conduct "very maturely."46 Wilkes proceeded to call on Beardmore in his confinement and urge him to bring suit for false arrest.47

Wilkes might not have been so enthusiastic had he known of the further measures which the ministers were deliberating. On November 18 Halifax signed another warrant, this time for "strict and diligent search for the authors, printers, and publishers of a seditious and scandalous weekly paper entitled *The North Britain (sic)....*"48 Such a general warrant, as it was called, was a traditional device employed by the Secretaries of State to bring suspected malefactors to justice when no specific names could be cited. The use of the general warrant was to cause the ministers a considerable amount of trouble later at the hands of the opposition, but on this occasion no actual arrests were made. Perhaps Grenville intervened in behalf of his brother, or perhaps the warrant was never intended to be executed. In any event, the actual use made of it was merely to intimidate Wilkes's printers, to whom it was shown privily. Shortly after November 18, Wilkes was twice forced to find new printers for the *North Briton.*49

Whether the ministers ever intended to prosecute Entick and Beardmore is not clear, but they soon proceeded with the same sort of intimidation they had used on the *North Briton.* The authors of the *Monitor* and their henchmen were released without trial after payment of bail. To hold a threat of prosecution and loss of bail over the journalists' heads seemed almost as effective a method of restraining opposition as prosecution, and it was certainly less risky than trying them publicly for sedition. No further use was made of the warrant against the *North Briton*.[50]

The warning of the ministry to the opposition journalists was plain, but Wilkes refused to heed it. The *North Briton* continued its reckless course of opposition to Bute and the peace. In February, 1763, Wilkes almost provoked the ministry into taking positive action. Number 38 of the *North Briton* took the form of a letter from the Pretender to his "cousin," Bute, thanking him for his invaluable services.[51] Such an intimation was tantamount to accusing Bute of treason; George III was especially incensed at this attack upon the loyalty of his tutor and minister, urging the Solicitor General to "act upon it."[52] The law officers, however, came to the decision that prosecution would not be advisable, and upon their advice no action was taken.[53] Thus the opposition papers were allowed to continue in operation throughout the period of Bute's ministry, except as far as their operations were restricted by the threat of ministerial prosecution.

iv.

In Versailles, meanwhile, Bedford had completed the negotiations for the preliminary terms for peace, which were signed on November 3, 1762, and the treaty was presented to the Parliament when it met on November 25. It was to be expected, after the long series of victories the British and their allies had won during 1762 and the propaganda Temple and Wilkes had disseminated, that there would be objections to a peace which made the slightest concession to France and Spain. Objections there were, and the opposition made the most of them in pressing arguments against the peace. On the whole, however, the peace, while admittedly not all that could have been wrung from France and Spain or even what Pitt would have obtained, was most advantageous to Great Britain. Thanks to Grenville, Bute had been restrained from giving up concessions which might have afforded the opposition too strong an argument. Even Wilkes was forced to admit that the treaty as it was presented was "the damn'dest peace for the opposition that ever was made."[54]

Thus in spite of the efforts of the opposition propagandists and the disappointed clamor of the mobs, most members of Parliament welcomed the peace. It glided through the Commons with little serious friction. Pitt inveighed against the treaty for three hours and forty minutes on December 9, accusing the ministers of having broken faith with the nation and betrayed the allies of the Crown. His main complaint, however, appeared to be that he could have done better. His harangue had little effect. On the division, the address was carried by a vote of 319 to 65.[55] The definitive treaty of peace was then drawn up and signed in Paris, February 10, 1763.

With the conclusion of the peace negotiations, the *Briton* and the *Auditor* were discontinued; they had served their purpose. The opposition papers, however, continued in operation. The *North Briton,* indeed, increased the ferocity of its attacks on the First Minister. It was the week after the signing of the peace that the letter from the Pretender to Bute appeared.[56] Anathemas on the peace whipped popular fury against the favorite to higher and higher levels. When the peace was first introduced in Parliament in November, 1762, Bute's carriage was assaulted by the mobs, pelted with clods of dirt, and followed with hisses.[57] His unpopularity increased as winter proceeded and spring approached. Bute's nerves began to give way under the strain, and his physical constitution was weakened by ill-health.[58] Finally in the midst of the clamor a new subject of contention was introduced in March in the cider tax.

In an effort to augment the national revenues, Bute hit upon the idea of an excise on cider. The task of presenting the bill in the Commons fell to Sir Francis Dashwood, the Chancellor of the Exchequer, who knew almost nothing of finance. The task of defending it, therefore, fell upon Grenville's shoulders. The excise, which had come so close to wrecking Sir Robert Walpole's ministry thirty years before, became again a rallying point for opposition. To the attack against the bill Pitt added his caustic tongue. When Dashwood introduced the motion on March 8, Pitt spoke against it, presenting an exaggerated picture of an army of excisemen invading farms and plundering cottages. Grenville rose to defend the measure and not only spoke on the tax but baited Pitt by making a lengthy digression on Pitt's extravagances during the war, which had made such a tax necessary. Returning at length to the tax, he argued its absolute necessity. In what other quarter, he asked the House, could a fresh source of revenue be found. "Tell me where, I repeat it, Sir, I am entitled to say to them, tell me where."

At this point Pitt took the bait, and proceeded to make Grenville ridiculous before the whole House. He sang over the words to a ditty which was then popular, "Gentle shepherd, tell me where," plainly mimicking Grenville's querulous tone. Thereupon "the whole House burst out in a fit of laughter, which continued for some minutes." Then he rose and belabored Grenville with ridicule, invective, and misrepresentation even beyond his usual style. When the angry Grenville rose to defend himself, Pitt merely gave him a sneer, bowed low to the Speaker, and sauntered slowly out of the House.[59] The bill passed the Commons by a comfortable majority, but Grenville's humiliation before the chamber was not forgotten. The nickname "Gentle Shepherd" remained with him for the rest of his life.

The cider bill brought the opposition to Bute's ministry to a head. Riots broke out in the southeasern "cider counties" and in London, instigated or at least encouraged by opposition leaders in Parliament. With the issue of the excise added to that of the peace, Pitt began to consider the prospects of active opposition with Newcastle and his group. He "was in the highest spirits" over the prospect.[60] Moreover, the Newcastle group was in high dudgeon over treatment which Bute had meted out. Devonshire had been dismissed from his office as Chamberlain upon his refusal to attend Cabinet Council, and in retaliation the Newcastle forces attempted to "strike terror" in Bute's ministry by the resignation of all "persons of high rank" among their group still in the King's service.[61] The result was not what they had anticipated. Only a few resigned, and instead of striking terror, they brought on a massacre of the innocents among their following. Not only were the leaders of the group stripped of public honors—Newcastle, for instance was dismissed from his posts as Lord Lieutenant and *Custos Rotulorum* of Middlesex, Nottingham, Sussex, and the town of Nottingham, and from the wardenship of Sherwood Forest[62]—but the most insignificant of their followers were deprived of place. "Whoever, holding a place, had voted against the preliminaries, was instantly dismissed," wrote Horace Walpole. "The friends and dependents of the Duke of Newcastle were particularly cashiered; and this cruelty was extended so far that old servants, who had retired and been preferred to very small places, were rigorously hunted out and deprived of their livelihood."[63] The Newcastle group in their resentment were ready to undertake opposition to Bute on almost any point.

With opposition rising on every side and his own health failing, Bute resolved to resign. He had accomplished his purposes, having made peace and having driven Pitt, Temple, and Newcastle from the government. By early March, he had made up his mind to resign. "I am afraid," he said, "not only of falling myself, but of involving my Royal Master in my ruin—it is time for me to retire."[64]

Bute had consistently declared during the winter that he intended to resign from the Treasury as soon as the peace was made and through the parliament. Yet "few had heard the declaration, and fewer believed it."[65] In late December and early January, after the preliminaries had passed the parliament, Bute still seemed to be consolidating his power in the ministry against Grenville and Egremont. His promise of the Treasury for Grenville seemed to have gone glimmering. When the Admiralty was almost completely remodelled without consulting Grenville as its head, rumors went the rounds that he was thinking of quitting the ministry altogether, and that Egremont would go with him.[66] When Bute finally decided in early March that the vessel was "safe in harbour,"[67] he turned not to Grenville but to Fox as his successor. The King balked at this idea; Fox was "of all men" the one George III would "be most grieved to see" in Bute's place. Why could not Grenville be made a peer and have the Treasury? What right would Fox have to complain, when he himself had said that any office of business was incompatible with the management of the Commons?[68] Bute continued for several days to urge that Fox be given the Treasury, but the King replied each time in terms of Fox's reputation as an unscrupulous politician. He had only accepted him as leader of the Commons, the King said, in order to keep Bute in the Treasury through the winter.[69]

Bute now turned to Fox for advice on choosing another successor. Without telling him that he was under consideration for the Treasury, the favorite asked Fox for suggestions. Fox replied at great length in a letter "wrote for Lord Bute" on March 11. He did not see how it was possible, he said, for Bute to retire within the year. Bute, however, had asked him to suppose him dead, and Fox proceeded on that supposition. He would then advise the King to put someone into the Treasury as a "stopgap"— presumably himself—until he should gain "experience of some men" to carry on his government. He particularly urged that Halifax, Egremont, and Grenville be either dismissed or demoted, since he felt they were not closely enough attached to the King and Bute, leaning too much toward Newcastle and Hardwicke! On Grenville he laid a particular ban:

> George Grenville is and will be, whether in the Ministry or in the House of Commons, a hindrance not a help, and sometimes a very great inconvenience to those he is joined with. He is a man of a very weak understanding, and I wish that I could impute to that alone what is wrong with him.... Weak and fearful as he is, had he been honest, he would not have brought you into the dilemma you was in in October last. When in a great office he withholds from the King and you all use of it to Government, you will say

it is a Catonical temper and a mulish resolution not to depart from what he first lays down. Let no such mule be in such an office. [70]

The King scorned Fox's suggestion that Gower, Shelburne, and Waldegrave[71] be given major office in the ministry, considering them not capable of holding such positions. Fox's "predilection" for them, he said, had driven him as far from the truth as his "aversion" to Grenville. "His whole attack" on Grenville was on account of his not using his department "for House of Commons jobbs." If Fox took the Treasury, the King asserted, "the very Judges must be fill'd by wretches that are unfit to decide the properties of freemen, because they can be the means of acquiring a vote in parliament." He begged Bute to try some other solution.[72] Yet within a few days, since the favorite professed to see no other solution, the King gave his reluctant consent to Fox's appointment. Grenville, he said, had "thrown away the game he had two years ago." Though he knew that he would rejoice in the first chance to be rid of him, he admitted that Fox was the only logical choice. "He cannot refuse it," said the King.[73]

In this last opinion the King miscalculated. When Bute sent Fox the offer to hand over the Treasury to him, the answer was precisely a refusal. "Mr. Fox is plainly, in his own mind, inclined to the Treasury," wrote John Calcraft, Fox's friend who served as intermediary between him and Bute, "but Lady Holland is so much against it and so miserable at the thoughts of it, that I could not help but keep my faith with her, and desist from persuading Mr. Fox to what she says would make her miserable and kill him."[74] Fox was known to be in poor health; his wife's wishes only reinforced what his better judgment already told him. "My health did not permit," he wrote later, "and I was obliged to claim and insist on the King's promise, that I should leave the H. of C. at the end of that sessions."[75]

Having refused the Treasury and having failed to persuade Bute to continue in it, Fox on March 17 again gave Bute his advice. Only four men, he said, could be considered for the Treasury: Halifax, Waldegrave, Northumberland,[76] and Grenville. Of these he inclined to Grenville, "if I can fairly say I incline to one to whom I have so many objections." He had lost the esteem of the Commons, he said; he was too timid and too poor a speaker to lead such a body. In view of Bute's good opinion of him, however, he "very reluctantly" gave the preference to Grenville.[77]

With such a suggestion Bute was now ready to comply, and the King had advocated that solution days before. Another problem presented itself, however. If Grenville took the Treasury and the Exchequer, as his experience in finance naturally suggested, Egremont's holding the seals would concentrate three of the most important offices of state in the hands of the stubborn brothers. One of the reasons in selecting Grenville was that he was "unconnected" and would be easy for Bute and the King to control. Yet Egremont had proved that he could be fully as recalcitrant as Grenville. Fox therefore suggested that Egremont be demoted and that Shelburne take his place. To such an arrangement Grenville politely but firmly refused to agree. As he had the year before, so now he refused to let his sole remaining family connection be sacrificed. Egremont, he stipulated, should quit the seals only by his own consent. Shelburne, he added, was not a proper replacement for Egremont. He was too young, too inexperienced, and had never held civil office. Besides, he was of a "new" family, "so recently raised to the peerage, however considerable [it] may have been in Ireland."78 Bute now attempted to remove Grenville's objections by bringing Pitt into the ministry with him; Pitt would surely be connection enough! Pitt, however, told Bute that "he would never have anything to do with his lordship." He was "now thoroughly connected with the Duke of Newcastle and his friends"79 and he was "determined to remain so." The favorite had no choice but to acquiesce in Grenville's demands. On April 1 he notified Grenville that Shelburne "in the handsomest manner wished to be omitted that the ground might be enlarged by more necessary people." Egremont was to retain the seals and Grenville was to have the Treasury, but only under stipulation. They were to form with Halifax, who was to be the other Secretary of State, a triumvirate to head the ministry and be responsible for policy. In short, Bute and the King were giving their full confidence to no one minister; they were placing the leadership of the government in the hands of a commission to do their bidding. Of this arrangement, Bute reported, Egremont and Halifax approved "extremely."80

The rumor went abroad that Bute's retirement and a new administration were imminent. The *North Briton* observed on April 2: "We may safely conclude that a change is at hand." There remained, indeed, only the filling of several minor posts in the government. Over them wrangles occurred between Bute and the King on the one hand and Grenville and Egremont on the other. On April 3 Bute was in "great uneasiness" over Grenville's insistence that Lord Digby, Fox's nephew, should not sit with him in the Treasury.81 Digby finally took a seat in the Admiralty instead.82 Throughout the period of the negotiations Egremont and Grenville kept in close consultation to gain the greatest possible strength in their new ministry.[83] Shelburne was placed at the Board of Trade, where he would be as little in the way as possible. Sandwich was placed at the head of the Admiralty by the King and Bute over Grenville's protests.[84] Given peerages, Fox and Dashwood were put out of Grenville's way both in the ministry and in the Commons.[85] Bute tried to persuade Bedford to accept the Presidency of the Council under Grenville, but the Duke replied that after the marks of ill-will he had received from Grenville and Egremont in the peace negotiations he would deserve to have his head examined if he joined such an administration.[86] The aged Lord Granville, now seventy-three, was made Lord President, instead.

At length on April 7 Halifax presented and Bute approved the list of ministers which the triumvirate had agreed upon. "Only the King's consent is wanting," reported one of Bute's friends. "Lord Bute resigns the Treasury tomorrow."[87] When April 8 arrived, all was in readiness. Bute therefore made a formal announcement of his resignation. Two days later, Grenville kissed the King's hands for the offices of First Lord of the Treasury and Chancellor of the Exchequer. The climb to the highest office in the land was accomplished.

NOTES

CHAPTER VI

[1] Newcastle to Hardwicke, May 21, 1762, Hardwicke MSS., Add. MSS. 35421, f. 263.

[2] Statement by Jonathan Scott, another of the *Monitor's* conductors, Wilkes Trial Papers, Add. MSS. 22131, f. 2.

[3] *Briton,* May 28, 1762; Almon, *Wilkes,* I, 91.

[4] Wilkes to Bute, February 9, 1762, Bute Correspondence, Add. MSS. 36796, f. 132. Wilkes had been returned for Aylesbury in 1757, and since that time he had been a supporter of the Grenvilles in the Commons.

[5] John Almon, *History of the Late Minority,* London, 1766, p. 58.

[6] See, for example, Temple to Wilkes, June 14, 1762, *Grenville Papers,* I, 457-458.

[7] Walpole to Mann, June 20, 1762, Toynbee, *Walpole's Letters,* V, 213

[8] MS. note by Wilkes, Wilkes MSS., Add. MSS. 30875, f. 16.

[9] See, for instance, Temple to Wilkes, June 14, 1762, *Grenville Papers,* I, 456-458.

[10] Milbanke to Rockingham, June 24, 1762, Rockingham MSS., 1, f. 155. On the power of the Secretary of State to act as a magistrate in cases of state crimes, see Florence M. Grier Evans, *The Principal Secretary of State,* Manchester, 1923, pp. 252-263.

[11] *North Briton,* July 10, 1765.

[12] Among the Murray MSS. are several letters from Temple to Wilkes during this period, readdressed to Temple in Wilkes' hand.

[13] George III to Bute, June 20, 1762, Sedgwick, *Letters,* p. 118.

[14] Denys Arthur Winstanley, *Personal and Party Government, A Chapter in the Political History of the Early Years of the Reign of George III, 1760-1766,* Cambridge, 1910, p. 119; Grenville's diary, *Grenville Papers,* I, 450.

[15] George III to Bute, June 21, 1762, Sedgwick, *Letters,* pp. 118-119.

[16] George III to Bute, July 8, 1762, Sedgwick, *Letters,* p. 121.

[17] George III to Bute, July 25, 1762, Sedgwick, *Letters,* pp. 124-125.

[18] Fox's memoir, Mary Eleanor Anne, Countess of Ilchester, and Lord Stavordale, editors, *The Life and Letters of Lady Sarah Lennox, 1745-1826,* 2 vols., London, 1902, I, 70.

[19] Minutes of Cabinet Council, July 26, 1762, Astle Collection, Add. MSS. 34713, ff. 110-112.

[20] Bute to Egremont, July 26, 1762, Sedgwick, *Letters,* pp. 127-128.

[21] Memorandum by Newcastle on a conversation with Viry, July 22, 1762,

Newcastle MSS., Add. MSS. 32941, ff. 18-25.

[22] George III to Bedford, September 4, 1762, Egremont MSS., 5, f. 2.

[23] Bute to Bedford, September 28, 1762, Sedgwick, *Letters,* pp. 138-140n. See Egremont to Grenville, September 26, 162, *Grenville Papers,* I, 475.

[24] Rigby to Bedford, September 29-30, 1762, *Bedford Correspondence,* III, 127-130.

[25] Minutes by Newcastle on a conversation with Cumberland, October 3, 1762, Newcastle MSS., Add. MSS. 32943, f. 30.

[26] Nivernois to Choiseul, October 9, 1762, cited in Sedgwick, *Letters,* p. 142.

[27] Minutes by Newcastle, October 3, 1762, Newcastle MSS., Add. MSS. 32943, f. 30.

[28] Rigby to Bedford, September 30, 1762, *Bedford Correspondence,* III, 132.

[29] Sedgwick, *Letters,* p. 142.

[30] Minutes by Newcastle, October 3, 1762, Newcastle MSS., Add. MSS. 32943, f. 30. Cf., p. 47 note 9.

[31] Newcastle to Hardwicke, October 7, 1762; Hardwicke to Newcastle, October 9, 1762, Newcastle MSS., Add. MSS. 32943, ff. 91, 120.

[32] Charles Lennox, third Duke of Richmond (1735-1806).

[33] Erskine to Bute, June 14, 1762, Bute's letters, Add. MSS. 36796, f. 143.

[34] Devonshire to Egremont, October 3, 1762, Egremont MSS., 29, f. 1.

[35] George III to Bute, c. October 5, 1762, Sedgwick, *Letters,* p. 143.

[36] George III to Bute, October 6, 1762, Sedgwick, *Letters,* p. 144.

[37] Fox to Bedford, October 13, 1762, *Bedford Correspondence,* III, 133-134; Fox to Granby, October 15, 1762, Historical Manuscripts Commission, *The Manuscripts of his Grace the Duke of Rutland, K. G.,* 4 vols., London, 1888-1904, II, 360.

[38] Grenville's narrative, *Grenville Papers,* I, 450-452, 483; Bute to Denbigh, October 13, 1762, Bute's Letters, Add. MSS., 36797, f. 14.

[39] Grenville's narrative, *Grenville Papers,* I, 484.

[40] Minutes by Newcastle on an interview with Halifax, October 18, 1762, Newcastle MSS., Add. MSS. 32944, f. 34-38. Newcastle suggests that one reason for Grenville's defection was that Bute would not give him control of the patronage in managing the Commons. f. 38. This Fox did get.

[41] Newcastle to Devonshire, October 14, 1762, Newcastle MSS., Add. MSS. 32943, f. 206.

[42] January 6, 1763, Sedgwick, *Letters,* p. 182.

[43] Walpole to Mann, September 26, 1762, Toynbee, *Walpole's Letters,* V, 248.

[44] Newcastle to Devonshire, October 9, 1762, Newcastle MSS., Add. MSS. 32943, f. 133.

[45] Jonathan Scott's information, Wilkes' Trial Papers, Add. MSS. 22131, f. 2; Almon, *Minority,* p. 60.

[46] *Grenville Papers,* II, 3.

[47] George Nobbe, *The North Briton,* New York, 1939, p. 133.

[48] Sealed warrant, Wilkes' Trial Papers, Add. MSS. 22131, f. 31.

[49] Wilkes to Churchill, December 1, 2, 1762, Wilkes MSS., Add. MSS. 30878, ff. 18, 70.

[50] Almon, *Minority,* p. 60.

[51] *North Briton,* February 19, 1763.

[52] George III to Bute, February 20, 1763, Sedgwick, *Letters,* p. 190.

[53] Charles Yorke to Hardwicke, February 23, 1763, Hardwicke MSS., Add. MSS. 35353, f. 312.

[54] Neville to Bedford, February 16, 1763, *Bedford Correspondence,* I, 202.

[55] *Parl. Hist.,* XV, 1240-1274. The claim made by Horace Walpole that wholesale bribery of the members was practiced in order to gain a majority for the peace (Walpole, *George III,* I, 199) deserves little serious consideration, since it is corroborated by no contemporary evidence, not even Walpole's own letters. See Namier, *Structure,* I, 225-229.

[56] See above, p. 181.

[57] Rigby to Bedford, November 26, 1762, *Bedford Correspondence,* III, 160.

[58] John Yorke to Royston, May 3, 1763, Yorke, *Hardwicke,* III, 493.

[59] Rigby to Bedford, March 10, 1763, *Bedford Correspondence,* III, 218-219; *Parl. Hist.,* XV, 1307-1308; Walpole, *George III,* I, 251.

[60] Newcastle to Hardwicke, March 12, 29, 1763, Yorke, *Hardwicke,* III, 456.

[61] Memorandum by Newcastle, November 2, 1762, Newcastle MSS., Add. MSS. 32944, ff. 206-215.

[62] Halifax to Newcastle, December 23, 1762, Rockingham MSS., 2 f.

[63] Walpole, *George III,* I, 233-234.

[64] John Adolphus, *The History of England from the Accession to the Decease of King George the Third,* 8 vols., London, 1840-1845, I, 117. Bute told Fox: "The end of my labors was solemnly determined even before I undertook them." March 2, 1763, Ilchester, *Letters to Fox,* p. 172.

[65] Walpole, *George III,* I, 255.

[66] Hardwicke to Newcastle, December 28, 1762; Newcastle to Devonshire, January 4, 1763, Newcastle MSS., Add. MSS. 32945, f. 412; 32946, f. 44.

[67] Bute to Fox, March 2, 1763, Ilchester, *Letters to Fox,* p. 172.

[68] George III to Bute, n.d. (early March, 1763), Sedgwick, *Letters,* pp. 197-198.

[69] George III to Bute, c. March 5, 1763, Sedgwick, *Letters,* pp. 197-1.

[70] Ilchester, *Fox,* II, 225-227.

[71] Granville Leveson Gower, second Earl Gower (1721-1803); William Petty, second Earl of Shelburne, later first Marquis of Lansdowne (1737-1803); and James Waldegrave, second Earl Waldegrave (1715-1763).

[72] George III to Bute, March 11, 1763, Sedgwick, *Letters,* pp. 199-200.

[73] George III to Bute, c. March 14, 1763, Sedgwick, *Letters,* pp. 200-201.

[74] Calcraft to Shelburne, March 15, 1763, Fitzmaurice, *Shelburne,* I, 146-147.

[75] To Sandwich, June 24, 1765, Ilchester, *Fox,* II, 230.

[76] Hugh Percy, first Earl of Northumberland, and later first Duke of Northumberland (1715-1786). Northumberland was Bute's son-in-law.

[77] Ilchester, *Fox,* II, 231.

[78] Grenville to Bute, March 25, 1763, *Grenville Papers,* II, 34-35.

[79] Williams, *Pitt,* II, 154-155; Newcastle to Devonshire, June 23, 1763, Newcastle MSS., Add. MSS. 32949, f. 191.

[80] Bute to Grenville, April 1, 1763, *Grenville Papers,* II, 40-41.

[81] Jenkinson to Grenville, April 3, 1763, Murray MSS.

[82] George III to Bute, April 10, 1763, Sedgwick, *Letters,* p. 214.

[83] Egremont to Grenville, April 5, 1763, Murray MSS.

[84] Memorandum by George III, August, 1765, Sir John Fortescue, editor, *The Correspondence of King George the Third from 1760 to December, 1783,* 6 vols., London, 1927, I, 170.

[85] Fox became Baron Holland and Dashwood Baron Le Despencer.

[86] Bedford to Bute, April 7, 1763, *Bedford Correspondence,* III, 228.

[87] W. G. Hamilton to J. H. Hutchinson, April 7, 1763, Historical Manuscripts Commission, *The Manuscripts of the Duke of Beaufort, K. G., the Earl of Donoughmore, and Others,* London, 1891, p. 247.

CHAPTER VII

COURTS LEGAL AND ROYAL, APRIL-SEPTEMBER, 1763

i

The *North Briton* was established for the express purpose of criticizing Bute's administration and combatting his propaganda organ, the *Briton*. With Bute's resignation, the reason for the existence of the opposition paper was removed. The *Briton* appeared for the last time with the issue of February 12, 1762, and its associate, the *Auditor,* predeceased it by four days. Bute was now out of office, having delayed after the making of the peace only to decide with the King upon his successors and to introduce his budget. Its purpose attained, the *North Briton* was apparently content. Wilkes gave every indication of intending to abandon his journalistic endeavors. As soon as the forty-fourth number of the paper made its appearance, he left the country with his daughter for France to place her in a Paris school, making no provision for the publication of a *North Briton* on the following Saturday.

Perhaps Wilkes conceived that there would be no further occasion for the services of his pen. It seems possible, and indeed quite probable, that he expected the King to call Pitt back into his councils.[1] No doubt Temple had learned from his brother-in-law of the overtures which Bute had made to him and had informed Wilkes of the matter. If Bute was retiring and was forced to come to Pitt for aid, it seemed certain that in the end Pitt must be called in to head the new ministry. The "great commoner's" popularity was growing even greater since the signing of the peace and the levying of the cider tax. There could certainly be no basis of popular support for a government by Bute's lieutenants. How could such a ministry withstand the onslaught of Pitt and Newcastle in a united opposition?

When Wilkes returned to England on April 11, however, he learned that Bute's lieutenants were to govern in spite of their unpopularity. The power in the new ministry had been settled not on Pitt but on three of

Bute's henchmen, Grenville, Egremont, and Halifax. Finding their hopes frustrated, the fiery journalist and his patron now faced the question of whether or not to continue their tirade against the new ministry. Although Temple and Wilkes can hardly have attributed Bute's resignation solely to the mob feeling which they had aroused, they realized its effectiveness. The methods which they had employed had been eminently successful. If by employing the same means they could contribute to driving this new coalition from power, the King might be forced to call on Pitt and Temple to form a ministry. The union of Newcastle and his faction with Pitt[2] left no other reasonable alternative.

Wilkes and Temple lost no time in making their decision. On April 13 an advertisement appeared in all the daily papers. The north Briton, it said, agreed that

> the Scottish minister has indeed *retired.* Is his influence at an end? Or does he still govern by the *three* wretched tools of his power, who, to their indelible infamy, have supported the most odious of his measures, the late ignominious *Peace,* and the wretched extension of the arbitrary mode of *Excise?* The North Briton has been steady in his opposition to a *single,* insolent, incapable, despotic Minister; and is equally ready to combat the *triple-headed, Cerberean* administration, if the Scot is to assume that motley form.

Bute, the piece asserted, was the guiding hand behind the new ministers, and he meant only to retire behind the curtain to a position which would permit his "dictating to every part of the King's administration."[3]

Thus at one stroke the *North Briton* declared war and opened fire on the Grenville ministry. The ministers were not long in giving him a more substantial target, the speech of the King at the prorogation of the Parliament on April 19. On his appointment to the Treasury, Grenville was obliged for the third time in twelve months[4] to apply to Temple for re-election to the Commons. On the evening of April 18, Grenville dispatched a messenger to Temple's house in Pall Mall with an application to his brother for re-election for Buckingham. As a compliment, he enclosed a copy of the speech which the King was to read to Parliament the following day. Temple, as usual, blustered that he would not give his brother permission, but Pitt, who happened to be with him, persuaded him to yield the point.

While Pitt and Temple were discussing the speech thus delivered, Wilkes arrived to consult with Temple on the *North Briton* which they had promised the public. The three men joined in a lively exchange of ideas on the weaknesses of the peace and criticisms of the speech, all of which Wilkes noted down. Then, returning to his home in Great George Street, Wilkes sat down and wrote from his notes, "with some additions of his own," the piece which was to become celebrated as Number 45 of the *North Briton.*5

The speech itself was concerned with praising the peace, which was described as being "so honourable to my crown, and so beneficial to my people." In addition, the King affirmed the resolution of his government to employ the strictest economy in order to reduce the burden of taxation. The praise of the peace was naturally couched in enthusiastic terms, but on the whole they were not grossly unwarranted. Although the speech was undoubtedly the work of Grenville and the other ministers, there can be no doubt that it embodied the views of George III on the peace. Ample proof of the fact is the violent personal exception which the King took to Wilkes's attack on the speech, even when particular care was taken that the attack should be directed solely against the ministers. Bute, Grenville, and the other members of the former administration had only carried out the ardent wishes of the King in the making of the peace.

In order to avoid any appearance of attacking the royal person, Wilkes took especial care at the beginning of Number 45 to emphasize that the King's speech had "always been considered...as the speech of the Minister." Such a doctrine was a commonplace among the members of Parliament; Wilkes in a later printing of the *North Briton* produced a long list of instances in which that idea had been expressed in the Parliament.6 The doctrine was probably fully as well known to the majority of the reading public which Wilkes addressed. Nevertheless, Wilkes took the precaution of carefully rehearsing these theories of constitutional government. No one should mistake that the attack was intended against the new ministers, not the King. He then proceeded to represent the King as greatly sinned against by his ministers, who had put falsehood in his mouth regarding the peace. The blameless character of the King, he asserted, only emphasized the blame of the ministers.

ii.

Number 45 was hardly in any respect more offensive than many of the previous issues of the *North Briton*. In fact, it fell far short of some of them. The ministers decided, however, that if legal prosecution of the paper was to be undertaken this was the time to do it. Bute had attempted to out-general Temple in the press and had failed miserably. The triumvirate could hope for little better fortune in the same game. With a united opposition against them, the press would be even more effective than it had been under Bute. If orderly administration was to be achieved, the opposition press must be muzzled. Since the mere threat of prosecution had failed to do the job, actual prosecution appeared necessary. The only alternative seemed to be to yield to Pitt and Temple, and this neither the King nor the ministers were willing to do. Thus Number 45 was singled out for legal prosecution.

Exactly what the ministers hoped to achieve by instituting prosecution is uncertain. They can hardly have thought popular opinion could be persuaded that Wilkes' attacks were actually libelous of the King. The mobs were too enthusiastically in his favor. Perhaps they hoped to ram a prosecution through friendly courts in spite of popular opinion. Or perhaps they hoped to raise an issue which would split the opposition asunder; no one understood better than Grenville the tenuous nature of opposition alliances. In any event, the change of administrations provided an excuse for the change in policy, and the King, who on several occasions had urged prosecution of Wilkes, would be sure to lend cordial support. Here was an opportunity to silence the opposition papers and diminish the effectiveness of the opposition at the outset of the new administration.

Though he may have suggested prosecution of Number 45, as he had suggested in the case of other numbers, no evidence has been found that George III had any part in the ultimate decision to prosecute Wilkes. While the ministry was preparing to arrest those connected with Number 45, the King was busying himself with the routine matters of his court. Writing to Bute on April 27 and 28, in the midst of the preparation of warrants and legal arguments, the King made no mention of either Wilkes or the *North Briton* and seemed unaware of the proceedings which were going on.[7] It would appear that the decisions were made entirely on the initiative of the triumvirate. Grenville's later statement that they acted "by his Majesty's commands" would indicate that as usual the King suggested prosecution to his ministers, but both the decision and the arrangements were left in their hands. Apparently the first notice the King received of the intended move was after Wilkes's arrest on the morning of April 30, when Egremont at length brought him the whole report.[8]

Once the decision was made to prosecute, the ministers proceeded with considerable caution. Number 45 appeared on Saturday, April 23. Having taken two days to come to a decision on the advisability of prosecuting, they sent on Monday morning to the law officers to inquire what action might be taken with assurance of success. Sir Fletcher Norton, the Solicitor-General, and Charles Yorke, the Attorney-General, took two days more to ponder the case. Then, April 27, they submitted a written opinion that Number 45 was "a most infamous and seditious libel, tending to inflame the minds and alienate the affections of the people from his Majesty and to incite them to traitorous insurrections against his government, and therefore punishable as a misdemeanor of the highest nature in due course of law by indictment or information."9

Meanwhile, anticipating this decision, Halifax had signed another general warrant, in much the same language as that of the preceding November, calling for the arrest of the authors, printers, and publishers of Number 45, which was termed "a seditious and treasonable paper."10 Unlike the former warrant, however, this one was to be vigorously executed. Under its authority some forty-eight people were taken into custody, including Kearsley and Balfe, the publisher and printer of Number 45. In their zeal, however, the government's messengers overstepped themselves; they also arrested Dryden Leach, whom they supposed to be a printer of the issue, but who had not printed a *North Briton* since November 27.

At the arrest of Wilkes, however, the ministers hesitated. Wilkes was a member of the House of Commons, and as such he was entitled to the privileges of that House. Thus he was immune from arrest except under certain ill-defined circumstances. Halifax sent to the law officers to know whether Wilkes might be arrested. On this ticklish question Yorke and Norton ventured to make only an oral affirmative answer. Halifax, however, was unwilling to proceed on such assurance and insisted on a written opinion. Thereupon Yorke consulted with his father, Hardwicke, who concurred in their opinion. On the morning of April 30 they finally delivered a written opinion that "the publication of a libel being a breach of the peace is not a case of privilege, and that the said John Wilkes may be committed to Newgate or to any other prison for the same upon the evidence laid before your Lordship."11

iii.

The way was now apparently clear. On the morning of April 30, Wilkes was arrested under the authority of the general warrant and brought before the Secretaries of State for examination. Here arose complications. Before being taken into custody, Wilkes managed to send word to Temple of his arrest and of its nature. Temple immediately proceeded to apply for a writ of habeas corpus in the Court of Common Pleas. Such a procedure was almost unique; most such writs, of course, were issued by the Court of King's Bench. Indeed, no habeas corpus had been issued by the Common Pleas since 1670.[12] The explanation for this unusual procedure was not legal but political. Probably Temple and Wilkes had considered the possibility, after the experiences of November, 1762, that the ministers might use a general warrant against the *North Briton*. Wilkes's consistent maintenance of anonymity assured that arrest, if it came, would be by general warrant unless his associates betrayed him. It was well known that the general warrant had no basis in Common or Statute law, though it was upheld by practice. Whether Parliamentary privilege would protect him would depend upon the light in which one interpreted his offense.

Thus prosecution would hinge not on well-defined legal principles but on the court's interpretation of disputed points. To obtain a habeas corpus in the King's Bench and bring Wilkes before that court would be to place the judgment in the hands of Lord Chief Justice Mansfield, the inveterate enemy of Pitt and his supporters. On the bench of the Common Pleas, however, sat Lord Chief Justice Charles Pratt, Pitt's loyal friend and supporter, who shared the "great commoner's" views in legal matters and who supplied him with many of his legal arguments in the Commons.[13] Perhaps Temple already knew that Pratt thought general warrants illegal. Certainly he knew that if a favorable decision could be obtained anywhere, it would be in the Common Pleas.

When Temple applied to that court for a writ of habeas corpus, Pratt granted it as a matter of course. The preparation of the document, however, took several hours, and it was not until five o'clock in the afternoon that it was served upon the messengers.[14] Meanwhile, the Secretaries of State had examined Wilkes and, despairing of gaining any information from him, had committed him to the Tower.[15] When the habeas corpus was served, Wilkes was out of the messengers' hands and under the authority of a different warrant; thus a new writ had to be obtained.

The warrant which committed Wilkes to the Tower was sworn out on the basis of testimony of the printers who had been arrested stating that Wilkes was the author of the offensive paper. Two significant changes were made from the general warrant under which he had been arrested. In the new warrant he was charged by name as being the author and publisher of Number 45, and the phrase describing the paper was changed from "a seditious and treasonable paper" to "a false and seditious libel."[16] The latter change was made after consultation with Hardwicke, who felt that the charge of seditious libel would be sufficient for prosecution.[17]

Apparently it was felt that the charge of treason, while it would clearly take the case beyond all question of Parliamentary privilege, would be difficult to prove in court. In view of the tremendous popular ferment which the arrest was stirring up in the City, extreme care had to be taken to insure against the chance of Wilkes's escape in the courts, for such a contingency would increase Wilkes's growing popularity even further and would lessen what little hold the ministry had upon the public mind. Thus if the case was to be tried before Pratt instead of Mansfield, as the ministers had already learned,[18] moderation would have to be followed in the charges in order to obtain a conviction.

The tumult caused by the arrest of the popular journalist was such as had not been seen in England since the riots over the Excise Bill in 1733. Newcastle wrote that "the city and suburbs are in the utmost alarm at these proceedings, which they call illegal and oppressive."[19] The excitement grew apace as the time approached for Wilkes to appear in court. When he was finally brought before Pratt on May 3, he made a short and rather fumbling speech in his own defense, at the close of which there arose "such shouts in the Hall and in the Court of Common Pleas that you would have thought the Seven Bishops had been acquitted."[20] Wilkes was remanded to the Tower while the court considered the evidence, with the case being adjourned until May 6.

Meanwhile, when Egremont reported to the King on April 30, he strongly urged that Wilkes should be dismissed from his post as colonel in the Bucks militia. He advised, however, that the King defer the action until Wilkes's papers were examined. Things might be found, he suggested, "so improper that Lord Temple's demission" as Lord Lieutenant might "accompany" that of Wilkes.[21] Here Temple's caution in having Wilkes return or destroy all his papers[22] paid dividends, and the ministers were disappointed. Egremont had to be satisfied with ordering Temple to notify Wilkes of his dismissal. Temple immediately complied, May 5, but he accompanied the notification with statements which the Secretaries considered too warm in commendation of Wilkes. "I cannot...help expressing the concern I feel," wrote Temple, "in the loss of an officer, by his deportment in command endeared to the whole corps."[23] The Secretaries had all the excuse they needed. On May 7 a letter, written in a clerk's hand and only signed by Halifax, notified Temple that the King had no further use for his services.[24]

This measure of revenge, however, was to be all that the ministers were to obtain immediately. When the Court of Common Pleas convened again on May 6, Pratt delivered the opinion that a libel was not a breach of the peace, but only tended to a breach of the peace. Therefore Wilkes was entitled by Parliamentary privilege to go free without bail. In handing down this decision, the court reversed the pronouncement that had been made in the case of the Seven Bishops, in which it had been decided that a libel was a breach of the peace.[25] It was apparent that the decision was not judicial but political in its motive. "The House of Commons," wrote Royston, "is much obliged to Lord C[hief] J[ustice] P[ratt], for I do not know that we ever claimed the privilege for ourselves which he had been pleased to allow us."[26]

No such cynical smirking was found among the London populace, which received the decision with a tremendous ovation. The cry "Wilkes and Liberty" was raised on a thousand tongues. The ministers had accomplished what they most feared. Failing to brand Wilkes as a traitor, they had made him a martyr to liberty. The popular hero now publicly declared that the Secretaries of State had robbed his house of his books and papers and demanded the immediate return of the "stolen goods."[27] The ministers of course replied that, notwithstanding his release on privilege, the King still desired that the Attorney-General prosecute Wilkes for libel. Those papers which did not lead to proof of his guilt, they said, would be returned to him in due course. Wilkes replied in an insolent tone, "If I considered you in your private capacities, I should treat you both according to your deserts." If they returned all papers not leading to proof of his guilt, "*the whole* will be returned to me."[28] Meanwhile, he applied to Sir John Fielding, the famous blind magistrate in Bow Street, for a warrant to search Egremont's and Halifax's houses. The application, of course, was refused, and there the matter ended.[29] The suits which he instituted against some of the governmental agents were more successful, but those against the principal ministers were still pending when Wilkes's ruin was finally encompassed in Parliament and in the courts.

Of more significance than the confiscated papers were those which Wilkes now began to print. Setting up a private printing press in his house, Wilkes ran off an edition of the *North Briton* in volume form, plainly defying the ministers in their prosecution. At the same time, he had his printer strike off several personal copies of a poem entitled "Essay on Woman," an obscene and blasphemous parody of Pope's "Essay on Man," which Wilkes and Thomas Potter had composed in one of their frequent debauches. The copies were intended solely for circulation among Wilkes's private friends, but they were to play a spectacular part in his disgrace in the Parliament.

iv.

The outcome of Wilkes's prosecution in the Common Pleas put the King in a quandary. His plans for eliminating the factions in the Parliament and establishing a strong ministry independent of "parties" was having exactly the opposite effect from that desired. Grenville's ministry had inherited the unpopularity of Bute's. While it could probably maintain its majority in the Commons when Parliament reconvened in the fall, the Wilkes affair had all but put an end to its popular prestige. The mob feeling which had driven Bute to retirement was rising against the triumvirate, and Wilkes was still free to fan it. The opposition, to be sure, was not united in its support of Wilkes; the prosecution had at least accomplished that much. But nevertheless the opposition as a whole benefitted from his successes, not only in popular prestige but in new, fresh issues to press against the ministers. There was even a possibility that such issues as Parliamentary privilege and general warrants might win enough converts in the Commons to deprive the ministers of their majority. In such a contingency, George III foresaw that he would have to abandon all his plans and call Pitt back into his councils.

In similar circumstances the practice of ministers under George II had been to strengthen themselves by admitting the leaders of certain opposition factions into the government. It will be remembered that Grenville gained his first position in the government by just such an arrangement.[30] Since the triumvirate had failed to suppress the opposition in the courts, the King now proposed, probably upon Bute's advice, to try to strengthen the ministry and weaken the opposition by admitting a few opposition leaders.

Of all the principal men in the minority, Hardwicke appeared to have maintained the most favorable position toward the ministers during the Wilkes controversy. While remaining outside the ranks of governmental supporters, he was nevertheless in favor of the prosecution of Wilkes. Although he insisted that he had "nothing to do in this affair," he gave the government the advantage of his advice in the legal matters which the controversy involved.[31] By his advice, moreover, Newcastle and their faction kept aloof from the affair, gave no support or aid to Wilkes, and refused to make political capital of his "sufferings."[32] Hardwicke thus appeared an ideal man to strengthen the ministry against Temple, Pitt, and Wilkes. Probably upon the advice of Bute, who had just returned to court for the first time since his resignation, the King dispatched Egremont on May 13 to sound out Hardwicke. Egremont made it plain at the start that the inclusion of Pitt and Temple in any government was out of the question; "he believed his master would run great risks before he would submit to them." Hardwicke gave Egremont to understand that, while he did not insist on the inclusion of Pitt and Temple, he did have certain "honourable connections, which some might represent under the odious name of faction." He was not to be obtained alone; his and Newcastle's followers must come in with him.[33] Such an arrangement would have upset all the King's plans for breaking up the factions in the Parliament. The negotiations were allowed to lapse.

The ministry, however, was becoming daily more unpopular, and the successes of Wilkes and his henchmen were feeding that unpopularity. On July 7, Dryden Leach brought suit before Pratt for damages against the governmental messengers for false arrest. The verdict was a foregone conclusion; Leach and his journeymen received damages amounting to three hundred pounds. In addition, Pratt pronounced as an *obiter dictum* that general warrants were illegal. The ministers entered a bill of exceptions against the opinion, as they were entitled to do, but this action tended even more to enrage the mobs and to increase the popularity of Wilkes and his supporters.[34] Pitt's enthusiasts, indeed, intensified this result by circulating and encouraging the tale that Wilkes was released because of the illegality of the general warrant, which was untrue.[35]

The situation of the ministry now seemed desperate. The King determined upon another attempt to bring in Hardwicke, for the death of the aged Granville in late July left a vacant place in the ministry. When the King informed them that he intended to make Hardwicke Lord President and to give Newcastle a place at court, the triumvirate remonstrated strongly against the measure. The King, however, remained firm in his intentions. On August 1, Egremont went again by the King's command and extended the invitation to Hardwicke with provision for Newcastle in the court. Also contemplated, it would appear, was a change which would have replaced Egremont as Secretary of State with Sir Joseph Yorke.[36]

Hardwicke, however, immediately refused the offer, saying, according to Grenville, that he and Newcastle "would never come into office, but as a party and upon a plan concerted with Mr. Pitt and the great Whig Lords, as had been practiced in the late King's time."[37] Such an arrangement was manifestly unsatisfactory. Hardwicke and Newcastle might stand aloof from Temple and Wilkes, but they remained firmly united with Pitt. Pitt, indeed, was not ardent in his support of Wilkes at this point. He told Newcastle that he "disapproved all these sort of papers, the North Briton, etc.; but that was not the question." Pitt was ready to abandon Wilkes while he caught up the issues Wilkes had provided. His real concern, he said, was for "liberty of the press" and "the privileges of the Houses of Parliament."[38] Yet he could not be weaned away from Temple. When Bute had approached him privately in June, the "great commoner'" had replied that he would never come in except as a "party" with Temple, Newcastle, and the rest.[39]

Hardwicke's refusal put the issue squarely to the King. It appeared useless to continue attempts at strengthening the triumvirate from the opposition ranks. Yet George III was not willing to discuss taking in the opposition as a "party." On August 3, he requested that his ministers give him ten days to consider the matter. He gave his promise that if no solution was worked out by that time for admitting new blood from the opposition, "he would lay aside all thoughts of it, and strengthen the hands of his ministers." That is, if he failed to bring in Hardwicke, Newcastle, or Pitt, he would fill the vacant positions with personal adherents of the triumvirate.

Grenville went to Wotton to spend the interval the King had requested and did not return to town until August 18. When he saw George III the next day, the King had made no plans, but he still seemed to be contemplating changes. By August 21, however, he had apparently resigned himself to the impossibility of strengthening the triumvirate; he was willing to continue with them and their adherents rather than turn to Pitt and Temple. He professed to Grenville that he was fully satisfied with his ministers and intended to give them every possible strength and support.[40]

v.

This assurance afforded only temporary encouragement, however, for on that same day Egremont was suddenly seized with a stroke of apoplexy and died within a few hours. The triumvirate was broken, and Grenville and Halifax found their position more precarious than ever. Decisive action was necessary. On August 23, having reached an agreement between themselves, they advised the King that he had three "options" in reconstituting the ministry: he could either "strengthen the hands of his present ministers," form a coalition of members of the ministry and the opposition, or "throw the Government entirely into the hands of Mr. Pitt and his friends." Naturally the ministers would have preferred the first alternative, though the second would likely have been acceptable; the King himself promised that he could never consent to take the third course.[41]

On the next day the Duke of Bedford, who had been outside the ministry since his refusal to join the triumvirate in office, made a play for office by going to the King in behalf of Pitt. The Grenville ministry, he advised George III, could not stand; the country would be ruined if he did not send for Pitt and his friends.[42] To take such a course would have been directly contrary not only to the King's promise to Grenville and Halifax but also to the course of action which he had been pursuing ever since Bute first took office. Yet historians have generally made it out that it was George's intention to follow Bedford's suggestion when he authorized Bute to make overtures to Pitt. They apparently deduce this conclusion from the fact that Pitt himself was given that impression. Both the behavior and the papers of the King, however, indicate that he was merely attempting to carry out the second "option" suggested by Grenville and Halifax. He was again seeking to wean Pitt away from the opposition factions. The King's personal relations with Egremont had been far from satisfactory since the formation of the triumvirate in April. His death, wrote George III, "encouraged me to attempt a coalition of partys."[43]

Following a series of secret negotiations, the nature of which is obscure, Bute paid a visit to Pitt, August 25, which was satisfactory to both. It is doubtful, however, that either of the men really understood the other's position. Pitt conceived that he was being called upon to form a new government and thought Bute was accepting terms upon which a whole new ministry should enter. Bute, on the other hand, was only accepting terms by which Pitt and a few friends would join a coalition ministry. This was obviously the version of the agreement which Bute carried to George III, for the next day the King informed Grenville that he intended to take Pitt into the management of his affairs, "declaring that he meant to do it as cheap as he could and to make as few changes as was possible." Yet Grenville, like Pitt, conceived that his brothers were to come in with a whole following, and he remonstrated with the King for going back on his promise.[44] It appears that none of the politicians, either within or without the ministry, had any conception of the idea which George III and Bute were attempting to put into effect. They could conceive of forming a ministry only along lines of family and factional ties; when the King tried to make them depart from their habitual paths, they misunderstood him and thought him fickle, if not downright dishonest.

This fact was to be amply apparent when Pitt, on the basis of his understanding (or misunderstanding) with Bute, was summoned to court on Saturday, August 27, to make arrangements with the King. The audience lasted for three hours. Pitt reviewed the whole political scene, giving his opinion on the peace, on the domestic and foreign state of the nation, and on the persons of "the great Whig families" then out of office, including Temple and Newcastle, whom he would insist upon restoring to the ministry. The King heard him out "with great patience and attention," only affirming now and then that on certain points he would have to consult his honor. It was obvious, however, that Pitt still had no intention of coming into a coalition ministry. Grenville and Halifax had been grievously weakened by the loss of Egremont, and Pitt was now pressing his advantage. When Pitt finished, George made no commitments, but only ordered Pitt to return on Monday, the twenty-ninth. The situation was as far from a solution as ever.

Pitt, however, left with the impression that the King had substantially agreed to terms upon which he should form a government. He began making preparations for the formation of a ministry, visiting Newcastle at his town house in Lincoln's Inn Fields and requesting the presence of Devonshire and Rockingham in town to consult with them.45 Grenville reported to Halifax that he understood Pitt had been given *carte blanche,* although he admitted that this was only rumor; the King had not spoken of the matter.46

In reality, George III had not agreed with Pitt's proposals. His statements that he would have to consult his honor should have revealed even to Pitt that he was dissatisfied. Immediately after the interview, Grenville found him "a good deal confused and flustered," as he might have been expected to be upon finding that the agreement between Bute and Pitt had not been what he thought. The King had not yet decided what should be done, however; in spite of Grenville's attempts to draw him out, he made no notice of Pitt's having been with him. Not until the following evening, when he had considered the whole matter and had discussed it with Bute, did George III summon Grenville and give him a full report of the audience with Pitt. Two points stuck in the King's mind: Pitt had refused to come into the government except in a "party" with Newcastle and his friends and supporters, and he insisted that Temple be given the Treasury. To submit to the first condition would involve giving up his ideas of creating a coalition ministry and would also entail breaking his word to Grenville and Halifax. The second condition would have given high preferment to the man who had engineered and directed the vicious attacks against his favorite, his ministers, and as the King felt, the Crown. Such terms, he told Grenville, were too hard. He had therefore decided that, since no coalition appeared possible, he would continue with his present ministers alone, giving them "the fullest assurances of every support and every strength he could give...towards carrying his business into execution." Grenville, he said, should be his sole advisor; Bute intended to "retire absolutely from all business whatsoever" and would leave town until the ministers should firmly re-establish themselves.[47]

Having thus made his decision, the King had to inform Pitt of it the following morning. It was unlikely that Pitt would understand in any event, but the manner in which George approached the subject made it doubly certain that he would misunderstand. Receiving him cordially, the King gave him an audience of nearly two hours. He began by speaking strongly of his honor; then he moved to the question of the Treasury, a logical step to him since Pitt had mentioned Temple for that position. The King suggested instead that Halifax should be First Lord; his ideas of coalition were appearing openly. Perhaps he was trying one last time to get Pitt to commit himself to a coalition, but Pitt only took a nibble at the bait. The paymastership, he said, was the position for Halifax. It was hard, but perhaps sacrificing Grenville's pride might turn the trick. The King replied that he had designed the Paymastership for "poor George Grenville; he is your near relation, and you once loved him." Pitt's only answer was a low bow; one might suppose it to mean either yes or no. Grenville in a subordinate, non-ministerial position would be tolerable, but Pitt would have the whole direction of the ministry, not a coalition. The choice was clear; all or nothing at all. The King finally brought Pitt to state just that idea by asking the provoking but insincere question: "Why should not my Lord Temple have the Treasury? You could go on then very well." Pitt took the bait and came forth with the desired reply:

> Sir, the person whom you shall think it fit to honour with the chief conduct of your affairs cannot possibly go on without a Treasury connected with him. But that alone will do nothing. It cannot be carried on without the great families, who have supported the Revolution Government, and other great persons, of whose abilities and integrity the public has had experience, and who have weight and credit in the nation. I should only deceive your Majesty if I should leave you in the opinion that I could go on, or your Majesty make a solid administration on any other foot.

The King here had the opportunity he sought to drive home his point. "Well, Mr. Pitt," he replied, "I see this won't do. My honour is concerned, and I must support it."

The audience and the negotiations with Pitt were at an end. Pitt went away saying that he had no idea upon what point the negotiations were broken off, but that could not be helped.48 The decision was made. George III had adhered to the aims which he had been seeking since his succession; he kept his weakened ministry rather than submit to be "given the law" by the factions in the Parliament.

vi.

Ironically, Pitt placed in the King's hands the means of strengthening the weakened Grenville ministry. In his audience, Pitt made the specific stipulation that Bedford, as author of the peace, "must have no office at all" either in the ministry or in the court.49 Bedford's resentment flared. A few months before he had declared that his sanity should be questioned if he joined the Grenville ministry; only days before he had declared that the country would be ruined if Pitt did not come in. Now, however, out of anger and resentment toward Pitt, he consented to take the position of Lord President and a seat in the Cabinet Council. Grenville thus gained the support of Bedford and his "Bloomsbury gang" faction in Parliament. By September 6 the arrangements with Bedford were made, and a majority in the Commons was assured.50

Meanwhile, to the King's surprise, Grenville asked that Egremont's vacant place as Secretary of State be filled by the Earl of Sandwich. That earl had been virtually forced upon Grenville as head of the Admiralty in April by the King and Bute. Grenville explained that he still did not consider Sandwich his friend; neither he nor Bedford was really his friend, but he felt they would lend strength to the ministry. The two, he cautioned, "might prove too strong for him." He relied on the King's "truth and honour" to sustain him. George III promised "that he would never fail him, nor forget his services."51 On September 9 the new ministers kissed hands for their offices, and a strong coalition was assured.

There remained the question of the relationship of Bute to the King and the ministry. The favorite had continued since his resignation to act as personal advisor to the King. When Egremont and Grenville gave evidence of their resentment of this arrangement, the King was indignant. "With what men am I not embarked?" he asked Bute in late April; "I thank God I have a friend...that comforts me and makes me look on my ministers as my tools solely in my public capacity."52 Bute seems to have realized, however, that his position behind the curtain was damaging to the public prestige of the ministry. Likewise, the knowledge of the ministers that they did not possess the full confidence of the King was damaging to the best interests of the government. When his efforts to secure Pitt for the King were unsuccessful, Bute realized that any further interference in the government on his part would only weaken the King's position. George III had promised Grenville his sole confidence, and for Bute to remain at court would arouse his suspicion and enmity. The favorite, therefore, announced soon after Pitt's second audience with the King that he intended to retire absolutely from public affairs, even giving up the Privy Purse, which he held as a personal favor to the King.[53]

Although Grenville made the natural request that no "secret influences" should prevail over his own advice as chief minister, available evidence indicates that he made no demands for Bute's retirement at this time.[54] It was not until September 6 that he learned of Bute's full part in the transactions with Pitt. According to the information he received, as he recorded it in his diary, Bute had been negotiating with Pitt to displace him as early as August 12.[55] Probably Grenville's real resentment and distrust of Bute began at the time of this intelligence. The only reason he gave the King for wishing his retirement on September 5 was the "great ferment" against him among the people, which the King readily admitted.[56]

Indeed, the idea that Bute's permanent retirement should be a condition *sine qua non* for the continuation of the new coalition apparently originated not with Grenville but with Bedford. The Duke had never forgiven Bute for curtailing his plenipotentiary powers in negotiating the peace. He had refused to join the administration so long as the favorite remained at court, and now that he had voluntarily retired for a time Bedford succeeded in persuading Grenville and Sandwich that Bute should be entirely forbidden the court.[57] By September 26 Sandwich was completely converted and was writing to Bedford urging him to speak to Grenville about hurrying up the favorite's departure. Grenville, he said, needed "a little spurring" on the point.[58]

By the time of this letter, George III had committed himself to banishing his favorite from court and having no communication with him whatever. Bedford could now be satisfied, but Grenville had other fears. The "secret influences" were removed and the strength of the ministry was assured, but Bedford might threaten his control of the ministry. Therefore Grenville exacted from the King a promise of support against his fellow ministers, and particularly Bedford. George III complied. When Grenville's fears of his fellows extended to attempting to place a peer of his own choice as keeper of the Privy Purse, however, the King called a halt. "Good God, Mr. Grenville!" he exclaimed, "am I to be suspected after all I have done?" Grenville explained that the King's insistence on his own nominee would give the public the impression that the ministers still did not have the confidence of the Crown, but George remained firm.[59]

Yet Grenville could console himself with the thought that he had a secure control of the ministry and the Commons even without this "nominal office." The affair of Wilkes and Number 45 had brought the triumvirate to the brink of ruin, but out of the August negotiations Grenville emerged with a stronger ministry in which he alone held the helm. Neither he nor his supporters had any doubt of the permanency of the arrangement. With the King's confidence and authority, ventured one of their adherents, "they will always be able to support themselves."[60]

NOTES

CHAPTER VII

[1] Wilkes even printed a *North Briton* for April 7, 1763, in praise of Pitt as the new minister. It was, of course, never published. See John Wilkes and Charles Churchill, *The North Briton,* 4 vols., London, 1772, II, 225-246.

[2] Upon learning of Grenville's appointment, Newcastle wrote to Hardwicke that there was "nothing to be done but to remain thoroughly united, and to unite absolutely with Mr. Pitt." April 10, 1763, Yorke, *Hardwicke,* III, 487.

[3] *London Chronicle, Public Advertiser,* etc., April 13, 1763; handbill, Newcastle MSS., Add. MSS, 32948, f. 123.

[4] Grenville was afraid when he was demoted to the Admiralty that Temple in his heat of opposition would refuse to allow his re-election (George III to Bute, October 11, 1762). Temple, however, "did not think it worth my while to give myself the least trouble on the matter" and let Grenville be returned uncontested. (Temple to Lady Chatham, October 26, 1762, Chatham MSS., 62, 53.)

[5] Almon, *Wilkes,* I, 93-95.

[6] Wilkes and Churchill, *North Briton,* II, 249.

[7] Sedgwick, *Letters,* pp. 230-232.

[8] Grenville's diary, *Grenville Papers,* II, 192; George III to Bute, April 30, 1763, Sedgwick, *Letters,* pp. 232-233.

[9] Yorke and Norton to Halifax, April 27, 1763, Wilkes Trial Papers, Add. MSS. 22132, f. 4

[10] Wilkes Trial Papers, Add. MSS. 22131, f. 37.

[11] Yorke and Norton to Halifax, April 30, 1763, Wilkes Trial Papers, Add. MSS. 22132, f. 12.

[12] Hardwicke to Royston, May 3, 1763, Yorke, *Hardwicke,* III, 92.

[13] Yorke, *Hardwicke,* III, 460. From Chatham MSS., 25, f. 74.

[14] Annual Register, VI (1763), p. 136; *Gentleman's Magazine,* XXXIII (1763), p. 240.

[15] Grenville wanted him thrown in the common prison at Newgate, as Norton and Yorke had suggested, but Halifax insisted on the Tower as the place where members of Parliament were customarily confined. George III to Bute, April 30, 1763, Sedgwick, *Letters,* p. 233.

[16] Warrant signed by Egremont and Halifax, Wilkes Trial Papers, Add. MSS. 22131, f. 48.

[18] Hardwicke to Yorke, April 30, 1763, Yorke, *Hardwicke,* III, 490.

[19] *Annual Register,* VI (1763), p. 136.

[19] To Hardwicke, May 1, 1763, Yorke, *Hardwicke,* III, 491.

[20] Yorke to Hardwicke, May 3, 1763, Yorke, *Hardwicke,* III, 493; Almon, *Wilkes,* I, 109-113.

[21] George III to Bute, April 30, 1763, Sedgwick, *Letters,* p. 233.

[22] See above, Chapter VI.

[23] Almon, *Wilkes,* I, 113-114.

[24] *Grenville Papers,* II, 55.

[25] Thomas B. Howell, *A Complete Collection of State Trials and Proceedings for High Treason and Other Crimes and Misdemeanors from the Earliest Period to the Present Time,* 34 vols., London, 1809-1828, XI, 989- 990.

[26] Royston to Birch, May 10, 1763, *Rockingham Memoirs,* I, 168. See also Hardwicke to Royston, May 10, 1763, Yorke, *Hardwicke,* III, 495.

[27] Wilkes to Egremont and Halifax, May 6, 1763, Wilkes MSS., Add. MSS. 30867, f. 206.

[28] Wilkes to Egremont and Halifax, May 9, 1763, Wilkes MSS., Add. MSS. 30867, f. 207.

[29] *London Magazine,* XII (1763), p. 265.

[30] See above, Chapter III.

[31] Hardwicke to Yorke, April 30, 1763, Yorke, *Hardwicke,* III, 490.

[32] Hardwicke to Newcastle, May 1, 1763, Yorke, *Hardwicke,* III, 491; Newcastle to Hardwicke, May 2, 1763, Newcastle MSS., Add. MSS. 32948, f. 211.

[33] Hardwicke to Newcastle, May 13, 1763, Newcastle MSS., Add. MSS. 32948, f. 275.

[34] Howell, *State Trials,* XIX, 1001-1003; Nuthall to Pitt, July 7, 1763, *Pitt Correspondence,* II, 230-235.

[35] Mackenzie to Jenkinson, July 16, 1763, *Jenkinson Papers,* p. 168; *Gentleman's Magazine,* XXXIII (1763), p. 346.

[36] Sir James Porter to Sir Joseph Yorke, November 21, 1763, H. M.C., *Beaufort MSS.,* p. 337. Porter says that Egremont "had resolved to quit" and "seemed to wish you as his successor."

[37] Grenville's diary, *Grenville Papers,* II, 191.

[38] Newcastle to Devonshire, August 11, 1763, Newcastle MSS., Add. MSS. 32950, f. 73.

[39] Newcastle to Hardwicke, June 30, 1763; Hardwicke to Royston, August 5, 1763, Yorke, *Hardwicke,* III, 509, 512-513.

[40] Grenville's diary, *Grenville Papers,* II, 192-193.

[41] Grenville's diary, *Grenville Papers,* II, 194-195.

[42] Memoranda by the King, August, 1765, Fortescue, *Papers of George III,* I, 167.

43 Memoranda by the King, August, 1765, Fortescue, *Papers of George III*, I, 167, 170, 174.

44 Grenville's diary, *Grenville Papers*, II, 195.

45 Hardwicke to Royston, September 4, 1763, Yorke, *Hardwicke*, III, 525-527; Pitt to Rockingham, August 28, 1763, *Rockingham Memoirs*, I, 171; Grenville to Oxford, September 1, 1763, Grenville Letter Book, Stowe MSS.

46 Grenville to Halifax, August 27, 1763, *Grenville Papers*, II, 95-97.

47 Grenville's diary, *Grenville Papers*, II, 197-201; from letter by Grenville, September 2, 1763, Murray MSS. The decision of the King to give up the whole idea of negotiations with Pitt was probably influenced by Bute, who also saw the disadvantages of calling a new "party" into the government. See note by W.J. Smith, *Grenville Papers*, II, 95. George III's promise that Grenville should be his sole adviser was a complete reversal of his position the preceding April, when he told Bute he looked upon his ministers "as my tools solely in my public capacity." Sedgwick, *Letters*, p. 233.

48 Hardwicke to Royston, September 4, 1763, Yorke, *Hardwicke*, III, 525-527.

49 Sandwich to Bedford, September 5, 1763, *Bedford Correspondence*, I, 238.

50 Grenville to Bedford, September 5, 1763; Bedford to Grenville, September 6, 1763, *Bedford Correspondence*, III, 242-245.

51 Grenville's diary, *Grenville Papers*, II, 205; Memoranda by the King, August, 1765, Fortescue, *Papers of George III*, I, 167; Grenville to Oxford, September 1, 1763, Grenville Letter Book, Stowe MSS.

52 Sedgwick, *Letters*, p. 233.

53 Elliot to Grenville, August 31, 1763, *Grenville Papers*, II, 101.

54 Grenville's diary, *Grenville Papers*, II, 201.

55 *Grenville Papers*, II, 204.

56 Grenville's diary, *Grenville Papers*, II, 204; Grenville to Strange, September 3, 1763, *Grenville Papers*, II, 106.

57 *Bedford Correspondence*, III, 114-137 *passim;* Fitzmaurice, *Shelburne*, I, 203. In 1765 Bedford reminded the King that he had entered the ministry upon the condition that Bute should retire from all councils. *Bedford Correspondence*, III, 280.

58 *Bedford Correspondence*, III, 250-251.

59 Grenville's diary, *Grenville Papers*, II, 209-211.

60 Porter to Yorke, November 21, 1763, H. M. C., *Beaufort MSS.*, p. 337.

CHAPTER VIII

THE PARLIAMENTARY WAR, 1763-1764

i.

Once Grenville had secured his position in the ministry by admitting Bedford and Sandwich to its inner councils, he could turn his attention again to Wilkes. Indeed, his subordinates had never forgotten him. Ever since Wilkes's release by Pratt in May, the journalist had been kept under close surveillance. A group of spies directed by Philip Webb, the Solicitor of the Treasury, and Nathan Carrington, the cleverest of the "terriers" employed by the government, had kept a constant watch on Wilkes's movements and had made periodic reports to Grenville.[1] Little by little information was ferreted out about the nature of the pieces which were being printed on the press in Wilkes's house in Great George Street. By the middle of July or thereabouts, Webb had learned of the printing of the "Essay on Woman" and was bending every effort to obtain a copy. Michael Curry, Wilkes's printer, was persuaded to hand over some pilfered sheets of the poem while Wilkes was away in Paris visiting his daughter.[2]

It was probably on receipt of this intelligence that Grenville consulted with the Attorney-General, Charles Yorke, on the best method of proceeding with a prosecution of Wilkes in the Parliament when it reconvened. If a charge of blasphemy could be added to that of libel and if both charges could be prosecuted before the ministerial majority in the Parliament, Wilkes might be effectively subdued. A major irritant to the ministers and a major grievance to the King could thus be eliminated. Yorke, who had played so large a part in the legal proceedings against Wilkes in April and May, approved the project of Parliamentary prosecution. Moreover, he pledged his support, although he was uncertain whether he could continue to serve as Attorney-General. The outcome of the negotiations then under way with his father, Lord Hardwicke, might determine that. Yet, whether in office or out, he promised that he would support the prosecution "to the utmost of his abilitys."[3]

The importance of the "Essay on Woman" to the ministers' plan of campaign against Wilkes is attested by their extraordinary efforts to obtain the full text of the poem. During August and most of September while Wilkes remained in Paris, they offered inducements to Curry; the printer refused their overtures. When Wilkes returned to London on September 26, however, he learned that the government had got wind of the printing of the poem. Believing Curry had betrayed him, he dismissed the printer from his employment, whereupon Curry in revenge turned over to Webb a full set of revised proofs, including the title-page, prefaces, the poem, ribald footnotes purporting to be the production of William Warburton, the distinguished Bishop of Gloucester, and three other parodies from Wilkes's unsavory collection.[4]

As if this mistake were not enough, Wilkes made another serious blunder at about the same time. Apparently the ministers were not determined on a course of prosecution in Parliament if Wilkes would listen to reason. Sandwich, an intimate friend of Wilkes and a former partner in the licentious orgies of the brotherhood of Medmenham Abbey, informed the journalist that the ministry was willing to forget his offenses if Wilkes would assent to certain terms of peace. Wilkes, however, felt secure in the protection of his friends. He rejected the offer scornfully, disdaining to accept any favors from the ministers. He told Sandwich, indeed, that he wished "to be understood as being devoted to the service of the opposition in any plan of writing that may be thought right."[5] The battle, in other words, would continue to the bitter end.

Having extended the olive branch and had it thrown back in their faces, the ministers now set about marshalling their support for the fight in the Parliament. While Sandwich prepared the case for the House of Lords, Grenville lined up his forces in the Commons. During the second week of October, he began sending out letters to the principal supporters of the ministry in that House urging them to be present when the Parliament convened about November 16. "There are many things likely to come on at the very beginning," he wrote. "I mean...the affair of Mr. Wilkes, which must be laid before the House the first day of the ensuing session."[6]

The minister intended that motions should be introduced in the Commons declaring that Number 45 was a false and seditious libel and that publication of such libels was outside the privilege of Parliament. Both questions were within the jurisdiction of the Commons. When privilege of Parliament was invoked by the courts and questioned by the government, it was the place of the Commons to pass on the question. There were precedents also for inquiry by the Commons into the publication of libels. Although Hardwicke ventured that "their determination will not be conclusive to a court of common law," it was nevertheless the prerogative of the House to consider the matter if it saw fit.[7] Grenville felt that it would lend strength to the ministerial cause if these motions could be introduced by someone not directly connected with the ministry. The prosecution would then lose some of the appearance of personal vindictiveness toward Wilkes on the part of the ministers. Accordingly, Grenville wrote on October 15 to his friend, Lord Strange,[8] one of the governmental supporters in the Commons, asking him to undertake the commission and requesting him to come to town to confer with the minister on the subject.[9] Apparently Strange declined to take so prominent a part in the proceedings, for negotiations were soon carried on toward the same purpose with one of the Lords of the Treasury, Lord North.[10] A talented orator and one of the most amiable and respected men in the House, North would give strength to the prosecution. He was at first reluctant, but as a member of the government he had responsibilities. By October 30 he had consented to perform the office.[11] The plans for the prosecution in the Commons were quickly formulated.

ii

When the Commons gathered in St. Stephen's Chapel, November 15, after hearing the King's opening speech, the long-anticipated Parliamentary battle began. Scarcely had the Speaker taken his seat when Wilkes sprang to his feet to complain of breach of privilege, while on the other side of the chamber Grenville rose to deliver a message from the King. Speaker Cust protested that no business could be done until a bill had been read according to precedent. A long and bitter debate ensued on the question of procedure, lasting nearly five hours. Pitt and his adherents contended that the question of privilege should take precedence over all others. North and Grenville took the opposite view, and angry words passed between Grenville and Pitt. At length, at six in the evening, the ministers beat an opposition motion on procedure by a division of 300 against 111, and the sides were defined.

Grenville then read the message from the King. It explained, of course, what every member of the House already knew: that Wilkes had avoided prosecution by pleading privilege of Parliament. The King wished the Commons to consider the whole case. After voting an address of thanks for the message, the members heard Number 45 and the evidence of the printer against Wilkes, most of which they already knew almost by heart.

Then North proceeded to his task. "The paper entitled '*The North Briton,*
No. 45,'" his motion read, "is a false, scandalous, and seditious
libel...tending to alienate the affections of the people from his Majesty...
and to excite them to traitorous insurrections against his Majesty's government." Here began a debate which lasted until nearly one o'clock in
the morning. Pitt refused to defend the paper from the charge of libel, but
he vigorously attacked the allegation that it tended to foment "traitorous
insurrections." Again and again he engaged North and Grenville, speaking, if Walpole may be believed, forty times. Toward one o'clock the
House divided on Pitt's motion that the words "and to excite them to traitorous insurrections against his Majesty's government" be deleted. The
minority still kept their original numbers, but the ministers prevailed, 273
to 111. The main question was then put and resolved in the affirmative
without a division. Grenville proceeded to order the paper to be burned
by the common hangman.

Only when this debate was over was Wilkes allowed to voice his
protest of breach of privilege. The members were tired and sleepy after
the long debate. Few paid Wilkes the courtesy to hear him out, and as
soon as he finished his short speech the House adjourned. No notice was
taken by the government of Wilkes's offer to waive his rights and submit
to trial by jury if the House would uphold his privilege. The prosecution
was now in high gear, and no compromise offered the slightest
temptation.12

While the ministers were thus successfully pursuing this phase of
Wilkes's prosecution in the Commons, another campaign was being
waged against the unfortunate journalist in the Lords. The plans for it had
been carefully laid. While Grenville arranged matters in the Commons
during October, Sandwich had drawn up a plan for the upper House.
From Grenville he obtained the "Essay on Woman" and the other poems
which Webb had procured.13 After careful study, Sandwich, Grenville,
and Northington, the Lord Chancellor,14 planned the means by which the
"Essay on Woman" could be incorporated into the campaign against
Wilkes. The Lord Chancellor felt that the mere charges of blasphemy and
impiety, while they might be prosecuted in the courts, would not be proper subjects to bring before the Parliament. There were other means to
effect the same purpose, however. Wilkes had mentioned on the title page
of the poem, in imitation of Warburton's edition of Pope's "Essay on
Man," that the notes were by Dr. William Warburton. Sandwich hastened
to the worthy bishop with the objectionable papers, and Warburton,
enraged at their contents, agreed to bring complaint against the poem as

a breach of privilege of the House of Lord in improperly mentioning his name. This, Northington agreed, would be sufficient cause to bring the matter before the Lords. The House would then take up the charges of blasphemy and impiety as a matter of course.15

Accordingly, when the King and the Commons had retired from the Lords' chamber after the opening speech, Sandwich revealed the surprise he had prepared for his fellow peers. Before the House took the King's speech into consideration, he rose and made complaint against the "Essay on Woman" and another poem which Curry had pilfered from Wilkes's collection entitled "The Veni Creator Paraphrased." It doubtless amazed and shocked some of the peers, who knew that Sandwich had often laughed with Wilkes over such coarse jests as the poems contained, to hear the Secretary droning the obscenities in a tone of righteous solemnity. His friend Sir Francis Dashwood, now Lord Le Despencer, remarked that it was the first time he had ever heard the Devil preaching. The pious Lyttelton was not so droll; he begged earnestly that the reading might stop, but his protests were drowned by cries of "Go on!" and Sandwich was allowed to finish his performance. Warburton followed him, foaming "with the violence of a Saint Dominic," and raging that "the blackest fiends in hell would not keep company with Wilkes when he should arrive there."16

A motion was then introduced that the papers, "highly reflecting upon a member of this House," were a breach of the privilege of the Lords and were "a most scandalous, obscene, and impious libel; a gross profanation of many of the holy scriptures; and a most wicked and blasphemous attempt to ridicule and vilify the person of our blessed Savior."17

The result was, of course, a foregone conclusion. No matter what his private sentiments, no one would have dared to defend the poems publicly. Temple ventured to object to the means by which the papers had been obtained, but he found little support among his fellow peers. The House was about to declare, on the evidence of Curry and the other printers who appeared as witnesses, that Wilkes was the author of the objectionable pieces. On the advice of Lord Mansfield, however, they adjourned the matter until November 17 in order to hear Wilkes in his own defense.18

iii.

Wilkes, however, was not able to appear before the Lords on November 17; dramatic events intervened. Rendered reckless by the outcome of the first day's events in the Parliament, Wilkes fought a duel on November 16 with Samuel Martin, whom he had maligned in the *North Briton* of March 5, 1763. November 17 found him flat in bed at home, with surgeons attending a serious wound in his side.[19] When he failed to appear, the Lords petitioned the King that proceedings should be instituted to bring Wilkes "to condign punishment."[20] The Court of King's Bench shortly hailed Wilkes to appear to answer a charge of blasphemy. On November 23, the Commons made ready to add another charge by introducing a motion "that privilege of parliament does not extend to the case of writing and publishing libels." Pitt and his followers fought the motion vigorously when it was debated on November 24. Appearing with his theatrical props of crutches and flannel bandages for his gouty leg, the orator fairly outdid himself in defense of privilege. His method was characteristic of the old Pitt, however; he took care to dissociate himself from any connection with the discredited Wilkes, saying that he "did not deserve to be ranked among the human species—he was the blasphemer of his God and the libeler of his King." Pitt saw that Wilkes's bark was sinking; it had been useful to him, but he did not scruple to abandon it to its fate when it could no longer be of service. The question of privilege might be made an asset to opposition; Wilkes could only be a liability.[21]

Pitt's ringing oratory was not sufficient to sway Grenville's strong majority, however. The motion carried by 258 votes to 133 and was communicated to the Lords, where it was passed on November 29. Then, following a joint conference, the two Houses on December 1 petitioned the King that proceedings should be instituted to bring the author of the *North Briton* Number 45 to punishment. Again Wilkes received a summons to the King's Bench.[22]

Grenville and his lieutenants were winning resounding victories over Wilkes in the Parliament, but among the mobs he remained the hero of the hour. On December 3, when the magistrates assembled at the Royal Exchange for the public burning of Number 45, a great riot broke out, the mob rescued the paper from the flames, and with the cry "Wilkes and Liberty" they trooped off to Temple Bar, where a bonfire was built and a jack-boot and a petticoat, symbols for Bute and the Princess Dowager, were consigned to the flames.[23] Apparently the rancors and prejudices which Wilkes had encouraged in the public mind were stronger than any shock at Wilkes's blasphemies, indecencies, and libels. Three days later, when Wilkes won a case in the Common Pleas against Robert Wood, the Undersecretary of State, for trespass in connection with the April arrest, a great crowd gathered. Cheering the verdict, they serenaded Wilkes with shouts of "Wilkes and Liberty" as he lay abed and then rushed off to jeer before the houses of Grenville and Halifax.[24] Clearly, the victories of the ministers in the Parliament were gaining them no popular support.

The proceedings against Wilkes continued in Parliament, however, albeit with delays because of his illness. December 16 was set as the date upon which he was to attend the Commons "in his place" to hear the charges against him. When his surgeons reported on that date that he was unable to attend, the House ordered that he attend on January 17 "if his health would then permit."[25] His health was better than he pretended, however. He managed to slip away from town in spite of the vigilance of ministerial agents, and Christmas Day found him in Calais on his way to Paris. He intended, he wrote Temple, to return to London by January 14.[26]

Once he reached Paris, Wilkes began to consider the fate which would greet him if he returned to England: expulsion from the Commons; a long imprisonment for libel and blasphemy, during which the fickle populace would forget "Wilkes and Liberty"; and possibly, without his privilege to protect him, a long sojourn in a debtors' prison. The prospect was hardly alluring. On the other hand, to remain in Paris would give him the prestige of martyrdom without its more unpleasant aspects, and he might return to England at a moment of his own choosing, when the political situation might be more promising. Thus when the Commons met on January 16 Wilkes's face was not to be seen. Instead, there appeared a letter from him, certified by two French physicians, stating that he was too unwell to travel.

The ministers were in no mood to trifle longer. The evidence of the physicians was brushed aside with the excuse that it had not been authenticated by a notary public, and on January 19 the House pressed on to a consideration of Wilkes's offense. On a motion to postpone the issue, Wilkes's friends were able to muster 102 votes against the ministry's 239, but thereafter their numbers dwindled rapidly. The debate lasted until nearly four in the morning; it was then resolved "with scarce a negative" that Wilkes should be expelled from the House.[27]

iv.

With Wilkes out of the way, the ministers might have looked forward to a quiet session. Wilkes's ruin in the Parliament was complete; his conviction in the courts was soon to follow. Pitt, aside from the question of privilege, was conciliatory toward the ministers. He was temperate in his criticisms of the peace at the beginning of the session, and he "spoke civilly, and not unfairly, of the ministers." Governmental supporters considered his speech on the address to the King in November worth fifty thousand pounds, for "it secures us a quiet session."[28]

The removal of Wilkes, however, had exactly the opposite effect. So long as "the blasphemer of his God and the libeller of his King" was the object for which the opposition fought, either directly or indirectly, many members who disliked the ministerial measures had hesitated to throw in their lot with those who were defending Wilkes. Now, however, the contest ceased to have any personal relation either to the Crown or the Deity, and the factions could unite against the government on a question of legal principle. Thus Pitt, Townshend, and other leaders in the opposition groups prepared for the thrust which they hoped would unseat Grenville and his friends.[29] In the early morning of February 15, 1764, the opposition introduced a motion providing "that a general warrant...is not warranted by law." The ministerial forces were not caught unawares, but their best efforts were necessary to avoid defeat. After three hours of debate, a division was taken at seven o'clock on a motion to postpone the question until February 17. Grenville was dismayed to find that the ministry prevailed by only ten votes, 207 to 197.[30]

Now came on the supreme test of the Grenville ministry in Parliament. Both the ministers and the opposition realized the magnitude of the occasion. The minority, indeed, was so sanguine of victory over Grenville and his associates that the bells of London were made ready for celebration, and bonfires awaited only the torch. An illumination was prepared for the top of the Monument, and Temple, who had sat in the gallery through the whole of the sixteen-hour session on the fifteenth, was so indiscreet as to have the fagots for two bonfires already lighted.

Both sides, meanwhile, beat the bushes for every possible supporter in the Commons. "One would have thought," wrote Walpole to his friend Lord Hertford, "that they had sent a search-warrant for Members of Parliament into every hospital. Votes were brought down in flannels and blankets till the floor of the House looked like the pool of Bethesda." Above, the galleries thronged with the gay colors of great ladies with their lords. The atmosphere was tense with excitement, for although the debate itself was dull, as detailed legal controversy was bound to be, the cheers and shouts of four hundred fifty men fired to enthusiasm and eager for a decision thrilled the air.[31]

Townshend and Charles Yorke[32] led the attack of the opposition, while Sir Fletcher Norton bore the brunt for the ministers. In bulldog fashion the new Attorney-General laid down legal maxims to match Yorke's sophistries and Townshend's flaming oratory, returning tenaciously to the attack, again and again. The courts, he informed his former colleague, would pay no more attention to a resolution of the Commons on such a point of law than they would to "the oaths of so many drunken porters in Covent Garden." Pitt and Grenville, meanwhile, glared at each other from opposite front benches and ran a race of silence to see who should answer the other. Playing his role to the limit, the "great commoner" thrice limped from the chamber in obvious pain, only to return wanly to his seat. At length at three in the morning he rose to the attack, but he was languid and exhausted. Walpole ventured that "in his life he never made less figure." Grenville answered him, laying down precedents and arguments with logical precision. At five o'clock came the test on a motion by the ministers to postpone consideration of the question for four months, when the Parliament would be prorogued. On the voice vote, the noes were so loud that the Speaker gave it to them. Tellers were appointed and a division was taken. The opposition announced first, at 218, but the ministry returned 232. The day was saved![33]

Thus dramatically and precariously did the Grenville administration weather the fiercest storm the opposition was ever to stir up against it. When the question of general warrants was finally settled in the Commons the following January, the opposition had suffered such a sharp decline that it was able to offer no effective protest.[34] The immediate effect of the defeat in February, 1764, was to damp completely the enthusiasm of the opposition and rob it of its one great cohesive issue. Had the opposition been able to maintain the numbers which it marshalled on this occasion it could doubtless have driven Grenville and his colleagues from office. But the force of the minority had been spent; Grenville never received a serious test in the Parliament thereafter.

v.

The Parliamentary war over privilege and general warrants brought defections not only among the rank and file of the government's supporters but within the court and the government as well. That of the most moment was Charles Yorke's. After the failure of the August negotiations with Hardwicke and Pitt, the Attorney-General was hard pressed by his family and Newcastle to resign from the Grenville ministry. Surveying the political scene and perhaps influenced by a conviction that general warrants were illegal, Yorke came to the conclusion that his greatest chance of fortune and honor lay not with Grenville but with his father and Pitt in the opposition. Accordingly, he resigned as Attorney-General, albeit with tears and misgivings, on November 3, 1763.35

The sacrifice did him little good and much harm. If he had calculated on going out to come in again with Pitt after Grenville's overthrow, he was soon disillusioned. Moreover, he felt himself obliged to make good his promises to Grenville and the King by supporting the ministry in the questions of privilege and the expulsion of Wilkes. Although he joined and even led the minority on the issue of general warrants, he was unable really to identify himself with the aims of Pitt and his group. Yorke's ambitions of becoming Lord Chancellor were known to all and were supported by his father and Newcastle, while Pitt was determined on placing Pratt on the woolsack in any coming ministry. Yorke thus became a divisive element between Pitt and the Newcastle-Hardwicke faction. Pitt complained that his presence in the opposition "might do more harm than good" and left him stranded. Indeed, the unstable "great commoner" attacked Yorke openly in the Commons and asserted that he himself "stood single" from all connections in the House.

Yorke's leaving the government at this crucial time virtually condemned him to the political wilderness. After the clash on general warrants, there seemed little chance that the opposition would be able to displace Grenville in the King's government. And even if Newcastle and his group gained the King's favor, it would have to be with Pitt's assistance or blessing, in which case Pratt would be given the preference over Yorke as Lord Chancellor. The realization of his ambition to be Lord Chancellor seemed farther away than ever. With his father soon to pass from the scene, he was out of favor with Pitt, was embarrassing to Newcastle, and was out of touch with Grenville, who felt himself strong enough now to do without him. For the house of Yorke, a decline had begun; the end was not yet in sight.36

Another change of camps attending the Parliamentary war caused a flurry on the political scene, though it was not of such moment as Yorke's defection. General Conway,37 a younger brother of the Earl of Hertford and a Lord of the Bedchamber, had been a regular supporter of Bute's and Grenville's ministries. But on the issues of privilege and general warrants he defied the ministers and voted with the minority. The King took the conventional avenue of disciplining officers who opposed his government; after the debate on general warrants Conway was dismissed from his command in the army and from his post in the King's household. In spite of the flurry it occasioned on the political scene, however, the action had little other effect than to insure the futile but meddlesome activity of Conway's friend Horace Walpole against the ministry. Grenville was to be annoyed by his carping criticisms for many a day afterward.38

As the political world settled down from the excitement of the great debates and Conway's dismissal, the last stages of the prosecution against Wilkes were brought to a close. His trial took place before Mansfield in the Court of King's Bench, February 20, 1764. Wilkes was convicted of writing and publishing both Number 45 and the "Essay on Woman," but since he was still in France and did not appear for the trial, no judgment was pronounced. Instead a writ was issued for his arrest. Finally, when he did not appear for judgment by November 1, 1764, he was declared an outlaw "according to the law and custom of the realm." The depth of Wilkes's degradation and disgrace had been reached!39

vi.

Meanwhile, the ministry had been occupied for some months on another project, the suppression of opposition in the daily papers. Not waiting for the defeat of their opponents in the Parliament, Grenville and his colleagues set about establishing a censorship of opposition in all the press as soon as the decision against the *North Briton* was obtained in November, 1763. A strict watch was set upon the daily newspapers to detect and prevent all objectionable material. On January 7, 1764, an anonymous letter warned the printer of an opposition daily that there was "an intention of overlooking the papers for some time past, in order to punish those who have inserted any letters that may have given offense. I give you this notice that you may be on your guard...." "We are much obliged to this correspondent for his hint," replied the printer, "and hope all who honour this paper with their favours will have a regard for the safety of the printer, who is of *no party*."40 The warning soon went the rounds of all the dailies. A contributor to the London *Evening Post* was informed, January 19-21, that his "Revolutionist" could not be printed. "It requires and must have some softening; for truths are told in so spirited a manner that we dare not run the risque of printing it."

Moreover, surveillance was backed with firmer action, and arrests were made when statements appeared which the ministers considered too unfavorable. Thus the editor of the *Evening Post* related in March that he had been arrested and fined. "But he hopes," he went on, "and will endeavor to avoid ever giving occasion to travel the same road again."41

Such was the effectiveness of the censorship campaign, indeed, that the opposition forces were virtually deprived of the newspaper as a propaganda instrument. The *Monitor,* it is true, continued to make its weekly appearance at least until March, 1765, but the continual threat of prosecution reduced the efforts of Entick and Beardmore to practical impotence. With privilege of Parliament withdrawn from those members who might be disposed to write and with the papers under such strict watch, Temple and the other directors were left only with the expedient of inserting into the dailies whatever editors were willing to risk printing in the form of anonymous letters. This method of procedure was developed and systematized until it became quite useful in the later controversies over the Stamp Act. In the spring of 1764, however, the censorship of the press was one more element contributing to the crippling and demoralizing of the Parliamentary opposition.

vii.

The story of the war in Parliament during the winter of 1763-1764 is the story of the Grenville ministry fighting for its life. What would have happened had the ministers not decided to prosecute Wilkes one can only conjecture. One imagines that the disappointment over the peace would soon have faded away and that Wilkes's power as a rabble-rouser would have faded with it. Viewed in this light, the prosecution was a grievous mistake. But mistake or not, once Wilkes was arrested and set free the ministers had to silence him, by fair means or foul. There could be no half-way measures and no turning back. It was, as Wilkes made plain in September, 1763, a fight to the death. The life of the ministry depended upon absolute victory.

Neither Wilkes's methods in combatting Bute and Grenville nor the ministers' methods in suppressing Wilkes were entirely ethical. They were unscrupulous, underhand, and decidedly not in a true spirit of fair play. Yet it would perhaps be a mistake to attempt either to justify or condemn them. It was simply a case of fighting fire with fire; the ministers proved the better firefighters.

The "Wilkes affair" is a significant chapter in the history of the liberty of the subject, but fully as significant is its place in the history of Parliamentary opposition. The contest which the government won so completely left the opposition in a crippled, exhausted, demoralized state. Such a situation would have been politically unhealthy at any time. It was particularly unfortunate in that it allowed the ministers to introduce, almost unopposed, the disastrous program of taxation of the American colonies.

NOTES

CHAPTER VIII

[1] See specimens of reports, *Grenville Papers*, II, 155-160.

[2] Affidavit by Michael Curry, August 3, 1763, Almon, *Wilkes*, I, 155-163.

[3] George III to Bute, n. d., Sedgwick, *Letters*, p. 235.

[4] Almon, *Wilkes*, II, 9-11; Wilkes to the electors of Aylesbury, October 22, 1764, Almon, *Wilkes*, III, 113-116; Horace Bleackley, *Life of John Wilkes*, London, 1917, pp. 120-121; George Rudé, *Wilkes and Liberty: a Social Study of 1763 to 1774*, Oxford, 1962, pp. 31-32.

[5] Onslow to Newcastle, September 29, 1763, Newcastle MSS., Add. MSS. 32951, f. 220.

[6] Grenville to Lord Strange, October 13, 1763 (form letter), Grenville's Letter Book, Stowe MSS.

[7] Hardwicke to Newcastle, June 8, 1763, Yorke, *Hardwicke*, III, 502.

[8] James Stanley, Lord Strange (1717-1771), eldest son of the Earl of Derby and M. P. for Lancashire.

[9] *Grenville Papers*, II, 135.

[10] Frederick North (1732-1792), eldest son of Francis, first Earl of Guilford. He afterward became second Earl of Guilford, August 4, 1790.

[11] North to Halifax, October 30, 1763, *Grenville Papers*, II, 151-152.

[12] *Journals of the House of Commons*, XXIX, 667-668; *Parl. Hist.*, XV, 1354-1361; Walpole, *George III*, I, 314-317; Walpole to Hertford, November 17, 1763, Toynbee, *Walpole's Letters*, V, 384-386.

[13] Sandwich to Grenville, October, 1763, Murray MSS.

[14] Robert Henley, first Baron Northington, afterwards first Earl of Northington (1708-1772). Northington was a personal adherent of the King and Bute.

[15] Sandwich to Grenville, November 5, 1763, *Grenville Papers*, II, 153-155.

[16] Walpole, *George III*, I, 312; Walpole to Hertford, November 17, 1763, Toynbee, *Walpole's Letters*, V, 387.

[17] *Journals of the House of Lords*, XXX, 417.

[18] *Parl. Hist.*, XV, 1346-1351; Walpole, *George III*, I, 309-314; Walpole to Hertford, November 17, 1763, Toynbee, *Walpole's Letters*, V, 387-388.

[19] Almon, *Wilkes*, II, 12-17.

[20] *Lords Journals*, XXX, 420-421.

[21] *Parl. Hist.*, XV, 1361-1364.

[22] *Parl. Hist.*, XV, 1365-1371, 1378-1380; *Annual Register*, VI (1763), p. 144.

[23] Walpole to Hertford, December 9, 1763, Toynbee, *Walpole's Letters*, V, 407-408; *Annual Register*, VI (1763), p. 144; *Scots Magazine*, XXV (1763), p. 632.

24 *Public Advertiser,* December 8, 1763.

25 *Parl. Hist.,* XV, 1386-1387; *Gentleman's Magazine,* XXXIII (1763), pp. 616-617.

26 Wilkes to Temple, December 25, 1763, *Grenville Papers,* II, 185-186.

27 *Commons Journals,* XXIX, 721-723; *Parl. Hist.,* XV, 1388-1399; Walpole, *George III,* I, 349-350.

28 Birch to Royston, n. d., *Pitt Correspondence,* II, 262 n.

29 Charles Townshend had gone into the opposition when he resigned as head of the Board of Trade in April, 1763, but he had remained silent during the debates on Wilkes and privilege. Walpole to Hertford, November 17, 1763, Toynbee, *Walpole's Letters,* V, 385.

30 Walpole to Hertford, February 15, 1764, Toynbee, *Walpole's Letters,* VI, 2-5; *Parl. Hist.,* XV, 1398-1400.

31 Walpole to Hertford, February 19, 1764, Toynbee, *Walpole's Letters,* VI, 7-9.

32 Yorke was now in opposition, having resigned his post as Attorney-General, November 3, 1763. Norton took his place, with William de Grey, M. P. for Newport, becoming Solicitor-General.

33 Walpole to Hertford, February 19, 1764, Toynbee, *Walpole's Letters,* VI, 9-12; *Parl. Hist.,* XV, 1400-1406.

34 *Parl. Hist.,* XVI, 6-15; *Annual Register,* VIII (1765), pp. 26-32.

35 Grenville's diary, *Grenville Papers,* II, 218-219.

36 Memoir by Philip, second Earl of Hardwicke, January, 1771, Hardwicke MSS., Add. MSS. 35428, ff. 1 ff; Basil Williams, "The Eclipse of the Yorkes," *Transactions of the Royal Historical Society,* Third Series, II (1908), 135-136, 150; Grenville's diary, *Grenville Papers,* II, 225-226 .

37 Henry Seymour Conway (1721-1795), M. P. for Thetford.

38 See *Grenville Papers,* II, 162-187, 224-258 *passim.*

39 Howell, *State Trials,* XIX, 1075-1077, 1099; *Gentleman's Magazine,* XXXIV (1764), p. 25.

40 *Gazetteer and London Daily Advertiser,* January 7, 1764.

41 *London Evening Post,* March 17-20, 1764.

CHAPTER IX

THE SUGAR ACT, 1763-1764

i.

The problem of John Wilkes and the opposition press was not the only one which faced George Grenville when he became First Lord of the Treasury in April, 1763. Both Newcastle and Bute in that office had watched wartime expenses expand the national debt to what they considered astronomical proportions. Newcastle had forced Pitt from office rather than expand the expense of the war in 1761. Bute had brought the war to a close just when it was succeeding everywhere because he feared the collapse of the fiscal structure if it continued. Now the problem of a balanced budget was Grenville's.

During the eight years from January 1755 to January 1763, the public debt had nearly doubled. Seventy-three million pounds in 1755, it had swelled to 137 million by 1763. The funds, borrowed at from three to four percent per annum, drew an interest of nearly five million pounds a year.1

What was worse, the debt promised to increase rather than diminish unless drastic action was taken. Pitt's wartime land tax of four shillings in the pound was still in force, as were all the other taxes of the war years,2 but even so the budget would not balance. The normal peacetime expenses of government had expanded quite apart from the national debt. In addition, the Crown had acquired vast new territories which would have to be organized and administered, entailing further expense. And finally, both new and old possessions would have to be protected, even though the war was over.

The territories acquired from France were a glorious addition to the extent of the empire, but in terms of shillings and pence they were long-term investments. It would be years before a British population there could protect itself. The Indians, incited by the remaining French in the areas, were still hostile to the British; financially, the territories were a liability. Bute, asserting the need for a standing army to protect both the new possessions and the old, stationed a force of 10,000 troops on the frontiers in March, 1763.[3] The wisdom of the action seemed amply borne out in the summer of 1763, when an Indian uprising under Pontiac threatened to drive the British settlers back to the Atlantic coast. But the expense of the troops was one more item in a budget already unbalanced.

Deficit financing in wartime was still relatively new, and not even the most able and experienced financiers of the day had any notion of its limits. No wonder the debt frightened them! Deficit financing in peacetime was unthinkable. A government with much greater parliamentary support than Grenville's would have paused before attempting it. But where could new sources of revenue be found? The landed interests of the country, the great territorial magnates who were the majority of members of both Houses of Parliament, had voluntarily borne the brunt of taxation during the war. A twenty percent tax on land revenues was the highest in history, and the landed interests were already murmuring that it should be lowered now that peace had arrived. That they would be willing to bear a greater burden of taxation in peacetime than they had during the war seemed totally unlikely. To increase the land tax above four shillings in the pound seemed beyond political possibility. Taxes would have to be found which would bear less directly on the landed interests.

Bute had reached a partial solution of this problem in the cider tax which Sir Francis Dashwood presented to the Commons in March, 1763. An excise on cider spread the taxation more evenly among the populace than did the land tax. It had one obvious disadvantage, however. The issue of excise was one which the opposition could turn to its own advantage, waxing loud in defense of personal liberties and raising mobs to support its contentions. Money had to be raised, but surely some type of tax could be found which would not bear on the landed gentry and still would not be ready-made as an issue for the opposition. An answer was finally found, or so it seemed, in an American revenue.

ii.

Parliamentary duties levied in America were not new. Thirty years before, Sir Robert Walpole's administration had passed the so-called Molasses Act of 1733, placing a duty of sixpence a gallon on all molasses imported into the Empire from foreign sources. The duty, however, was not designed to raise a revenue. By levying a duty of sixpence a gallon on French and Spanish molasses imported by New England rum distillers, Parliament intended to protect the sugar producers of the British West Indies from foreign competition. The rate proved prohibitive—or at least uncollectable. Colonial merchants calculated the costs of smuggling, with such risks as it bore, as less than half the sixpence a gallon of the duty. The result was widespread smuggling and almost no revenue. Part of the picture, of course, was the fact that British admiralty and customs officials made little effort to suppress the smuggling. Hence the low cost of the business. But even so the cost roughly approximated the differential between British and foreign molasses, thus serving the purpose of protection. For thirty years, planters, merchants, and officials had lived comfortably with a system which served their mutual interests, however it winked at disobedience of the law.

It seems likely, however, that these pragmatic arrangements were unrecognized by the men dealing with the nation's financial problems in 1763. Grenville saw only that it was costing eight thousand pounds a year to collect only two thousand pounds of revenue.[4] The law was being flouted and revenue was being lost. In March, 1763, as First Lord of the Admiralty in Bute's administration, he introduced in the Commons a bill to use British ships-of-war to enforce the trade laws. New powers were given to the vice-admiralty courts, both in the colonies and in Great Britain, and all commanders of British warships were authorized to act as customs officers in suppressing smuggling.[5]

This act, which passed the Lords and received the Royal assent after Grenville assumed the Treasury, took the trial of smugglers out of the hands of friendly colonial juries and put it into those of customs officers. One can hardly imagine an arrangement more certain to arouse the ire of colonial importers.

The government intended by tightening the collection process to get more revenue, yet from the very nature of the acts the sums collected were certain to remain small. The Treasury was soon considering the idea that Americans might bear a greater share of the burden of imperial protection and administration. Grenville's secretary to the Treasury Board, Charles Jenkinson, preserved among his papers a memorandum written in his own handwriting but signed with the initial "G". Dated February 25, 1763, the treatise suggested among other things that the colonies should be reorganized on a uniform pattern established by Parliament, and that the several colonial governments be supported by a Parliamentary tax, either an import or an export tax. It is unlikely that this was Grenville's memo; only a peer would normally sign only one initial. Grenville always initialled documents "GG." But someone was submitting suggestions to the Treasury which, if an attempt had been made to implement them, would surely have set off tumultuous colonial opposition.[6]

But in their second meeting as a Board, the new Lords of the Treasury took up the question of how the troops in America were to be supported.[7] The total charge for the twenty-one battalions which Bute had stationed in North America and the West Indies was estimated at £224,903.17.06 per annum.[8] Could the colonies be expected to contribute this much toward their own protection? And if so, by what means?

Lord Egremont, the Secretary of State, wrote to the Board of Trade on May 5, inquiring "in what mode, least burthensome and most palatable to the colonies, can they contribute towards the support of the additional expense which must attend their civil and military establishments."[9] Apparently at this point the ministers still entertained the idea of paying not only the troops but royal officials as well out of customs revenues from the colonies. In the end, however, they limited their attempts solely to the support of the military establishment. The tax measures they enacted, even if they had been enforced, would not have raised enough revenue to pay the whole cost of the troops. No need to raise another, more troublesome question.

At this point the main question was not how much Americans should pay or what establishments they should support. The real problem was to find the necessary money. The Treasury also asked other agencies of the government for advice. On May 21 Charles Jenkinson wrote to the Commissioners of the Customs. The Lords of the Treasury, he informed them, had observed that the revenues from America and the West Indies amounted "in no degree to the sum which might be expected from them." The customhouse was directed to "endeavour to find out the causes of this deficiency" and to advise the Treasury "in what manner the revenue may be better collected in the future."[10] The most obvious reason for low revenues from the Molasses Act was smuggling. Grenville's bill of the preceding March was now supplemented by a letter from Egremont to the colonial governors calling on them to be vigilant in their efforts to control smuggling. All possible measures should be taken to prevent illegal trade and especially the smuggling of foreign goods into the colonies.[11] Meanwhile the Commissioners of the Customs, replying on July 21 to Jenkinson's letter, offered three propositions. First, the non-resident collectors of the customs, most of whom lived in England on large salaries while their ill-paid deputies supported themselves on bribes, should be compelled "to a constant residence at their respective stations." This, said the Commissioners, was "not only necessary to the observance of the laws but likewise a proper preparatory step to such further laws and regulations as may hereafter be thought fit to be established."

Secondly, they advised that the collectors be prevented from taking any fees whatever, substituting instead "a poundage out of their respective remittances." This would prevent the bribing of officers to connive at smuggling and give the collectors an active interest in increasing the revenue.

Thirdly, and most important, they suggested that the prohibitive duties on certain foreign items of trade much in demand in the colonies, notably molasses, should be lowered to a point the trade would bear and thus be made to produce a revenue.12

This was the sort of recommendation Grenville had been waiting for. The Treasury Lords met the following day to consider the proposals. Grenville's colleagues, Lord North, Sir John Turner, Thomas Hunter, and James Harris,13 agreed with the First Lord that the recommendations should be implemented as soon as possible. The last two proposals would require action by Parliament; the Treasury simply informed the King of its intention to bring the ideas before that body.14 The first provision, however, needed only a directive from the Treasury. Accordingly, Jenkinson sent an order to the Commissioners of the Customs to "write immediately to such of the said officers as are absent from their respective stations directing them to repair thither forthwith upon pain of dismission." The Commissioners were also ordered to "prepare proper instructions to be sent to all the officers of the customs in America and the West Indies, enforcing in the strongest manner the strictest attention to their duties."15

Having taken this action, the Treasury wrote on July 29 to request more of the customhouse's ideas on collecting the revenue. What "further checks and restraints to be imposed by Parliament...will most contribute" to the collection of revenue in the colonies?16 The customhouse officers took a month and a half to study the request. Then, on September 11, they submitted that the Molasses Act of 1733 had been "for the most part either wholly evaded or fraudulently compounded" and recommended the imposition of more drastic penalties for smuggling.17 They elaborated in a further memorandum on September 16. If the duties were lowered so as to "diminish the temptation to smuggling," they said, the revenue could be increased. Then such smuggling as continued could be ended by bonding all ships putting in or out of American ports, by making the penalties for smuggling payable only in specie rather than in depreciated colonial paper money, and by carefully examining all foreign ships putting out from Britain to the colonies.18

Here again were concrete proposals for Parliamentary action. When the Lords of the Treasury met on September 22, they sent instructions to the Commissioners of the Customs to prepare a bill incorporating their measures for suppressing smuggling.[19] At the same time Charles Jenkinson and his fellow Secretary to the Treasury, Thomas Whately, were given the task of determining how great a duty the colonial molasses trade with the French islands would bear and still produce a revenue. A great mass of material on the trade was compiled by the Secretaries during the fall of 1763, both statistics on the trade and opinions of merchants and colonial agents.[20]

iii.

By mid-December, 1763, the news was abroad in London that the Treasury intended to lower the duty on molasses and make it produce a revenue. Jasper Mauduit, the London agent of the Massachusetts Bay colony, wrote home that the Treasury had first considered a duty of fourpence per gallon in place of the sixpenny duty. Now it appeared that the officers would be satisfied with twopence. He would attempt, he volunteered, to get it reduced to one, but it would not be more than two.[21]

But Mauduit was overly sanguine. Whately computed from the material which he and Jenkinson had collected that the colonies consumed about 80,000 hogsheads of molasses a year. At a hundred gallons a hogshead and a threepenny duty per gallon, a revenue of a hundred thousand pounds a year could be raised. A twopenny duty, of course, would have brought in two thirds as much, and a penny duty one-third—other things being equal. The question was, at what point would the amount of the duty begin to reduce the volume of trade and therefore the duty? Whately calculated that a twopenny duty would not affect the volume of importation at all, considering the differential in cost between British and foreign molasses. A threepenny duty would affect the flow, reducing importation by a ratio of nine to seven. But even so, the higher duty would produce £77,775 compared to £66,667 for a twopenny duty. Thus Whately and Jenkinson recommended the higher duty.[22]

Mauduit apparently heard of this decision, for he submitted a memorial to the Treasury in February, 1764, "representing against the imposition of an higher duty than 2d on french molasses." A threepenny duty, asserted the agent for Massachusetts, would be "destructive of the distilleries in that province, a heavy burthen on the fisheries, and a means of promoting the distilleries lately set up by the French." The Treasury considered the memorial, February 27, but Whately's calculations were more convincing. The Board dismissed Mauduit's contentions without comment,[23] and plans moved ahead for the presentation of the threepenny duty to Parliament in March.

Meanwhile, as the time approached for the presentation of the budget to Parliament, Grenville had to decide precisely to what use the American revenues were to be applied. The ministers had suggested the preceding May that the Americans might be required to support both the civil and military establishments in the colonies by Parliamentary taxes.[24] In January, 1764, they were apparently still entertaining that idea. On January 23, estimates of the civil establishments of all the colonies in America and the West Indies were read before the Treasury Board.[25] By February 11, however, Mauduit was able to report to the Massachusetts legislature that Grenville had decided the revenues should be applied solely to the support of the army in the colonies.[26]

Why Grenville decided not to try to support the royal governments in the colonies from Parliamentary taxation one can only speculate about. Perhaps he recognized that there would be fierce opposition from the colonies, since the measure would have deprived the colonies of a means of control over royal officials. Or perhaps that credits him with greater insight than he had. The explanation may lie in simple arithmetic. The revenue from the revised molasses duty would not even cover the cost of the army.[27] Why antagonize the colonies by talking about extending it to the royal governments?

There seems to have been little strenuous opposition to the measure. The Massachusetts Assembly did not even see fit to give Mauduit any instructions on the matter. He reported that he did not think it proper to oppose it without authorization. "Nor," he added, "do I find the least disposition in the other agents to oppose it."[28] It would seem that lowering an existing duty did not provoke arguments of "no taxation without representation." They awaited the Stamp Act.

iv.

Nor did there seem to be much to fear from the opposition in Parliament. Pitt retired to his estate at Hayes as soon as the debates on general warrants were over.[29] He came forward no more that session. Without Pitt's magnetic leadership, the opposition was certain to shrink in size. Moreover, there was no real issue around which the remaining leaders could rally their forces. Certainly Grenville's budget offered few points for attack. He planned no new taxes; he would raise all the necessary funds for the coming year without resorting either to borrowing or to further demands on the purses of the British populace. Few members of the Commons would object to lowering a colonial duty to make it pay and take a load off their shoulders.

Some, of course, might oppose simply for opposition's sake. Thus when the opportunity arose to introduce the budget while both Charles Townshend and Charles Yorke were absent, Grenville seized it. On March 6, 1764, Lord Hardwicke died after a lingering illness. Electioneering had already begun between government and opposition for his position as High Steward of Cambridge University. Since Newcastle's resignation, Cambridge had been regarded as a stronghold of the opposition, for in addition to Hardwicke as High Steward, Newcastle himself was Chancellor. If the government could capture the High Stewardship, Grenville and his colleagues would gain political stature. Sandwich had already established himself as the government's candidate, while the opposition put forward Hardwicke's eldest son, Lord Royston. As soon as Hardwicke died, both sides set off to Cambridge to marshal their forces for the election. Charles Yorke naturally went to support his brother, and Newcastle felt the contest of enough moment to withdraw his nephew Townshend from the Commons and send him into the fray.[30]

When Grenville introduced his budget on March 9, therefore, the opposition benches were largely empty. For two hours and forty minutes the First Minister expounded the measures by which he would raise the full supplies for the coming year. He did so with ability and even wit; even Newcastle conceded that he "entertained the House." Horace Walpole complained that he answered questions "with more art than sincerity," but without influential men to lead the way there were few to object. "There were a few more speeches, till nine o'clock, but no division," reported Walpole.[31]

Grenville was pleased. "The general state of the supplies for the year has been opened in the House of Commons here," he wrote the following day, "and the plan which has been proposed for raising them has met with no opposition.... The state of the House of Commons appears much more favorable to his Majesty's administration, and the minds of men seem to be much less heated than they were...." At the rate matters were progressing, he commented, the ministers would be able to finish the public business and close the session before Easter.[32]

The polling at Cambridge was to occur on March 22; Grenville needed to get his budget approved before that. So on March 14 he moved that the bill for revision of the Molasses Act, or the Sugar Act as it was to be called, be committed for debate in the Commons on Thursday, March 2. Newcastle was furious. Grenville had set the date "on purpose," he complained to Yorke, "to prevent Mr. Townshend's being in the House."[33] But Newcastle's fury made little difference in the House of Commons. The second reading of the bill raised no more difficulties than the first, and with the third reading on April 5 the bill went to the House of Lords. There, as a money bill, it was passed with little discussion or debate.

Among the rank and file, indeed, members of the Commons were almost unanimously in favor of Grenville's measure. Sir James Porter, a friend of the Yorkes and ordinarily in opposition, was singing the Minister's praises. "When I heard Mr. Grenville in the House of Commons I think as to matter I never observed any go so deep, and with more thorough knowledge," he wrote.[34] Grenville had "displayed his abilities and knowledge of the situation of this country in a very eminent degree. This the opposition allow, and they go still further, and own that if the country can be saved in the loaded state in which he found it, he is the man with his economy to do it."[35]

Even Newcastle was forced to admit that Grenville had gained credit and support. "His praise," he wrote, "is sounded thro' the whole Kingdom." The country gentlemen were "returning home with the greatest encomiums of the man who, in the terrible situation of the Kingdom, can pay debts and raise near eight millions for the current service of the year without any new tax or any new loan." Yet the old Duke recognized the weakness in Grenville's plans: the deficit in revenues was to be made up by borrowing from the sinking fund. "What he pays with one hand, he borrows with the other," he told Legge, "and leaves an immense unfunded debt, as must, if not soon provided for, destroy the credit still more than it is and leave this Kingdom a bankrupt country." Still, he conceded that Grenville, however unfounded his acclaim, "has certainly, for this time, gained some credit by his performance."[36]

Among the measures which made up Grenville's budget for 1764, the Sugar Act was perhaps the least significant so far as revenue was concerned. Of the estimated budget of nearly eight million pounds, the American duty was expected to contribute less than eighty thousand. Yet in its results the Sugar Act was to be the most significant measure the Commons passed in 1764, for it inaugurated the program of seeking a revenue in America which was to lead eventually to rebellion and independence. The central feature of the bill, of course, was the adjustment of the duty on molasses and sugar which Whately and Jenkinson had prepared. But that was only one item in a general plan, which also called for duties on Madeira and other foreign wines directly imported into the colonies, wines imported through Great Britain, foreign coffee and indigo, foreign silks and other fabrics, and coffee and pimento of British colonial produce exported to places other than Great Britain.[37] Of these six categories, all except the adjustment of the duties on molasses and sugar were intended purely as mercantile regulatory measures, as the Navigation Acts had always been. Only the molasses duty was calculated to raise any revenue.

The Sugar Act took its name from the revenue portion of the measure, but actually only six of its articles pertained to taxes of any kind. The more than forty remaining articles embodied the recommendations of the Commissioners of the Customs for tightening collection of revenue. They provided for extensive changes in commercial and customs regulations which in the aggregate constituted almost a revolution in the commercial relations between Great Britain and the colonies. Minute regulations were prescribed for the loading of ships, their putting up bond before clearing port, their course and manner of sailing, and many other incidentals relative to the shipping of goods. Stringent penalties, moreover, were provided for violation of the new rules, amounting even to forfeiture of ship and treble the value of its cargo.[38]

The act was signed by the King in April, 1764; it was not to go into effect until the last day of September. The interval gave the colonists and their agents nearly five months in which to agitate against the measure and to concoct arguments against it. Admittedly there were many objectionable features from the point of view of a colonial merchant. Any tax was objectionable, for it cut into profits. It was particularly so when even its framers conceded that it might reduce the volume of trade as well. The mercantile regulations, moreover, were involved and troublesome. In some cases they threatened to cut out profitable trade with foreign ports. The propaganda which colonial agents circulated in London, however, followed the line which Mauduit's memorial to the Treasury in February had taken. The Sugar Act, they claimed, would destroy not only the colonial distilling industries, which were dependent on molasses, but the New England fishing industry as well!

Actually, the act had none of the dire effects which Mauduit had predicted. His forecasts were mere propaganda; probably neither he nor the colony he represented took them seriously. Fish continued to be caught, cured, and marketed in the same manner as before the act went into effect. Molasses continued to be imported in increasing quantities, mostly from the French islands.39 The customs service was put on a paying basis, though the revenues for the first year of the act's operation were not as great as had been anticipated.40 But in spite of the fact that few adverse effects were felt directly from the act, it generated an atmosphere of discontent among influential portions of the colonial population. Protests against the duties continued throughout Grenville's administration. They were to be successful in bringing about a further reduction in the duty level after Grenville was dismissed from office.

The colonial merchants, however, were not alone in protesting Grenville's commercial restrictions; merchants in London and other ports in Great Britain also objected to them. Traders with North America and the West Indies suffered like their brothers in the colonies from the mercantile regulations. In addition, the West Indian merchants were injured by the competition of the foreign West Indian products which the new law allowed. When the cry was later raised against the Sugar Act in the colonies, there were many voices closer to Westminster to echo it.

vi .

Two other important steps regarding America were taken during the first years of Grenville's administration. Grenville had little directly to do with the first of them, the "Proclamation Line of 1763." In view of Pontiac's uprising, it seemed inadvisable to allow further settlement of the trans-Appalachian region until the area could be secured against Indian attack and a proper government organized. So a proclamation tried to alleviate conflict between Indians and settlers for the time being by forbidding colonists to settle in "all land and territories lying to the westward of the sources of the rivers which fall into the sea from the west and southwest."41 Naturally a storm of protest arose in the colonies, especially among speculators who had already invested in trans-Appalachian land.

Apparently, Grenville had little to do with either the formulation or the promulgation of the decree. It was largely the work of Halifax, Shelburne, and Hillsborough,42 who succeeded Shelburne at the Board of Trade in September, 1763. Yet, although he did little more than give the measure his approval before it received the royal assent, October 7, 1763, Grenville evidently was in agreement with the measure, for in a pamphlet either written or inspired by him he defended it vigorously.43

The other measure affecting the American colonies was an act prohibiting the issuing of paper money by the colonial governments. The

New England colonies had been forbidden to issue bills of credit as long before as 1751, but the colonies to the south still enjoyed the privilege. Why Grenville decided to impose this prohibition is not clear. Perhaps the idea was suggested by Henry McCulloh, the North Carolina land speculator who had first suggested the idea of revising the Molasses Duty. During 1763 a letter from McCulloh to James Pownall, a secretary to the Board of Trade, found its way before the Lords of the Treasury. McCulloh represented the tremendous difficulty of carrying on public business, collecting quit rents, and negotiating simple commercial transactions in North Carolina because of the depreciation of paper money in the colony. Whatever the origin of the idea, Grenville decided that it would be advisable to put colonial finances on a "sound money" basis. The thought of attempting to carry on public business in depreciated paper was naturally distasteful to a conservative financier. So, near the close of the session of Parliament in 1764, he introduced a bill "to prevent paper bills of credit, hereafter to be issued in any of his Majesty's colonies or plantations in America, from being declared legal tender in payment of money." Paper money in the colonies, the act asserted, had so depreciated that "debts have been discharged with a much less value than was contracted for, to the great discouragement and prejudice of the trade and commerce of his Majesty's subjects, by occasioning confusion in dealing and lessening credit in the said colonies and plantations."[45]

No doubt Grenville was sincere in a desire to improve the financial situation of the colonies. The inflated paper currency had often worked hardships on creditors in the colonies, and Grenville intended to remedy the situation. The remedy, however, was worse than the ill, for the lack of paper money worked a hardship on almost everyone. Burdened with an unfavorable trade balance with the mother country, the colonists were virtually forced to resort to paper money or to invent some other medium of exchange. While the picture the colonists painted in 1764 and 1765 of an economy reduced to the stage of simple barter was undoubtedly exaggerated, it was nevertheless true that the Currency Act accomplished more ill than good for the colonies.

Aggravating discontent over the Sugar Act, the Proclamation of 1763, and the Currency Act was a post-war depression which swept the colonies in the winter of 1764-65. It probably had little to do with any of the new measures but to wartime expansion of credit and inevitable contraction and bankruptcies with the return of peace. The natural reaction of the colonial merchants, however, was to cast the whole blame on the Sugar Act and the other measures of the Grenville administration.[46]

Economic unrest thus aggravated the effect of propaganda against the Parliamentary measures. Already a few isolated individuals were pondering whether Parliament had the right to levy taxes on the unrepresented colonies.[47] This was the prepared ground into which Grenville in the spring of 1765 cast the seeds of rebellion in the form of a new Parliamentary tax bill. It was to be known to history as the Stamp Act.

NOTES

CHAPTER IX

1 Statement of the public debt, January 5, 1763, Treasury Papers, Class I, 434, ff. 1-2, Public Record Office.

2 Estimate of the ways and means for 1764, n.d., Treasury Papers, I, 434, f.33.

3 Sir Jeffrey Amherst to Welbore Ellis, April 26, 1763, Egremont MSS., Public Record Office, 24, packet 2.

4 Grenville to Walpole, September 8, 1763, *Grenville Papers* 114.

5 *Commons Journal*, XXIX, 620, 623.

6 Add. MSS. 38335, ff. 14-33. Thomas C. Barrow identifies the author as Lord Grosvenor, who originally submitted the proposal to Lord Bute. *William and Mary Quarterly*, 3rd Series, Vol. XXIV, January, 1967, pp. 108-126. Barrow quotes the whole manuscript.

7 Treasury minute, April 22, 1763, Treasury Papers, XXIX, 35, f. 70.

8 "Estimate of the charge of 21 Battalions proposed for service in North America," n.d., Egremont MSS., 24, packet 3.

9 Board of Trade Papers, Class I, 17, f. 31, Public Record Office.

10 Treasury Papers, XI, 27, f. 282.

11 See, for example, Egremont to Sharpe, July 9, 1763, Maryland Historical Society, *Archives of Maryland,* Baltimore, 1883 ff., XIV, 102-103.

12 Commissioners of the Customs to the Lords of the Treasury, July 21, 1763, Treasury Papers, I, 430, ff. 346-349. The third recommendation was not a new one. In 1761 Henry McCulloh, a North Carolina land speculator and Crown official, had suggested to Bute that the molasses duty might be lowered and made to produce revenue. (Henry McCulloh, *Miscellaneous Representations Relative to Our Concerns in America Submitted (in 1761) to the Earl of Bute,* edited by William A. Shaw, New York, 1905, p. 12.) Charles Townshend also suggested the idea while at the Board of Trade.

13 North had served as a Lord of the Treasury since June, 1759, and Turner since May, 1762. Hunter and Harris were new to the board, having taken their seats when Grenville became First Lord. Joseph Haydn, *The Book of Dignities,* London, 1894, p. 157.

14 Lords of the Treasury to the King, n.d., Treasury Papers, I, 430, ff. 332-334.

15 Jenkinson to the Commissioners of the Customs, July 25, 1763, Treasury Papers, XI, 27, f. 304; Treasury minute, July 22, 1763, Treasury Papers, I, 430, f. 344.

16 Treasury Minute, July 29, 1763, Treasury Papers, XXIX, 35, f. 135.

17 Commissioners of the Customs to the Lords of the Treasury, September 11,

1763, Treasury Papers, I, 430, ff. 339-342.

[18] Commissioners of the Customs to the Lords of the Treasury, September 16, 1763, Treasury Papers, I, 426, ff. 289-295.

[19] Treasury minute, September 21, 1763, Treasury Papers, XXIX, 35, f. 164; Thomas Whately to the Commissioners of the Customs, September 23, 1763, Treasury Papers, XI, 27, ff. 319-320.

[20] This material is preserved in the Liverpool MSS., Add. MSS. 38021, *passim.*

[21] Mauduit to the Speaker of the Massachusetts House of Representatives, December 20, 1763, *Collections of the Massachusetts Historical Society,* Boston, 1792 ff., First Series. VI, 193.

[22] Note in Whately's handwriting, n.d., Treasury Papers, I, 434, f. 52.

[23] Treasury minute, February 27, 1764, Treasury Papers, XXIX, f. 320.

[24] Above, fn. 9.

[25] Treasury minute, January 23, 1764, Treasury Papers, I, 423, ff. 11-16.

[26] Mauduit to Speaker, February 11, 1764, *Collections of the Massachusetts Historical Society,* First Series, VI, 194.

[27] Estimate of the ways and means for 1764, n.d., Treasury Papers, I, f. 33.

[28] Mauduit to Speaker, February 11, 1764, *Coll. of Mass. Hist. Soc.,* First Series, VI, 194-195.

[29] Walpole to Hertford, February 19, 1764, *Letters of Horace Walpole, Fourth Earl of Orford,* edited by Mrs. Paget Toynbee, 16 vols., London, 1903-1905, VI, 21.

[30] Newcastle MSS., Add. MSS. 32956-32957, *passim;* Winstanley, *Government,* pp. 284-287.

[31] Newcastle to Townshend, March 10, 1764, Newcastle MSS., Add. MSS. 32956, f. 342; Walpole to Hertford, March 11, 1764, Toynbee, *Walpole's Letters,* VI, 25. Walpole gives the length of the speech as two hours and forty minutes; Newcastle says three hours and a quarter.

[32] Grenville to Northumberland, March 10, 1764, Grenville Letter Book, Stowe MSS.

[33] Newcastle to Charles Yorke, March 15, 1764, Newcastle MSS., Add. MSS. 32957, f. 87. The vote at Cambridge was indecisive, and the matter was not finally settled in Hardwicke's favor until almost a year later.

[34] William Gordon, April 13, 1764, H. M. C., *Beaufort MSS.,* p. 339.

[35] Porter to Sir Joseph Yorke, April 16, 1764, H.M.C., *Beaufort MSS.,* p. 340.

[36] Newcastle to Legge, March 23, 1764, Newcastle MSS., Add. MSS. 32957, f. 230.

[37] 4 Geo. III, c. 15, sec. i-vi .

[38] 4 Geo. III, c. 15, sec. vii-xivii.

[39] See Oliver M. Dickerson, *The Navigation Acts and the American Revolution*, Philadelphia, 1951, pp. 86-87, 173.

[40] From September 29, 1764, to October 10, 1765, the North American revenues amounted to about £20,000. Treasury Papers, I, 430, f . 228.

[41] *Annual Register,* VI (1763), p. 211.

[42] Wills Hill, first Earl of Hillsborough (1718-1793).

[43] *The Regulations Lately Made Concerning the Colonies, and the Taxes Imposed Upon Them Considered,* London, 1765, pp. 20-21. For studies of the preparation of the proclamation, see Charles Walworth Alvord, *The Mississippi Valley in British Politics,* 2 vols., Cleveland, 1917, I, 157-210; R. A. Humphreys, "Lord Shelburne and the Proclamation of 1763," *English Historical Review,* XLIX (1934), 241-246.

[44] McCulloh to Pownall, June 2, 1763, Treasury Papers, I, 434, f. 123.

[45] 4 Geo. III, c. 34.

[46] Edmund S. and Helen M. Morgan, *The Stamp Act Crisis: Prologue to Revolution,* Chapel Hill, 1953, p. 31.

[47] Morgans, *Stamp Act Crisis,* pp. 34-39.

CHAPTER X

THE STAMP ACT, 1763-1765

i.

As they prepared the Sugar Act, it became obvious to Grenville and his colleagues in the Treasury that the old Navigation Acts, no matter how they were revised and enforced, could not raise enough revenue to support the troops stationed in America. Whately's most optimistic projection envisioned only a third of the annual cost in revenue. The Lords of the Treasury, while they worked at suppressing smuggling, enforcing customs collecting, and making laws yield revenue, also pondered what new taxes might safely be imposed to augment the revenues from America.

In July, 1763, Henry McCulloh, who had already suggested one if not two of Grenville's American measures, wrote to Charles Jenkinson with a suggestion for another, a stamp duty. Telling over "a brief state" of the taxes then in force in some of the colonies, McCulloh informed the Secretary to the Treasury that "a stamp duty on vellum and paper in America, at sixpence, twelvepence, and eighteenpence per sheet, would, at moderate computation, amount to upwards of sixty thousand sterling per annum; or, if extended to the West Indies, would produce double that sum."[1]

Stamp duties, of course, were nothing new; they had been used in England since the reign of William III. As employed in Great Britain, a moderate levy yielded an annual revenue of about a hundred thousand pounds.[2] The tax had several merits. It did not bear heavily on any particular segment of the population, and thus avoided complaints of discrimination or favoritism. The cost of collection was small in comparison with other types of levies, a feature which would appeal to the economy-minded Treasury. And, as McCulloh envisioned it, a stamp duty might yield a sizeable revenue in America.

Naturally, the idea of extending the stamp duties to the colonies had occurred to many people before 1763. Several had formally suggested it to the government. In 1739, for instance, Sir William Keith, the Governor of Pennsylvania, urged the idea on Walpole's ministry.[3] McCulloh himself had submitted a proposal for an American stamp tax to Halifax when the latter was President of the Board of Trade in Pitt's administration.[4] At the end of the Seven Years' War, Bute received suggestions on how to raise funds for the occupation of the newly conquered territories. Governor Dinwiddie of Virginia proposed in January, 1763, that an ideal method would be "a stamp duty on all bonds, obligations, and other instruments of writing...similar to that duty in Great Britain."[5]

Thus the idea which McCulloh suggested in July, 1763, was neither new nor the invention of any one person. It was the sort of idea, however, that Grenville and the Treasury were seeking: a fair tax which could make up the gap between the cost of the American troops and the revenue which the Sugar Act would raise. The Americans would at least come closer to paying the cost of their own defense.

There was, of course, the old requisition system, Parliament requesting of the colonial assemblies that they vote funds and levy troops for defense. But the recent war had proved that colonial assemblies, even when facing military threat, would not honor Parliamentary requisitions. Pitt had been able to persuade the colonial assemblies to raise troops and appropriate funds only by promising to reimburse them after the war. Even then some of the colonies refused to give any aid. Among the papers Grenville's Treasury examined in 1763 was a memorial by Arthur Dobbs, Governor of North Carolina, telling of his assembly's flat refusal in 1762 to vote troops requested by the ministry.[6]

Pontiac's rebellion simply reemphasized the worthlessness of the system in the eyes of the Treasury. When asked for troops to put down the uprising, only four colonies even made a gesture toward complying. New York, Connecticut, New Jersey, and Virginia felt threatened; the other colonies, most of them safer from attack, refused to grant any assistance whatever. Surely it was fruitless to expect the colonies to contribute to their defense in time of peace.[7]

Stamp duties, on the other hand, seemed the ideal answer. What group on either side of the Atlantic could offer substantial objections to them? The duty would almost administer itself; the stamps had only to be sold. By September 8 Jenkinson had convinced the Treasury Lords to pursue the idea. But how would a stamp duty operate in America? They knew roughly how the tax operated in Great Britain, though it was not their province to know the intricacies of the tax laws. But would such a duty operate the same way in America?

One man to consult on the matter was obviously Henry McCulloh. He had been resident in the colonies on three occasions, twice as a colonial customs official.8 But even so he was not acquainted with the detailed workings of stamp tax legislation. So on September 8 Jenkinson called in Thomas Cruwys, the solicitor to the Stamp Office. He could give legal and technical form to a bill based on McCulloh's knowledge of the colonies. Cruwys was instructed "to consult Mr. McCulloh on a plan for a general stamp law throughout America and the West Indies."9

Cruwys had already written out a plan of the bill when he met McCulloh on September 14. But he knew almost nothing about colonial conditions; not surprisingly, McCulloh's ideas were "quite different" from his. For three hours they talked, with Cruwys "taking down divers minutes." The next day, having drawn up a "full account" of his conference, he went to Sir James Calder, one of the Commissioners of the Stamp Duties. Then, with Calder's approval of his prospectus, he took the material to Grenville.10

With this much of the picture of a colonial stamp duty before them, the Treasury decided that the idea was worth developing. At their next meeting, September 22, they gave the project official form by directing Jenkinson to "write to the Commissioners of the Stamp Duties to prepare the draught of a bill to be presented to Parliament for extending the stamp duties to the colonies."11 The stamp office, of course, turned the job of drafting the bill over to Cruwys, with Calder as his immediate supervisor. Jenkinson retained final supervision, at one point insisting on keeping Cruwys on the job when Calder thought he had served his purpose.12

Grenville all this time was preoccupied with aligning his new ministry after the death of Egremont and with arranging for Wilkes's prosecution in Parliament. He paid little attention as Cruwys shaped what was to be the most momentous measure of his whole political career. The American duties, we should keep in mind, were minor matters of administration, safely delegated to underlings such as Cruwys, almost ignored by the historian. The stamp measure was almost never mentioned at this stage in the correspondence of the ministers. Much more important political questions absorbed their attention.

Sometimes, of course, Grenville had to turn his attention to the stamp duty, just as he had to deal with a myriad of other minutiae of administration. On October 10, Cruwys submitted a long list of articles which McCulloh proposed should be stamped and the duties on each, which Grenville perused and approved.13 Two days later, another list of "duties in general exclusive of Mr. McCulloh's" was drawn up, fourteen large sheets of three columns each, and a copy was submitted to the Treasury, which approved.[14] At the same time, the stamp office submitted Cruwys' rough draft of a form for the legislation. Some items were tentative, reflecting Cruwys' lack of familiarity with colonial conditions. For example, he suggested that "if there are any inns of chancery or universities or academies" in the colonies, a two shilling entrance fee might be charged, and that two pounds two shillings might be levied on entrance to an inn of court, "if there are any inns of court."[15] Yet such information as was lacking could easily be supplied. Whately informed Cruwys that his plan had been approved by the Treasury and gave him orders "to prepare the form of a law." At the same time, Grenville ordered McCulloh to "purchase all the American and Plantation laws forthwith" and take them to Cruwys, who said he would "want them," and to settle with Cruwys on the form of a bill.[16]

Both McCulloh and Cruwys now proceeded to draft bills, which were submitted to the Treasury on November 19. Three days later, Cruwys learned that his plan had been accepted and McCulloh's rejected. Perhaps the Treasury considered McCulloh's proposals too sweeping. He envisioned a revenue of £500,000 annually, and he proposed that the funds raised be applied to the support of troops, presents to the Indians, and the creation of a colonial civil list.[17] In any event, after November 22 the work proceeded along the lines which Cruwys had outlined.[18]

ii.

Although Cruwys and McCulloh continued to work on a stamp bill throughout the winter of 1763-64, Grenville decided when the time came to draw up his budget for 1764 that he would not include the measure. On March 9, after introducing the act revising the customs and commercial regulations, he presented a resolution: "Toward further defraying the said expenses [of the military establishment in the colonies] it may be proper to charge certain stamp duties in the said colonies and plantations."[19] The following day Cruwys was notified to cease work on the bill, as it would not be introduced that session.[20]

The reasons for Grenville's postponement of the Stamp Act are not entirely clear. Unfortunately, no record was made of his exact words to the Commons. Moreover, and still more important, the reports of those who were in the chamber and who wrote while memory of the speech was fresh do not agree in all material points. They express not what Grenville said but merely the impression his hearers formed of his general meaning. It seems fairly certain, however, that he told the Commons the postponement was owing, either in whole or in part, to the desire of the ministry to sound out the colonies on the matter of stamp duties and to hear their objections.21 Some objections Grenville had already heard. Colonial agents and others from the colonies were muttering that Parliament had no constitutional right to tax the colonies. Grenville headed these off at once; he "strongly urg'd not only the power but the right of Parliament to tax the colonys, and hop'd in Gods name as his expression was that none would dare dispute their sovereignty."22

Otherwise, however, he was not only ready to hear objections; he also told the Commons that he would be willing for the colonies to "suggest any better mode of taxation."23 Grenville doubtless meant by a "better mode" another tax by Parliament which would raise revenue and be acceptable to the colonies. The colonial agents, however, were to interpret the offer as an opportunity to return to the unsatisfactory requisition system.

Another reason which influenced the postponement was probably not mentioned by Grenville in his speech, but both Whately and Jenkinson were aware of it. Grenville felt that McCulloh was not sufficiently conversant with all of the colonies to serve as the sole guide for apportioning duties. Such reliance on the old speculator would be particularly dangerous when there might be questions of constitutional right involved. The tax, if it was to be imposed at all, would require careful study and consideration of all the facts. Therefore, Grenville told his secretaries if not the Commons that the act would be postponed until further information could be obtained from the colonies on the conditions there.24

Still a third reason suggests itself, though apparently none of the Treasury officials voiced it. Grenville was able to postpone the imposition because there was no immediate need for it. The ways and means for 1764 were already in sight without a stamp duty. If there was the least chance of trouble, it would cost nothing to go slowly on the measure and consider each step. The 1765 budget would be soon enough to include the stamp tax.

Was Grenville's offer to hear colonial objections sincere? If it was, was it not also curiously naive? Surely he was experienced enough to know that no tax measure would be accepted without grumbling. It would have been fatuous to hope to flatter the colonies while the secretaries gathered the necessary information. A year, he must have known, would allow additional time to concoct arguments to safeguard pocketbooks. Likely no popular assent was possible. But in a year's time, responsible leaders in the colonial assemblies could examine the alternatives and see that his stamp act was the most practical and least painful way of raising the necessary revenue. Assent—or at least absence of overt disapproval—by the legislatures might head off the arguments that Parliament could not tax unrepresented areas of the empire. Perhaps Grenville intended to set the precedent of consulting the legislatures before Parliament taxed them. If so, the result was to be far different.

Having announced (or implied) that he would receive the complaints of the colonies, Grenville received a delegation of colonial agents on May 17, 1764, to discuss the measure. The minister reiterated the arguments he had given the Commons. A stamp tax was the most equitable of all "inland" duties; it would require the fewest officials and cost the least to collect. When Israel Mauduit, brother of the Massachusetts agent, asked for a list of the duties to be employed, Grenville replied that the bill was "not yet thoroughly digested," but that in general it would follow the duties in force in Great Britain. He repeated his wish to consult the colonies and expressed his confidence that when they had "fully considered" the measure "upon its proper grounds and principles, and no other method should on the whole be suggested so proper for America in general, it would be a satisfaction to him to carry it into the House with their concurrence and approbation."

As for the requisition system, Grenville showed plainly that he had no intention of including it among the "better modes of taxation" he was inviting the colonies to suggest. He spoke of the difficulties which "would have attended" apportionment among twenty-six colonies on the continent and in the West Indies. There is no indication in the reports of the colonial agents that this was a change from his position in his March 9 speech.[25]

One important item of information the colonial agents did not report to their assemblies: the total revenue which the act was expected to raise in the colonies. Israel Mauduit apparently asked Grenville for this information in private, and though the minister was able to make no definite statements, he unofficially conjectured it "might probably raise from 80 to 100,000 pounds."[26] Why Mauduit failed to report this information to the Massachusetts assembly one can only guess. Perhaps he considered it unimportant, since it was only an unofficial estimate.

It appears that only two of the colonial assemblies even considered an alternative tax by Parliament. The Pennsylvania assembly told its agent in September, 1764, that it was considering a Parliamentary tax which would "fully preserve the rights of the Crown in America and the liberties of the colonists."27 What the plan was he did not say, however, and it was never approved by the assembly.

The Connecticut assembly apparently brought a plan to a more advanced stage, proposing a tax on the importation of slaves and on the exportation of furs. Such a tax, the assembly maintained, would be more suitable than a stamp duty. Those not wanting slaves could avoid the tax, while the duty on furs would bear most heavily on the portion of the population most directly protected by the standing army the tax would support. But this proposal also never advanced beyond the assembly-house walls.28

iii.

Meanwhile, in London, having halted Cruwys' work on March 10, Grenville turned his attention to other matters. Aside from the hearing which he gave the colonial agents on May 17, he was absorbed with questions of foreign relations and of personal differences within the ministry.29 In late June, tired and ill from endless personal squabbling with Sandwich, Halifax, and Bedford, he took a ten-day vacation at Wotton to rest. In these "regions of sleep and repose," as his bored secretary, Charles Lloyd, called them,30 Grenville was disturbed by a letter from Jenkinson, who was attending to the business of the Treasury in Westminster. Amid the news, domestic and foreign, there were "two or three points of Treasury business" which he wanted the minister to "turn" in his mind while he was in the country. One was the matter of a colonial stamp duty. The summer was slipping away, and nothing was being done toward preparing the measure.

"In the last session of Parliament," he wrote, "you assigned as a reason for not going on with the Stamp Act, that you waited only for further information on that subject. This having been said, should not Government appear to take some step for that purpose? I remember your objections to it; but I think the information may be procured in a manner to obviate those objections, and without it we may perhaps be accused of neglect."31

Grenville's repose was disturbed. "By the number of letters that were dispatched from hence yesterday Mr. Grenville might very well have imagined himself in Downing Street," wrote Lloyd. The minister was prevented from writing by an eye inflammation, but Lloyd reported that he would take the points Jenkinson had mentioned "under consideration" and discuss them when he returned to London.32 Yet Grenville was not greatly concerned about the stamp duty. In the many letters he dispatched from Wotton, including daily letters of business from July 4 until he returned to town on July 9, no mention was made of the matter.[33]

Soon thereafter, however, the ministers took steps to get the precise information on colonial documents and procedures which Grenville felt he needed to draft a stamp bill. On August 11, Lord Halifax, who as Secretary of State for the Southern Department had charge of American affairs, sent out circular letters to the governors of all the colonies asking for lists of all the documents normally used in business and legal transactions in each colony. The information, the letters stated, was to be used by the ministry in drawing up a stamp duty.[34]

About the same time, Whately wrote to his friend John Temple, the Surveyor-General of the Customs in Boston,[35] requesting more extensive information. There had been, he knew, a stamp duty in the Massachusetts colony. How much revenue did it produce, and what were the chief articles taxed? "What objections may be made to it, and what additional provisions must be made to those in force here?" Since duties on legal documents would make up a large proportion of the bill, as they did in England, Whately was naturally interested in colonial legal procedures. He was a barrister himself, having left his practice only to become Secretary to the Treasury in 1763. He wanted, if Temple would procure them, the names of the Massachusetts courts and "the respective instruments and proceedings used therein." "Have you any fines and recoveries," he asked. "Have you any inferior courts that hold plea to a certain sum only? What appeals do you have from one court to another? and are your writs the same as are mentioned in our stamp acts?" Grenville had directed that every fact be obtained and weighed, that no tax should be laid on blindly.

As summer faded and autumn advanced, the information poured in from the colonies. From the governor of every colony from Quebec to Trinidad came long lists of the documents and instruments used there.[37] Jenkinson and Whately at last were receiving the information they needed. On November 15, Whately called Cruwys, McCulloh, and Bretell, the Secretary to the Stamp Commissioners, to the Treasury offices to go over the new information and revise the lists of duties. For four hours that day and five hours the next they pored over the problem, settling each duty. The four men assembled again December 6 and considered additional duties suggested by the continuing influx of information.[38]

By December 7, 1764, the four men had completed their draft of the bill. Whately had written an explanation of the differences between the

British and the proposed American duties. On that day they attended a meeting of the Lords of the Treasury, and for four hours they discussed the measure before the Board. "The rates in England," Whately explained, "cannot be the measure for fixing those in the colonies; the same instruments are not always used in both countries and on other instruments a duty which is light in one may be heavy in the other." For that reason. duties on legal proceedings were lower than those in England, for they would frequently amount to "considerable sums paid by one person," and the people of the colonies were really poor. The "multiplicity" of their litigation, asserted Whately, was "the consequence of their poverty." Admiralty court assessments were higher in the colonies because smuggling involved such considerable sums of property, but a corporation tax had been omitted. There were few corporations in America, and those concentrated in a few colonies. If they were taxed, those colonies would object, "for nothing will occasion more murmuring than that one should be subject to a duty from which others are exempted." Duties on indentures were also omitted, for they would be "a grievous tax upon labor already too dear."39

In short, Whately had done all he could to make the stamp duties as equitable and as little burdensome to the colonists as possible. If the Treasury approved, he said, there was little left to do but to copy the table of rates and "draw the necessary clauses for management and distribution." Grenville and his associates, however, were still not willing to accept the measure as final. Cruwys came away from the meeting with two folio sheets of suggested changes which the Treasury felt would make the act more palatable to the Americans.40

The "general plan," however, was settled, and the remaining work on the bill was routine. The Treasury approved the amended bill on December 17, but small adjustments still had to be made. Until the end of January, 1?65, Cruwys was consulting with Whately and making "amendments and additions" to the draft.41 As a final measure of caution, Whately sent a copy of the bill to Charles Yorke in February to make certain that everything was in legal order. The former Attorney-General had no complaints.42 The drafting of the Stamp Act was complete.

iv.

The care which the Treasury and its agents bestowed on preparing the details of the stamp duty was well advised, for discussion of the power of Parliament to tax the unrepresented colonies had grown both heated and widespread during the summer and autumn of 1764. Grenville had been somewhat disturbed in March by the discussion of the rights of Parliament. His anxiety, indeed, had been enough to cause him to take the precautions of postponing the act and giving it a year's additional consideration. When Jenkinson devised the method of eliciting information from the colonies, he had consented to go on with the preparation, but the constitutional question still troubled him. By late November, the newspapers learned that the ministers were considering giving the colonies representation in the House of Commons.[43] The representatives, so the notices ran, would be delegates of the several assemblies in the colonies, and their votes would be restricted to issues which "immediately concern[ed] the interest of America only."[44] The project was soon abandoned, however, apparently because Grenville came to realize that such a move would never be approved by the Commons.[45]

But if the colonies were not to be given some sort of representation, was it safe to impose taxes on them? Grenville and the Treasury began to study with minute care Parliament's taxing power. A detailed list of all the acts of Parliament which had imposed duties of any sort on the colonies from the reign of Charles II through 1764 was prepared and examined by the Treasury.[46] Likewise, all the acts "relating to imports and exports to and from the plantations and to the shipping employed there" were considered by the Board.[47] The charters of all the colonies and other documents "establishing internal regulations in the plantations" were examined for their bearing on the right of taxation.[48] And in addition to the question of whether or not they had the power to tax the colonies, the Lords of the Treasury pondered that of whether the colonies were able to bear the tax. Lists were compiled of the debts which each colony had incurred during the war, of how much had been paid and how much remained to be paid on each, and of the arrangements made for paying off the debts and how long it was expected to take. The expenses of each of the colonies were computed, and the measures by which they were met were enumerated.[49]

It was probably about this time that Jenkinson drew up for the Treasury's perusal a memorandum on the advisability of the act from a logical and constitutional viewpoint. The measure, he maintained, was both expedient and just. "All who are entitled to protection ought equally to bear the burthen of it, and...they who have the management of that protection can be the only judges of what that burthen should be." Even when added to the revenue from the Sugar Act, the stamp duty still would not defray the cost of protecting America. As for the colonists' contention against taxation without representation, Jenkinson considered it untenable. Taxation of the colonies by Parliament was a matter of long-established precedent; the Post Office Act (9 Anne), the Greenwich Hospital Act (2 George II), and the Molasses Act (6 George II) were instances. Furthermore, members of Parliament did not represent particular places, but "the dominions of the Crown of Great Britain at large." The Americans complained that a stamp duty would subvert the power of the colonial assemblies, but Jenkinson asserted that there would be no such result. The act would merely exercise a function of which the colonial assemblies were incapable, that of providing for the common defense of the whole group. Nevertheless, he thought it would be "discreet" if Parliament would assure the colonies that it would not exercise its power where the assemblies were competent. And even if it should, surely the Americans could never prefer "these little legislatures" to "the immediate protection of the Parliament of Great Britain," which was "more valuable, more conducive to the security of their liberty and their propertys than the protection of their own legislatures."[50] This was, no doubt, what the Lords of the Treasury wished to hear, but it says little for Jenkinson's understanding of the colonial mind!

Grenville also sought advice from the legal experts of the realm. No doubt he discussed the matter long and earnestly with Northington, the Lord Chancellor. On December 23, he had a conversation with Lord Mansfield, which prompted the Lord Chief Justice also to look into the matter. The following day he wrote Grenville not only affirming that Parliamentary sovereignty extended unquestionably to colonial taxation, but even suggesting that he have someone investigate "the origin of the power of the colonies to tax themselves and raise money at all."[51] Such a view was, of course, extreme; perhaps it should have been a signal to Grenville that the judges were not necessarily the safest counsellors on such sensitive issues. Nevertheless, Grenville felt justified in proceeding with his plans to introduce the bill. With study, advice, and mature consideration to back him, he made up his mind to go on in spite of the arguments of the colonists.

In late December and throughout January, while Cruwys and Whately labored, it was rumored in the newspapers that the ministry had "totally laid aside" the idea of a stamp duty.[52] The colonial agents, however, were better informed. Advised of the intention of the ministers, they were busy meeting and consulting "as to the mode and measure of opposition to be given to the Stamp Bill." All had instructions "to support the rights and privileges of the Colonies and to dispute, as it were, the power of

Parliament." Most of the colonies had signified to their agents their will-
ingness to comply with "proper requisitions" from London, and the
agents felt that if Grenville and the administration knew of their intention
it might help "to ward off the intended blow." Accordingly, they selected
a delegation of four of their number, Richard Jackson, Benjamin
Franklin, Jared Ingersoll, and Charles Garth, to call upon the minister.

The meeting which resulted on February 2, 1765, amounted only to
polite fencing between the minister and the agents, with neither party giving an inch of its position. Grenville gave them a "full hearing" and spoke
"with great tenderness and regard for the happiness of the Colonies." He
assured the agents that he was eager to pursue only such measures as
would give "universal satisfaction," but that he was obliged to bring the
resolution of the preceding March before the Commons. If the House
thought any other method of raising the money "more eligible," he
assured them that he would not "object to it." Regarding the requisition
system, however, he was discouraging. The agents assured that "uneasiness and jealousies" might be avoided and the money more easily collected by following methods the colonies were accustomed to. But
Grenville, remembering the wartime experience with requisitions, asked
if the colonies would be able to agree to the "proportions each colony
should raise." With twenty-six colonies, some of them newly acquired,
the apportionment of quotas would be certain to raise "uneasiness and
jealousies" too. The agents admitted that there would be no agreement
among the colonies, and Grenville asserted that no one in London had
sufficient information to apportion quotas. (He might have added also
that no one had sufficient gall!)

Richard Jackson, who was also Grenville's Secretary to the Exchequer,
was agent for Connecticut and Pennsylvania; he made the more material
objection that the stamp measure would subvert the powers of the colonial assemblies. Grenville, having already satisfied his own mind on this
point, said that "no such thing was intended nor would he believed take
place."[53]

Obviously nothing was to be gained by such negotiations. The agents
were convinced that no means of raising a revenue would do except a
colonial levy on the requisition principle, while Grenville was equally
convinced that the requisition system would not work and that a stamp
duty was the best and fairest means of gaining the required revenue. The
positions were irreconcilable. Apparently the agents recognized the fact,
for no more negotiations were attempted. Four days later, Grenville introduced the stamp bill in the House of Commons.

v.

The Parliamentary opposition, meanwhile, had declined even further in strength since the end of the 1764 session. A lack of leadership had been evident in the debates on the Sugar Act. Few among the opposition saw possibilities in the American measures; the Cambridge University election had been of more consequence than debating Grenville's budget.[54] It appeared futile to oppose measures which were so popular in the House. The new session offered no better prospect. There would be, said Townshend, "no general warrants to arraign, no extraordinary measures, and no grounds of debate but the army, the navy, and the several disputable speculations which may occur about the state of the debt and the condition of the public credit." When Parliament met again, he asserted, the opposition would have declined greatly in strength.[55]

Nevertheless, the leaders of the opposition met in May at Newcastle's estate at Claremont to draw up a plan of action for the 1765 session. A program was drafted and unanimously approved, but the issues it outlined envisioned little success. Another debate on general warrants, an attack on dismissing officers for their votes in Parliament, and criticism of popular foreign and domestic policies did not promise strong support. When Parliament, which had been prorogued until June, was further prorogued until January, what enthusiasm there was for the plans evaporated.[56]

By autumn it was evident, as Lord Barrington observed to another of Grenville's supporters, that the opposition's leadership had "neither abilities nor union."[57] By January, almost all their leaders were either disillusioned, disaffected, or dead: Pitt, Yorke, Townshend, Hardwicke, Devonshire. The severest loss was Pitt. The "great commoner" had been offended that the opposition allowed Grenville's adverse comments on his conduct of the war to go unchallenged in the Commons. As early as June he had been reported as saying that "all opposition was to no purpose." He would "oppose all measures he thought wrong, whoever were the ministers; and let George Grenville do right, he would support him."[58] Grenville heard about the same time that Pitt was talking in friendly tones about the ministry and disclaiming the opposition. He even "talked as if he wished to act in office with the Government, and...his language to Mr. Grenville was, that he was necessary to any Administration, and had conducted the King's business wisely through the last session of Parliament."[59]

Pitt, indeed, seemed to feel that the King might at any moment call him back to head the ministry, and he was keeping himself ready and unattached. He knew of no one in the opposition, he said, who "would join with him or act upon his plan and principle if there was to be a change of administration."[60] By August he was displaying outright hostility to Townshend and Yorke, although he was still on friendly terms with the other opposition leaders.[61] In October, however, Pitt definitely repudiated all connections with the minority and declared himself to be single and determined to act "under the obligation of principles, not by the force of any particular bargains."[62]

Charles Yorke, meanwhile, made himself unacceptable to the remainder of the opposition, particularly the City elements, by patronizing a certain Dr. Hay, a member of the Commons, who made a violent attack on the Common Council of the City during the 1764 session. Pitt, many of whose warmest supporters were City merchants, repudiated Yorke and his actions, and Newcastle, embarrassed, gave him little support. Yorke, in turn, refused to pledge his support to the opposition,[63] and by mid-November was negotiating with Grenville and Northington for one of the government legal offices, either Attorney-General or Master of the Rolls.[64] Although he did not accept either office—with characteristic irresolution he wavered for days before refusing— he did accept a patent of precedence over the Solicitor-General "as a mark of the King's personal grace...for his past services."[65] There were no "stipulations for the future," but Yorke had virtually pledged himself to the support of the ministry.

Townshend was also tired of the political wilderness. Deeply offended because his pamphlet, *A Defense of the Minority,* was received unenthusiastically by the opposition, he made overtures to Grenville even before the debates on general warrants, expressing eagerness to serve with Grenville and Halifax, though "he did not like the rest of the Administration."[66] In June, after the meeting at Claremont, he sent word to Jenkinson that he was a "free man, bound to no party system."[67] In November he was still trying. "With respect to himself," wrote Jenkinson, "Mr. Townshend said that the Pay Office, and being a Cabinet Councillor (which he was, he said, before) would satisfy him."[68] The ministers neither assented nor refused, and Townshend was kept dangling. In such a state, he was unlikely to cause much disquiet in the House of Commons!

Indeed, the opposition virtually had no leadership in the Commons other than Beckford and his noisy City group. Both Hardwicke and Devonshire had died during the previous year. Newcastle and Cumberland, disillusioned with opposition, were toying with the notion of approaching Bedford about an alliance to form a new ministry.[69]

Cumberland suggested that they abandon all hope of Pitt and coalesce with the "Bloomsbury Gang." Newcastle, however, feared an alliance of Pitt and Bute should they take such a course, and he finally chose to go on hoping for Pitt's cooperation.[70] Cumberland at this point gave up on opposition, and Newcastle resolved to attend the House of Lords as little as possible during the coming session.[71] Rockingham, leader of the younger opposition set, was optimistic, but he was too shy and halting a speaker to lead opposition in debate.

Meanwhile, the repressive measures of the ministry had put an effective bridle on the press as an instrument of opposition or even discussion of public policy.[73] Alderman Sir William Baker, a North American merchant and one of Beckford's City faction in the Commons, met with other members of his group in November to discuss setting up a weekly sheet in the Temple-Wilkes style. They found, however, that no one was willing to take the risk of writing for the opposition except the ineffective Walpole. "There is such a backwardness, or rather shyness, in the others who can write," John Almon observed to Temple, "that nothing can be done." Moreover, the publisher reported that a "terrible panic" had "seized all the printers and publishers both in and out of the City."[74] Pamphlets continued to appear against general warrants, the budget, and other issues of ministerial policy, but the opposition weeklies were effectively silenced.[75] This meant that the Stamp Act, certainly the most fateful measure of Grenville's administration, would be introduced and debated with little organized discussion in the press.

vi.

It was thus a subdued and docile House of Commons which Grenville reminded on February 6, 1765, of the resolution to lay a stamp duty on the American colonies. In a "pretty lengthy speech," he explained the measure in an "able" and "candid" manner. The necessity of levying it and the objections which had been offered to it were examined and discussed, the minister urging the House to give the bill "a most serious and cool consideration" and not be influenced by discussions going on "out of doors." In the absence of propaganda weeklies, opponents of American taxation hit upon the technique of writing anonymous letters to the daily papers. The letters, bearing American datelines but likely written by colonial agents in London, foretold dire consequences which a stamp duty would have. But is seems that none of their arguments were given much credence by the House.

Those who spoke against the bill were mainly limited to the City contingent and their allies and to the colonial agents who had seats in the Commons. Beckford, Richard Jackson, Sir William Meredith, Colonel Isaac Barre, "and some others" spoke. Barre, an Irishman who had served with the army in America, flashed thunder and lightning as he praised the "sons of liberty" in America who had defended and would still defend their liberties. Beckford, however, was the only speaker to question the power of Parliament to tax the colonies.

Despite their vehemence, however, the group in opposition to the bill was small. When toward midnight they forced a division on a motion to adjourn the debate, they were able to muster only forty-nine votes against 245 for the government. Charles Garth informed the South Carolina colony that he would try to bring in colonial petitions against the act when it was debated in committee, but he warned that the numbers of the division augured little success for the attempt. The power of Parliament to tax the colonies had been asserted by the minister, he wrote, and was "so universally agreed to that no petition disputing it will be received."[76]

Garth's prediction proved correct. When the act was read the first time before the House in Committee of Ways and Means, February 13, Sir William Meredith offered a petition of the Virginia assembly against the bill. When he had stated the contents of it, a debate arose as to whether it should be received or rejected. Contention centered around a precedent of 1732 against receiving petitions on revenue bills. But the ministers declared also that no petition could be received "that should hint at questioning the supremacy and authority of Parliament to impose taxes in every part of the British Dominions." At length the debate ended with the petition's being rejected without a division. Jackson and Garth also tried to bring in petitions, but they met the same fate. On February 15 the act was read a second time and committed to the Committee of Supply.[77]

The main questions concerning the bill were thus settled. The House would not accept the petitions against it because they were on the wrong sort of points; they did not object to features of the bill itself or offer alternative measures, but questioned the power of Parliament itself. When the act came to its third reading, these issues were already settled, and the bill was sent on without opposition to the Lords. In that House, according to the *Parliamentary History,* it passed "without debate, division, or protest."[78] On March 22 it received the royal assent by commission, since George III at the time was suffering an attack of the malady which eventually left him mad. If the act was a mistake, the King was not to blame.

vii.

The Stamp Act has sometimes been treated as an act which applied only to the thirteen continental colonies which later revolted, but such an impression is mistaken. It applied as well to Newfoundland, the Canadian provinces, the Floridas, and the West Indies. Likewise the standard American accounts emphasize the duty which the act imposed on court papers, newspapers, almanacs, pamphlets, land grants, advertisements, liquor licenses, and commissions of all kinds. That these duties were important is undeniable. They were not, however, either the chief source of revenue or the main cause of irritation and resentment among the colonists. They were merely troublesome, not really burdensome. Their importance in arousing resistance lies in the fact that they extended irritation to large segments of the population, which allowed those who really bore the burden to rouse them to action in a cause in which their own economic interests were slight.

The group which bore the heaviest burden of stamp duties were the merchants and shippers. One clause levied the bulk of the burden imposed on them, a clause calling for duties on "any note or bill of lading which shall be signed for any kind of goods, wares, or merchandise to be exported from, or any cocket or clearance granted within the said colonies or plantations."79 That the real burden of the stamp duty was intended to fall upon trade and shipping through this clause is shown by the long list of ships' and merchants' papers that had to pay a duty, by the use of the navy and customs officers provided to enforce the act (which spread hostility against the navy and customs officers to others besides the New England distilling interests), and by the concentration of the supplies of stamps not necessarily in the areas of greatest population, but in those of greatest ocean trade.80 In addition to this clause, the duties on negotiable paper put new and heavy expense on credit transactions, and since nearly all colonial shipping business was done on credit this put another heavy burden on the merchants and shippers.

Unfortunately for the home government, these interests were among the most articulate and influential in the colonies. They were, moreover, not solely American; the North American and West Indian merchants in London and other British ports came in for a heavy share, probably the bulk, of the burden of these duties. Here is the explanation for the fact that the City merchants led by Beckford, Baker, and Meredith opposed the Stamp Act in Parliament. It imposed a direct burden of taxation on their own trade! This was the group which had financed the *Monitor;* had led in the support of Wilkes, Temple, and Pitt; and had opposed the Grenville ministry on every one of its major measures. It should have surprised no one that this group would lead opposition to the act once it was passed and perhaps encourage and foster protest in the colonies.

Nevertheless it was generally felt in March, 1765, that Grenville had spared no efforts to make the act palatable to the Americans. Jared Ingersoll, agent for Connecticut, wrote that the minister had made every effort "to hear patiently, to listen attentively to the reasonings [of the Americans] and to determine at least seemingly with coolness and upon principle the several measures which are resolved upon."[81] "I see Mr. Grenville's credit gains every day," Newcastle observed in late March, "notwithstanding Sir William Baker's *private opinion* that he is ignorant and mistaken."[82] "The opposition is dwindling down to nothing. and Mr. Grenville...is the man of consequence, and...does the business. Let them say what they will, Mr. Grenville, I say, will have *champ libre,* and nobody will oppose him."[83]

Grenville enhanced his reputation even further in the Commons on March 28 when he announced that the Bank, on the security of the land tax, French war indemnities, and sinking fund surplus provided for in the budget, had arranged to lend the Treasury £1,700,000 at three percent interest. With this, Grenville moved that one-fourth of the redeemable debt at four percent be paid off. Reducing the interest on that portion of the national debt would further save the Treasury money. "This will certainly *sound* well," observed George Onslow, one of Newcastle's followers, "tho' it is not near so great a thing as you may be sure G. Grenville made of it."[84] Meanwhile, the details of administration of the Stamp Act had to be arranged before the act went into effect on November 1. The newspapers were soon advertising that "young gentlemen" would be appointed as stamp collectors in America as soon as "proper materials" could be prepared. At this, Nathaniel Cotton, a clergyman friend of Grenville's who had sailed to America as a naval chaplain, wrote the minister on March 30 suggesting a further step to court the acquiescence of the Americans to the Stamp Act. The colonists, he said, were "rather out of sorts" because of the duties Grenville had levied. "In order to make the Stamp Act more eligible and more cordially received," Cotton suggested that "some of the appointments should take place among themselves." This would "have a tendency to engage them more heartily in it, when they enjoy a salary under the Crown." When the "principal inhabitants" found that "they or their sons" might benefit from appointments, they would "chearfully act in concert with those who are sent from hence."[85]

The stamp collector was to receive three hundred pounds a year, which was considered a genteel salary. Grenville might have used the appointments to increase his influence among the members of Parliament. Cotton's suggestion seemed so sensible, however, that Grenville decided he would select the whole number of stamp collectors from among the colonists. Surely this measure would foster acceptance of the act. When the news was sent out, applications poured in from the colonies. Throughout May and June the Lords of the Treasury were occupied in selecting suitable collectors. The task was not completed until the last meeting of Grenville's Treasury, when two collectors and six inspectors of stamps were appointed.[86] It was also provided, at the suggestion of the Commissioners of the Customs, that the collectors should have eight percent of all monies collected under the act for "themselves, their servants, and their under-distributors."[87] The Treasury was trying to make sure the colonial stamp collectors were interested in their work!

The Treasury dealt with one more objectionable feature of the act before Grenville left office. Jenkinson and Whately had received complaints from the colonies that the act would drain precious cash out of the colonies. The money, of course, was to be spent in the colonies to pay for supplies for the troops there. Nevertheless, it was to be turned in to the Exchequer, and few Americans troubled to look beyond that fact.[88] Jenkinson therefore took steps in April, 1765, to prevent the revenue's ever leaving American shores. "It concerns nobody but the Receiver General of the Customs and the persons who have contracted to remit the pay of the troops," he told Grenville. It was proper, he said, that directions be given by a minute of the Treasury, and he accordingly drew up such a minute for the Treasury's approval.[89] Thus on July 9, while finishing up the last business of the Treasury, Grenville and his board read Jenkinson's proposal and gave their directive. The duties, they commanded, should not be remitted into the Exchequer but should be paid to the Deputy Paymaster in America "to be immediately applied to defray the subsistence of the troops and any military expenses incurred in the colonies."[90] Surely now there could be no complaints!

viii.

One more major act concerning America remained for the Grenville administration to enact after Parliament approved the Stamp Act. In April, 1765, with Grenville as Newcastle predicted having *champ libre,* the ministers pushed through Parliament a measure calling for additions to the mutiny act of that session to provide for the quartering of troops in the colonies. His Majesty's troops, the act provided, were to be quartered in barracks furnished by the colonies, and in inns, in ale-houses, and in other public places of lodging at the expense of the colonial governments when barracks were not available. In the event that neither barracks nor public houses proved sufficient, then "and upon no other account" the governor and council of the respective colonies might appoint agents to select "such and so many uninhabited houses, outhouses, barns, and other buildings, as shall be necessary." In addition, the colonies were to furnish certain necessary utensils and certain stapes such as salt, vinegar, and rum or beer.[91]

The measure was in line with the ministerial policy of having the colonies contribute to the support of the army which was to protect them. Probably it was designed to fill the gap between the cost of the troops and the revenue from American duties. It appears to have been mainly the production of Halifax and Welbore Ellis, the Secretary at War, to whom General Gage had applied for the changes in order to house his soldiers. Grenville had serious objections to the idea of quartering soldiers in private homes. The idea, proposed by Halifax and Ellis, seemed to Grenville "by far the most likely" of the American measures "to create difficulties and uneasiness, and therefore ought certainly to be thoroughly weighed and considered before any step is taken in it." "The quartering of soldiers upon the people against their wills," he advised the King, "is declared by the petition of right to be contrary to law."[93] Hence care was to be taken to place the administration of the quartering of troops strictly in the hands of the colonists and to avoid entirely the stationing of men in private, inhabited homes. Moreover, it was intended that the act would encourage the building of barracks in which to house troops, thus furthering the project which the colonies had suggested throught their agents, that of taxing themselves to support the army.

ix.

It is an obvious fact that Grenville's American measures failed in their objective of integrating the colonies into a scheme of British imperial taxation. To say that his measures were not adjusted to the realities of the time is to state the self-evident, in view of the results which followed. But while the defects of the program are patent to the observer of today, they were hardly so obvious in the spring of 1765. Grenville had followed a course which seemed to him, to the government's supporters, to most of the opposition, and even to the colonial agents a fair if not a wise one. He had consulted the opinion of Parliament and found it overwhelmingly in his favor. He had sought the consent of the colonies, and while it was not forthcoming, there were definite indications that the measures would be passively accepted as necessary evils. One thing seems clear: while several of the measures of colonial regulation and taxation caused objection and complaint in the colonies, it was only with the enactment of a tax which bore heavily upon influential elements in both the colonies and Great Britain, elements which were already in opposition to the government at Westminster, that there grew up an organized, effective resistance to Parliamentary measures in America. If one measure can be singled out as the starting point of the resistance movement which led to revolution, it must be the Stamp Act.

NOTES

CHAPTER X

[1] McCulloh to Jenkinson, July 5, 1763, *Grenville Papers,* II. 374n.

[2] Survey of the stamp duties in Great Britain, n.d., Treasury Papers, I, 430, f. 80.

[3] William Edward Hartpole Lecky, *History of England in the Eighteenth Century,* Second Edition, 8 vols., New York, 1888-1890, II, 341.

[4] McCulloh to Newcastle, ——, 1757, Newcastle MSS., Add. MSS. 32874, ff. 308-310.

[5] Dinwiddie's suggestions "Concerning the settlements in North America," January 17, 1763, Liverpool MSS., Add. MSS. 38308, ff. 297-301.

[6] Treasury Papers, I, 433, f. 332.

[7] Charles R. Ritcheson suggests that Grenville may have questioned the constitutionality of the requisition system, since it provided revenue for the Crown independently of Parliament. See *British Politics and the American Revolution,* Norman, Oklahoma, 1954, pp. 11-12. This idea and Ritcheson's contention that Grenville had formulated and was operating on a consistent plan of imperial organization in his American measures finds little or no support in Grenville's papers. However, cf. Chapter IX, note 6.

[8] For a study of McCulloh and his American ventures, see Charles G. Sellers, Jr., "Private Profits and British Colonial Policy: the Speculations of Henry McCulloh," *William and Mary Quarterly,* Third Series, VIII (1951), 535-551.

[9] List of charges for services in drafting the American stamp bill, unsigned, presented to the Treasury October 29, 1765, Hardwicke MSS., Add. MSS. 35911, f. 18.

[10] List of charges, October 29, 1765, Hardwicke MSS., Add. MSS. 35911, f. 18.

[11] Treasury minute, September 22, 1763, Treasury Papers, XXIX, 35, f. 15; Jenkinson to Commissioners of the Stamp Duties, September 23, 1763, Rockingham MSS. 8, f. 3.

[12] List of charges, October 29, 1765, Hardwicke MSS., Add. MSS. 35911, f. 19.

[13] List of articles and duties, Hardwicke MSS., Add. MSS. 35910, ff. 136-159.

[14] List of charges, October 29, 1765, Hardwicke MSS., Add. MSS. 35911, f. 19.

[15] "Mr. Cruwys's scheme for an American stamp bill persuant to the Commissioners of Stamps order dated 30th Sept.1763," Hardwicke MSS., Add. MSS. 36226, ff. 353-356.

[16] List of charges, October 29, 1765, Hardwicke MSS., Add. MSS. 35911, f. 19.

[17] Minutes by Cruwys on a conversation with McCulloh, October 12, 1763; list of articles proposed by McCulloh to be taxed, October 10, 1763; "Mr. McCulloh's preamble clause of appriation *[sic]*," November 9, 1763, Hardwicke MSS., Add. MSS. 35910, ff. 136-159, 205.

[18] List of charges, October 29, 1765, Hardwicke MSS., Add. MSS. 35911, ff. 20-21.

[19] *Commons Journals,* XXIX, 935.

[20] List of charges, October 29, 1765, Hardwicke MSS., Add. MSS. 35911, f. 22.

[21] Cecilius Calvert to Horatio Sharpe, March 11, 1764, *Archives of Maryland,* XIV, 144); Charles Garth to a South Carolina committee of correspondence, June 5, 1764, Lewis B. Namier, "Charles Garth, Agent for South Carolina," *English Historical Review,* LIV (1939), 646. See Morgans, *Stamp Act Crisis,* and "The Postponement of the Stamp Act," *William and Mary Quarterly,* third series, VII (1950), 359-360.

[22] Eliphet Dyer to Jared Ungersoll, April 14, 1764, *Papers of the New Haven Historical Society,* 9 vols., New Haven, 1865-1918, IX, 291.

[23] Whately to Ingersoll, n.d. (late April, 1764), *New Haven Society Papers,* IX, 294.

[24] Jenkinson to Grenville, July 2, 1764, *Grenville Papers,* II, 373; Whately to Ingersoll, n.d. (late April, 1764), *New Haven Society Papers,* IX, 294.

[25] Garth to a South Carolina committee of correspondence, June 5, 1764, Namier, "Garth," *English Historical Review,* LIV, 646-647; Jasper Mauduit to the Massachusetts assembly, May 26, 1764, Massachuestts Archives, XXII, 375, quoted in Morgan, "Postponement," pp. 359-360; MS. by Israel Mauduit, n.d., *Jenkinson Papers,* pp. 306-307.

[26] *Jenkinson Papers,* p. 305.

[27] Benjamin Franklin to Richard Jackson, September 22, 1764, *Pennsylvania Archives,* Harrisburg, 1852 ff., Eighth Series, VII, 5644.

[28] *Public Records of the Colony of Connecticut,* 15 vols., Hartford, 1850-1890, XII, 670.

[29] See Grenville's diary, *Grenville Papers,* II, 495-504, and below, Chapter XI.

[30] Lloyd to Jenkinson, June 30, 1764, *Jenkinson Papers,* p. 304.

[31] July 2, 1764, *Grenville Papers,* II, 372-375.

[32] To Jenkinson, July 3, 1764, *Jenkinson Papers,* pp. 307-308.

[33] Grenville Letter Book, Stowe MSS.

[34] For example, Halifax to Sharpe, August 11, 1764, *Archives of Maryland,* XIV, 108-109.

[35] Temple (1732-1798) was a distant cousin of Grenville's, born in Boston of parents who were both of the younger line of Stowe Temples. Grenville used his influence in 1760 to obtain for Temple the position of Surveyor-General of the Customs for the northern district of America. See *Coll. of Mass. Hist. Soc.,* Sixth Series, IX, xv.

[36] Whately to Temple, August 14, 1764, *Coll. of Mass. Hist. Soc.,* IX, 22-23.

[37] Colonial governors to Halifax, October 14-November 26, 1764, Treasury Papers, I, 430, ff. 175-291.

[38] List of charges, October 29, 1765, Hardwicke MSS., Add. MSS. 35911, f. 22.

[39] Preamble to Whately's bill, submitted December 7, 1764, Hardwicke MSS., Add. MSS. 35910, ff. 311-323.

[40] Minutes by Cruwys, December 7, 1764, Hardwicke MSS., Add. MSS. 36226, ff. 373-374; Whately's bill, December 7, 1764, Hardwicke MSS., Add. MSS. 35910, f. 23.

[41] List of charges, October 29, 1765, Hardwicke MSS., Add. MSS. 35911 ff. 25-29

[42] Whately to Yorke, February 16, 1765, Hardwicke MSS., Add. MSS. 35911, f. 1; Yorke to Whately, February 17, 1765, Murray MSS.

[43] *St. James's Chronicle,* November 24-27, 1764.

[44] *London Evening Post,* December 4-6, 1764.

[45] William Knox, *Extra Official State Papers,* 2 vols., London, 1789, II, 31.

[46] Treasury Papers, I, 433, ff. 360-365.

[47] Treasury Papers, I, 433, ff. 366-373.

[48] Treasury Papers, I, 433, ff. 374-379.

[49] Treasury Papers, I, 433, ff. 380-383, 402.

[50] Memorandum by Jenkinson, n.d., Liverpool MSS., Add. MSS. 38339, ff. 131-135.

[51] *Grenville Papers,* II, 478.

[52] *Westminster Journal,* December 22, 1764; *London Evening Post,* January 24-26, 1765; *Gazeteer and New Daily Advertiser,* January 28, 1765.

[53] Ingersoll to Fitch, February 11, 1765, *Collections of the Connecticut Historical Society,* Hartford, 1860 ff., XVIII, 324-325; Garth to a South Carolina Committee of Correspondence, February 8, 1765, Namier, "Garth," *English Historical Review,* LIV, 649.

[54] See above, pp. 170-171.

[55] Townshend to Newcastle, April 30, 1764, Newcastle MSS, Add. MSS. 32958, f. 248.

[56] Newcastle to Legge, May 7, 1764, Newcastle MSS., Add. MSS. 32958, f. 307.

[57] To Buckinghamshire, September 24, 1764, Historical Manuscripts Commission, *Report on the Manuscripts of the Marquess of Lothian Preserved at Blickling Hall, Norfolk,* London, 1905, p. 252.

[58] Townshend to Newcastle, April 28, 1764; Newcastle to John White, June 19, 1764, Newcastle MSS., Add. MSS. 32958, f. 26; 32960, f. 17.

[59] Grenville's diary, *Grenville Papers,* II, 504.

[60] Newcastle to White, June 19, 1764, Newcastle MSS., Add. MSS. 32960, f. 17.

[61] Memorandum by Newcastle, August 12, 1764, Newcastle MSS., Add. MSS. 32961, f. 187.

[62] Pitt to Newcastle, October —, 1764, *Pitt Correspondence,* II, 296.

[63] Newcastle to Cumberland, May 5, 1764; Newcastle to Lord John Cavendish, August 21, 22, 1764, Newcastle MSS., Add. MSS. 32958, f. 307; 32961, ff. 291, 309.

[64] Correspondence between Northington and Grenville, November 16-26, 1764, *Grenville Papers,* II, 461-470.

[65] Hay to Grenville, November 26, 1764, *Grenville Papers,* II, 470.

[66] Grenville's diary, *Grenville Papers,* II, 482.

[67] John Bindley to Jenkinson, June 13, 1764, *Jenkinson Papers,* p.302.

[68] Jenkinson to Grenville, November 20, 1764, *Grenville Papers,* II, 465.

[69] Bedford was at odds with Grenville and Halifax over the amount of time which France was to be allowed to pay the sums she owed Britain under the Peace of Paris. See Grenville's diary, *Grenville Papers,* II, 502, 510-515; Sackville to Townshend, n.d., *Stopford-Sackville MSS.,* 61.

[70] Minute by Newcastle on a conversation with Cumberland, November 14, 1764, Newcastle MSS., Add. MSS. 32963, f. 365.

[71] Newcastle to the Bishop of Norwich, March 21, 1765, Add. MSS. 32966, f. 82.

[72] Charles Watson-Wentworth, second Marquis of Rockingham (1730-1782) was by now the acknowledged lieutenant of Newcastle in their faction of the opposition.

[73] See above, pp. 159-160.

[74] Almon to Temple, November 12, 1764, *Grenville Papers,* II, 457-460.

[75] On the pamphlet warfare, see Walpole, *George III,* II, 3-9.

[76] Ingersoll to Fitch, February 11, 1765, *New Haven Society Papers,* IX, 309-312; Garth to a South Carolina committee of correspondence, February 8, 1765, Namier, "Garth," *English Historicial Review,* LIV, 650.

[77] Garth to a South Carolina committee of correspondence, February 17, 1765, Namier, "Garth," *English Historical Review,* LIV, 650-651; *Commons Journals,* XXX, 121, 148.

[78] XVI, 40. The *Parliamentary History* probably relies for its information on a speech of Edmund Burke in 1776, which considerably distorts the picture of the debates in the Commons. No evidence yet appears to contradict the assertion that there was no debate in the Lords.

[79] 5 George III, c. 12.

[80] See Dickerson, *Navigation Acts,* pp. 191-192.

[81] Ingersoll to Fitch, March 6, 1765, *New Haven Society Papers,* IX, 319.

[82] Newcastle to Onslow, March 21, 1765, Newcastle MSS., Add. MSS. 32966, f. 79.

[83] Newcastle to Rockingham, March 26, 1765, Newcastle MSS., Add. MSS. 32966, f. 110.

[84] Onslow to Newcastle, March 28, 1765, Newcastle MSS., Add. MSS. 32966, f. 115.

[85] Murray MSS.

[86] Treasury minute, n.d. (July, 1765), Rockingham MSS., 28.

[87] Treasury minute, July 5, 1765, Rockingham MSS., 28.

[88] Benjamin Hollowell to Jenkinson, November 20, 1764, *Jenkinson Papers,* p. 340; Temple to Whatley, September 10, 1764, *Coll. of Mass. Hist. Soc.,* Sixth Series, IX, 26.

[89] Jenkinson to Grenville, April 13, 1765, *Jenkinson Papers,* p. 360.

[90] Treasury minute, July 9, 1765, Rockingham MSS., 28.

[91] 5 George III, c. 33.

CHAPTER XI

THE REGENCY BILL, APRIL-MAY, 1765

i.

At the time the American Stamp Act received the royal assent in late March, 1765, George Grenville's ministry apparently enjoyed the most secure position of power that any government had held since the accession of George III. Control in the Parliament was virtually uncontested. The opposition had dwindled to a small group of disunited and dispirited elements, having little energy, no important issues, and no leaders of weight to rally around. Pitt still remained in gloomy seclusion at Hayes. Visitors found him "not without his complaints of the American tax being not sufficiently objected to,"[1] but he refused to come forward himself. Townshend and Yorke, Newcastle and Cumberland had virtually abandoned all ideas of opposition. Moreover, as we have seen, the ministry's campaign against the opposition press had virtually eliminated the newspaper as an effective propaganda instrument. In the Commons, Grenville could command overwhelming majorities. The minority, if not completely inarticulate, was at least impotent.

There were still divisions and jealousies among the ministers of the type which had been exhibited the previous summer among Grenville, Halifax, and Bedford.[2] Yet they proved no threat to the power of the government in Parliament. They could still present a united front against the opposition. Nor was unpopularity a real threat. The City commercial interests remained hostile to the administration, and the mobs at their command were no more friendly to the ministers than they had been during the Wilkes affair. But there were now no such combustible issues and no Wilkes to fan flames of discontent and mob violence.

The weakness of the ministry lay in its position with regard to the King. George III had never liked his ministers since the crisis of August, 1763, when Bedford and Grenville turned their venom on his friend and counsellor, Bute. For a year and a half he had endured them because there seemed no acceptable substitute. But he had undergone many agonies in

the process. When Bute returned to court in the spring of 1764 after passing the winter, as he had promised, at his estate at Luton, Bedford
accused him of breaking his agreement not to interfere in governmental
affairs. Thereafter, the King complained that whenever the ministers
"thought themselves in danger from Parl-y opposition they were submis-
sive, but when once they thought themselves secure of that then their
whole attention was confined not to the advantage of the country but to
making themselves masters of the Closet." George III may have had no
coherent theory of kingship and the prerogatives of the Crown, but he was
quick to resent anything that resembled dictation from his ministers.
Grenville, however, insisted that he should have the exclusive privilege of
naming his colleagues in the government. "No office fell vacant in any
department," complained George III, "that Mr. Grenville did not declare
he could not serve if the man he recommended did not succeed." When
the Lord Lieutenancy of Ireland fell vacant in 1764, Bedford recommended one of his adherents, Lord Weymouth. George III objected,
whereupon Halifax and Sandwich added their recommendations for
Weymouth "in a slight manner." Grenville, however, pressed Weymouth's
claims "with eagerness," in spite of a long list of objections which the
King produced. Forced to admit that he was not well acquainted with
Weymouth, Grenville nevertheless insisted on his appointment as long as
Bedford wished it. The King declared this statement "the most extraordinary reply that ever was avow'd by a man who pretended to make the
advantage of the State his only rule of action."[3]

The height of Grenville's insolence in the King's eyes was his insistence that all members of the government consult him as head of the ministry before they presumed to speak to the King on business. As Grenville
saw it, orderly business required centralized control by the chief minister.
George III, however, saw it as a violation of the Crown's prerogatives.
George was incensed when Grenville reprimanded the Surveyor-General
of the Board of Works, Thomas Worsley, for taking business of his office
directly to the Closet. Worsley was an old friend of the King and Bute,
who had brought him into Parliament for Orford in 1761. The King
thought it absurd for him to be forbidden the Closet by anyone, whether
he came on business or not. Grenville, however, declared that "he would
not serve another hour" if people presumed to speak to the King on business "without his previous consent."[4]

The frustrations which this conflict of positions brought on preyed on
the King's mind. He was forced to continue with Grenville and the other
ministers. The negotiations of August, 1763, had demonstrated the futil-

ity of attempting a coalition ministry, and he refused to call on one of the opposition factions. By flattery and cajolery he tried to win the ministers over. He tried to play them against one another. But despite their private disagreements, they presented a solid front to the King. At length, in late 1764 the King's mental stability began to be affected.

Grenville observed in his diary in late December that the King was having unusual difficulty making ordinary decisions. This may have been the first indication of a phase of depression. In the first of the New Year Grenville noted repeatedly the King's "cold and distant" attitude. On January 13 the King's physician, Sir William Duncan, informed the minister that George III "had a violent cold, had passed a restless night, and complained of stitches in his breast."5

This seems to have been the first serious appearance of the "madness" which was to affect the King periodically over the next several decades and eventually leave him entirely mad. In the 1940's an American psychiatrist, Manfred S. Guttmacher, working from the records of George III's physicians, reached the conclusion that the King was a victim of manic-depressive insanity. More recent investigation has concluded instead that the ailment was porphyria.6 The King's physicians were naturally anxious to keep the situation as confidential as possible. Throughout the duration of this episode of the malady, Grenville was informed and apparently believed that it was a simple cold,7 while rumor had it that the King was afflicted with tuberculosis.8

George III's state of mind fluctuated greatly from time to time. On some days he was so ill that Grenville was not even permitted to speak to him on public business. On other days, he was admitted to find the King "perfectly cheerful and good humored, and full of conversation." The alternation of states of mind continued with greater or less intensity into February and March, with his condition at the time of the passage of the Stamp Act being so serious as to require assent by commission for him. Toward the latter part of March, however, he began to mend, and by April 3 he was able to hold a public levee.9

ii.

All during his illness, George III was haunted by fear of death, and he foresaw only chaos for the Kingdom if he died. His children were still quite young; a regency would inevitably result in factional divisions among the royal family if it were not arranged before his death. When he met with Grenville after the levee on April 3, he told the minister that he would have a regency bill drawn up as soon as he was fully recovered. He had already consulted with Bedford and Northington, he said, and he had decided upon a meeting of the Cabinet Council for the following day at the Lord Chancellor's house.[10]

Grenville was somewhat upset to learn that the King had consulted the other ministers in advance of him—precedence was a point of some concern with him—but he was more concerned by the type of measure the King desired. The natural model for a regency bill was the one which had provided for George III's own minority during the reign of his grandfather when his father, Frederick, Prince of Wales, had died in 1751. By this act the young prince's mother, Augusta, Princess Dowager of Wales, was named as regent and was to be assisted by a council of the chief ministers of state and four members whom George II appointed under his sign manual, whose names were not to be known until his death.[11] George III now told Grenville that he approved of the plan of 1751, "except that he wished to have the power of naming the regent left to himself, by instruments in writing, without specifying the particular person in the Act of Parliament." The King professed to believe that by such a course he could "prevent any faction or uneasiness in his family upon this subject." For this reason also he said that he thought it inadvisable to include the Princes of the Blood (his uncle, the Duke of Cumberland, and his younger brothers) in the Council of Regency.[12]

Grenville expressed his approval of the idea of a regency and the King's "goodness" in thinking of it, but he wisely withheld comment on the proposal to name the regent secretly. The plan was fraught with considerable political difficulty. There was, first of all, the obvious likelihood that George III would select Bute as regent. Bedford especially, but Grenville also, were antagonistic toward Bute; they felt they had been ill-treated at his hands. More important, however, he had been the focus of the tempest of popular hatred which Temple and Wilkes had stirred up. His appointment as regent, or that of his close friend the Princess Dowager, would be the signal not only for a great popular upheaval against the government but for renewed and invigorated efforts by the opposition in Parliament. The issue, however trumped up it may have been, had been explosive in 1761-1762, and it could be again. Grenville and his colleagues would have to move with caution.

Walpole pointed out, perhaps with some truth, that the King's conduct showed a loss of confidence in his ministers. Rather than consulting the ministers, he was dictating to them. Walpole saw in this a return of the Favorite to the inner confidence of the King—probably correctly.[13] In any event, Grenville and Bedford probably were convinced that Bute now had the King's ear.

Such were the considerations on the ministers' minds when the Cabinet Council met on April 5. Since their hold on the King's confidence was so tenuous, they could not afford to thwart his wishes openly. Yet to allow the proposal to go before Parliament as it was would simply invite attack by the opposition. A compromise was clearly necessary, and the Cabinet Council rose to the occasion. Their decision was embodied in a minute of the Council to the King, duly signed by Northington, Bedford, Halifax, Sandwich, Egmont, Mansfield, and Grenville. Approving entirely of the proposal for a regency on the King's plan, they nevertheless declared that they understood "his Majesty's idea of reserving to himself the power of appointing a regent [was] meant to be restrained to the Queen, or any person in the Royal family, usually residing in Great Britain." To this minute the King gave his endorsement.[14]

Bute was definitely excluded by this agreement; Grenville and Bedford had gained half their objective. But what of the Princess Augusta? Surely as the King's mother she was a member of the royal family. But the ministers left that problem for another day. If they had at this point hit upon the novel idea which they later propounded—that the Princess was not a member of the royal family—they did not mention it to the King.

Grenville told the Council that there might be "some delicacy and difficulty" in explaining the regency matter to Parliament in the King's speech "with precision and distinctness." The Council, he said, ought to decide on the wording while all the members were present. The other ministers, however, decided that Grenville could frame the address alone. Grenville went to Wotton for a few days during the Easter recess, leaving Halifax and Mansfield to supervise the drafting of the bill by the Attorney-General.

Yet the few days of recess, April 6 through 17, were not free of concern about the bill itself. Halifax and Mansfield insisted they needed a copy of the speech in order to draw up the bill.[15] Grenville replied with an overtone of annoyance that he had not intended to reduce the address to writing until he returned to town, but he would try to prepare it and bring it when he came. In the meantime the minutes of the Cabinet Council and the text of the 1751 act would have to suffice.[16]

When he saw the King on April 18, Grenville presented and George III "entirely approved" the draft of the speech from the throne. But the details of the bill were far from being finished. The King had changed his mind and decided to include the royal princes in the Regency Council, although he still wanted the right to appoint four more members of the council. This would give him the right to appoint nine councillors, a number equal to that of the principal officers of state. Northington succeeded in persuading the King to be content with appointing five. Grenville, however, could not persuade him to name the regent in the bill; "His Majesty did not alter his opinion in that particular." When George finally asked what the real difficulty was, if the measure would be opposed in the House of Commons, Grenville replied that he believed it would be opposed, but the main difficulty "was from a cause much more remote." Probably the King understood what Grenville would only hint at; he steadfastly and even heatedly refused to abandon his position when both Grenville and Bedford tried to persuade him.[17]

Two days later, April 24, the King rode in state to the House of Lords and addressed the assembled Parliament, asking for a regency bill on the agreed plan. The address of thanks was attended to quickly, but there were still signs of an approaching storm. Beckford declared that he would "oppose this Act in every step of it, and must oppose the address as implying a general approbation of it." More members assented to the address while reserving the right to oppose the bill. No division was called on the address. As Grenville observed to the King, "it appeared very plainly that the plan of opposition was to let the address go, but to resist the provisions of the bill to the utmost."[18] With such a prospect, the ministers and the King realized that the bill ought to be framed so as to offend the opposition as little as possible and still accomplish its purposes. The speech from the throne had not mentioned how the King's nominations to the Regency Council would be made. George III decided to depart from the 1751 bill. It might be very disagreeable, he told Halifax on April 26, if the opposition should move to include the names of the Princes of the Blood and his ministers have to refuse the proposal. It seemed to him, therefore, that it would be best to include his uncle and brothers by name rather than naming them secretly by appointment.[19]

iii.

The reasons which the King gave his ministers, however, were only supplementary to his desire to placate the Duke of Cumberland. He and his uncle had been on less than friendly terms ever since the accession, for Cumberland violently disapproved of Bute and his policies. The Duke, indeed, had taken an active part in opposition primarily on that account. For several months, however, Cumberland had been disillusioned with the opposition and had ceased his activities in its behalf. The King now had a job for him. On April 7 he had put out his first feelers, giving his uncle an audience and informing him of the proposal for a regency bill, which the Duke approved. Cumberland felt all through the conference that the King had something on his mind which he could not bring himself to say.20 In all probability, George had intended to ask him to act as intermediary with William Pitt in forming a new ministry. It seems almost certain that the frustrations and unpleasantness of his relations with Grenville and Bedford had driven the King into his state of depression. Now that he had recovered sufficiently to undertake business, he was determined to be rid of his ministers. But at this time he did not force himself to a decision, and he let the opportunity pass.

Yet if Cumberland was to serve as his emissary in secret negotiations for a new ministry—and on whom else could he call?—he must not be offended by being left off the Council of Regency. This, in light of the fact that Cumberland had been named President of the Regency Council in the Act of 1751, would be an unforgiveable slight. Indeed, the Duke already gave evidence that he felt the omission keenly. When the King approached him through Lord Northumberland about undertaking the negotiations, Cumberland was evasive. Northumberland, after all, was one of Bute's lieutenants, his son having married the daughter of the Scottish earl. And Cumberland was also disturbed by the possibility of the Princess Dowager's being made regent, which would open the way to Bute's return to power.21 When Northumberland was again sent to the Duke on April 24, after unpleasant encounters had taken place between the King and Grenville and Bedford over the appointment of the regent by name, Cumberland was more direct. He simply refused to discuss undertaking the negotiations so long as he and his nephews were "totally left out" of the Regency Council.22

Faced with this situation, George III was forced to continue for a time with Grenville and his colleagues, even though they had added a new resentment to his original disfavor by opposing his wishes on naming the regent. If the regency bill was to be passed during that session of Parliament, it appeared that Grenville's ministry would have to direct it. Yet the foundations could be laid for negotiations by placating Cumberland in the bill. The King set about this on April 26, ordering his ministers to meet again in Cabinet Council to consider naming the Princes of the Blood. The Cabinet, however, thought that the question should not be theirs to decide; rather, it should be determined by the King himself in a royal message to the Parliament. Halifax and Sandwich were dispatched to discuss the matter with the King, but this was not possible until Sunday, April 28. George III had retired to Richmond with Bute (a significant development!) and refused to be disturbed.

When Halifax and Sandwich finally saw the King, he agreed to inaugurate the new matter in a message, and he agreed with Northington the same day that the five princes, to be named in the bill, should be substituted for the five secret nominations which had formerly been envisaged. Appointments by the King were to take place only in the event of the deaths of the princes.23 The details of the bill were thus arranged.

iv.

Grenville, however, was disturbed by the manner in which the King had gone about the arrangements. Rather than negotiating with the ministers through Grenville as their head, George III had simply called in whichever of the ministers seemed most concerned and left Grenville to keep up with developments as best he could. In a ministry already rent with jealousies and divisions, George's policy of "divide and rule" was calculated for success, but Grenville was naturally quick to resent it. When the King informed him of the arrangement made with Northington, the First Minister, though he must have approved of the provision, bristled and replied "that he really had been honoured with so little of His Majesty's confidence in this important business, that he was at a loss to form any opinion upon it, or to know what it was that had drawn upon him this degree of His Majesty's displeasure."24

To protest thus against George III's ideas of the function of ministers and their relationship to the sovereign would have been affront enough to the King had Grenville been content to rest there. He compounded the insult, however, by embarking on one of those lengthy lectures the King so much detested. He pointed out the trouble to which he had gone in preparing the bill and the difficulties he anticipated in carrying it through the Commons. In such circumstances, he said, it would be doubly difficult if the King continued to withhold his "confidence and approbation from him." The result of the encounter, of course, was not to convince the King but to disturb and enrage him and doubtless to strengthen greatly his determination to rid himself of Grenville.25

For the present, however, the regency bill was the question at hand. The following day, Halifax introduced the bill in the House of Lords. It took their lordships somewhat by surprise, Halifax reported, but on the whole it was not unacceptable. Few other than Temple and the Duke of

Richmond gave evidence that they would oppose.26 When the ministers moved the following day to commit it to a committee of the whole, debate immediately arose. Lyttelton questioned the constitutionality of the method of appointment, while Shelburne thought the whole measure unnecessary and unwise.27 Yet after lengthy debate the opposition failed to draw any appreciable support. Only seven lords joined Temple and Shelburne in opposing the measure. Newcastle and his followers gave it their support, apparently because the bill so closely paralleled the Act of 1751, which the old Duke had had a hand in preparing. The slenderness of the minority so enraged Temple that he declared he would attend the House no more while the regency bill was under consideration.28 The bill, meanwhile, was duly committed and ordered to be considered on May 2.

Lyttelton then moved that the House present an address to the King requesting that he name the regent in the bill. The motion found little support, even though Lyttelton accompanied it with a speech which lasted all evening and part of the following day. Out of the debate on the motion, however, came two important questions, posed by the Duke of Richmond.29 Had the Queen been made a naturalized citizen by her marriage; and if not, would she be eligible for the regency? Still more problematical, precisely who actually belonged to the royal family?30

The consideration of these questions was the first order of business on May 2 when the Lords resolved themselves into a committee of the whole on the regency bill. The first question Northington dismissed with the firm contention that the Queen had been naturalized by her marriage and was eligible for the appointment. On the second question the ministers had apparently reached no agreement. Perhaps they had not even considered the matter. Bedford had maintained in the House the day before that only those in the direct order of succession composed the family, a definition which would have excluded both the Queen and the Princess Dowager.31 Northington now expressed the opinion that even the judges would not be able to determine who composed the royal family; indeed, he maintained that the fittest person for the decision could not give his report "if from this time he was to live two hundred years."32

In the midst of this ministerial confusion, Richmond brought forward a motion that the King be allowed to appoint the Queen, the Princess Dowager, or any descendants of George II usually resident in Great Britain. This would have avoided the troublesome definition of the royal family, but it included the Princess Dowager, whom Bedford and other ministers were determined to exclude. Bedford and Halifax advanced the argument that only the Queen and those in the direct line of succession should be eligible, and they mustered enough support to defeat Richmond's motion without a division.[33]

It was now clearly necessary for the ministers to come to a decision on the matter of who was to be eligible. Grenville, Halifax, and Bedford met for supper after the Lords adjourned to thresh the question out. Halifax reported that the King had given his permission for the phrase "born in England" to be used as a qualification if the ministers thought it necessary. This clearly gave the King's sanction to the omission of his mother. It was already settled in the speech, of course, that the Queen should be personally named. Grenville expressed extreme surprise at the concession the King had made, and well he might. How Halifax had persuaded George III one can only guess. It seems probable, in the light of later developments, that George did not fully understand what the concession would entail. Perhaps Halifax convinced him that if the Princess's name were included the Commons would insult her by taking it out. But it seems probable also that Cumberland may have required the exclusion of the Princess as a price for undertaking negotiations for a new ministry.[34] This would seem the more persuasive reason. The King must have realized that the exclusion might cast a shadow on his mother's reputation, but he was willing to take the risk in order to placate Cumberland and clear the way for replacing his oppressive ministers. In any event, the ministers decided with the King's permission that the Queen and the descendants of George II should be the only persons eligible for the regency. When the King was informed of the decision the next morning and was told that if the Princess's name were included the Commons would strike it out, he gave his approval.[35] Grenville apparently attributed the concession solely to the persuasiveness of the ministers' argument and suspected nothing.

On May 3, the ministers were thus able to present a united front to the House of Lords. Richmond's motion of the previous day was amended by omitting the Princess Augusta's name, allowing the King to appoint "the Queen or any person of the Royal Family descended from the late King, now and usually resident in England." Richmond expressed himself "perfectly satisfied," and the motion passed the House by unanimous consent. May 5 was appointed for a third reading, after which the bill was to go to the Commons.[36]

Yet the ministers themselves were not unanimous. When Grenville met Northington the next day, the Lord Chancellor was much disturbed about the omission of the Princess and fearful of the attack which might be waged in the Commons. He apparently influenced the King to the same opinion, for when Grenville entered the closet after Northington on May 5 he found George now much disturbed about the injustice being done to his mother. For the moment concern for his mother outweighed his dislike for his ministers. The Chancellor, he told Grenville, agreed with him (had convinced him would probably be more correct) that it was a "mark of disrespect" to the Princess and that "a motion against it would be made by the opposition." It would be strange, he asserted, for the opposition to propose and the ministers refuse her inclusion. Northington had told him that nothing could be done in the Lords, but could not a message be sent to the Commons asking that she be included?[37]

v.

Grenville was now caught in a trap. Whichever way he proceeded, he would either incur the disfavor of the King or be hotly attacked in the Commons on an issue which would rally support for the opposition. Opposition could be expected on the issue of the Princess whether she were included or excluded. If her name were included, the opposition would have an obvious point for attack. If it were omitted, the group of government supporters who were attached to Bute would oppose her exclusion, and opportunists among the opposition would join them. The safest course for Grenville, it appeared, was to avoid inconsistency and let the Princess remain excluded. If the House insisted on her inclusion, he could yield gracefully, and his position would be little impaired. It would be far more difficult to defend her inclusion in case the opposition rallied substantial support against it, and to yield before such pressure and publicly insult the Princess would be unthinkable.

The King, however, now wished to have the Princess included, which would complicate the situation and give the opposition the opportunity for which it was waiting. Grenville tried to explain how impolitic it would be to propose the alteration and in what a poor light it would cast the ministers. He reminded the King that the situation would not have arisen if he had heeded the advice of his ministers and appointed the regents by name. George entreated with great agitation and emotion, even with tears, that a message be sent to the Commons asking for his mother's inclusion, but Grenville remained firm. The minister conceded, however, that if the House wished to include the Princess among the eligible he would offer no objection.[38]

This, then, was the plan which Grenville and the other ministers agreed

upon. It seems, on the whole, the best strategy they could have devised at
this point for getting the regency bill smoothly through the Commons.
The objection was that the maneuver added one more resentment to the
growing hoard which George III was collecting against his ministers.

The House of Lords returned to consideration of the regency bill as
appointed on May 6. It was read the third time and passed, whereupon it
was sent to the House of Commons for its concurrence. That same day it
was read for the first time in the lower House, which heard it without
comment and appointed the following day for its second reading.[39]
Before the second reading took place, however, Lord John Cavendish[40]
introduced a motion for an address to the King requesting that he name
the regent in the bill. The question was obviously intended to test the
strength of the opposition in the House. It was debated for some time, but
the opposition showed its weakness both by its lack of spirit in debate and
its lack of numbers in the vote. It allowed the motion to be defeated without a division. The opposition was showing surprisingly little strength.

When the bill was read the second time, the minority engaged in "more
lively debate and produced some good speeches." But when the question
for commitment was put, Conway and some other opposition leaders
were for it and it passed without a division. Grenville felt that everything
had gone in a manner agreeable to the King.[41] From his own point of
view, however, there were some objections. The weakness of the opposition was a welcome sign, of course, but there were defections among the
government's supporters. John Morton, member for Abingdon and an
intimate of the court of Princess Augusta, had notified Grenville that he
intended to introduce a motion that the Princess's name be included in the
bill. Grenville had already promised the King that he would not oppose
such a motion, but he was by no means eager to see it introduced. It
would not only be personally unwelcome to himself and to Bedford, but
it would produce an awkward and unpleasant situation for the minister
when the measure was returned to the Lords for concurrence. When he
saw the King on May 8, Grenville suggested that the Princess inform her
friends in the House that she was satisfied with the arrangement as it
stood. The King, however, replied that though the solution seemed plausible there was nothing he could do to put it into effect. Apparently either
he knew that the Princess was not satisfied or he refused to interfere now
that the matter was about to be settled to his own liking. Grenville had no
choice but to promise again that the ministers would not oppose the
motion.[42]

The Commons sat as committee of the whole on the regency bill on

May 9, and the ministers came prepared for Morton's unwelcome motion. The opposition first tried its hand with a motion which would have restricted the regency to the Queen alone. The ministers struck it down by a vote of 258 to 68.[43] Then Morton rose on the government side of the House and moved that the Princess Dowager's name be included among those who were eligible for the regency. Grenville was surely not pleased—Lord Villiers of the opposition claimed that he could read his displeasure "in his looks and manner"[44]—but he took his pill without a murmur. "I am very sure," he told the House, "that his Majesty...will see with pleasure any proper compliment which this House shall think fit to pay to his Royal mother the Princess of Wales...." He added that he would "certainly concur" in expressing the respect in which the House held the King's mother.[45]

With the ministers in acquiescence if not in active support and with the opposition surprised at the sudden turn of events, the motion went virtually unopposed in debate and was passed without a division, although Bedford's "Bloomsbury Gang" refused to participate in the vote. The following day the debates were brought to a close, the bill was passed without a division on the third reading, and the troubles of the ministers went again to the House of Lords.[46]

vi.

Grenville and his colleagues now found themselves in an awkward position. They had forced the peers to jump through the hoop one way. Now against their will they were obliged to make them jump through the other way. When the bill was re-introduced in the chamber, May 13, Sandwich had the unhappy obligation to move the adoption of the Commons' amendments. He made the best of an embarrassing situation. Halifax's original proposal, he said, had had his hearty approval, but the whole purpose was to ascertain who should be eligible for the regency. He hoped, therefore, that the Lords would agree to the amendments of the Commons. Parliament could not exclude the Princess if it would be disagreeable to her or to any of the royal family. The object now was to be unanimous in restoring the Princess's name.[47] Bedford and Halifax, meanwhile, kept their seats, embarrassed and silent.[48]

Yet the ministers fared not so badly with their lordships. Richmond, of course, could not forbear taunting them with the fact that the Commons' amendment before them was exactly the same as his own which they had defeated in the Lords. But there was no opposition in debate except by

Newcastle and Portland.[49] The bill passed without a single negative vote, and the King and House of Commons were so notified. When the King went in state to the House of Lords and gave his assent, May 15, the regency bill ceased to trouble the ministers.[50]

The task which the King had set for his ministers had been accomplished, and the final arrangement was that which George III had wished. If, as some thought, an injustice had been done to the Princess Augusta in the process, it was the lesser of two evils. At least there had been no debate on the Princess's personal virtue; such debate might well have ensued had her name been included in the bill from the first. Grenville had been placed in a situation which no one could have handled satisfactorily. He had handled it as smoothly and gracefully as possible under the circumstances. But the King, as we have seen, had determined to change his ministers even before the regency bill was presented to the Parliament. The altercations with Grenville and Bedford over including the Princess had strengthened that determination, and the successful passage of the bill did not alter it. At the very time that George III gave his assent to the regency bill, the Duke of Cumberland was preparing to open negotiations for the formation of a new ministry.

NOTES

CHAPTER XI

[1] Onslow to Newcastle, March 19, 1765, Newcastle MSS., Add. MSS. 32966, f. 69.

[2] See *Grenville Papers,* II, 301-307, 502, 505, 510-515.

[3] Memoranda by the King, August, 1765, Fortescue, *Papers of George III,* I, 164, 171.

[4] Memorandum by the King, August, 1765, Fortescue, *Papers of George III,* I, 170.

[5] *Grenville Papers,* II, 533, III, 112-115.

[6] Manfred S. Guttmacher, *America's Last King,* New York, 1941, pp. 75-86; John Brooke, *King George III,* New York, 1972, pp. 336-341; Stanley Ayling, *George the Third,* New York, 1972, pp. 122-125.

[7] See Grenville's diary, *Grenville Papers,* III, 115-125, 167.

[8] Walpole to Hertford, April 18, 1765, Toynbee, *Walpole's Letters,* VI, 198.

[9] Grenville's diary, *Grenville Papers,* III, 115.

[10] Grenville's diary, *Grenville Papers,* III, 125.

[11] 24 George II, c. 24.

[12] Grenville's diary, *Grenville Papers,* III, 12.

[13] Walpole, *George III,* II, 104.

[14] Minute of the Cabinet Council, April 5, 1765, Fortescue, *Papers of George III,* I, 73; Halifax to Grenville, April 5, 1765, *Grenville Papers,* III, 16.

[15] Halifax to Grenville, April 9, 1765, *Grenville Papers,* III, 16-17.

[16] Grenville to Halifax, April 10, 1765, *Grenville Papers,* III, 17-19.

[17] Grenville's diary, *Grenville Papers,* III, 127-130.

[18] *Lords Journals,* XXXI, 151-152; Grenville to the King, April 24, 1765, *Grenville Papers,* III, 21-22.

[19] Grenville's diary, *Grenville Papers,* III, 131.

[20] Cumberland's statement, *Rockingham Memoirs,* I, 187.

[21] See Mary Bateson, editor, *A Narrative of the Changes in the Ministry, 1765-1767. Told by the Duke of Newcastle in a Series of Letters to John White, M.P.* (Camden Society Publications, New Series, vol. 59), London, 1898, pp. 5-6.

[22] Cumberland's statement, *Rockingham Memoirs,* I, 189-190. The Duke mistakenly dates the latter conversation with Northumberland on April 17 rather than April 24. The events of several weeks he antedates by seven days.

[23] Grenville's diary, *Grenville Papers,* III, 131-138.

[24] Grenville's diary, *Grenville Papers,* III, 138.

[25] Grenville's diary, *Grenville Papers,* III, 138-141.

[26] Halifax to the King, April 29, 1765, Fortescue, *Papers of George III,* I, 78-79.

[27] Walpole, *George III,* II, 111-114; Fitzmaurice, *Shelburne,* I, 325-328.

[28] Walpole to Hertford, May 5, 1765, Toynbee, *Walpole's Letters,* VI, 220-221.

[29] Charles Lennox, third Duke of Richmond (1735-1806).

[30] Phillimore, *Lyttelton,* II, 666-673; Walpole, *George III,* II, 116-117.

[31] Walpole to Hertford, May 5, 1765, Toynbee, *Walpole's Letters,* VI, 221.

[32] Halifax to the King, May 2, 1765, Fortescue, *Papers of George III,* I, 81.

[33] Halifax to the King, May 2, 1765, Fortescue, *Papers of George III,* I, 81.

[34] Newcastle, *Narrative,* pp. vii, 5-6.

[35] Grenville's diary, *Grenville Papers,* III, 148-150.

[36] Halifax to the King, May 3, 1765, Fortescue, *Papers of George III,* I , 72-73; Newcastle, *Narrative,* p. 8; Onslow to Newcastle, May 4, 1765, Newcastle MSS., Add. MSS. 32966, f. 330.

[37] Grenville's diary, *Grenville Papers,* III, 151-152.

[38] Grenville's diary, *Grenville Papers,* III, 153-157.

[39] Grenville to the King, May 7, 1765, *Grenville Papers,* III, 23.

[40] Younger brother of the fifth Duke of Devonshire and son of the old leader of the opposition (1732-1796).

[41] Villiers to Grafton, May 10, 1765, *Autobiography and Polictical Correspondence of Augustus Henry, Third Duke of Grafton,* edited by Sir William Anson, London, 1898, pp. 76-77; Grenville to the King, May 10, 1765, *Grenville Papers,* III, 24-25.

[42] Grenville's diary, *Grenville Papers,* III, 158.

[43] Grenville to the King, May 9, 1765, *Grenville Papers,* 25-30.

[44] Villiers to Grafton, May 10, 1765, Grafton, *Autobiography,* p. 77.

[45] Grenville to the King, May 9, 1765, *Grenville Papers,* III, 29-32.

[46] Grenville to the King, May 11, 1765, *Grenville Papers,* III, 34-37.

[47] Walpole, *George III,* II, 149-150.

[48] Walpole to Mann, May 14, 1765, Toynbee, *Walpole's Letters,* VI, 236.

[49] Newcastle, *Narrative,* p. 9.

[50] Walpole, *George III,* II, 154; *Public Advertiser,* May 16, 1765.

CHAPTER XII

THE DOWNFALL, MAY-JULY, 1765

i.

The King, if anything even more determined to replace his ministers, had only postponed further attempts while they pushed the Regency Bill through the Parliament. He made no use of the Duke of Cumberland as emissary between April 24, when Cumberland had broken off the earlier negotiation out of resentment at being omitted from the Regency Council, and the final passage of the bill. But as soon as the House of Lords gave its assent to the revised bill, effectively removing Cumberland's objections, George III dispatched Northumberland posthaste to the Duke. The Grenville ministry had served its purpose; now it must go. Late in the evening on May 13, Northumberland knocked on Cumberland's door with the King's plans for a new ministry. George III, the Duke learned, wished him "to see whether Mr. Pitt and Lord Temple, with the other great Whig families, could not be brought to form a strong and lasting administration."[1]

With "the utmost secrecy and celerity," as the King enjoined, Cumberland now undertook the commission to negotiate a new ministry. Newcastle and Rockingham, the leaders of that portion of the opposition he called the "great Whig families," he found quite willing to form a ministry provided that Pitt was at their head. The Earl of Albermarle[2] was then dispatched to Pitt's bedside at Hayes with the King's proposals. Pitt and Charles Townshend were to be the Secretaries of State, as Pitt himself had proposed in August, 1763. Whether Pitt was pleased, neither man recorded. Northumberland was to head the Treasury, with Newcastle and Temple settling the Presidency and the Privy Seal between them. Egmont was to remain at the Admiralty.

All these arrangements Pitt accepted without demur, but he had his conditions: restore the dismissed army officers in the Commons to their commands; give Pratt "ample justice and favor," presumably a peerage;

repeal the cider tax; declare general warrants illegal; implement a merit system of army promotion rather than the existing one based on "dancing attendance," as Pitt put it; and renew the alliance with Frederick the Great which Bute had broken off in 1762.[3] In short, all the major issues on which Pitt had opposed Grenville's policies were to be readjusted in Pitt's favor! One should note that at this point Pitt did not even mention a repeal of the American stamp tax.

In conversations with Cumberland on May 15 and 16, Temple also agreed to the King's proposals, but only tentatively pending George III's acceptance of Pitt's conditions. Cumberland advised the King to accept them, reporting Temple's coolness as the chief threat to the negotiation.[4]

Meanwhile, other developments placed more stress on the King, aggravating his emotional instability and his resentment of his ministers. The House of Lords, after passing the Regency Bill on May 13, also read another bill sent up by the commons to impose a tariff on Italian silks. English weavers were seeking protection of their depressed industry. As it was drawn, however, the bill would have entirely excluded oriental silk shipped to England by way of Italy. Bedford opposed the measure, and as no one ventured a word in its defense, it was thrown out on the first reading.[5]

The next day, three or four thousand outraged weavers from Spitalfields gathered at the palace at Richmond and petitioned the King for redress. George was already disturbed and depressed over his disputes with his ministers and his clandestine negotiations to replace them. He promised the weavers he would do all he could to give them relief. When Grenville saw him the next morning, he was still "uneasy, and very much disturbed" about the uprising, urging Grenville to do something in Parliament. Grenville replied that it was too late; the session was virtually closed.[6]

That day petitioning turned into rioting. The weavers followed the King's carriage when he went to the Lords, shouting against the peers. When Bedford's carriage appeared it was pelted with stones, and the Duke himself was injured. Following his carriage to Bloomsbury, the mob surrounded Bedford House, tearing down the outer wall and continuing to riot until the troops were called out and the Riot Act read on the 17th. George III had to select a commander for the troops, causing him more anguish.[7] All this because of Bedford!

The ministers had no inkling of the negotiations under way with Pitt and Temple until the 16th, when Grenville went to the King with the draft of his speech to prorogue the Parliament. George III said that he would look at it some other time; for the present he would simply have the Parliament adjourned. When the surprised minister asked the reason, the King replied that it was the confusion of the riots. But, protested Grenville, that was over, and besides what could Parliament do about it? That was the business of law enforcement. There was no more business to attend to. What reason could he give for continuing the session? The country would think that the King was keeping Parliament in session to approve writs for a new election, that he intended to change his ministers!

Aha! Once Grenville broached the question, the King could not dissimulate. Badly upset, he fumbled, "Mr. Grenville, I will speak to you another time about that: I promise you I will speak to you; you may depend on it I will speak to you." With "emotion and disorder," Grenville recorded in his diary, the King ended the audience.[8] The secret was out!

That evening Bedford, Halifax, and Grenville dined with Sandwich and discussed tightening their lines of defense. The first task was to rid themselves of any internal divisions. This was to be the crucial test of the ministry, and they had to stand united. Halifax and Grenville, who had not been on the most cordial terms in the ministry, frankly avowed their discontents and agreed to act in concert, as did Bedford and Sandwich. Whatever the King was preparing, the ministers stood united to face it.

ii.

Secrecy was no longer necessary. George III called in Cumberland on Saturday afternoon, May 18, and told him he would accept Pitt's conditions. The Duke was to go to Hayes in person for the negotiations, and if he pleased he might take the Guards with him so everyone would know negotiations were under way! So on Sunday morning Cumberland and Albemarle rode out to Hayes, sending a note to Temple to meet them there. They rode to disappointment. Cumberland spent an hour and a half tete-a-tete with Pitt, explaining at length the King's "sincere desire" to see him in his service and deploring the actions of the Grenville ministry. The Duke assured him that all his conditions had been accepted, and Pitt seemed satisfied.[9] He even began talking as if he were already the King's first minister.[10]

When Temple arrived, however, the atmosphere changed abruptly. He was concerned over the influence behind the King in making the change. Plainly, he felt, it was his arch-enemy, Bute; proof was the naming of Northumberland, Bute's lieutenant, for the Treasury. Both Pitt and Temple at length declined to have anything to do with the negotiation as long as there was any indication that Bute would have influence in the proposed government. Pitt had always insisted on control in any ministry; when his competitor behind the scenes would be the hated Scottish favorite who had forced him from power in 1761, it would be intolerable.

Pitt never explained why the negotiation collapsed; a statement to Jemmy Grenville that there would be no "settling an administration upon my own plans" was as close as he ever came. And everyone in public life, virtually, had a different answer: his health, his pride, his insistence on never again leading where, as he put it, he could not "guide." Cumberland, after having spent an hour and a half urging Northumberland on Pitt, proposed Temple for the Treasury instead, but it was no use.[11]

Thus Cumberland had the unpleasant duty of reporting to the King that Pitt and Temple, upon whom George had based all his hopes, would not come into his service. The King was reduced to extremities. His cloak of secrecy had been lifted by his own words to Grenville. Now his only hope of ridding himself of his oppressors had dissolved. How could he face Grenville and the other ministers and ask them to remain? It was too great a humiliation. In his distress he sent Cumberland on the forlorn errand of persuading Lyttelton to form a ministry with Townshend and Conway. If Grenville's brothers refused, perhaps his cousin would accept. But Lyttelton and Townshend, whom the King designed for the Exchequer, both declined, and the project was quickly abandoned. Cumberland returned once more to the King, this time with the advice which George III dreaded to hear: Grenville and his colleagues must be retained.[12]

iii.

Since the moment Grenville learned that the King was negotiating to replace him and his colleagues, relations with the King had been strained. Grenville simply refused to adjourn the Parliament to await his dismissal. He would not whet the knife which would cut his throat; that, Grenville insisted, must be performed by his successor. Bedford told the King that Bute was the instigator of the weavers' riots and lectured him sternly on the perfidy of his favorite. Even Northington spoke "warmly and strongly" to George about the change, at least as Grenville recorded it.[13] These were the men to whom the King now had to submit himself, hand and foot. It was a bitter task, but bitterer were to come.

Meanwhile, other developments improved Grenville's personal situation. While the negotiations with Lyttelton ran their abortive course, Lord

Temple surveyed his personal and political situation. He saw in it little promise. The opposition he had orchestrated to Grenville was virtually dead. The ease with which the ministers handled the Parliament in the Stamp Act and Regency Bill debates proved that conclusively. Scarcely any issues for attacking the ministry were visible anywhere on the horizon. Even if there had been issues, Grenville had so collared the means of propaganda with which Temple was familiar that he no longer had a medium for rallying support. Further opposition seemed hopeless. And now there seemed little chance of entering a ministry in his own right; the negotiations were concluded, and still it was Grenville, not Pitt and Temple, who presided over the government. Indeed, it appeared that Grenville rather than Pitt held the key to the family's success. Temple was old and childless. When he died, either Grenville or his son would inherit his title and estates. Who could say that a reconciliation with his brother might not result in his joining the Grenville ministry? In spite of everything, it seemed, the man who would wield power was not the spectacular brother-in-law but the workaday brother. The path of personal and family prestige seemed to lie not with Pitt but with Grenville.

It did not take Temple long to decide that an approach to his brother was the move to make. On May 20, Augustus Hervey, a friend of the Grenville family, approached George with the obviously inspired suggestion that he reconcile with his brother. Grenville was not unwilling, but he declined to make the first move. Temple was not to be put off. Later in the day, Hervey brought direct word from the Earl that he felt he and Grenville had grounds for reconciliation, since they now had "equal reason to complain" of Bute, the point on which they had broken. Grenville thereupon agreed to see his brother. On May 21 they met, but "many difficulties arising in the course of the conversation upon past matters, they parted without agreeing." Of what the "difficulties" were neither man left record. The following day, however, whatever conditions had been made were apparently met. Temple sent a letter to Downing Street at eight o'clock in the morning, and himself followed at nine. There was a "meeting...of the most friendly kind, and upon the foot of the most perfect reconcilliation," and Temple paid a pleasant visit to Mrs. Grenville and the children.[14] A wound nearly four years old was finally healed.

iv.

While these family developments, which were to have momentous political consequences, were taking place, George III mustered his fortitude and faced his minister again. But he did not have the courage to tell Grenville the whole truth. When he received the minister in the closet, May 21, after Grenville had had his first interview with Temple, his scrupulous honesty for once apparently failed him. He told Grenville that he had had no design to change the Treasury or the Exchequer, but only departments of government which were not under Grenville's care. The First Minister must already have learned from Temple how flagrantly untrue that was! Pressed to know whether he and his colleagues would remain in the King's service, Grenville replied that he would have to consult his fellows, only saying that, with the opinion of the public what it was, it would be more than ever necessary that Bute should have not voice in the conduct of affairs.[15]

That evening the ministers met at Bedford house to settle on the terms they would require of the King. The impatient George III could not wait them out. Scarcely an hour after they met, a message from the King summoned Grenville peremptorily, and the meeting was adjourned without a decision. In the audience which ensued, Grenville asked pointedly whether his Majesty was retaining him with any sense of reluctance. George III probably winced inwardly, but he replied that he had none, that Grenville had always behaved toward him "in the most respectful and becoming manner."[16]

However, one may doubt that George III considered the ultimatum which his ministers presented to him at noon the next day either respectful or becoming. They offered five stipulations. Bute was to have no influence whatever in the government; Stuart Mackenzie, Bute's brother, was to be removed as Privy Seal of Scotland; the Marquis of Granby was to be made commander-in-chief in the place of the Duke of Cumberland; Lord Holland was to be dismissed as paymaster; and the ministers were to have full control over Ireland.[17] In addition to the two blows against Bute, they would revenge themselves on Cumberland for his part in attempting to replace them and on Holland for intrigues against them.[18] The Irish demand was to insure their control of the appointment of a new Lord Lieutenant.

When Grenville delivered these demands at noon on May 23, the King simply asked if they were Grenville's as well as the other ministers' and if they were *sine qua non*. Grenville replied that he would never have brought them if he had not agreed with them or "if they had not thought them all indispensably necessary." George III promised an answer in the evening, doubtless with an inward sigh; some of the requirements cut to the quick. He was able to avoid the insult to Cumberland by persuading

Granby not to accept the post of Commander-in-Chief. Holland was little able to command his sympathy. Even the demand that Bute should have no influence was no more than he could have expected from Bedford and Grenville. Bute had clearly intrigued more than once to have them replaced. But to wreak vengeance on Bute by insulting his brother was more than he had expected from Grenville. It was evidence to the King of Bedford's spite. Perhaps Grenville would give it over.

Meeting Grenville at eleven o'clock that evening, the King suggested that Mackenzie be allowed to keep the office shorn of all power—as a pure sinecure. Grenville, however, stood firm with Bedford; he insisted that even the nominal office in Mackenzie's hands would indicate to the public the continued influence of Bute in government. Even the King's desperate plaint that he would disgrace himself, that he would have to break a promise to Mackenzie of the office for life, did not shake Grenville. Finally the King yielded the point for the time being, but doubtless with decreased respect for Grenville, who he felt had made himself wholly subservient to Bedford's vindictive campaign against Bute.19

v.

Cumberland, meanwhile, was still trying to construct a new ministry. He again approached Temple, inquiring if he would accept the Treasury if the offer came directly from the King. Temple replied that he could not until he had conferred with Pitt, and he offered little hope even then. His reconciliation with Grenville, he explained, placed him under no obligation or restraint, but he might have his "delicacies," and Pitt might also. Cumberland urged him to go immediately to talk with Pitt, but when he learned that the King had accepted Grenville's terms he let the matter lapse.20 On May 24 Lord Frederick Campbell took Mackenzie's place as Privy Seal for Scotland, and Charles Townshend finally gained a place in Grenville's administration in Holland's vacant paymastership.21

George III's attempts to replace his ministers, it appeared, had utterly failed. Grenville and his colleagues were more firmly entrenched in power than ever. There was virtually no group willing to form a ministry to replace them. Newcastle and Rockingham had refused to proceed without Pitt to handle the Commons, and Pitt and Temple had refused even after every condition they asked had been granted. The only other plausible leader whom the opposition might have employed was Charles Townshend, whom Grenville had now pacified with the lucrative paymastership. Little wonder that the ministers felt themselves able to deliver an ultimatum, or that the King felt he had no choice but to accept it!

Not surprisingly, the stress of these events took their toll on the King's health. On May 24, after the final tiff with Grenville over Mackenzie's removal, the royal physicians were ordered to attend the King. He went to the House of Lords the following day to prorogue Parliament, but he returned directly to Richmond without seeing his ministers. Sunday, May 26, the King and Queen did not attend chapel or hold a drawing-room, evidence that something was amiss. The physicians gave out that the King was "not very well."

Likely George III wrote at this time an undated letter to Lord Bute, bemoaning his captivity and wishing he could be "a private man that I might with my own arm defend my honour and freedom, against men whose families have formerly acted with more duty to the Crown than these wretches their successors...." He complained that "every day I meet with some insult from these people; I have been for near a week as it were in a feaver my very sleep is not free from thinking of the men I daily see." His mind, he said, was "ulcer'd by the treatment it meets from all around it."22

Slowly, however, the King recovered his equilibrium and adjusted to the situation. May 29 he held a levee. When Grenville saw him in the Closet before the Council met, he was at least civil and Grenville found his behavior "not remarkable." He refused, however, to allow Grenville to nominate a new member of the Queen's household to replace Lord Weymouth, who had been appointed Lord Lieutenant of Ireland. The King said that the post, Master of the Queen's Horse, was "no office of state, that the Queen had thought of a person for it, and...it was reasonable for her to please herself. Mr. Grenville bowed and said no more." By May 31, Grenville observed that he was "more easy and less reserved," talking easily about business.

It was obvious to the ministers, however, that the King's correct politeness covered an icy hostility. He would only speak to Grenville when he was spoken to, rather than opening the conversation himself as he had always done. Grenville observed on June 7 that he spoke without waiting for him to begin, and seemed "civiller" than he had been, but Grenville did not flatter himself "that it proceeds from anything but disguise." He openly showed his displeasure when informed that Jemmy Grenville's eldest son was to come into Parliament for a vacant seat.23

Relations with the family continued to improve, if not those with the King. On May 30, Temple, George and Jemmy Grenville, and their wives all went to Hayes to dine with Pitt and Lady Chatham. Pitt "expressed pleasure" at the reconciliation of the family, but reserved judgment as to whether this was a political reconciliation. At his request, the family agreed that politics would not be a subject of discussion. The newspapers, of course, took note of the meeting and speculated on its political meaning. Perhaps there was to be a constitution of the wartime ministry on a Grenville family plan. "This union of so respectable a family, it is hoped, will produce something favourable for the public," commented one daily. Others were less sanguine. It was said, reported one paper, that Pitt had declared he would accept no office so long as S[cottis]h interest bears such uncontrolled direction."24 Despite all of Grenville's and Bedford's efforts, many still felt that Bute's was the guiding hand in the government.

Bedford himself carried his concerns about Bute directly to the King. In an audience on June 12, he remonstrated strongly concerning George III's obvious lack of confidence in his ministers. Reminding the King of his promises of "countenance and support," he accused him of giving public countenance to his "most bitter enemies." This likely referred to public favor shown the Duke of Devonshire. Was not Bute, he asked, interfering against the ministers? What must the public think? The King did not attempt to deny his lack of confidence, only asserting that he had kept his word with regard to Bute. Bedford declared that if the King could not give his "favor and countenance" to his ministers, he should "transfer to others" their authority—although he quickly added that such authority would be worthless without the support of his present ministers.25

If the Grenville ministry still retained any of the King's confidence, this harrangue surely dissipated it! Angry and humiliated by Bedford's remonstrances, George III took him at his word that he should "transfer to others" the authority of his ministers. He sent forthwith for Cumberland again to resume negotiations for a new administration.26

Bedford's remonstrance was thus the match which set off a new explosion of negotiations; this time they were to succeed, and the Grenville ministry was to be replaced. On whose authority was Bedford's fatal step taken? As early as June 1, Bedford and Sandwich had agreed that "some concert" should be held among the ministers to remedy the "unpleasant" situation.27 But apparently no action was taken in concert. Grenville, the faithful diarist, would surely have recorded any meeting held to plan such strategy. Certainly some of the other ministers knew of the proposed complaints, for the idea was "pubblickly talked of" by Bedford's following.28 But the fact that Northington heard not one word of the matter until the King informed him[29] indicates that Bedford did not speak for all the ministers. It would seem that Bedford formed the resolution either without the knowledge of his colleagues or (less likely) with the acquiescence of some but not all.[30]

vi.

The first result of the incident was yet another attempt to bring Pitt into the King's service at the head of a ministry. At the King's behest, Cumberland attended him on Sunday, June 16, and they decided to send the Duke of Grafton to Hayes. Grafton undertook the mission the next morning, finding Pitt with gout in both feet but quite ready to talk with the King. Returning to London that evening, Grafton reported that Pitt was ready to treat.[31]

Thus on June 19 Pitt had an audience of between three and four hours with the King. On arrangements for domestic politics there was no disagreement. The terms which the King had been ready to accept in May he was ready to accept again. He had some doubts, however, on Pitt's request for an alliance with Prussia and Russia. When Pitt asserted that it was a *sine qua non*, George asked him to consider the matter thoroughly and attend him on Saturday, June 22.[32]

Grenville received news of these events at Stowe, where he had retreated with Temple and Lyttelton for a few days. Sandwich wrote on June 15, "the common talk of the town is that our political life is not to last many days."[33] Grenville already knew of the offer to Pitt, having talked with his brother-in-law as soon as Grafton notified Pitt of the King's wishes.[34] It appeared that a family ministry was about to be formed. The rumor spread in London. "A royal and noble company will shortly pay a visit to Lord Temple at Stowe," reported the *London Evening Post*.[35]

While Grenville remained at Stowe with Temple, the other ministers in London were troubled. Sandwich wrote, June 19, reporting Pitt's audience with the King and requesting Grenville to come back to town. Grenville replied the next morning that he did not think his presence in town either necessary or wise. It would have the appearance, he said, of an attempt to "embarrass" the King "in the arrangement which he is now endeavouring to form." Whatever arrangement was made, he told Sandwich, it would "come on, or go off, just the same whether I am there or not."[36] The other ministers, however, feared that Grenville was about to abandon them for Pitt and Temple, an idea which Grenville certainly must have been considering. To Sandwich's continued requests that he come to town, Grenville replied on June 21 that he had not made up his mind about the situation and that when he returned to town, "which you know will be in a few days," he would require to be left "at full liberty to act as I shall think necessary."37 Whichever way the cat jumped, Grenville wanted to be ready.

Sandwich's letter of June 20 also informed Grenville that the King regarded his ministers as having resigned with Bedford's remonstrances of the twelfth. George III, Sandwich reported, thought the ministers would have further demands upon him if he kept them in his service. Sandwich had replied that they required only the King's confidence and favor.38

Pitt, meanwhile, proceeded with assurance in his negotiations with the King. When the appointed audience arrived, June 22, they reached a virtual agreement. No arrangement was made as to membership in the ministry, however, until the King conferred with Temple. To him Pitt wrote immediately after the audience that affairs had "advanced considerably." "Upon the whole," he wrote, "I augur much good, as far as intentions go: and I am touched with the manner and *Royal frankness,* which I had the happiness to find."39 At this point Pitt was obviously confident of Temple's support and assured that he would shortly take up the reins of government. Temple's audience, set for ten o'clock on June 25, would be the final hurdle in the path to office.

But Temple was still disturbed about the influence behind the King's desire for a change. He still believed that Bute and Cumberland were dominating the King's actions. Was not Cumberland engineering this whole negotiation? Even if Bute were off the scene, as he and Pitt had demanded, Cumberland would be fully as objectionable as private adviser to the King. Temple was disturbed by the prospect. On Sunday, June 23, he set out for town, but he requested Grenville to come to see him on the morning of the audience. Grenville went to Pall Mall for breakfast with him on June 25 and found him in "great agitation." When he had his audience, Temple declined not only to take the Treasury, which Pitt had proposed, but to take any office at all. The ostensible reason he gave was the difficulty of conducting the Commons, since he himself was in the Lords, as were all the other principal officers proposed except Pitt, and he would not be able to attend regularly owing to the uncertain state of his health.40 Temple was quick to add, however, that he was also constrained by considerations "of a tender and delicate nature, ...which he therefore desired not to explain."41

In all probability, Temple referred to the influence which Cumberland

and Bute appeared to have on the negotiations. He could not say outright to the King, "Your uncle and your friend are objectionable and must not meddle in the government," but to plead "tender and delicate" objections was almost as direct. "Delicate" was the word the eighteenth-century politician generally applied to personal obligations and relations, and "tender" referred to the close connection of Bute and Cumberland to the King. Temple told Grenville afterward, "The plan of the provisional administration was, I think, Butal-Ducal."[42] Temple's objection to Cumberland's influence, indeed, became an open secret among his political associates. When the Duke died in late October, 1765, even the ministers considered that "Lord Temple's great objection" was "removed."[43]

It does not appear that Temple's reconciliation with Grenville played any part in his refusal to take office. Likely Grenville would have come in with him, or at least would have supported the government without office. Temple announced publicly that the reconciliation had had nothing to do with his refusal.[44] Pitt and Temple apparently had agreed to give Grenville an office. The negotiation, asserted Charles Townshend, "did not break off on Mr. Grenville's account."[45] Indeed, if the list of the proposed ministry which was circulated to the papers was correct, they planned for Grenville to keep his office as Chancellor of the Exchequer, while Temple took the Treasury. That would have meant his managing the Commons in Pitt's absence.[46] But with Temple's refusal, all such plans evaporated.

Pitt's decision was sealed with Temple's. The evening after Temple's audience, Pitt notified Grafton, through whom the negotiation with him had begun, that he would be unable to serve the King. "It is with extreme concern," he wrote, "that I am to acquaint your Grace, that Ld. Temple declines to take the Treasury. This unfortunate event wholly disables me from undertaking that part which my zeal, under all the weight of infirmities, had determined me to accept."[47] The following morning he gave the same report to the King, greatly lamenting Temple's refusal but declining absolutely to enter office without him.[48]

Many historians have been perplexed by Pitt's refusal to take office without Temple. He was not a politician of great stature, it is argued; his main importance in the eyes of his contemporaries was that he was Pitt's cohort. But this greatly underestimates Temple's political acumen, not to say genius. The propaganda war he directed against Bute in 1762-63 is a pertinent example. Pitt and Temple together made a near-perfect statesman-politician, with Pitt supplying the broad aspects of statesmanship while Temple attended to the detailed manipulation of people, patronage, and propaganda which insured success to the politician. Pitt alone, however, was a rather inept politician. He had proved it before, and he would prove it unquestionably in his third ministry, when he took office with Temple in opposition. Pitt was one of the most imposing orators ever seen in the House of Commons and a statesman of great verve and ingenuity, but he lacked the knack of managing men and attending to detail. It would be rash indeed to assume that Pitt himself did not realize this lack in his personality. The wonder seems to be not that he refused to take office without his indispensable partner in 1765, but that he agreed to undertake a ministry without him a year later. Their long friendship and family connection and the fact that Temple had given him financial assistance may have played a part, but it seems plausible that Pitt refused to take office without Temple because he felt he could not do without him.

vii.

George III was doubtless disappointed at Pitt's refusal, but he was not altogether surprised. When he had first written to Cumberland on June 12 about negotiating with Pitt, he expressed doubt that Temple and Pitt could be obtained. There had been no thought, however, of going back to the Grenville-Bedford group on his knees again. Admittedly no strong government could be formed of Newcastle, Rockingham, Grafton, and the other members of the opposition, but this would not matter greatly, argued the King. The Parliament had been prorogued and need not meet again until the winter; any government could tide the country over until then. It might be strengthened in many ways before that time. "The world will see," wrote the King, "that this country is not at that low ebb that no administration can be form'd without the Grenville family."49

Now once again Cumberland was pressed into service, this time to negotiate with Newcastle and the opposition without Pitt. They proposed a system which would put Rockingham in the Treasury, give the seals to Grafton and either Townshend or Conway, and make the other of the latter two Chancellor of the Exchequer.50 Many of the opposition, however, did not consider it wise to enter government without Pitt. They had visions of being excoriated by his invective before the House of Commons. When eighteen opposition leaders gathered at Claremont on June 20, only twelve approved of forming a ministry without Pitt.51

The opposition was weak enough without being divided to boot. Cumberland was ready to give up. He told Newcastle that if the opposition failed, the King, who was adamant that he would not go back to Grenville and Bedford, would have no choice but to turn the government over to Bute and his friends. Newcastle was able to persuade him, however (rather easily, one would think, knowing Cumberland's feelings about Bute), that if the opposition took office and followed the program Pitt had outlined, the "great commoner" would probably support them. No need for Bute! So on this unsupported assumption arrangements proceeded. Bute's friends would be proscribed, Pratt would have the peerage Pitt had designed for him, and other arrangements were completed for the minor offices, always with an eye to avoid what might offend the titan at Hayes.[52] "If, as I am persuaded will be the case, those measures which Mr. Pitt has prepared are followed," ventured Newcastle, "Mr. *Pitt* cannot and I dare say will not oppose."[53]

viii.

Grenville did not learn of these negotiations until July 2,[54] but knowing about them would have done him no good. King and opposition leaders were so eager that nothing would stand in their way. Grenville's fate was sealed. But while the new ministry was constructed, he went on with the routine business of government. Only July 9 the Treasury Board dealt with the last details for implementing the American Stamp Act. Then the next day the blow fell. At half-past ten, a letter arrived from the Lord Chancellor:

> Dear Sir,
>   I have this moment received His Majesty's commands to signify to you his pleasure, that you attend his Majesty at St. James's this day, at 12 o'clock, with the seal of your office.
>   I am very unhappy in conveying so unpleasant commands....[55]

After twenty-seven months as First Lord of the Treasury and Chancellor of the Exchequer, Grenville presented himself at noon at St. James' Palace. George III opened their last official conversation by saying he understood that Bedford, in his June 12 harangue, had resigned in the name of the ministers, giving the King liberty to form a new ministry. Grenville replied that though he had not resigned or even intended to resign, he was apprised that the King so understood the matter. He wished to know, however, what had brought the royal displeasure upon him. The King replied that his ministers no longer gave him advice, but commands.

When Grenville asked whether, as his opponents charged, he had ever been disrespectful to the King, George was even emotional in his reply. "Never, Mr. Grenville, never," he cried; "it is a falsehood." Grenville reported that he repeated this once or twice.[56]

Taking a new tack, the minister reviewed his whole association with Bute in office and the successes of his administration since Bute left— "success far beyond Mr. Grenville's most sanguine hopes, notwithstanding which he had the mortification to see his services unacceptable, and himself lost in His Majesty's confidence by the malice of his enemies." To the King's protest that Bute had had no part whatever in the changes at hand, Grenville replied that he was glad a person whom the King honored "with his favor and confidence" had not given him such advice, "had not advised a measure which would be productive of so much weakness and disorder to his government."

As a parting word, Grenville advised the King not to draw a line between his dominions in Britain and America. News had already reached his ears of riots in Boston against the Stamp Act.[57] The colonies, Grenville told him, were "the richest jewel of his Crown;" it would be ruinous to take any step toward surrendering sovereignty over them. For his own part, he pledged himself to maintain his stand on America steadfastly, both in and out of Parliament. Anyone who did less, he asserted, would be a "criminal and a betrayer of his country."

Throughout the whole audience, Grenville observed, the King's conduct was pleasant and civil, "imputing no blame, but giving no word of approbation." If there was any twinge of conscience for thus coldly dismissing his honest, hard-working, sincere servant, Grenville did not discern it. Having given his advice, the minister submitted his last business for the King's attention, gave him the last papers to sign, thanked him for his justice in clearing him of the "aspersions of his enemies," and withdrew.[58] In the days which followed, Rockingham and Newcastle and their followers constructed their administration. Grenville was never again to return to office.

NOTES

CHAPTER XII

[1] Cumberland's statement, *Rockingham Memoirs*, I, 191.

[2] George Keppel, third Earl of Albemarle (1724-1772), was a personal friend and adherent of Cumberland.

[3] Cumberland's statement, *Rockingham Memoirs*, I, 191-193.

[4] Cumberland's statement, *Rockingham Memoirs*, I, 194-198; Grafton, *Autobiography*, p. 45.

[5] Walpole, *George III*, II, 154.

[6] Walpole, *George III*, II, 154-155; Grenville's diary, *Grenville Papers*, III, 163-164.

[7] Ellis to the King, May 17, 1765, Halifax to the King, Fortescue, *Papers of George III*, I, 94-97.

[8] Grenville's Diary, *Grenville Papers*, III, 165; Gilbert Elliott's memorandum, *Jenkinson Papers*, p. 369.

[9] Newcastle, *Narrative*, p. 14; Cumberland's statement, *Rockingham Memoirs*, I, 200-202.

[10] Grafton, *Autobiography*, p. 46.

[11] Newcastle, *Narrative*, p. 14.

[12] Newcastle, *Narrative*, pp. 15-16; Walpole, *George III*, II, 170-172.

[13] Grenville's diary, *Grenville Papers*, III, 171-172.

[14] Memorandum by Grenville, May 21, 1765; Grenville's diary, *Grenville Papers*, III, 42-43, 183; Hervey to Grenville, May 21, 1765, Murray MSS.

[15] Grenville's diary, *Grenville Papers*, III, 177-180.

[16] George III to Grenville, May 21, 1765; Grenville's diary, *Grenville Papers*, III, 40, 181-182.

[17] Memorandum to the King, May 22, 1765, Astle Collection, Add. MSS. 34713, f. 239; *Grenville Papers*, III, 41.

[18] Holland to Bute, August 27, 1765, Ilchester, *Fox*, II, 294.

[19] King to Egmont, May 23, 1765, Fortescue, *Papers of George III*, I, 113-115; Grenville's diary, *Grenville Papers*, III, 184-187.

[20] Newcastle, *Narrative*, pp. 19-20.

[21] Grenville's diary, *Grenville Papers*, III, 188.

[22] Sedgwick, *Letters*, p. 336.

[23] Grenville's diary, *Grenville Papers*, III, 188-194; Gilbert Elliott's diary, *Bedford Correspondence*, III, 284.

[24] *London Evening Post*, May 28-30, 1765; *Westminster Journal and London Political Miscellany*, June 1, 1765.

[25] Bedford to Marlborough, June 13, 1765; minutes by Bedford, June 12, 1765, *Bedford Correspondence,* III, 286-290.

[26] King to Cumberland, June 12, 1765, Fortescue, *Papers of George III,* I, 118-119.

[27] Sandwich to Bedford, June 21, 1765, *Bedford Correspondence,* III, 286.

[28] Newcastle, *Narrative,* p. 21.

[29] Northington to the King, June 12, 1765, Fortescue, *Papers of George III,* I, 117.

[30] The version of the matter given by Horace Walpole (*George III,* II, 182-183) must be wholly discounted. In addition to his not being in a position to obtain authentic information on the incident, he was always ready to say the worst of Grenville and Bedford.

[31] Newcastle, *Narrative,* pp. 21-22; Grafton, *Autobiography,* pp. 52-53.

[32] Newcastle, *Narrative,* pp. 22-23; Albemarle to Grafton, June 19, 1765, Grafton, *Autobiography,* pp. 83-84.

[33] Sandwich to Grenville, June 15, 1765, Murray MSS.

[34] Grenville to Temple, June 13, 1765, Murray MSS.

[35] June 15-18, 1765.

[36] *Grenville Papers,* III, 52-56.

[37] Sandwich to Grenville, June 20, 1765; Grenville to Sandwich, June 21, 1765, *Grenville Papers,* III, 56-60.

[38] *Grenville Papers,* III, 57.

[39] Pitt to Temple, June 22, 1765, *Grenville Papers,* III, 60-61.

[40] The other principal officers proposed were Grafton as Secretary of State, Newcastle as President, Northumberland as Chamberlain, Lyttelton as Privy Seal, and Shelburne as President of the Board of Trade. All of these, of course, also sat in the Lords.

[41] Grenville's diary, *Grenville Papers,* III, 200-201; cf. Newcastle, *Narrative,* p. 24.

[42] Temple to Grenville, July 2, 1765, *Grenville Papers,* III, 64.

[43] Hervey to Grenville, November 1, 1765, *Grenville Papers,* III, 106. See G. M. Imlach, "Earl Temple and the Ministry of 1765," *English Historical Review,* XXX (1915), 317-321.

[44] Phillimore, *Lyttelton,* II, 676.

[45] To Lord Townshend, July 3, 1765, Astle Collection, Add. MSS. 34713, f. 254. A copy in the Stowe MSS. in Grenville's handwriting was printed in *Grenville Papers,* III, 65.

[46] *Public Advertiser,* June 26, 1765; *Lloyd's Evening Post,* June 24-26, 1765.

[47] Pitt to Grafton, June 25, 1765, Grafton, *Autobiography,* pp. 53-54.

[48] Newcastle, *Narrative,* p. 24; Grenville's diary, *Grenville Papers,* III, 202.

49 King to Cumberland, June 12, 1765, Fortescue, *Papers of George III,* I, 118.

50 Newcastle, *Narrative,* p. 25.

51 Memorandum by Newcastle, *Rockingham Memoirs,* I, 218-220.

52 Newcastle, *Narrative,* pp. 27-29.

53 Newcastle to Ashburnham, June 27, 1765, Newcastle MSS., Add. MSS. 32967, f. 142.

54 Grenville's diary, *Grenville Papers,* III, 205. As late as July 3, the *Public Advertiser* reported: "We hear large wagers are laid in the West End of the town that there will be no change in the ministry before the meeting of the Parliament."

55 *Grenville Papers,* III, 71.

56 Whately to Grenville, June 19, 1765, Murray MSS.

57 Grenville's diary, *Grenville Papers,* III, 211-216.

CHAPTER XIII

THE VALLEY OF INDECISION, JULY 1765-JANUARY 1766

i.

The ministry which Newcastle, Rockingham, and their followers formed in July, 1765, has been called the Rockingham Ministry, but in many ways its leader, if it had one, was outside the government and unconnected with it. For in its formation and throughout its short existence, the "Rockingham" government centered about the absent person of William Pitt. On July 6, Newcastle elaborated to Rockingham the idea which he and Cumberland had agreed upon, that of conforming personnel and policy to Pitt's ideas. "I would humbly propose," he wrote, "that the plan of administration should in general be made as palatable to Mr. Pitt and as agreeable as possible to his notions and ideas." For this purpose, Grafton, who was "the person Mr. Pitt chose to be Secretary with him," was to be made Secretary of State, and it was planned that he should "keep up his correspondence with Mr. Pitt and acquaint him with the execution of those measures which he (Mr. Pitt) proposed to the King."[1] Conway was selected as the other Secretary of State and was entrusted with the conduct of the House of Commons. Jemmy Grenville, the member of the clan least offensive to Newcastle and the one most devoted to Pitt, was placed in the Vice-Treasureship of Ireland. While the other offices were filled with men from their own following, Newcastle and Rockingham took care not to offend Pitt. Rockingham took the Treasury, with William Dowdeswell as Chancellor of the Exchequer, and Newcastle took the relatively passive position of Privy Seal, leaving the conduct of the "responsible" offices to his "boys."

At granting Pratt a peerage they hesitated. Pitt wished to see Pratt Lord Chancellor, but not so Newcastle. He designed the office for Charles Yorke, but the King would not have that. So George III's friend Northington kept the Great Seal, and Yorke was placed again as Attorney-

General with a promise from the King that he should be Chancellor within a year.[2] Without the Chancellorship, a peerage for Pratt would be troublesome. Yorke and Rockingham considered it precarious to reward a judge for a decision in court on a point of law. Newcastle, however, pressed urgently for a barony for Pratt. "The world is running mad again for Mr. Pitt," he wrote to Rockingham. "Pray, my dear lord, for your sake as well as for the sake of the whole, do not despise it [Pratt's peerage] and show the King the necessity of it. ... We shall have *undoubtedly* an able *supporter* in the House of Lords, and he is not the least nearer or perhaps not so near the Great Seal as without it."[3] Pratt, therefore, was given his peerage as Baron Camden, and the new ministers hoped that Pitt would be appreciative.

The "great commoner," however, was not so easily won, When Rockingham tried to obtain Pitt's friend Shelburne for the Board of Trade, which he had held under Grenville, Pitt advised Shelburne not to take the office, and Shelburne refused.[4] Nor was Pitt pleased when Sir Fletcher Norton was turned out to make room for Yorke as Attorney General. He wrote to Norton that "he was not turned out by *his* advice, and that were he minister he should be glad of the assistance of such advices."[5] (Pitt regularly referred to himself in correspondence in the third person—a stuffy style even in the eighteenth century!) Perhaps when the Parliament met Pitt would support the new ministers; for the present, however, he gave them no public support. They could only hope.

Pitt, indeed, appeared firmly united with Grenville and Temple. On July 16 the public learned that Pitt had paid a long visit to Stowe for political consultation with his brothers-in-law.[6] Pitt and Grenville had a long private conversation—"long enough," Horace Walpole sneered, "for one of them to have made a speech in—in short, four hours."[7] Lord Digby commented to Lord Holland on the interview:

> All this will make one think that these people, tho' widely separated of late, may unite, and that will produce an extraordinary scene. This new ministry give out that Pitt will support them, and have preferred Pratt to make the world believe it, but many people doubt what part he may take yet. I was told that he had already been displeased at their making so free with his name.[8]

No one knew the course Pitt would take, but it was obvious the new ministry was adrift without him. "Here is a new political arch almost built," Lord Chesterfield wrote to his son on July 15, "but of materials of so different a nature, and without a keystone, that it does not, in my opinion, indicate either strength or duration. It certainly will require repairs, and a keystone, next winter; and that keystone will and must necessarily be Mr. Pitt."9 Grenville was less metaphoric but fully as skeptical. "I do not see that this measure is likely to contribute to the establishment of a firm and stable government, nor to the happyness and honour of the King and his people," he told one of his supporters. If it were stronger, he said, it would make his "retreat infinitely more happy" and would give him "comfort and satisfaction" in his status as a "private man."10 That, at least, was the proper thing to say! But all agreed that Rockingham and company were on shaky ground. "The Newcastle Party are now in office," Whately wrote to his friend John Temple in Boston; "how long they will continue so is another question."11

In the City there was disappointment that Pitt and Temple had not formed a government. There were even regrets at the passing of Grenville's ministry, and the merchants began to fear that "these people would not get on well."12 Pitt's City supporters sat and waited to see what their idol would do. On July 18, however, Pitt set out for his new estate of Burton Pynsent in Somersetshire, and nothing was heard from him for weeks.13 Grenville was passing the word that Pitt in his conversation at Stowe "had absolutely expressed his disapprobation of the ministry to him very strongly,'14 and the information quickly spread. In late August the Common Council of the City of London, presenting the King an address of congratulation on the birth of a prince, expressed its lack of confidence in the ministry, and the commercial towns of Exeter, Bristol, and Canterbury promptly followed suit.15 The government, men were saying, would not last until winter.

ii

While Newcastle and Rockingham were forming their ministry, Grenville set about organizing propaganda against them. The problem was not easy, as the opposition had found during Grenville's administration. The laws on seditious libel had been extended to such lengths that the publication of weekly propaganda sheets such as Temple and Wilkes had run no longer was safe. Newcastle and Rockingham would be able to use legal prosecution as effectively as Grenville. Some writers opposing the Stamp Act, however, had begun using the expedient of anonymous letters to the daily papers. This became the medium of Grenville and Temple's attack. Even before Grenville was dismissed, a letter appeared in several papers over the signature "Anti-Sejanus." Throwing the whole blame of the change of government on Bute, whom he compared by implication with the hated favorite of the reign of Tiberius, Anti-Sejanus attempted to show that Rockingham and Newcastle were the tools of Bute. The ministers being dismissed, he said, had been tried at the same tribunal at which Pitt, "the delight and ornament of this Kingdom," had been "tried and sentenced." Their offence was the same as his, that of "serving the public too well, and gaining too much credit with the nation."[16]

During the rest of July, several Anti-Sejanus letters took care to associate Pitt and Temple and to assert their disapproval of the ministers.[17] The attack, however, continued to center on the accusation that the new ministers were Bute's puppets. Their youth and inexperience in public office seemed to give the charge credibility. When in late July the ministers began turning out all Grenville's supporters in lesser posts of government, Anti-Sejanus again asserted this was Bute's animus at work.

The ministers, of course, did not allow Anti-Sejanus to go unanswered. "A Weaver in Spitalfields"—a remarkably articulate weaver!—answered his first two letters, and thereafter government writers appeared using a variety of names: "Libertas," "Veritas," "Moderantius," and others. Anti-Sejanus also had friends, among whom was "Cato," who seemed particularly to follow Temple's line of thought, attacking Bute and the ministers while refraining from defending Grenville's record.[18]

During August and September, Grenville himself took up direction of propaganda efforts against the ministers. He had directed pamphlet warfare against Temple and Pitt while he was in office, with Whately, Lloyd, and William Knox his principal writers.[19] Now, out of office, he directed his pamphleteering against the new ministry. Charles Lloyd and Frederick Hindley were kept busy during August and September writing pieces, which were transmitted to Grenville at Wotton for perusal and correction.[20] On September 11 and 12 he met with his writers in London to plan strategy for propaganda as the opening of Parliament approached.[21] If, as the ministers announced, the government planned to follow Pitt's ideas of undoing all Grenville's measures, Grenville would fight him in the press.

At the same time, he set about rallying all his friends and supporters in the Parliament for the battle which he anticipated in both houses when the Lords and Commons assembled. The number of Grenville's adherents had grown over the past four years. When he broke from Pitt and Temple in 1761, he could truthfully say that he had "no friends" or "great connections."22 Even when he took the Treasury, he could call few of his associates in office his "friends" and certainly not his followers. He frankly told the King in August, 1763, that Bedford and Sandwich were not his friends.23 Two years at the head of the ministry, however, had sufficed for Grenville to draw about him a personal following of his own, somewhat in the fashion that Newcastle had built his faction with the governmental patronage. By the spring of 1766, Rockingham calculated that Grenville commanded the loyalty and votes of nearly fifty men in the House of Commons; Temple in the Lords, acting with Bedford, made the group's influence felt there. Rockingham's vote-counting estimated sixty-nine men in the Commons controlled by Grenville and Bedford together,24 and Sir William Meredith, one of Newcastle's troops in the House, placed the estimate as high as eighty-four, forty-three of whom were Grenville's and forty-one Bedford's followers.25

The leaders among Grenville's band were mostly men with whom he had served in office. Lord North, Sir John Turner, Thomas Hunter, and Whately had all served with him in the Treasury. John Proby, Baron Carysfort in the Irish peerage, was Grenville's son-in-law, had been one of his Lords of the Admiralty, and was one of his ablest debaters. Robert Maxwell, Earl Farnham, and Grenville's brother-in-law, Thomond, were also Irish peers. Since the peers of Ireland were not in the House of Lords, they were eligible to represent British constituencies in the Commons. There were also a number of sons and heirs of noblemen, still commoners by law and eligible to sit in the Commons, but accorded by courtesy the next highest title of their fathers. In addition to Frederick, Viscount North, heir of the Earl of Guilford, there was John Manners, Marquis of Granby, son of the third Duke of Rutland. James Stanley, Lord Strange, and John Stewart, Lord Garlies added the weight of courtesy titles. The younger son of a Marquis or Duke was also by courtesy addressed as a lord, although still a commoner. Thus Lord Frederick Campbell, brother of the Duke of Argyll, and the Duke of Rutland's brother, Lord Robert Manners, were members of the band. And finally there were Grenville's personal friends: Augustus Hervey, Robert Nugent, and Hans Stanley.26

Grenville took care to maintain close contacts with these leaders as the autumn approached. In mid-September, when his wife Elizabeth's chronic bilious complaint attacked and the couple spent several weeks at Bath "taking the waters," he wrote to many of his political friends advising them of the situation and requesting them to keep in touch with him there.27 As the opening of Parliament neared, there would be more and more to discuss among the opposition leaders, for the resistance to the Stamp Act in America was reaching the proportions almost of a rebellion, and there began to be talk of repeal.

iii.

The first news of the disturbances in America over the Stamp Act reached London in early June, 1765, and was published in the *St. James's Chronicle,* June 6. As the summer progressed, news trickled in that the resistance was increasing and spreading. Whately informed Grenville on August 8 of the resolutions of the Virginia Assembly against parliamentary taxation and the Stamp Act.[28] Grenville considered them "too extraordinary" to escape the particular notice of the Parliament, and he began to lay his plans for a debate on the Stamp Act when the Commons assembled.[29]

The ministers realized all too well the importance of the American riots. Yet what was to be done about them? The Lords of the Treasury met August 20 and again August 23 without reaching any conclusion.[30] Another meeting, September 2, resulted in the profound decision by the Lords of the Treasury that "all acts of the British Legislature extend and are in force in every part of his Majesty's dominions."[31] Twelve days later a circular letter enjoined all colonial governors to "give your aid and assistance to the Distributors of the Stamps within your government."[32]

The truth was that the ministers did not know what to do about the situation in America. While they did nothing, news poured in to the Board of Trade, the Treasury, and various individual ministers about the spreading riots and the impossibility of selling or even protecting the stamps which arrived in the colonial ports from England.[33] In mid-October, with trade falling off with the colonies because of American non-importation agreements, the ministers began to be seriously disturbed. They considered how the act might be enforced but could arrive at no practical suggestions. "To recommend in the mildest manner the obedience to the last act of Parliament; to lay before them [the colonies] the consequence of their disobedience...; to execute by fair means, not by military force; to give them reason to hope that...the Parliament may be induced to give some relief" by "a proper application to his Majesty"—these were the suggestions for quelling a mass uprising which threatened to swell into rebellion![34]

Perhaps a little more practical was another proposal which Rockingham and Newcastle considered in October: that of allowing the colonies to import gold bullion from Spanish America in order to give them specie with which to pay the Stamp duties. Newcastle hoped also that Spanish ships might be allowed to trade with the colonies and set up a triangular trade instead of a direct one with British America. "Otherwise," he said, "the great stagnation of our trade with North America and the exportation of our woolen manufactures thither will not be put upon the foot it was before Mr. Grenville gave those fatal orders." Rockingham, however, decided that the proposals "would not quite do our business."35

iv.

While his ministers floundered, George III was also uneasy. Rockingham and Newcastle had been his last resort for ministers, and almost from the first he had been dissatisfied with them. He could not have been ignorant of the low esteem in which they were held by the political world. Moreover, Temple's worst fears about Cumberland were realized by the King himself, for the Duke became the sole intimate link between the ministers and the throne, and in that position he was able to "dictate" to the King more effectively than ever Grenville and Bedford had. Cumberland was "the head and soul of all," Robert Mackintosh reported to Temple. "The error, 'tis now said, is discovered, of having so totally surrendered regality into those hands. and the fatality of the mistake is felt; which produces wishes as well as opinions of the necessity of being delivered."36

Newcastle and Rockingham were forced to submit to Cumberland's domination, for they were dependent on the Court for their support. Newcastle saw the problem clearly. The ministry, he told Albemarle, Cumberland's lieutenant,

may have a considerable majority in both houses: but that majority must be made up of their enemies, creatures of the last two administrations, and such as are influenced only by their employments and their interest. Such a majority will last no longer than they find the administration carries everything clearly and roundly. The moment there is the least check, *they* return to their vomit and vote according to their consciences (if they have any) or at least consistently with their manner of voting during this reign."37

With the situation which was developing in the colonies, it appeared doubtful the ministers would be able to carry "everything clearly and roundly." The King, resentful of Cumberland and without confidence in the ministers, again took secret steps to change his government. Entirely unbeknown to his ministers, George III opened negotiations with the Grenville family through the avenue of the Queen and her secretary, General Graeme.[38] Early in October, Temple was notified secretly of the King's wish to change his ministers. He drew up a tentative plan for a ministry, which he sent to Graeme by his friend Humphrey Cotes. When the whole plan for administration had been committed to writing by Cotes and Mackintosh, it was presented to the Queen. Cotes, informing Temple of the developments, expressed "real satisfaction" at the Queen's "good sense and discernment" and thought that "at least" the proposals would "bring forth the King's *real* sentiments."[39]

At Stowe, Temple was less pleased with the agency of Graeme and the Queen. He had "the highest opinion of the Queen's amiable qualities and prudent conduct," he instructed Mackintosh to say. Could he have said otherwise? He desired "always to be stated to the King as full of the most dutiful and affectionate attachment, and should have the greatest pleasure in contributing to the honour, ease, and felicity of his government." Although "having much indulged the thoughts of retirement," he declared that he "would cheerfully sacrifice his private enjoyments and undertake the publick service, if he can do it upon such clear ground as may allow him to hope of success in it." All this was the necessary obsequious flattery of the royal person. But he showed his distrust of secret negotiations, as he had in his interviews with Cumberland. He declared that "no consideration on earth can induce him to engage in administration unless he is assured he enters upon it with the King's full cordiality and confidence." He therefore wished for "no negotiations," and was "averse to any interposition whatsoever;" instead, he wished "to receive the King's pleasure from himself."[40] The "great commoner" had been summoned to the King's presence; surely his noble brother-in-law deserved no less!

Temple was apparently sure of Grenville's support, although in his correspondence with his political supporters during these days Grenville reveals no inkling of the negotiations. But Temple was not certain of Pitt. "The determinations of his mind since he went into Somersetshire I know not," he told his agents, "but whenever he is called upon as before, I take it for granted he will give them with the same duty and zeal." "Mr. Pitt is in my notions indispensable," he said, "and you know I think too much regard cannot be shewn him."[41]

Temple's requirements left the King in a quandary. He could not afford to call Temple to court and negotiate personally with him, for such public action would destroy the little confidence the Parliament had in the Rockingham ministry. Success with Temple was by no means so well assured that the King could afford to jeopardize the reputation of the government he had. But Temple said he wanted "no negotiations" with anyone other than the King. For the moment George III apparently laid aside the idea of a Grenville family administration, for no further overtures were made to Temple. The Earl had overplayed his hand! In late October, Whately reported a rumor about town that there might be a coalition of the Rockingham ministry with Bute and his followers, but he gave the report "little credit."[42] For another week affairs remained in suspense. Then on October 31 Cumberland died suddenly. With his removal from the scene, George III had less objection to the Rockingham ministry. They, however, had lost their link with the court party. A void in Parliamentary support had to be filled and the ministry strengthened. The report soon gained currency that Pitt and Temple were immediately to be called into government.[43] Presumably this would mean office for Grenville too.

v.

The ministers, however, were not thinking of calling Temple and Grenville; Pitt was their only objective. From Burton Pynsent, Pitt gave little hint of his feeling on the matter. He had told Grafton in August that he neither approved nor disapproved of the ministry, though he did not regard Newcastle's direction of affairs (or "Claremont," as he expressed it) as an "object of confidence or expectation of a solid system for the public good."[44] Now he was talking in riddles about his connections with Grenville and Temple. "Quarrels at court, or family reconciliations, shall never vary my fixed judgment of things," he told Thomas Walpole, who was buying his Hayes estate.[45] "All I can say is this, that I move in the sphere only of measures."[46]

Pitt's opinions on measures were probably a riddle to himself at this point. In his seclusion in Somersetshire he was pondering the problem of the American Stamp Act riots. At Burton Pynsent and then at nearby Bath, where he carried his gouty legs in mid-November, he read pamphlets such as those of Daniel Dulany of Maryland and discussed the question of Parliamentary right with men whose opinion he respected, notably the new Baron Camden.[47] His wrestling with the question extended well into December before he decided what "measures" he would support.

Meanwhile, however, Newcastle heard the rumors that Pitt "differed very much from my Lord Temple," and he "took the liberty" of advising George III that it would be "of great service" if Pitt "could, in any degree, be connected with his Majesty's present administration, either in the House of Commons or in the House of Lords."[48] With the loss of Cumberland as link to the Court, it was more necessary than ever to have the popular approval which Pitt's membership and support could bring. Rockingham, however, was reluctant to approach the "great commoner," and plans to send the Duke of Grafton to Bath with an invitation to join the administration were abandoned.[49]

Newcastle had to be satisfied with giving out that the measures the ministry intended to pursue in Parliament were "exactly conformable" to Pitt's ideas. As evidence, he tried to get Pitt's friends lined up. On December 5 he wrote to George Cooke, one of Pitt's City supporters in the Commons, asking that he second the address in response to the King's opening speech in Parliament. Cooke immediately sent to Bath for advice, and Pitt counselled refusal. "I confess it appears to me, that nothing would be less suited to your situation...than to be held out to the world as connected with the Duke of Newcastle," he wrote back on the seventh.

> "When his Grace does me the honour to say that anything is 'exactly conformable to *my ideas*,' he is pleased to use the name of a man, who has never communicated his ideas to the Duke of Newcastle upon the present state of affairs; and who is finally resolved never to be in confidence or concert again with his Grace."

When his ideas "in their true and exact proportions," were made public, Pitt declared, he would announce them himself.[51] In other words, he had not yet fully made up his mind about "measures."

By December 15, however, he had made his decision on the American question, or so George Onslow learned from William Beckford. "Beckford declares he is thoroughly and unalterably averse to the late people," he reported, "and that he talkt of coming up the first day if he thought it possible for them to think of carrying a question against us."[52] Encouraging, yet the ministers still did not know precisely what Pitt thought about the matter, and the opening of Parliament was only two days away. They knew only that he differed "thoroughly and unalterably" with Grenville.

vi.

The Parliament met December 17 only for a short session, intended merely to approve writs of election for the new ministers. George III was deeply disturbed by the American situation; he had told Conway it was "undoubtedly the most serious matter that ever came before Parliament."[53] But the speech from the throne said only that "matters of importance" had "lately occurred in some of my colonies in America which will demand the most serious attention of parliament." That would come after the Christmas recess, when the vacancies in the House would have been filled.[54]

Grenville and Bedford had known for some weeks that the ministers intended to postpone considering the colonial riots; they had even heard that they would try "if possible to repeal the American tax."[55] This they were resolved to oppose from the very beginning. A "congress" of all the old ministry except Halifax met with Grenville at Bath in late November and planned their strategy; the report went abroad that they intended "a most vigorous attack" when the Parliament met.[56] Newcastle and Rockingham expected and feared an attack on them for "not supporting the honour and right of Parliament,"[57] and they decided to mention the American riots in the King's speech only after news arrived on December 11 of "nothing less than a rebellion at New York."[58]

Thus it was no surprise to the ministers that when the address to the King came to be debated, Grenville offered an amendment which virtually declared the American colonies to be in open rebellion. He called for an expression of "just resentment and indignation at the outrageous tumults and insurrections" in America, "resistance...by open and rebellious force to the execution of the laws...." And he moved an amendment to the address calling for

> such measures as shall be necessary for preserving the legal dependence of the colonies upon this their mother country; for enforcing their due obedience to the laws; for maintaining the dignity of the crown, and asserting the indubitable and fundamental rights of the legislature of Great Britain.[59]

Why, he demanded, had the King been advised to speak so leniently? The address, he cried, "seemed as if it was drawn by the captain of the mob."[60]

Grenville was embarrassed to find, however, that he was unsupported except by his own following and that of Bedford. The court party, on whom he had relied for support, stood solidly against him, and several of them spoke in vigorous support of the ministers. Cooke, moreover, joined the attack, justifying the actions of the colonists and taking Grenville to task for "fixing the name of rebellion on all because a tumultuous set of people had been riotous." Cooke was known to be in the confidence of Pitt, and his statements were taken by many in the House to be straight from the "great commoner" in Bath. Faced with such opposition, Grenville was prevailed upon by his former Attorney General, Sir Fletcher Norton, to withdraw his motion, and the address was passed without dissent.61 Two days later, Rigby and Grenville introduced a motion in a thin House to call for the papers regarding the American riots. The motion was lost, 70-35, even though Grafton acceded to a similar motion by Bedford in the Lords. The following day Grenville lost a motion, 77-35, that the House adjourn not to the fourteenth of January, as the ministers proposed, but to the ninth.62 It appeared that the ministers had the Parliament well under control.

vii.

The ministers were sure of their followers, but they did not know which way to lead them. The talk of the town over Christmas was that Pitt, Temple, and Grenville were about to form "a wise and permanent administration," but no one could say if it were true. As Lord George Sackville observed, the ministers had "no reason as yet to imagine" that Pitt was "averse to them, and the majority in both houses does not call for any immediate alteration."63 But if alterations were not imperative, decisions were. The most important was the American matter.

Rockingham had already concluded that revisions would have to be made in the Stamp Act. Twenty-eight London merchants, chaired by Barlowe Trecothick, met on December 6 with the First Lord to press for redress of grievances. Out of the meeting came a "general letter" sent to all the "out-ports and manufacturing towns" of the country. It asked every town to make "a regular application to Parliament...for granting every ease or advantage the North Americans can with propriety desire...."64

The merchants' petitions poured into the Treasury in the weeks which followed, but the question still remained: what "ease or advantage" might the Americans be granted "with propriety"? Should only certain provisions of the Stamp Act be relaxed or revoked? Should the whole act be repealed? Should the ministers go even further and accede to the colonial argument that Parliament had no right to tax the colonies? When the ministers met to discuss the matter two days after Christmas, Rockingham suggested revision. He had been in contact with the merchants and knew which clauses of the act were causing the most discontent among influential men on both sides of the Atlantic. The stamp duties "might be paid in currency rather than specie," he said. More important, merchants could be brought into line by "exempting from stamp duties the cockets and clearances and the bonds given in pursuance of the Act of Navigation."[65]

Others among the ministers, however, wanted total repeal. There was general agreement that there should be "a declaratory law of the legal rights of Parliament," which was "to assert the authority of Parliament in general words."[66] But they could reach no decision on whether to repeal or modify.[67]

Something had to be decided, and soon! Grafton and Conway insisted that Pitt be consulted, and Thomas Townshend, Newcastle's nephew, was sent down to Bath. He was to seek Pitt's opinion "what it might be proper to do in the American affairs," and at the same time he was to be invited to join the ministry. Pitt replied that he would give his opinion only to the King or to the Parliament. The ministers, he said, had already made too free with the little encouragement he had given them. He was ready to take office with Grafton, Conway, and Rockingham, but only on two conditions: he "must have the power to offer my Lord Temple the Treasury," and Newcastle must be excluded. Only if Temple refused the Treasury would he consent to Rockingham's retaining it.[68]

These were hard terms for Rockingham and Newcastle to swallow. Newcastle had the stronger stomach. "I have ever been so much of the opinion that it was for the service of his Majesty and the nation that Mr. Pitt should be employed that I could not suffer myself to be the avowed obstacle to it," he told a friend. Accordingly on January 8 he went to the King and offered to resign his post in order for Pitt to be brought in.[69] Rockingham, however, was unwilling to take the chance of losing the Treasury; he preferred to go on without Pitt. In spite of the insistence of Grafton, Conway, and Newcastle, the First Lord prevailed; on January 10 it as decided that "the idea of writing to Mr. Pitt immediately" would be abandoned.[70]

So the reopening of Parliament on January 14 found the ministers in as great a state of indecision as ever. The King tried to be encouraging. "If you continue firm, I don't doubt of success," he wrote Rockingham, "but if you in the least seem to hesitate the inferiors will fly off."[71] But how could one not seem to hesitate when he knew not where he was headed? The session reopened, and the ministers waited for Pitt to rescue them from their "valley of indecision."

NOTES

CHAPTER XIII

[1] Rockingham MSS., 1, f. 239.

[2] Narrative by Hardwicke, January, 1771, Hardwicke MSS., ADD. MSS. 35428, f. 19.

[3] Newcastle to Rockingham, July 12, 1765, Rockingham MSS., 1, f. 246.

[4] See Rockingham to Shelburne, July 11, 1765; Shelburne to Rockingham, July 11, 1765, *Rockingham Memoirs,* I, 234-236; Pitt to Shelburne, December _ , 1765, *Pitt Correspondence,* II, 359-361.

[5] *Rockingham Memoirs,* I, 230.

[6] *London Evening Post,* July 13-16, 1765.

[7] Walpole to Holland, July 18, 1765, Ilchester, *Letters to Fox,* p. 241.

[8] July 18, 1765, Ilchester, *Letters to Fox,* p. 239.

[9] Dobree, *Chesterfield's Letters,* VI, 2358.

[10] Grenville to Hans Stanley, July 12, 1765, Murray MSS.

[11] July 12, 1765, Temple-Whately Letterbook, Stowe MSS.

[12] Upton to Holland, July 16, 1765, Ilchester, *Letters to Fox,* p. 236.

[13] *London Evening Post,* July 18-20, 1765. In January, 1765, Pitt was bequeathed an estate of between 3,000 and 4,000 pounds a year by Sir William Pynsent, a Somersetshire knight who was an admirer of Pitt and particularly of his opposition to the Cider Tax. See Stanley Ayling, *The Elder Pitt,* New York, 1976, pp. 311-312.

[14] Hopkins to Grafton, August 12, 1765, Grafton, *Autobiography,* p. 56.

[15] Lloyd to Grenville, August 29, 1765, *Grenville Papers,* III, 80-81.

[16] *St. James's Chronicle,* July 6-9, 1765: *London Evening Post,* July 6-9, 1765.

[17] *Public Advertiser,* July 11-20, 1765.

[18] *London Evening Post,* July 25-27, 1765. Temple, while personally reconciled with Grenville, was not reconciled to all his measures. At this time he was amusing himself by "abusing Mr. Grenville's administration in the grossest terms, and [saying] there was hardly an article of it that must not have been changed or amended." Sackville to Irwin, July 29, 1765, H.M.C., *Stopford-Sackville MSS.,* I, 101.

[19] See Walpole, *George III,* II, 6-9.

[20] Grenville to Frederick Hindley, August 26, 1765; Grenville to Lloyd, August 26, 1765; Lloyd to Grenville, August 26 and September 2, 1765, Murray MSS.

[21] Grenville to Hillsborough, September 8, 1765, Murray MSS. At this time Grenville also arranged for the purchase of a house in Bolton Street, Piccadilly, which he kept until his death.

[22] Newcastle to Devonshire, October 31, 1761, Newcastle MSS., Add. MSS. 32930, F. 226.

[23] Grenville's Diary, *Grenville Papers,* III, 205.

[24] Lists by Rockingham of the minority on the repeal of the Stamp Act, Rockingham MSS., 54.

[25] List by Meredith, February 22, 1766, Newcastle MSS., Add. MSS. 32974, f. 169. Cf. Namier, *England,* pp. 243-245.

[26] Lists by Rockingham and Meredith, cited above.

[27] Grenville to North, September 4, 1765; Grenville to Hillsborough, September 8, 1765; Grenville to Strange, September 5, 1765, and several others in draft in Murray MSS.

[28] *Grenville Papers,* III, 78-79.

[29] Grenville to Whately, August 13, 1765, Murray MSS.

[30] Treasury minutes, fall, 1765, Rockingham MSS., 28.

[31] Memorandum by Rockingham, September 2, 1765, Rockingham MSS., 49.

[32] Charles Lowndes to the colonial governors, September 14, 1765, Treasury Papers, I, 442, f. 223.

[33] Letters read before the Treasury Board on the American riots, fall, 1765, Newcastle MSS., Add. MSS. 33030. P. D. G. Thomas, *British Politics and the Stamp Act Crisis,* Oxford, 1975, pp. 130-134.

[34] "Memoranda on N. America--Stamp Duty," October 13, 1765, Newcastle MSS., Add. MSS. 32970, f. 314.

[35] Newcastle to Rockingham, October 22, 1765, Newcastle MSS., Add. MSS. 32971, f. 13; Rockingham to Yorke, October 24, 1765, Hardwicke MSS., Add. MSS. 35911, f. 63.

[36] Mackintosh to Temple, August 30, 1765, *Grenville Papers,* III, 82-83.

[37] September 15, 1765, Newcastle MSS., Add. MSS. 32969, f. 392.

[38] Major General David Graeme (1716-1798), M. P. for Perth and private secretary to the Queen.

[39] Cotes to Temple, October 13, 1765, *Grenville Papers,* III, 92-95.

[40] Notes by Mackintosh, October 13, 1765, *Grenville Papers,* III, 97-98.

[41] Temple to _____ (Mackintosh or Cotes), October 13, 1765, *Grenville Papers,* III, 96; Grenville Letterbook, Stowe MSS., 7, II.

[42] Whately to Grenville, October 25, 1765, Murray MSS.

[43] Hervey to Grenville, November 2, 1765, *Grenville Papers,* III, 105-106.

[44] Pitt to Grafton, August 24, 1765, *Pitt Correspondence,* II, 321-323.

[45] Walpole (1727-1803), a younger son of Horatio, Lord Walpole, was at this time M. P. for Ashburton and a merchant in the City.

[46] Pitt to Walpole, November 5, 1765, *Pitt Correspondence,* II, 328-329.

[47] Williams, Pitt, II, 182. On Dulany, see Morgans, *Stamp Act Crisis,* pp. 71-87.

[48] Newcastle to Grafton, November 4, 1765, Newcastle MSS., Add. MSS. 32971, f. 289.

[49] Winstanley, *Government*, pp. 251-252.

[50] Cooke to Pitt, December 5, 1765, *Pitt Correspondence*, II, 338-342.

[51] Pitt to Cooke, December 7, 1765, *Pitt Correspondence*, II, 342-343.

[52] Onslow to Newcastle, December 15, 1765, Newcastle MSS., Add. MSS. 32972, f. 251.

[53] King to Conway, December 5, 1765, *Rockingham Memoirs*, I, 256.

[54] *Parl. Hist.*, XVI, 83-84.

[55] Grenville to Bedford, November 28, 1765, *Bedford Correspondence*, III, 323.

[56] Chesterfield to his son, November 28, 1765, Dobree, *Chesterfield's Letters*, VI, 2685-2686.

[57] Memorandum for Rockingham by Newcastle, December 10, 1765, Newcastle MSS., Add. MSS. 32972, f. 190.

[58] Onslow to Newcastle, December 11, 1765; Rockingham to Newcastle, December 12, 1765, Newcastle MSS., Add. MSS. 32972, ff. 202-203, 214.

[59] *Parl. Hist.*, XVI, 88-89.

[60] Conway to the King, December 17, 1765, Fortescue, *Papers of George III*, I, 201-202.

[61] Cooke to Pitt, December 17, 1765, *Pitt Correspondence*, II, 350-353; Conway to the King, December 17, 1765, Fortescue, *Papers of George III*, I, 202.

[62] Conway to the King, December 19, 1765, Fortescue, *Papers of George III*, I, 205; Walpole, *George III*, II, 205.

[63] Sackville to Irwin, December 23, 1765, H.M.C., *Stopford-Sackville MSS.*, I, 103.

[64] Circular letter, December 6, 1765, Rockingham MSS., 26.

[65] Memorandum in Rockingham's hand, n.d., Rockingham MSS., 49.

[66] Memorandum in Rockingham's hand, n.d., Rockingham MSS., 49.

[67] Winstanley, *Government*, p. 256; Adolphus, *History of England*, I, 197-198.

[68] Newcastle to the Archbishop of Canterbury, January 11, 1766, Newcastle MSS., Add. MSS. 32973, ff. 112-113; Winstanley, *Government*, pp. 256-257. Cf. Grafton, *Autobiography*, pp. 62-63.

[69] Newcastle to Page, January 10, 1766; "minute of what I propose to say to the King," January 8, 1766, Newcastle MSS., Add. MSS. 32973, ff. 55, 127.

[70] Rockingham to the King, January 10, 1766, Fortescue, *Papers of George III*, I, 218; Rockingham to Newcastle, January 11, 1766, Newcastle MSS., Add. MSS. 32973, f. 100.

[71] January 10, 1766, Fortescue, *Papers of George III*, I, 218.

CHAPTER XIV

REPEALS, REVERSALS, AND REVISIONS, 1766

The ministers were undecided as to their course when January 14 arrived, but both Grenville and Pitt had made up their minds. Grenville and his former colleagues in the ministry had determined upon a pitched battle in both Houses from the beginning of the session. Sandwich reported to Bedford, January 6, that he had consulted with Grenville and Halifax and that they were "all of opinion that a question and a division is very advisable in both Houses the first day of the session." Sandwich was unconcerned, moreover, that agents of the ministers might open his letter. "If they should know that we are determined to give them no rest, it is a matter of little consequence."[1]

At Bath, Pitt also had come to a resolution. His gout had abated, and he was preparing to depart for Hayes when he wrote his friend Thomas Nuthall, "If I can crawl, or be carried, I will deliver my mind and heart upon *the state* of America."[2] What opinions his mind and heart held he still did not say, but Grenville and his friends could guess that they would not be what they wished to hear.

The King's speech when the Parliament reassembled was a virtual admission of the ministers' indecision. He did little more than appeal for advice on the "occurrences" in the colonies. The House of Commons had retired to debate their address and Robert Nugent was speaking when Pitt entered. All eyes were immediately upon him. "A peppercorn in acknowledgement of the right" of taxation, Nugent was saying, was "of more value than millions without." When Nugent finished in this vein, Pitt got the Speaker's eye. The House was in agitation. The "great commoner" seldom rose so early in the debate! As the members became quiet, Pitt was explaining his position. "I stand up in this place single and unconnected," he announced. Turning to Grenville, who sat two seats from him, he severed their reconciliation with a single blow. "As to the late ministry," he thundered, "every capital measure they have taken has been entirely wrong!" But Conway and the other ministers fared little better. Pitt had "no objection" to them; he had even advised them to take office

255

when they had consulted him. But he could not give them his confidence. "Pardon me, gentlemen," he said with a bow; "confidence is a plant of slow growth in an aged bosom; youth is the season of credulity. By comparing events with each other, reasoning from effects to causes, methinks I plainly discover the traces of an over-ruling influence." By this, as he elaborated, he meant Bute and Newcastle.

Having disposed of Grenville and the ministry, Pitt turned to the question at hand. He had been ill in bed when the Stamp Act was passed, he said. "If I could have endured to have been carried in my bed, so great was the agitation of my mind for the consequences, I would have solicited some kind hand to have laid me down on this floor, to have borne my testimony against it." This was certainly news to all those who had been urging him so long to give a hint of his opinions! But now, having made up his mind, he gave more than a hint. "It is my opinion," he cried, "that this kingdom has no right to lay a tax upon the colonies." The power of Parliament was "sovereign and supreme in every circumstance of government and legislation whatsoever," he admitted, but "taxation is no part of the governing or legislative power." Taxes, he asserted, could only be granted by representatives duly elected. He proceeded to lay out the arguments and much of the language of Daniel Dulany's pamphlets. The idea that the colonists were "virtually represented" in the Commons he dismissed contemptuously; it did not "deserve a serious refutation." The Parliament might bind the colonies "by her laws, by her regulations and restrictions in trade, in navigation, in manufactures—in every thing, except that of taking their money out of their pockets without their consent."

Pitt's distinction between external and internal taxation was one which would not stand analysis. Grenville was quick to attack it as contrary both to logic and to all legal precedent. It is conceivable that had the Parliament implemented Pitt's recommendations there might have been no revolution, but it is equally irrelevant. His position was out of tune with the time and with the temper of Parliament. The arguments were accepted eagerly enough in America, but not as considered and thoughtful policy; they were rather means to an end, the ready means which men grasped gratefully with little consideration of logic or legality. The Congress was to learn under the Articles of Confederation that the power to tax *was* the power to govern; without it they could only negotiate with the all-powerful States.

Grenville rather than Pitt expressed the thinking of the House. "Protection and obedience are reciprocal," he argued. "Great Britain protects America; America is bound to yield. If not, tell me where the Americans are emancipated! When they want the protection of this kingdom, they are always very ready to ask it." Grenville went straight to the illogic of Pitt's argument. "I cannot understand the difference between external and internal taxes," he declared. "They are the same in effect, and only differ in name. That this kingdom has the sovereign, the supreme legislative power over America, is granted. It cannot be denied; and taxation is part of that sovereign power. It is one branch of the legislation." With a long list of precedents, he proceeded to demonstrate to the House that representation had never been a requisite for taxation.

Turning to Pitt, Grenville almost accused him of treason. "The seditious spirit of the colonies owes its birth to the factions in this House," he cried. "Gentlemen are careless of the consequences of what they say, provided it answers the purposes of opposition." Men who bade the House "expect disobedience" from the colonies, he asserted, were "but telling Americans to stand out against the law, to encourage their obstinacy with the expectation of support from hence."

Pitt rose heatedly to defend himself, and though he had already spoken once on the motion and was clearly out of order, he was met with cries of "go on!" and was permitted to speak. "I have been charged with giving birth to sedition in America.... Sorry I am to hear the liberty of speech of this House imputed as a crime. But the imputation shall not discourage me. It is a liberty I mean to exercise." Then the House sat aghast as Pitt, in the heat of this personal duel with his brother-in-law, went far beyond his prepared position. "The gentleman tells us America is obstinate; America has resisted!" he declaimed. "Three millions of people so dead to all feelings of liberty as voluntarily to submit to be slaves would have been fit instruments to make slaves of the rest."

Yet Pitt realized that he could not debate the question of Parliament's legal right with Grenville. He was not, he said, "armed at all points with law cases and acts of Parliaments, with the statute-book doubled down in dog's ears.... I would not debate a particular point of law with the gentleman; I know his abilities. I have been obliged to his diligent researches." On constitutional principle, however, he stood firm in maintaining that Parliament could not place internal taxes on the colonies. "If the gentleman does not understand the difference between internal and external taxes, I cannot help it," Pitt declared, deliberately mistaking Grenville's meaning; "but there is a plain distinction between taxes levied for...revenue and duties imposed for the regulation of trade."

"Upon the whole," he concluded, "I beg leave to tell the House what is really my opinion. It is, that the Stamp Act be *repealed absolutely, totally* and *immediately.* That the reason for the repeal be assigned, because it was founded upon an erroneous principle." The sovereignty of Parliament, he suggested, might be "asserted in as strong terms as can be devised," and it might extend to "every power whatsoever except that of taking their money out of their pockets without their consent."[3]

Edmund Burke, anxiously awaiting an opportunity to deliver his own maiden speech in the House, said these exchanges of Grenville and Pitt were "an altercation of several hours" and that both men were "heated to a great degree; Pitt as much as contempt, very strongly marked, would suffer him."[4]

Meanwhile, Temple in the House of Lords had delivered himself of the same sort of sentiments as Grenville had expressed in the Commons, and he had come to the Commons gallery in time to hear Grenville reply to his brother-in-law. Pitt's "heat" and "contempt" were no doubt increased by seeing Temple beyond the Bar of the House, conspicuously "smiling and condemning everything Mr. Pitt says and applauding the sentiments and behavior of Mr. Grenville."[5] Grenville also took the occasion of the debate to complain of "aspersions" on him which had appeared in the press and which he felt it becoming to "wipe off" in the House. Temple was vastly pleased with his whole performance. The following day he wrote Grenville:

> I heard you last night, so much to your honour, give the lye direct to the vile misrepresentations which had been so industriously propagated against you, and I feel so much pleasure in it that I must beg you will accept of a small pittance of a thousand pounds transferred this day to your account at Mr. Coutts's in testimony of my joy and conviction.[6]

ii.

The ministers now had their cue from the "great commoner," but it was such a cue as they dared not respond to. Unsure of the support of the court and faced with the violent opposition of Grenville and his supporters in the Commons, what hope had they of forcing so radical a proposal through the Parliament? To repeal the Stamp Act as a measure of expediency might have been plausible, but to lead the legislature to renounce its right of taxation of the colonies was beyond the realm of political possibility. Moreover, Pitt had unmistakably declared his lack of confidence in the ministry; if Rockingham did not choose the plan he had suggested, Pitt's supporters and admirers probably would fall away.

There seemed only two alternatives open to Rockingham: he could either persuade Pitt to join the government and counteract those baneful words spoken in debate, or he could go to the King, confess his inability to go on, and throw up the reins of government. He chose to try the former course. "Your Majesty's present administration," he wrote to George III the day after the great debate, "will be shook to the greatest degree if no further attempt is made to get Mr. Pitt to take a cordial part." The chances appeared better than they had been two weeks before, for Pitt and Temple had now openly differed on the American question. Rockingham agreed with Grafton and Conway that Pitt "might be separated" from Temple and Grenville by an invitation to take office.[7]

When Grafton visited Pitt the following day, he found that Pitt was indeed "separated" from Temple, but the separation did not lessen Pitt's sense of obligation to Temple or his feeling that his brother-in-law was a necessary ally in a ministry. Grafton asked whether, if Pitt entered the government, he would still require that Temple be offered the Treasury. Pitt replied that the question was cruel; he could not come into office unless Temple was invited also, but he himself was not on such terms with him that he could propose it to Temple. The ministers would have to approach him through the "proper channel." Pitt declined to say what he would do if Temple refused. He further required Newcastle's total exclusion from the ministry and extensive changes in personnel, amounting to dissolution of Rockingham's government and reconstitution under Pitt.[8]

These terms were even harder than those Pitt had required on January 2, and again Rockingham and the King thought them too much. Perhaps George III did not want Pitt in office because he was offended by his defense of American resistance. Grenville recorded in his diary on January 31 that "the King expressed himself angrily against Mr. Pitt, and said he was glad he had not committed his dignity by seeing him.[9] In any event, when Rockingham visited Pitt, January 18, he informed the "great commoner" that the King "could not think it proper" to invite Temple to join his ministers and Pitt in office, since "his Lordship differ'd so much in measures with his present Ministers."[10] Thus the second attempt to gain Pitt was abandoned by Rockingham. He chose to gamble on the support of the court and the favor of the King.

Meanwhile, on January 17 Conway, Grafton, Dowdeswell and Townshend met at Downing Street with Rockingham to decide what to do about the Stamp Act. "The ideas we join in," Rockingham wrote to

Charles Yorke after the others had left, "are...a declaratory act in general terms, afterwards to proceed to considerations of trade, etc., and finally to a determination on the Stamp Act, i.e. a repeal."[11] The plan was precisely what Pitt had suggested in the Commons, with one significant exception. Pitt had recommended that the sovereignty of Parliament be "asserted in as strong terms as possible," but he had specified that the power of taxation be denied. The "declaratory act" now envisaged in "general terms" would neither affirm nor deny the power of taxation, while legislative supremacy would be asserted. In this statement, the ministers hoped, all but extremists on both sides would find common ground.

Rockingham talked with Pitt on January 21 and came away with the impression that Pitt did not oppose declaring the rights of Parliament. "Mr. Pitt declared strongly for the repeal of the Stamp Act," Newcastle recorded Rockingham as reporting, "but as to...asserting the right of the Parliament, Mr. Pitt did not seem so strong as he was the other day in his speech."[12] Accordingly, a declaratory act, the ministry decided, would be drawn up "in general terms," to be followed by arguments of the expediency of repeal from considerations of trade and finally by a motion for repeal. Rockingham was careful to keep the declaratory act in unoffensive generalities. Attorney General Yorke insisted that Parliament's right be declared "as well in cases of taxation as in all other cases whatsoever,"[13] but for the moment Rockingham stood his ground. "It is our firm resolution in the House of Lords," he told Yorke, "that that word must be resisted."[14]

iii.

The ministers laid their plans to displease as few members of the Parliament as possible, but they neglected the King's opinion. George III was dissatisfied with his weak ministry and offended by their plans to repeal the Stamp Act. He repeatedly suggested to his friends in the ministry, Northington and Egmont, that there should be a union with Bute and his followers to carry out a revision and enforcement of the Stamp Act in spite of Pitt. Newcastle and Rockingham, however, knew what a tempest the opposition could raise around Bute's name; they rejected the idea as often as it was raised. Very well, said the King, the ministers could "either go on or give up," but he no longer took responsibility for procuring them support. Bute's followers in the King's service as minor officials asked if they would be dismissed for opposing the ministers on repeal. In one of his now infrequent letters to Bute, George told him on January 10 that he could not approve if Bute's followers in office tried to "overturn" his ministers; "that conduct alone could make me think myself at liberty as a man of honour to be forever detach'd from them." But to oppose out of conscience was different. "As to my friends differing from Ministers where they think their honour and conscience requires it, that I not only think right, but am of opinion it is their duty to act so; nay I think it is also incumbent on my Dear Friend to act entirely so also."15

Thus George III gave his personal followers in the Parliament permission to follow their consciences on the Stamp Act even before Pitt made his declarations on January 16. Immediately thereafter, he tried to get Bute's followers and his own personal adherents to form an administration alone, but that attempt was unsuccessful.16 He then began to think once more of calling Temple, Grenville, and Bedford into his service. Northington had told him that if the Grenville brothers came in he would be "a slave for life," and George III was inclined to agree with him.17 But Pitt was preaching virtual treason, and the ministers seemed determined to court him. To whom else could he turn?

By January 28, an indirect negotiation was under way to "feel out" Grenville and Bedford on the subject. The agents were Northington and the Scottish Earl of Marchmont for the King and Lord Hyde for Grenville and Bedford.18 Marchmont, Hyde reported on January 28, had conferred with Northington and the King on the matter and was "satisfied with what passed." "I forbode good from the secrecy," Hyde observed. "A continuation of things would require none; a change possibly ought not yet to be divulged. I am happy in thinking that they both conclude you are the fittest man for the place from which you was dismissed." At the same time, Hyde took the initiative in another direction. "I have removed some rubbish (erroneous prejudice) and have had Lord Bute sounded on a conciliation plan, a coalition of the ablest men; a negotiation safe for him, worthy of majesty, auspicious for the nation. It might be attended with permanency."19

Three days later, Bute's friend Lord Suffolk20 approached Grenville in the House of Commons. If "a message were brought from the King" to Grenville and Bedford "thro' Lord Bute," how would they receive it? Grenville replied that the question was "of great delicacy,...as I did not know the party who proposed it." He therefore declined to negotiate except with "principals," and he suggested to the young lord that he ask the person giving him the commission to reveal himself. That evening Suffolk reported that the agents were Marchmont and Northington. The Lord Chancellor, said Suffolk, was ready to "open the door" for Grenville and Bedford to "negotiate an administration with the King himself immediately."

Grenville and Bedford sent word by Suffolk that they would receive any message the King should send, "by any person whatever," with "all respect and duty." They could do no less, Grenville decided. To give "a more negative answer" might throw Bute and his influence behind the Rockingham government "upon the important question of asserting the sovereignty of Great Britain over America, which once gone is irretrievable, and which in the present situation by Lord Bute's defection from the ministry there is a very fair prospect of preventing."21

Meanwhile, Hyde also was in contact with Marchmont and had fresh reports. The King, he said, was professing himself "strenuously for supporting and asserting the right of Great Britain to impose" the Stamp Act; he was "against the repeal of the Bill, but thought perhaps it could be modified." This, Grenville commented, was precisely the line of thought that Bute was publicly giving out.22 There might be some likelihood of an accommodation with Bute to defeat the repeal.

George III agreed, but he could not be certain of the best course. Would Grenville modify the act as the King wished, or would he insist on enforcing it in its original form? The King's indecision and stress brought on one of his attacks. On February 1 he was "feverish" and sent for his physicians. The following day he was in much agitation, and he exclaimed to his doctors that he was "willing to do anything for the good of his people, if they would but agree among themselves." Guttmacher called this a psychological projection of his own indecision.23

Grenville and Bedford heard nothing more of the negotiation until February 9, although Northington talked as though it was still pending.24 Meanwhile, Temple, Bedford, and Bute in the Lords managed to defeat in committee two government motions on America.25 Grenville learned on February 9 that Bute wanted an interview with him. Grenville replied that he was "ready to receive any proposition Lord Bute thinks proper to make."26 Three days later he and Bedford met Bute at the home of his friend Lord Eglinton.27 The ex-ministers considered the interview as what it probably was intended to be: a preliminary interview to a negotiation with the King. They informed the favorite that if the King would allow them "to tread the same paths" they had followed in office, they would do all they could "to assist his Majesty in this present critical time." Grenville averred that there was "no disposition" by either of them "to look back to what is past, or consider any thing but what is *now* best for the King's service."28 Bedford personally declined to take any office—he was in ill health and almost blind—but both he and Grenville pledged their cooperation with Bute "for the service of their King and country." If the King were "inclined to pursue the *modification* instead of the *total repeal* of the Stamp Act," Grenville and Bedford were at the King's service. Grenville warned, however, that if the Stamp Act were repealed, he would never again consent to enter the government.29

If the ex-ministers considered this interview with Bute an indication that the King had made up his mind to engage their services in office, they were mistaken. George III had still decided nothing, but his thoughts were inclining toward Rockingham. For more than a week Grenville and Bedford heard nothing from Bute. At length on February 18 they sent to the King through his brother, the Duke of York, to know what had happened to the negotiation. By this time the King had made his decision. He replied to his brother's inquiries that he did "not think it constitutional for the Crown personally to intefere in measures it has thought proper to refer to the advice of Parliament."30 He would continue with the Rockingham ministry.

iv.

While the King was debating and negotiating with Grenville and Bedford, a battle was going on in the Parliament. Conway fired the opening salvo on February 3 by introducing the Declaratory Act. Few men in the House of Commons were prepared to deny that the Parliament had, as the resolution declared, "full power and authority to make laws and statutes of sufficient force and validity to bind the colonies and people of America...in all cases whatsoever."31 Both Grenville and Pitt, however, opposed the resolution, although for different reasons. Grenville maintained there was no need for it. If Parliament had the right to legislate for and levy taxes on the colonies, as he maintained it did, there was no necessity to declare it. The Stamp Act had already done so. And if the ministers meant to repeal the Stamp Act, as Conway soon announced that they did, there was no use trying "to deceive mankind into a belief that we mean to establish a right we avow we do not mean to exercise."

Pitt rose immediately to second Grenville's last contention. It was "absurd," he agreed, "to vote the right in order not to exercise it." The resolution, he contended, was as much an invasion of American rights as the Stamp Act if it was to apply to taxation. "If liberty be not countenanced in America," he warned solemnly, "it will sicken, fade, and die in this country."32 On the whole, however, Pitt was conciliatory toward the min-

isters. Even Grenville observed that he "spoke with much more moderation than usual."[33] The House, after debating until three in the morning,
passed the resolution without a division. In the Lords, Pitt's allies,
Camden and Shelburne, attacked the assertion of Parliament's right of
taxation, but on the division they could muster only five lords against a
ministerial majority of 125![34]

The majorities, however, by no means indicated the strength of opin-
ion in favor of repeal of the Stamp Act. As Newcastle observed, the
Declaratory Act "might as well be followed by an act to enforce the
Stamp Act as by a bill to repeal it."[35]

The following day, February 4, Rockingham lost a motion in the Lords
that the government "recommend" rather than "require" the colonies to
make satisfaction to the sufferers in the Stamp Act riots. Bute and Temple
rallied sixty-three lords against the ministry's sixty. The ministers seriously considered resigning, but upon deliberation decided to continue as
if they believed themselves in full possession of the King's confidence.[36]

They spread the report that the King himself favored repeal, but this
protection was quickly removed. Lord Strange learned from the King that
he favored modification rather than repeal and only favored repeal in
preference to total enforcement.[37] The whole town soon knew that the
King differed with his ministers on repeal.

Grenville, meanwhile, was trying not to offend anyone who might support him in the final fight against repeal. On February 5 he offered resolutions calling for compensating the victims of the colonial riots and voting them the approbation of the House. Even Pitt supported the resolutions. A third motion, calling for indemnity to those who had not "taken
out stamps" on documents which required them, had a good prospect of
succeeding also, but it was objected to by Gilbert Elliott and some of
Bute's friends. Grenville immediately withdrew the motion, even though
his friends urged him to a division. He thought it "more prudent," he said,
to "give up the words objected to" than to furnish Bute's followers with
"a pretense for leaving him in the main question of repeal when it should
come."[38]

But with ministers in retreat in both Houses, Grenville now committed
an error in tactics. On February 7, in an effort to embarrass the government and perhaps force them from office, he tried to commit the
Parliament that all laws in the colonies be enforced before proceeding to
modify the Stamp Act, which he admitted was necessary. Even many of
the opponents of repeal thought it inexpedient to vote on this question
before settling whether the Stamp Act should be enforced or repealed. Of

course, few members could object in the abstract to enforcing the laws, but many questioned whether this law was enforceable. The debate was long and heated. Pitt thundered personal abuse at Grenville, adding insult to the injury by sauntering out of the House as his brother-in-law rose to answer him. Grenville, angry, answered "as if he was present" and, according to Grenville, at least, gained "great applause." But when a division was finally called on Charles Yorke's motion to adjourn, to everyone's astonishment the ministers polled a majority of 140, 274 to 134.39

Pitt tried to make some amends by writing to Grenville the next day, apologizing for leaving the House and assuring him that it did not "mark the least want of personal regard to Mr. Grenville, [he] being in truth not in a condition to remain in the Committee, and having requested leave to retire." Grenville replied very stiffly, obviously not in the least mollified, thanking him formally for his assurances but saying that he wished Pitt "could have heard his answer."40

Whether it was warranted or not, men both within and without the Parliament took the division in the Commons as an indication of renewed life in the Rockingham ministry. The stock market, which had fallen three to four percent with the defeats of the ministers, rose as quickly as it had sunk, and men began to say that "the ministry may now stand their ground."41

With greater confidence, then, the government prepared to present the Parliament the petitions of merchants and witnesses' testimony on the state of trade with America. Repeal was the object, Newcastle wrote on February 15, but not for Pitt's reason. Newcastle was not concerned about the wrong done to America but the harm to British trade and the threat of riots in Great Britain.

> It was the opinion of the King's servants...that nothing but the repeal of the Stamp Act could possibly restore quiet and peace in America and recover to this country those valuable branches of trade which are at present totally lost, and which, if not soon recovered, will be attended with the most fatal effects here at home. And [they]...will produce as great riots, tumults, and insurrections in the great manufacturing towns here as have been in any part of America.... If the repeal of the Act should be passed in the House of Commons and be rejected in the House of Lords, I dread the consequence of what may happen even here in the capital.42

The task, therefore, was to convince the Parliament that even though the right undoubtedly existed to tax the colonies, the Stamp Act was harming British trade, threatening British tranquility, and taking money out of the members' own pockets. To this end, Conway paraded some forty North American merchants and colonial agents before the bar of the Commons. Visiting Americans gave eye-witness reports of the American riots and assured the members that the act could not be enforced without additional troops. Benjamin Franklin's carefully rehearsed performance made a great impression and was quickly published. Conway, meanwhile, laid before the House all the correspondence from stamp distributors and colonial governors describing the tumults in America.[43]

Grenville too brought in petitions and witnesses to convince the House that modification, not repeal, was the only reasonable course.[44] At length on February 21 the last witness was heard and the last petition presented. As the news spread that the resolution to repeal was to be introduced, all England was tense. Friday evening, February 21, crowds of people milled outside Westminster Palace as the debate proceeded inside, and scores of City merchants packed the lobby of St. Stephen's Chapel.[45]

Inside, the House sat in committee with West India merchant Rose Fuller in the Chair. Conway set the stage by introducing the motion for repeal. Charles Jenkinson put the case for Grenville and the opposition by moving that the words "explain and amend" be substituted for the word "repeal." The debate, Conway wrote to the King, "was not animated, as generally happens upon most important subjects when they have been long the subject of discussion." Grenville supported Jenkinson's motion, speaking "strong and well," and was backed by his friends Robert Nugent, Gilbert Ellis, and Lord Strange. Pitt and Cooke were the chief cohorts of the ministers. Finally Jenkinson's motion was put to a vote and a division taken. The opposition mustered 167, their largest number during the whole course of the fight on repeal, but the ministers were stronger. They reported 275, a majority of 108![46]

As the teller for the noes reported the total for the ministers, a great shout went up from the merchants in the lobby and was echoed by the crowds outside. The battle was not over, but the opposition had shown its weakness in the first skirmish; London and England did not wait to rejoice. When the House adjourned at two o'clock Saturday morning, after the resolution for repeal had passed without a division, the crowds gave a tremendous cheer for Conway. At Pitt's appearance they uncovered their heads and followed his chair out of respect. But when Grenville appeared they hissed and pressed in on him scornfully. Grenville, "swelling with rage and mortification" as Horace Walpole told it, seized the nearest man by the collar. Fortunately the fellow was good-humored enough. "Well," he cried, "if I may not hiss, at least I may laugh!" Laugh he did, and the whole crowd joined him.[47]

Yet despite the overwhelming majority of the ministers and the humiliation at the hands of the mob, the stubborn Grenville refused to concede the fight. While England rejoiced in the resolution to repeal, Grenville announced that he would fight the measure to the very last. Newcastle suggested to Rockingham that he spur up their managers in the Commons, lest Grenville catch them off guard.[48] Thus at every stage Grenville outdid himself to oppose the progress of the bill. And at every stage his followers fell away. On February 24, after an angry speech in which he denounced the repeal as "a servile, mean, and contemptible bill,"[49] he lost a motion to send the bill back to committee by 240 to 133.[50] On the final reading of the bill, March 4, he again crossed swords with Pitt, but Conway reported that "the debate was not most interesting." The ministerial majority on this occasion was 250 to 122.[51]

In the Lords, however, the sides were more evenly matched, and until the very end the issue was in doubt. Led by Temple, Mansfield, Bute, and Bedford, the opposition ran the gamut of legal and constitutional argument. Camden and Shelburne espoused the ideas Pitt had expounded in the Commons. Between Mansfield and Camden, the two Chief Justices, there occurred a running battle on the constitutional issues involved. The ministers, however, concentrated on the commercial issue. Newcastle and Grafton hammered away at the contention that if the Stamp Act were not repealed, Britain's trade would be undone and the country with it.[52] The ministers carried the motion for commitment of the bill, March 11, by 73 to 61,[53] a margin much too close for comfort. It must have been with a sigh of genuine relief that Rockingham wrote to the King, March 17: "Lord Rockingham humbly presumes to acquaint his Majesty that the Repeal of the Stamp Act has passed the House of Lords—without division."[54]

v.

The Stamp Act was the first of Grenville's major measures to fall under the axe of the Rockingham ministry. Others were quickly to follow. While repeal of the Stamp Act was still before the Commons, the first steps were taken toward repeal of another measure Grenville had played a major role in passing. On February 26, the ministers presented petitions from the cider counties of Cornwall, Devon, Somerset, Gloucester, Worcester, Hereford, and Monmouth. Citizens of those counties respectfully petitioned for repeal of the Cider Act of 1763.[55] On March 7, Dowdeswell as Chancellor of the Exchequer brought in a resolution for the repeal of the act, which Pitt immediately seconded. Once again Grenville and Pitt locked horns over the excise issue; this time Grenville was probably careful to avoid using the words "tell me where!" In 1763 Grenville had had a governmental majority to back him against Pitt, but now the roles were reversed. Although Grenville was solidly supported by his friends, the motion for repeal was carried on a voice vote. Dowdeswell then brought in a substitute bill which placed the duties on cider not on the producers, as the old act had done, but on the retailers of cider.[56] Thus applied, the act was far more equitable, for it bore more equally on the whole population, and it obviated the objectionable searches of private homes which the old act had necessitated. Both the repeal and Dowdeswell's new act slipped through the Commons without further difficulty. In the Lords, Temple, Mansfield, and Lyttelton abandoned Grenville and voted for repeal of the Cider Act.[57]

The deficiency in ways and means which the repeal of the Stamp Act caused was made up by Dowdeswell and Rockingham in a window tax. Keeping the land tax—in spite of the advice of Rockingham's financial advisers[58]—at four shillings in the pound, the Treasury added an additional burden on the landed interests by enacting a graduated window tax. Grenville and his lieutenants, Nugent, Lord Carysford, and Lord North, opposed the measure "with great ability" and were able to divide 112 against 162.[59] Yet the figure they made before the landed gentry, satisfying as it was, must have been poor compensation for the reversal of their tax measures.

One reversal, however, Grenville himself took a major part in executing. In return for his support on the Stamp Act, the most important issue in Grenville's thinking, Temple probably required Grenville to support him in one of his great aims, that of declaring general warrants illegal. Temple was apparently sincere in regarding general warrants and the seizing of private papers as flagrant invasions of individual liberty. Grenville now joined him in the crusade which he himself had defeated two years before. When Pitt announced in the Commons, April 24, that he would bring in a bill to declare general warrants illegal, Grenville rose immediately to declare his own support. Men were amazed to see Grenville "applauding Pitt in every word."[60] When the bill was introduced the following day, the resolution passed without a division.[61] Half of Temple's program was accomplished.

On April 29 Grenville, "in a very elaborate speech," introduced a motion to declare seizure of private papers illegal in all cases except treason and felony. Attorney General Yorke, whose father Hardwicke had strongly defended the government's action in the *North Briton* case, now "spoke exceeding well...& strongly against Mr. Grenville's motion," Onslow reported to Newcastle, "which makes me wonder it was so generally agreed to."62 With support from Pitt, however, the bill carried on a final reading May 14 by a division of 55-16. In the house of Lords, however, the measure was lost.63

On the repeal of another of Grenville's measures, Pitt remained silent. In an effort to solidify the tie they had made with Trecothick and the North American merchants, the ministers brought in a bill, April 30, to repeal the Sugar Act molasses duty and replace it with a duty of a penny a gallon on both foreign and British molasses. Beckford and the West Indians merchants opposed the bill. Pitt, privately admitting that he favored the penny duty,64 tried to act as mediator among the ministers, Grenville, and Beckford. Grenville spoke vigorously in defense of his threepenny duty. "The Americans themselves," he said, "had never asked to pay less than twopence." A penny a gallon was the amount that was usually paid to customs officers to connive at smuggling!65 Nevertheless, the combined arguments of Grenville and Beckford could not overcome the ministers' assertions that the measure was necessary to restore trade with North America. On May 8, the repeal of the Sugar Act and the substituted penny duty passed their crucial vote in committee. The following day they were reported to the House and began an easy course through Parliament.66 Grenville's American taxes had been done away with.

vi.

When the Parliament was prorogued in May, 1766, all of Grenville's measures which had been regarded as grievances had been either repealed or revised. Yet in spite of the popularity of the repeals and revisions, the Rockingham government was as much without support as ever. For both the initiative in proposing the changes and the leadership in passing them had been largely Pitt's, and it was to Pitt rather than Rockingham that men gave the credit. Without popular or Parliamentary support, the government began to crumble. Grafton, offended that Pitt had not been allowed to come into office on his own terms, had resigned as Secretary of State in April.67 His place was difficult for Rockingham to fill. The man he chose added little prestige to the ministry, for the Duke of Richmond had little experience or ability for the post. In addition, the

King complained that Richmond's appointment had been forced on him against his will.

By the end of June, the government was on its last legs. The ministers, men learned, were sharply divided among themselves. Richmond and Conway had united against Rockingham and Newcastle and were opposing them at every turn, "upon occasions serious and trifling."[68] Northington was the next to abandon the stricken vessel. On July 6, he went to the King to resign the Great Seal. Before Rockingham and the rest of the ministry could gather their wits, the King informed them that he had sent for Pitt, July 7, to form a new administration.[69]

When he received Pitt, July 12, the King probably learned from him the plan on which he intended to build his ministry. Certainly he learned that Pitt wished to have Temple at the Treasury, for the following day he had Temple summoned to London. The King, Northington wrote Temple, wished "to have a conversation" with him "on the subject of giving force and effect to his Government."[70]

At this summons, Temple set out from Stowe in the early morning of July 14, knowing nothing of Pitt's plans or of the political situation except that a negotiation for a new ministry was proceeding. On his way from Stowe he had an hour's conversation with Grenville at Wotton. The brothers agreed that Grenville's claim to office should not be pressed.[71] But even with this concession, Temple found himself unable to accept the terms which Pitt offered. In an interview with the King July 15 and another with Pitt the following day, Temple learned the type of ministry the "great commoner" planned. The basis of the administration, Temple contemptuously informed Grenville, was to be the "rump" of the Rockingham government, "strengthened by the particular friends of Mr. Pitt, the whole consisting of all the most choice spirits who did the last Session most eminently distinguish themselves in the sacrifice of the rights and honour of the whole Legislature and Kingdom of Great Britain." Conway and Grafton were to be Secretaries of State, and Camden was to be Lord Chancellor.

Pitt would not hear of Temple's bringing in any of his family or political connections. He was willing to allow Lyttelton to sit in the Cabinet Council as a special favor to Temple, but he could have no office. Temple's suggestion that Gower be Secretary of State "could not be thought of." While he was requested to take the nominal headship of the ministry and one of its most responsible posts, Temple was to have no say whatsoever in policy or personnel. He was expected, he complained, to be "a capital cypher, surrounded with cyphers of quite a different complexion, the whole under the guidance of that great Luminary, the great Commoner, with the Privy Seal in his hand."72 He had been willing, he wrote to his sister, to sacrifice George's "pretensions" to office, "as he was himself, to Mr. Pitt's indisposition towards him," but he emphatically declined, as he put it, *"to go in like a child, to come out like a fool."*73

If Pitt was unwise in treating Temple thus, he showed even less wisdom in the days which followed. For the ministry which he selected had little other cohesive force than Pitt's own personality. Grafton took the Treasury, with Charles Townshend as his Chancellor of the Exchequer. Conway was again Secretary of State, although he was transferred from the Southern to the Northern Department to curtail his using the patronage,74 and his place was taken by Pitt's friend Shelburne. Camden became Lord Chancellor, while among the King's personal friends Northington became Lord President of the Council and Egmont retained the Admiralty.

Pitt's decision to take the Privy Seal was probably wise. Ill and aging, he could also plead the necessity of exercising general supervision of the ministry as an excuse for not taking a "responsible" office. But his decision to accept the King's offer of a peerage was a collosal mistake. In so doing he not only deprived his ministry of the effect of his oratory in the Commons; he deprived it of the tremendous popularity of the "great commoner." For the tumultuous adulation which the public heaped on William Pitt was denied to the new Earl of Chatham. "There is no solitude so obscure as not to resound with the clamour against the new peer," Whatley reported to Grenville in early August. "Those who remember that against Lord Bath say it was nothing to this."75 "If the new peer has not gained as much ground in the Closet as he has lost in the public," Lord Trevor observed, "he must soon have but a very narrow and tottering basis left to stand upon."76

Yet despite the public clamor and the loss of his popularity, the new Lord Chatham did not despair. He asserted that he "had the King's entire confidence and that he had not the least doubt or suspicion that he should lose it." He was "sensible of the run there was against him," but "if his Majesty was pleased...to continue his confidence to him, he would never desert the King, but support him in all events, broke and old as he was." He even boasted, Newcastle reported, that he "had not the least doubt of success, and that his administration would be a permanent one."77 How empty that boast was time would soon tell!

NOTES

CHAPTER XIV

[1] *Bedford Correspondence*, III, 324-325.

[2] January 9, 1766, *Pitt Correspondence, II, 362*.

[3] *Parl. Hist.*, XVI, 90-108; *Pitt Correspondence*, II, 363-373n.; Sackville to Irwin, January 17, 1766, H.M.C., *Stopford-Sackville MSS.*, I, 104; Sarah Osborn to John Osborn, January 17, 1766, *Letters of Sarah Byng Osborn, 1721-1773*, edited by John McClelland, Stanford University, 1930, p. 93; Walpole, *George III*, II, 260-268; West to Newcastle, January 14, 1766, Newcastle MSS., Add. MSS. 32973, ff. 133-135.

[4] Burke to O'Hara, January 18, 1766, *Burke Correspondence*, I, 231-232; Ayling, *Elder Pitt*, p. 434.

[5] Sackville to Irwin, January 17, 1766, H.M.C., *Stopford-Sackville MSS.*, I, 104.

[6] *Parl. Hist.*, XVI, 102-103; Temple to Grenville, January 15, 1766, *Grenville Papers*, III, 227.

[7] Rockingham to the King, January 15, 1766, *Rockingham Memoirs*, I, 270-271.

[8] Memorandum by the King, January 18, 1766, Fortescue, *Papers of George III*, I, 237-239; Memorandum by Newcastle, January 20, 1766, Newcastle MSS., Add. MSS. 32973, ff. 194-196; Grafton, *Autobiography*, pp. 64-66.

[9] Grenville's Diary, *Grenville Papers*, III, 355.

[10] Minutes by Newcastle on Rockingham's conversation with Pitt, January 20, 1766, Newcastle MSS., Add. MSS. 32973, ff. 194-196.

[11] Rockingham to Yorke, January 17, 1766, Hardwicke MSS., Add. MSS. 35430, f. 31.

[12] Minutes by Newcastle on a conversation of Rockingham with Pitt, January 23, 1766, Newcastle MSS., Add. MSS. 32973, ff. 237-240.

[13] *Rockingham Memoirs*, I, 287.

[14] Rockingham to Yorke, January 25, 1766, Hardwicke MSS., Add MSS. 35430, ff. 37-38. Cf. draft of the letter, in slightly different form, in *Rockingham Memoirs*, I, 287-288.

[15] The King to Bute, January 10, 1766, Sedgwick, *Letters*, pp. 241-246.

[16] See *Jenkinson Papers*, pp. 404-408.

[17] The King to Bute, January 10, 1766, Sedgwick, *Letters*, p. 244.

[18] Hugh Campbell, third Earl of Marchmont (1708-1794) and Thomas Villiers, first Baron Hyde, afterwards first Earl of Clarendon (1709-1787). Hyde was the younger brother of Lord Jersey, Grenville's intimate friend, and was one of

Grenville's followers in the House of Lords. He held the post of Joint Paymaster-General in Grenville's administration.

[19] Hyde to Grenville, January 28, 1766, Grenville MSS., Add. MSS. 42084, f. 7.

[20] Henry Howard, twelfth Earl of Suffolk (1739-1799).

[21] Minutes and observations by Grenville, January 31, 1766, Astle Collection, Add. MSS. 34713, ff. 263-264. Cf. *Grenville Papers*, III, 355-356.

[22] Grenville's diary, *Grenville Papers*, III, 353.

[23] Grenville's diary, *Grenville Papers*, III, 357; Guttmacher, *America's Last King*, p. 89.

[24] Grenville's diary, *Grenville Papers*, III, 359.

[25] Newcastle, *Narrative*, pp. 47-48; Sackville to Irwin, February 10, 1766, H.M.C., *Stopford-Sackville MSS.*, I, 106.

[26] Paper by Cadogan, February 9, 1766, Grenville MSS., Add. MSS. 42084, f. 17. Cf. *Grenville Papers*, III, 360 n.

[27] Alexander Montgomerie, tenth Earl of Eglinton (1722-1769).

[28] Memorandum by Grenville "delivered by me to Mr. Cadogan" on the February 9, 1766 conversation, Grenville MSS., Add. MSS. 42084, f. 19.

[29] Minutes by Bedford, February 18, 1766; MS. note, n.d., *Bedford Correspondence*, III, 326-329; Grenville's diary, *Grenville Papers*, III, 361-363.

[30] Minutes by Bedford, February 18, 1766, *Bedford Correspondence*, III, 329; the King to Yorke, February 18, 1766, Fortescue, *Papers of George III*, I, 273.

[31] *Parl. Hist.*, XVI, 164.

[32] Documents on debates on the Declaratory Act and the repeal of the Stamp Act, *American Historical Review*, XVII (April, 1912), p. 572.

[33] Grenville's diary, *Grenville Papers*, III, 357.

[34] Rockingham to the King, February 3, 1766, Fortescue, *Papers of George III*, I, 253.

[35] Newcastle to the Archbiship of Canterbury, February 2, 1766, Newcastle MSS., Add. MSS. 32973, f. 344.

[36] Newcastle, *Narrataive*, pp. 47-48.

[37] The story of this confused negotiation may be found in Memoranda by the King, February 10 and 11, 1766, Fortescue, *Papers of George III*, I, 268-270; Grenville's diary, *Grenville Papers*, III, 362; notes by the King, n.d., in *Rockingham Memoirs*, I, 301-302, and Rockingham MSS., packet 161.

[38] West to Newcastle, February 6, 1766, Newcastle MSS., Add. MSS. 32973, f. 363; Grenville's diary, *Grenville Papers*, III, 358.

[39] Sackville to Irwin, February 10, 1766, H.M.C., *Stopford-Sackville MSS*, I, 107; West to Grenville, February 7, 1766, Newcastle MSS., Add. MSS. 32973, f. 373; Grenville's diary, *Grenville Papers*, III, 359.

[40] Pitt to Grenville, February 8, 1766; Grenville to Pitt, February 8, 1766, Grenville MSS., Add. MSS. 42084, ff. 13-15.

[41] Sackville to Irwin, February 10, 1766, H.M.C., *Stopford-Sackville MSS,* I, 107.

[42] Newcastle to the Archbiship of Canterbury, February 15, 1766, Newcastle MSS., Add. MSS. 32974, f. 5.

[43] *Commons Journals,* XXX, 503-598; *Parl. Hist.* XVI, 136-160; Newcastle MSS., Add. MSS. 33030, *passim.*

[44] "The great question can't come on before Tuesday, if then, as G. Grenville has his evidence to examine." Onslow to Newcastle, February 15, 1766, Newcastle MSS., Add. MSS. 32974, f. 9.

[45] Walpole, *George III,* II, 299; Rockingham to the King, February 21, 1766, Fortescue, *Papers of George III,* I, 275.

[46] Conway to the King, February 22, 1766; Rockingham to the King, February 21, 1766, Fortescue, *Papers of George III,* I, 273-275; West to Newcastle, February 21, 1766, Newcastle MSS., Add. MSS. 32974, f. 49; *Commons Journals,* XXX, 598.

[47] Walpole, *George III,* II, 299.

[48] Onslow to Pitt, February 25, 1766, *Pitt Correspondence,* II, 395; Newcastle to Rockingham, February 23, 1766, Newcastle MSS., Add. MSS. 32974, f. 69.

[49] Onslow to Pitt, February 25, 1766, *Pitt Correspondence,* II, 395.

[50] *Commons Journals,* XXX, 602.

[51] *Commons Journals,* XXX, 627; Conway to the King, March 5, 1766, Fortescue, *Papers of George III,* I, 277. Pitt on this occasion chided Grenville on his recent courting of Bute, of which he said a "bird" had told him. Grenville replied he had also heard the birds sing of a meeting Pitt had had with the favorite in August, 1763. West to Newcastle, March 4, 1766, Newcastle MSS., Add. MSS. 32974, f. 135.

[52] *American Historical Review,* XVII, 577-586.

[53] Grafton to the King, March 12, 1766, Fortescue, *Papers of George III,* I, 280-281.

[54] Fortescue, *Papers of George III,* I, 284.

[55] *Commons Journals,* XXX, 609.

[56] Conway to the King, March 7, 1766, Fortescue, *Papers of George III,* I, 277-278; *Commons Journals,* XXX, 641.

[57] Newcastle, *Narrative,* p. 53.

[58] David Hartley to Rockingham, October 28, 1765, Rockingham MSS., I, 294.

[59] Onslow to Newcastle, April 18, 1766, Newcastle MSS., Add. MSS. 32974, f. 425; Sackville to Irwin, April 25, 1766, H.M.C., *Stopford-Sackville MSS.,* I,

110; *Commons Journals,* XXX, 749.

60 West to Newcastle, April 25, 1766, Newcastle MSS., Add. MSS. 32975, f. 26.

61 Rigby to Bedford, April 24, 1766, *Bedford Correspondence,* III, 333-334; *Commons Journals,* XXX, 772-773.

62 Onslow to Newcastle, April 29, 1766, Newcastle MSS., Add. MSS. 32975, f. 50.

63 "Parliamentary proceedings," May 2, 1766, Newcastle MSS., Add. MSS. 30883, f. 9.

64 "As to molasses, I have little to say; I think a penny best." Pitt to Nuthall, May 11, 1766, *Pitt Correspondence,* II, 420.

65 Harris to Hardwicke, April 30, 1766, Hardwicke MSS., Add. MSS. 35607, f. 255.

66 *Commons Journals,* XXX, 783-808.

67 Grafton, *Autobiography,* pp. 73-74.

68 William Gerard Hamilton to Temple, July 1, 1766, *Grenville Papers,* III, 255-258.

69 Newcastle to Ashburnam, July 10, 1766, Newcastle MSS., Add. MSS. 32976, ff. 52-54; Newcastle, *Narrative,* p. 77.

70 July 13, 1766, *Grenville Papers,* III, 263.

71 Grenville to Bedford, July 15, 1766, *Bedford Correspondence,* III, 340; Grenville's diary, *Grenville Papers,* III, 376-377.

72 Temple to Grenville, July 18, 1766, *Grenville Papers,* III, 267-268.

73 Temple to Lady Chatham, July 27, 1766, *Pitt Correspondence,* II, 469. See also *Grenville Papers,* III, 263-278; Grafton, *Autobiography,* pp. 94-95; *Pitt Correspondence,* II, 441-442, 448, 467-470.

74 The Southern Department, wrote Rockingham, "includes a great patronage, and would have been of use to our friends if it had been in a real friend's [i.e., Conway's] hands." Rockingham to Newcastle, July 26, 1766, Newcastle MSS., Add. MSS. 32976, f. 254.

75 Whately to Grenville, August 7, 1766, Grenville MSS., Add. MSS. 42084, f. 136.

76 Trevor to Grenville, August 17, 1766, Grenville Letter Book, Stowe MSS.

77 Minutes by Newcastle on a conversation with Chatham, September 7, 1766, Newcastle MSS., Add. MSS. 32977, f. 41.

King George III

CHAPTER XV

THE OPPOSITION TO CHATHAM, 1766-1767

i.

The new Earl of Chatham, in forming a "ministry of all talents" which ignored the family factions in the Parliament, defied the principles on which politics had been organized during the political lifetimes of all those on the scene in 1766. It was the radicalism of Chatham's concept which moved Lord Temple to reject his offer of the Treasury, since he was expected to take the most responsible post in the government without the support of any of his family or friends in the Grenville following. In a letter to Lord Trevor, "shown by me to my brother Ld Temple on Saturday 19 July 1766 before it was sent and entirely approved by him," Grenville explained that his

> brother's refusal was owing to his resolution not to stand as a capital cypher in a most responsible situation surrounded with other cyphers of a different complexion, under the absolute guidance of Mr. Pitt in contradiction to the public opinions which he had declared last sessions & in support of new measures which he foresees he may probably not approve. His wish was union but not obedience which neither his rank nor fortune will allow him to admit of & which he had the greatest reason to expect would not have been proposed to him by one to whom he would not have proposed it. I rejoice extremely that he has expressly declined making any mention of me upon this occasion which I think is much more for his dignity as well as mine, as what he has done cannot now be attributed to that motive or any personal views for his own family. In this situation it is not pretended that there is any change of *measures* & the only change of *men* is to bring in some of Mr. Pitt's immediate dependents who joined to the rump of the last administration are to compose the present ministry. My sentiments as to the *measures* are still the same & as to the *men* I cannot think the change proposed will give either temper, stability, or union to the King's councils."[1]

The Grenvilles had developed an overblown notion of their rank and fortune and of the respect due them, perhaps owing to a nagging awareness of their parvenu status among the great families. But they put their finger on the chief motivation of the King. When he signed the warrant creating Pitt Earl of Chatham, he expressed his confidence that the new lord would "zealously give his aid towards destroying all party distinctions and restoring...subordination to government."[2] George III, first with Bute's direction and advice and then on his own, had been striving since the beginning of his reign to build an administration independent of the factions in the Parliament. Chatham's "ministry of all talents" seemed to suit his purposes admirably. With a government composed simply of able men rather than "friends" and "connections," the King and Chatham embarked. Yet in the course of Chatham's ministry the "parties" in the Parliament were not destroyed. Instead, the Grenville, Bedford, and Rockingham factions were brought finally into a united opposition to Chatham's government as a result of the Earl's own measures.

Grenville was outraged that Chatham, "having formerly insisted that he would not be responsible unless he was suffered to guide, at present insists upon guiding without being responsible in any shape...." He was taking "an office where he cannot officially be responsible for any thing," Grenville complained, and he jibed that Chatham would "issue his mandates" from the House of Lords "thro' the firmness & wisdom of the Rochefort General [Conway] & the consistent steadiness of Mr. Chas. Townshend...."[3] Wit was not Grenville's forte; sarcasm was his weapon.

Whatever the abilities of his managers in the Commons, from the beginning nothing went right for the minister. In mid-August, Lord Egmont resigned the Admiralty because he did not approve of Chatham's foreign policy.[4] Chatham tried to fill his place with Lord Gower, Bedford's lieutenant in the Lords and Temple's friend. But although he was eager for office, Gower declined when he learned that the offer was restricted only to himself and that other members of the Bedford and Grenville groups would not be taken care of. "The evident purpose of all this," observed Grenville, who was privy to the negotiation, was "to break and divide us, if possible."[5] Chatham was obliged to call on Sir Charles Saunders, a friend of the Rockinghams. The Marquis, who already had friends in the ministry, was offended by the "manner of the appointment,"[6] but the vacancy was filled.

Several of Grenville's band did accept positions in Chatham's ministry. Lord North became Joint Paymaster-General and Lord Granby Commander-in-Chief. Lord Hillsborough wrote to tell Grenville that he was becoming First Commissioner of the Board of Trade. Grenville congratulated him but warned that the office was not likely to amount to as much as formerly, since it was "stripped of its fundamental and constitutional powers of representation" and "reduced to a mere board of report." He told Lord Trevor that the real power in colonial administration had been turned over to a new Secretary of State for the Colonies, Shelburne, whom he had never liked, perhaps because George III and Bute had forced him on Grenville's administration in 1763.[7]

More disturbing to Chatham than personnel problems was the failure of his first venture in foreign policy. Ever since Bute had allowed the treaty with Frederick II of Prussia to lapse in 1762, Pitt had advocated its renewal as a counterpoise to the rising power of Bourbon France and Spain. Once in office he immediately set about to negotiate an alliance with Prussia, in which Russia was to be included. Frederick, however, was too deeply involved in the tangled web of Polish politics to be concerned over Britain's fears of France and Spain. He replied that he no longer wanted alliance with a country in which a change of ministers might mean a revolution in foreign policy.[8] Chatham had staked much on the negotiation; its failure was a serious blow to the prestige of his ministry.

The failure in foreign policy, moreover, was accompanied by the commission of an illegal, if necessary, act at home. The economy was distressed by a succession of bad harvests, with rising grain prices threatening many with starvation. Riots broke out in many parts of the country. Chatham by an Order in Council placed an embargo on the export of grain, even though the price had not reached the point at which the action was legally justified. The measure could readily be defended on grounds of necessity, but it was still illegal. The ministers would have to seek a retroactive dispensation when the Parliament opened, and opposition could take advantage of their vulnerability.[9]

ii.

The opening of Parliament was set for November 11, an unusually early date, and Grenville was primed for attack. "If I were to judge of your feelings by my own," he wrote to Whately, "I can easily believe you are sorry to be called out of the country so early as the 11th of November."[10] The Bedford and Rockingham groups, however, were not enthusiastic for opposition. Rockingham and Newcastle were not disturbed about the illegality of the embargo. The old Duke, indeed, had attended the Privy Council when the decision was taken, and approved the decision.[11] Rockingham had early expressed his eagerness "that we and our friends should be quiet, and that our only object should be to keep up a good-humoured correspondence with those parts of the present system who were parts of ours." For the sake of their friends in office, they would not oppose, "and perhaps at some day we may feel the benefit of this moderation."[12] Their sentiments did not change as November arrived.[13]

Now Bedford was not anxious to take up cudgels against Chatham. He informed Grenville that neither he nor his friends would oppose the address, which would approve the embargo, and he even expressed doubt "whether it would not be very improper *to give any disturbance whatever*."[14] Grenville and Temple, however, were not inclined to be so favorable to their brother-in-law. Early in August, Grenville declared that he had never engaged to support Chatham, since he had "so long and so highly disapproved of Mr. Pitt's public conduct, his principles, and his measures." Yet he declared that if Chatham would change his sentiments, "as he has done so frequently," and follow a program "really for the public service," he would "not do as he has done by me, and oppose it from personal rancour and jealousy."[15]

Grenville did not deny that Chatham's grain embargo was "really for the public service." As did almost everyone else, he recognized its necessity. But he also recognized its illegality, that it was an act of prerogative of the Crown at variance with the law of the land. As such it would require an act of indemnity from Parliament for those who had advised and executed it. After having "given all the attention to this question which I am able," he decided that if the government did not move the indemnity bill, he would.[16]

In the King's speech to the Parliament the embargo was mentioned, but neither the speech nor the address referred to its illegality. Camden, indeed, had persuaded the Privy Council that it was not illegal, since the Crown always had the power to save the whole, the *salus populi*.[17] He repeated the same doctrines in the Lords in the debate on the address, provoking a hot attack by Mansfield and Temple, who demanded a bill of indemnity for the ministers' action. Yet they could not muster enough support to call a division.[18]

In the Commons, however, Grenville had better sport. Beckford, "copying after his friends," repeated Camden's constitutional doctrines, which savored of the reign of Charles I more than that of George III. Grenville immediately had his words taken down by the clerk, and the

House was about to proceed to censure him when the frightened Beckford recanted. Conway, seeing a storm rising, was forced to promise the bill of indemnity which his comrades in the Lords had refused.[19]

Yet despite his success in disconcerting the ministers, Grenville found himself unsupported on the floor except by his own followers. The Rockinghams and Bedfords took no part. "We had not above 100 members in the House & my friends were all gone except two or three, so that this great point was carried against the present ministers by those who act with the court."[20] In the midst of the debate, Grenville inquired of Rigby what the Bedfords were going to do. "We are going to do nothing," Rigby replied, "but, so help me God, as I am a man of honour, it is not by my advice."[21] But even without active support, Grenville continued to harrass the ministers. When their indemnity bill was brought in, admitting that the embargo was not justified by the "strict rules of law," Grenville brought them to logical exactness and further concession by obliging Conway to give up the word "strict." "So," said Lord George Sackville, who now counted himself among Grenville's band, "we all went to dinner in good humour."[22] Grenville could feel that he had accomplished his aim, that of putting "an effectual stop to that alarming plea of necessity for the exercise of a power by the Privy Council to suspend or supersede the laws & Constitution, a plea which has more than once brought us to the brink of slavery and destruction." It was, he wrote, "the same plea of necessity used by officers of the Crown a few months ago for the suspending of the execution of the Stamp Act, not only in America, but even here in England, before the consent of the Parlt was obtained for the repeal of it."[23]

Chatham still came off well, for the ministers had not had to face the united opposition of Grenvilles, Bedfords, and Rockinghams. But his good fortune was not to continue long. Soon after the opening of Parliament, he offended the Rockinghams by forcing Lord Edgecumbe to resign the Treasurership of the Household to make room for a new political adherent, Sir John Shelly. The Rockinghams demanded satisfaction, and when none was forthcoming they resigned from the government in a body: Portland, Scarborough, Bessborough, Monson, Meredith, Saunders, and Keppel. Chatham, undismayed, filled up the places with friends of Bute when the Bedfords refused his overtures.[24] Yet he had made dangerous enemies in the Rockingham group, and the Bedfords were at liberty also to oppose. Moreover, the connection with Bute was damning to Chatham in the eyes of many members of Parliament. Men smiled at each other when Lord Mount Stuart, Bute's heir, moved Charles

Jenkinson's new writ of election when he took a seat at the Admiralty,[25] On learning of Jenkinson's intention to join the Chatham ministry, Grenville gave instruction that his former Secretary to the Treasury should never be admitted to his house again.[26]

Immediately after the negotiation with Chatham was over, the Bedford group moved to make *cause commune* with the Grenvilles. Rigby wrote Grenville, December 1: "I can't refrain, from the satisfaction I feel, from informing you that I think it infinitely most probable...that I shall not differ from you on any publick measures."[27] Lyttelton, meanwhile, informed the Rockinghams of Temple's and Grenville's "inclination to unite" with them against Chatham. But Temple's terms, reported Hardwicke, were too high: "the Treasury for himself and his brother—that is, the *power.* Lord Rockingham is quite *averse* to a coalition on such terms."[28]

No agreement could be reached. Yet Rockingham was not averse to opposition, with or without the Grenvilles. He did not agree with those, he said, who declared "that any opposition to Lord Chatham and Lord Bute is to make G. Grenville minister."[29] Newcastle asserted that he was for opposition even if it made Grenville minister. "I see so little that I like in the present Administration & I think Lord Chatham's behaviour so wrong both to the publick and the party...," he wrote, "that it would not break my rest if even George Grenville should get the better of him, and succeed him."[30]

During the Christmas recess, there was an attempt by Lyttelton to negotiate a union between the Grenvilles and the Rockinghams. He had a meeting with Newcastle, Rockingham, and Bessborough, at which he pressed "mightily our junction with My Lord Temple and Mr. Grenville; that one of them two *[sic]* must be at the Head of the Treasury," Newcastle recorded the following day. "My Ld Rockingham told My Lord Lyttelton very plainly, that that was what we could not consent to...; that our whole conduct had been to shew the impropriety of Mr. Grenville's measures. ...after that it was not consistent with their Honor and Consciences to be bringing Mr. Grenville again in to that office." But he "most extremely approved" opposition in conjunction with the Grenvilles, and he thought "Mr. George Grenville the most useful man of them all." He would not object to his having some lesser office which "did not carry the minister with it."[31] There was as yet no formal coalition or communication between the groups, but nevertheless they were united by a common determination to oppose. Chatham chose this moment to launch an attack on the rights of the East India Company, one of the most powerful corporations in the world.

iii.

By British victories in the Seven Years' War, the East India Company had become the virtual ruler of the vast conquered territories of Bengal, Orissa, and Bihar. More recently, Lord Clive had negotiated a treaty which gave the company the revenues of the territories, which were fabulously wealthy, in return for a tribute paid to the Mogul Emperor at Delhi and a pension to the Nabob of Bengal. Sensing tremendous profits, the stockholders of the company met in September, 1766, and in spite of the opposition of the company's directors voted an increase in dividends from six to ten percent.[32] This was partly in defiance of the Chatham government, which, it was reported, was contemplating an investigation into the rights of the company to the territorial revenues and into its affairs in general. Such a procedure seemed highly advisable to the ministers when East India stock began a course of violent fluctuation reminiscent of the South Sea Bubble.[33] Few were surprised, therefore, when Beckford introduced a motion in the Commons, November 25, that the House examine into the affairs of the company.[34] From the first there were danger signals for the ministry. Rockingham and his followers believed that the company was being attacked without cause. Grenville and Bedford maintained that even Parliament had no right to invade the charter rights of a corporation. Thus all three opposition factions joined in the attack on the motion when it was introduced, with Grenville bearing "a very principal share with an universal applause." Nor was a united opposition the only bad omen for the ministers, for Charles Townshend "inclined much to the same side" as Grenville. Townshend, deeply involved in speculation in East India stock—he had pocketed some £7,000 in profits by April, 1767—did everything he could to prevent an inquiry. "I hear that Lord Chatham is very angry with Charles Townshend," Jenkinson reported.[35]

When Beckford continued his campaign, December 9, with a motion that copies of all the grants made to the company and other papers relative to its affairs be laid before the Commons, the opposition gave further evidence of its unity. Burke and Yorke, the two principal debaters of the Rockingham following in the Commons, fought side by side with Grenville. The debate was not altogether pleasant for Grenville, however, for among Beckford's supporters on the floor were now three former members of his band. Lord North and Lord Granby engaged him in debate, and there was a "small altercation" with Granby. But worse, his close friend, Robert Nugent, for whom he had named his eldest son,[36] had now joined the administration and took part in the debate against him.[37]

In spite of the opposition's unity and the signs of ministerial disunity, Chatham carried his motions with safe majorities. When the Parliament rose for the Christmas recess, December 15, the Earl retired to Bath with the gout but with little other worry. Yet, as Grafton observed, there were many difficulties in view, though Chatham refused to recognize them. In addition to the "union of parties, sufficiently powerful to embarrass every measure," there were "internal dangers." Chatham and most of the ministers wished to examine the East India Company's right to its revenues, but Conway and Townshend wanted to come to an immediate settlement with the company without entering the contentious question of charter rights.[38]

The "internal dangers" which faced the ministry became plain to all when Chatham was unable to return to Westminster for the reopening of Parliament, January 16. Townshend frankly avowed his difference of opinion with his leader, agreed with Grenville's declaration that "the East India Company had a right to its revenues," and announced that a negotiation was under way.[39] With Chatham's concurrence, the ministers postponed consideration of the matter until the company presented its proposals, but when the Commons returned to the matter in March the ministers fared little better. On March 6, Beckford presented the company's proposals to the House and moved that the papers which had been presented to the Commons should be printed. In this move he was met by the united opposition of Rockingham, Bedford, Grenville, and their friends, joined by both Townshend and Conway. The motions eventually carried in both Houses, but not without considerable difficulty, and the dissension in the ministry was clearly revealed.[39]

Worse, in March the involvement of Townshend in the company's stocks became public knowledge. Much of his speculation had been carried on with public money entrusted to him when he was Paymaster of the Forces. Horace Walpole's outrage was typical: "What! and can a Chancellor of the Exchequer stand such an aspersion? Oh! my dear sir, his character cannot be lowered."[40]

Embarrassed but still intact, the administration soldiered on. The next stage of the East India negotiations was a prolonged bargaining between the company and the ministers, with Shelburne taking the initiative. Contrary to the belief of Rockingham and other members of the opposition, Chatham had nothing to do with the affair. In the end, the settlement which Townshend and Conway presented to the Commons on May 1 was a complete deviation from the "right forward road" Chatham had outlined. It took no notice of the vexed question of territorial rights of the company. In return for commercial concessions, the company simply paid the state £400,000 annually for two years.[41]

One more problem remained with the company. Once the directors had engaged to pay revenues into the Exchequer, the government, to protect the state's revenue, was soon forced to limit the percentage of dividends stockholders could vote. Again the ministers found themselves divided against a united opposition, with Grenville and Townshend leading the fight against limitation. It took all the weight Bute's friends could throw into the scales to bring the measure through the Parliament.[42] By this time Chatham was in the throes of a terrible mental depression. His minions were able to avoid defeat of the East India bill, but only by adopting the opinions of their opponents, trimming their sails to the breeze stirred up by the opposition.

iv.

Meanwhile, Grenville and the opposition had brought the ministers down to defeat on another issue. Townshend in late February submitted a budget to the Commons which proposed continuation of the land tax at four shillings in the pound, where it had stood since the Seven Years' War. Grenville decided it would be a popular move and a blow at administration to try to reduce the tax. A general election was due the next year; a reduction of the land tax over ministerial opposition would be a real feather in the cap of its opponents. The Rockinghams also approved of the idea, but they did not want Grenville to get any credit from proposing it. The Rockinghams decided that Dowdeswell, as a former Chancellor of the Exchequer, should move the reduction before Grenville had the chance, if possible, "in order to intercept the possible *popularity* falling to G. Grenville."[43] Such was the feeling of some of the group against Grenville that Admiral Keppel announced "if Mr. Dowdeswell moved" the reduction, "he believed he would be for it, but if Mr. Grenville moved it, he should certainly be against it."[44]

So on February 27, when Townshend introduced his budget calling for a four-shilling tax, Dowdeswell immediately moved that it be reduced to three. Grenville was undisturbed by motives such as those which prompted the Rockinghams. He joined strongly in support of Dowdeswell's motion, followed closely by Rigby. When the division was taken, Townshend and the ministry found themselves in the minority by eighteen votes, 206 to 188. "What may be the consequences, nobody can tell," observed Newcastle.[45] For the present, however, the opposition had a major triumph. For the first time since the fall of Walpole, the government had been defeated on a major measure. And in spite of Rockingham's precautions, Grenville gained a considerable amount of popularity. The country gentlemen came crowding around him in the House, "shaking him by the hand and testifying the greatest satisfaction."[46]

Yet despite defeat, the ministers did not resign. They continued in their employments, conceding to the opposition whenever necessary to avoid further defeats, and continually hoping for the reappearance of Chatham from his forced retirement. In the East India debates they made concessions damaging to their prestige, while the opposition remained united. Indeed, the Rockinghams and the Grenville-Bedford coalition had a considerable amount of success in remaining united without a formal alliance, even on questions on which they were fundamentally disagreed. On May 13, Townshend submitted resolutions to the House concerning the behavior of the colony of New York, which had refused to obey Grenville's "Quartering Act" of 1765. The colony, his resolutions stated, had been disobedient; therefore the act of its assembly declaring the refusal to comply was declared void, and the governor of the colony was forbidden to assent to any bill of the assembly until after the "Quartering Act" was fully complied with.[47]

Neither the Rockinghams nor the Grenville-Bedfords approved the resolutions. Rockingham's followers considered them too strong. Conway, indeed, joined his friends outside the ministry in attacking his colleague, Townshend. The resolutions, he asserted, were "violent, dangerous, and ineffectual," and he thought the offense "a trifling one."[48] Grenville, on the other hand, thought the resolutions too feeble. Speaking "very long and with great abuse on the administration," he demanded that in addition to the proposed punishment the government should prescribe "that no person should have any office whatsoever that did not swear and subscribe to the superiority of Great Britain as he took the oaths of allegiance."[49] When Grenville introduced a motion to call for such an oath, the Rockinghams joined the ministry to defeat it, 150-51. When the main question of opposing the resolutions came, however, means were found whereby all the opposition groups could vote together. Grenville moved simply that the Mutiny Act for the colonies should be "amended and enforced," and all three groups joined in support of the motion. The ministry defeated it by eighty-two votes, but the opposition groups preserved their unity in a difficult question.[50]

Now came on the most important of Charles Townshend's American measures in the 1767 session, that of taxing the colonies by a customs levy. In a debate on a motion of Grenville's, January 26,[51] Townshend had declared Chatham's distinctions between internal and external taxation of the colonies were "perfect nonsense."[52] In April, when he brought in the bulk of his budget, he declared he would make up the deficit caused by the reduced land tax "by amelioration of our revenues and by an American tax," and Grenville hastened to compliment him.[53] On May 13, when Townshend finally opened to the House his plan of American taxation, Grenville was less pleased. While Townshend professed himself "clear in the opinion that this country had a power of taxation of every sort and in every case," he announced that he would defer to colonial opinion and levy only such taxes as were considered "external." He then proceeded to outline a number of "trade regulations" on paper, glass, lead, paints, and tea, the proceeds of which were to be applied to the "administration of justice and the support of civil government in such of the...colonies and plantations where it shall be found necessary."[54]

What the response of the Rockingham and the Bedford groups was to the act is unknown. Apparently no record of the debates in committee, June 2, was preserved. The Duke of Grafton wrote years later that "the right of the mother country to impose taxes on the colonies was then so generally admitted that scarcely anyone thought of questioning it."[55] But Grenville was openly critical of Townshend's pretense that the Americans would accept the tax as a regulation of trade and an external tax. If it served their purpose, he warned, the Americans could be logical and well as illogical. "They will laugh at you for your distinctions about regulation of trade." He warned then, as he would warn again, that Britain would have either to stand up for the whole power of taxation over the colonies or give it all up. But the House proceeded with Townshend's plan, and revolution came a step nearer.[56]

v.

When the Parliament rose, July 2, 1767, Grenville's following and the other opposition groups were no closer to a formal union among themselves than they had been when the session began. On many questions they had fought and voted together against the ministers, but the Rockingham group had come to no agreement with the Bedfords and Grenvilles on a plan of opposition. Lack of unity was not the wish of any party; all desired to cooperate. Mainly what divided them were questions of personnel: which men should have which offices if Chatham was turned out?

When Townshend's land tax was defeated, the opportunity for union seemed to have arrived. Rockingham's rigidity was the barrier. Political coalition must be based on compromise, and Rockingham insisted on stolid consistency. "The proof of our consistency turns upon two points: the one Lord Bute, and the other G[eorge] G[renville]," he wrote to Newcastle; "and our conduct toward the one and the other decides our character."[57] He refused to be instructed by Newcastle's vast political experience, insisting that neither Grenville nor Temple should have office in a coming ministry. Grenville proved unexpectedly conciliatory, declaring that neither he nor his brother wanted office; he himself wanted only a seat at the Cabinet Council in order to "be of service to the public." He declared, moreover, that he would "never think of reviving any of those measures which had been set aside and overruled in my Lord Rockingham's administration, particularly with regard to North America."[58]

Newcastle's frustration with Rockingham spilled out in a letter to Albemarle.

> I am sorry to see that nothing I say has the least weight with Lord Rockingham. Who desires him to treat with Lord Temple or Mr. Grenville? I do not. I desire him to treat with the Duke of Bedford, & see whether the Duke of Bedford's friends cannot bring this negotiation to bear, including Mr. Grenville. I think Mr. Grenville necessary; his Lordship does not.[59]

Rigby, speaking for the Bedfords, insisted on Grenville's having the Treasury in this "shadow cabinet," since it would be impossible to find another capable man "in whom both parties would concur; and that therefore the whole now depended upon that single point of Mr. Grenville coming in the Treasury." With that the negotiation broke off, and Bedford went away complaining "that my Lord Bute and my Lord Chatham must continue to govern this country because one man must not be permitted to have that office for which he is the most proper person."[60]

No further attempt was made at union during that session of Parliament, but soon after the Houses rose there was a further opportunity. This time the prospect was not a "shadow cabinet" but an actual ministry. Chatham continued in his state of depression, unable to transact business or even to advise his colleagues. Hopes for his speedy recovery began to fade. Early in July, the King called Rockingham with the intention of strengthening the remains of Chatham's administration by adding a few of Rockingham's friends. He ended, however, by asking the

Marquis to submit a complete plan of administration.[61]

A new negotiation was therefore set on foot. Again Grenville was conciliatory. He and Temple declined any place in the government. They would give their support, however, if a "becoming share" of places were left open for their friends and if the ministers would pledge themselves to "assert and establish" the superiority of Great Britain over the colonies. This last condition was the stumbling block for Rockingham. Rigby as Grenville's agent presented his terms when the Rockingham and Bedford groups met at Newcastle's town residence in Lincoln's Inn Fields on July 20. Rockingham, in spite of Grenville's pledge the previous March, strongly reasserted by Rigby, jumped to the conclusion that "reasserting and establishing" the supremacy of the mother country might mean reenacting the Stamp Act. Bedford drew up an amended declaration which was to be submitted to Grenville, but Rigby, probably abusing his agency for Grenville, asserted that it would never be accepted. After nearly four hours of wrangling, the group left the question unsettled and proceeded to the distribution of offices.

Here it was Rockingham who provided the stumbling block. He insisted, against all Bedford's arguments, that Conway must remain Secretary of State and manage the Commons. Neither man would give an inch of his position. To Newcastle's dismay, Rockingham and Bedford met the morning afterward and agreed in regarding "the negotiation absolutely at an end." Another meeting of the groups on the evening of July 21 brought no better results; the leaders parted with the declaration "that each party was from that time discharged from any engagement to each other, and at full liberty to take whatever part they pleased."[62] Thus the attempt failed, and Rockingham reported to the King that he was unable to serve him in forming a government. The King was then able to persuade Grafton and Conway to remain in the administration without Chatham's leadership, a task they had hitherto refused to undertake.[63] Rockingham, regretting the failure of the negotiation, cast the whole blame on Grenville and tried to persuade his friends that consistency had required them to refuse his terms "for our own honour."[64] The Bedfords, however, blamed the breach wholly on Rockingham's insistence on Conway as Secretary of State, and Newcastle was inclined to agree with them.[65]

All through the autumn the opposition remained divided, engaging in mutual recriminations. Still, when Parliament opened the situation did not augur particularly ill for them. Ministerial unity had, if anything, been strengthened by the sudden death of Charles Townshend in September, but administration was still leaderless. Northington spoke gloomily in his cups of the weakness of the ministry.[66]

As events turned out, if the ministry was weak the opposition was weaker. The cause was sheer misunderstanding. Though they had no formal agreement, the opposition groups were willing to act together when Parliament opened November 24. But in the atmosphere of uncertainty preceding the opening, Bedford heard a rumor that Rockingham had told a friend he would never sit in a Cabinet Council in which Grenville had a place. Bedford was incensed. He informed Grenville of the alledged proscription as soon as the latter arrived in town, and Grenville's ire was up too. Unfortunately for the opposition, neither man took the trouble to authenticate the rumor. In the debate on the address to the King's speech when Parliament opened, Dowdeswell came as close to Grenville's declaration of the preceding July as Rockingham's opinions would permit. But Grenville, intent on his resentment, failed to recognize the conciliatory note in Dowdeswell's speech. He stood and delivered his soul against the Rockinghams. He was more convinced than ever, he declared, of the necessity of asserting the authority of the mother country. But there were "persons of contrary sentiment" in the House, he cried, surveying Rockingham's followers, "whom he would never support in power nor cooperate with." Indeed, he declared that he would keep "the same distance from them that he would from those who opposed the principles of the Revolution."[67]

These vitriolic words from a bitter man who mistakenly considered himself betrayed spelled the death knell of opposition. Rockingham, highly insulted, refused to explain the falseness of the rumor, either to Grenville or to Bedford, whose followers had said not one word in his defense.[68] The Rockinghams were irretrievably divided from the Bedfords and Grenvilles. The fruit of the breach was soon apparent. The politicians of the Bedford group were not the sort to remain indefinitely in the political wilderness. When Grafton offered places in the ministry, they accepted with alacrity. Bedford declined office because of his failing eyesight, but his followers were well provided for. Gower took the Presidency and Weymouth replaced Conway as Northern Secretary of State. Lord Hillsborough filled the new Secretaryship of State for the Colonies. Rigby was placed as Vice Treasurer for Ireland, and Sandwich became Joint Paymaster.[69]

The accession of the Bedfords to office brought an end to all opposition in the Parliament. Early in December the members began to leave town, weary of seeing the ministers carry everything before them. "Mr. Grenville comes down alone, and never communicates with anyone," wrote one of Newcastle's correspondents. "Administration seems perfectly easy, and opposition perfectly indolent."70

Thus ended Grenville's part in an attempt by the Parliamentary opposition to defeat the King's ministers and force the closet themselves. It ended in failure for the opposition and triumph for the King's program of choosing his own ministers. Yet the fortunes of the opposition to Chatham's administration taught men many lessons. The fact that successful opposition requires unity of command, with liaison between the component corps, and that unity requires compromise and coalition, was forcefully demonstrated. Some politicians learned the lessons offered; some did not. But the lessons were there. The opposition to Chatham was a significant chapter in the development of the concept of a "loyal opposition."

NOTES

CHAPTER XV

[1] Stowe MSS. 7, II letterbook.

[2] The King to Pitt, July 29, 1766, *Pitt Correspondence*, III, 21.

[3] Grenville to Fife, July 31, 1766, Stowe MSS. 7, II letterbook.

[4] Newcastle to Portland, August 16, 1766, Newcastle MSS., Add. MSS. 32976, f. 423.

[5] Grenville to Temple, August 20, 1766, *Grenville Papers*, III, 305.

[6] Rockingham to Newcastle, August 29, 1766, Newcastle MSS., Add. MSS. 32976, f. 488.

[7] Grenville to Hillsborough, August 9, 1766; Grenville to Trevor, August 10, 1766, Stowe MSS. 7, II letterbook.

[8] *Pitt Correspondence*, III, 15-143 *passim;* Williams, *Pitt*, II, 224-226.

[9] Denys Arthur Winstanley, *Lord Chatham and the Whig Opposition*, Cambrldge, 1912, pp. 72-73.

[10] Newcastle to Grantham, September 25, 1766, Newcastle MSS., Add. MSS. 32977, f. 160-161.

[11] Grenville to Whately, September 21, 1766, Stowe MSS. 7, II letterbook.

[12] Rockingham to Newcastle, August 29, 1766, Newcastle MSS., Add. MSS. 32976, f. 488.

[13] Albemarle to Newcastle, November 6, 1766, Newcastle MSS., Add. MSS. 32977, f. 332.

[14] Bedford's journal, *Bedford Correspondence*, III, 353-354; Grenville to Temple, November 10, 1766, *Grenville Papers*, III, 337.

[15] Grenville to Lloyd, August 8, 1766, *Grenville Papers*, III, 299.

[16] Grenville to Mansfield, November 10, 1766, *Grenville Papers*, III, 339-340.

[17] Newcastle to Grantham, September 25, 1766, Newcastle MSS., Add. MSS. 32977, f. 160.

[18] Walpole to Mann, November 13, 1766, Toynbee, *Walpole's Letters*, VII, 72-74; Sackville to Irwin, December 9, 1766, H.M.C., *Stopford-Sackville MSS.*, I, 115.

[19] Conway to the King, November 11, 1766, Fortescue, *Papers of George III*, I, 415-416; Sackville to Irwln, December 9, 1766, H.M.C., *Stopford-Sackville MSS.*, I, 115; Grenville's diary, *Grenville Papers*, III, 382-383.

[20] Grenville to Buckinghamshire, November 22, 1766, Stowe MSS. 7, II letterbook.

[21] Grenville's diary, *Grenville Papers*, III, 384.

[22] Sackville to Irwln, December 9, 1766, H.M.C., *Stopford-Sackville MSS*, I, 115-117.

[23] Grenville to Chalmers, October 5, 1766, Stowe MSS. 7, II letterbook.

[24] Winstanley, *Chatham and the Opposition*, pp. 75-87.

[25] Rockingham to Newcastle, December 4, 1766, Newcastle MSS., Add. MSS. 32978, f. 169.

[26] Grenville's diary, *Grenville Papers*, III, 393.

[27] Grenville MSS., Add. MSS. 42084, f. 217.

[28] Hardwicke to Yorke, November 28, 1766, Hardwicke MSS., Add. MSS. 35362, f. 48.

[29] Rockingham to Newcastle, December 8, 1766, Newcastle MSS., Add. MSS. 32978, f. 222.

[30] Newcastle to Rockingham, December 9, 1766, Newcastle MSS., Add. MSS. 32978, f. 238.

[31] Wedderburne to Grenville, September 25, 1766, *Grenville Papers*, III, 323-325; Rigby to Bedford, September 25, 1766, *Bedford Correspondence*, III, 344-346.

[32] "A short account of what passed yesterday with the Marquess of Rockingham, Ld. Bessborough, and myself," by Newcastle, December 18, 1766, Newcastle MSS., Add. MSS. 32978, ff. 398-400.

[33] Lucy S. Sutherland, *The East India Company in Eighteenth-Century Politics*, Oxford, 1952, pp. 138-157.

[34] Flood to Charlemont, n.d., *Pitt Correspondence*, III, 144; Grenville's diary, *Grenville Papers*, III, 389.

[35] Ayling, *Elder Pitt*, p. 31; Namier and Brooke, *Townshend*, pp. 158-162. No doubt Grenville was sincere in his defense of the rights of corporations, but Townshend was not the only Member of Parliament whose financial dealings helped him rationalize support of the Company. Since 1752, Temple had been a director of the corporation. East India Company directors to Cobham (Temple at that time), April 6, 1752, Stowe MSS., Box 110 (informs Cobham of a meeting of the body.)

[36] George Nugent Grenville, afterwards third Earl Temple and first Marquis of Buckingham (1753-1813).

[37] Harris to Hardwicke, December 9, 1766, Hardwicke MSS., Add. MSS. 35607, f. 332. Nugent wrote to Grenville, December 4, informing him of his decision to accept office and hoping that his "change of situation" would produce "no abatement" of their friendship. Grenville noted the letter in his diary, but without the spiteful exclusion accorded Jenkinson. Whether it affected their friendship is uncertain, but if any further correspondence passed between them it was not preserved. *Grenville Papers*, III, 349, 394.

[38] Grafton, *Autobiography*, p. 109.

[39] Minute by West, March 6, 1767; Rockingham to Newcastle, March 7, 1767;

Newcastle to West, March 8, 1767, Newcastle MSS., Add. MSS. 32980, ff. 215, 220, 230, 234; Grenville's dairy, *Grenville Papers,* IV, 213-214.

[40] Walpole to Mann, March 19, 1767, Namier & Brooke, *Townshend,* p. 167.

[41] Grafton, *Autobiography,* p. 125: Sutherland, *East India Company,* pp. 162-176.

[42] Newcastle to Mansfield, May 28, 1767; Newcastle to Hardwicke, May 31, 1767, Newcastle MSS., Add. MSS. 32982, ff. 148, 192-194; Grenville's diary, *Grenville Papers,* IV, 225; Grafton, *Autobiography,* pp. 125-126; Sackville to Irwin, June 11, 1767, H.M.C., *Stopford-Sackville MSS.,* I, 123-124.

[43] Rockingham to Newcastle, February 21, 1767, Newcastle MSS., Add. MSS. 32980, ff. 138-139.

[44] Newcastle to Rockingham, February 22, 1767, Newcastle MSS., Add. MSS. 32980, ff. 144-145.

[45] Minute by Onslow, February 27, 1767; Newcastle to Caryl, February 28, 1767, Newcastle MSS., Add. MSS. 32980, ff. 178, 191.

[46] Grenville's diary, *Grenville Papers,* IV, 212.

[47] *Commons Journals,* XXXI, 364.

[48] Bradshaw to Grafton, May 14, 1767, Grafton, *Autobiography,* p. 177.

[49] West to Newcastle, May 13, 1767, Newcastle MSS., Add. MSS. 32981, f. 378.

[50] West to Newcastle, May 13, 15, 1767, Newcastle MSS., Add. MSS. 32981, ff. 375, 395.

[51] Grenville introduced a motion that, in order to do away with colonial objections to Parliamentary taxation, the colonies be required to maintain the troops there by their own taxes. He was completely unsupported in the House by his own personal following. Onslow to Newcastle, January 26, 1767, Newcastle MSS., Add. MSS. 32979, f. 343; Harris to Hardwicke, January 26, 1767, Hardwicke MSS., Add. MSS. 35608, ff. 1-2; Jenkinson to Lowther, January 27, 1767, Liverpool MSS., Add. MSS. 38205, f. 132.

[52] Harris to Hardwicke, January 26, 1767, Hardwicke MSS., Add. MSS. 35608, f. 2.

[53] Harris to Hardwicke, April 19, 1767, Hardwicke MSS., Add. MSS. 35608, ff. 14-15.

[54] West to Newcastle, May 1. 1767. Newcastle MSS.. Add. MSS. 32981, f. 375; *Commons Journals,* XXXI, 394.

[55] Grafton, *Autobiography,* p. 127.

[56] Sir Henry Cavendish, *Debates of the House of Commons during the Thirteenth Parliament of Great Britain,* edited by J. Wright, 2 vols., London, 1841, I, 217.

[57] March 15, 1767, Newcastle MSS., Add. MSS. 32980, f. 297.

[58] Minutes by Newcastle, April 1, 1767, Newcastle MSS., Add. MSS. 32981, ff. 1-3.

[59] Newcastle to Albemarle, March 30, 1767, Newcastle MSS., Add. MSS. 32980, f. 440.

[60] Minutes by Newcastle, April 1, 1767; Newcastle to Albemarle, April 3, 1767, Newcastle MSS., Add. MSS. 32981, ff. 1-3, 24. The complete story of the negotiation may be found in Newcastle MSS., Add. MSS. 32980, ff. 374, 376, 384, 386, 410, 418. 424, 438, 440, 450, 454, and 32981 . ff . 1-3, 24; Grenville's diary, *Grenville Papers*, IV. 218-221.

[61] Winstanley, *Chatham and the Opposition*, pp. 152-160.

[62] Memoranda by Rockingham, n.d., Rockingham MSS., 1, ff. 536-539; Grenville to Lyttelton, July 19, 30, 1767; Whately to Lyttelton, July 30, 1767, Phillimore, *Lyttelton*, II, 723-731; Grenville to Rigby, July 20, 1767, Astle Collection, Add. MSS. 34713, f. 291; Newcastle, *Narrative*, pp. 123-147; Whately to Sackville, July 21, 1767; Rigby to Grenville, July 21, 1767, *Grenville Papers*, IV, 71-86.

[63] Grafton, *Autobiography*, pp. 150-153.

[64] Rockingham to Dowdeswell, September 9, 1767; Rockingham to Portland, September 15, 1767, Rockingham MSS., 1, ff. 551, 554.

[65] Newcastle, *Narrative*, p. 158.

[66] Fetherstone to Newcastle, November 8, 1767, Newcastle MSS., Add. MSS. 32986, f. 311.

[67] Minutes by Newcastle, November 25, 1767, Newcastle MSS., Add. MSS. 32987, f. 113.

[68] Rockingham to Newcastle, November 2, 1767, Newcastle MSS., Add. MSS. 32987, f. 119.

[69] Lloyd to Grenville, December 22, 1767, Murray MSS.

[70] West to Newcastle, December 3, 1767, Newcastle MSS., Add. MSS. 32987, f. 149.

Charles Watson-Wentworth, 2nd Marquis of Rockingham

By Courtesy of the National Portrait Gallery, London
Artist: Joshua Reynolds

CHAPTER XVI

ELDER STATESMAN, 1768-1770

i.

The last three years of his life saw Grenville in a new role in the House of Commons. Detached in a measure from active politics, seeking no office or preferment, he chose rather to act as counsellor and elder statesman. The most experienced man in the House in point of service to the Crown and the only one who had been at the head of the government (all the others were in the Lords: Newcastle, Bute, Chatham, and Rockingham), he was thoroughly versed not only in parliamentary procedure but in constitutional law. In this position, he consciously maintained an aloofness from the opposition factions in order to sustain his status as impartial adviser and elder statesman. Although he often disagreed with the ministers, he did not carry disagreement to the point of factious opposition. Having laid his opinion before the House in debate, he was likely to withdraw even before a vote was taken. The days of pursuing opposition through division after division were over.[1]

His restraint was largely owing to the state of his health. His speeches in the House were often interrupted by fits of violent coughing, and on occasion he spat up blood. Nor was the health of his wife Elizabeth such that he could concentrate his full attention on politics. Her chronic bilious condition reached an acute state in these years, necessitating frequent absences for Bath and seaside "cures" and resulting in her death in late 1769. Grenville's band of supporters dwindled as it became obvious that office and patronage were not to be had by following him.[2] Yet Grenville, unable to command large numbers for opposition and unable to bear the strain of acrimonious debate, still gave the Commons his experience and counsel in a troubled time. They were much needed, for during those years the Parliament dealt with two great constitutional issues: the Middlesex election and the renewed taxation of America.

ii.

After an absence of over four years, John Wilkes returned to England early in 1768 to throw the political world into turmoil again. His time was well chosen, for the country was in the grip of agricultural distress, commercial depression, and social unrest. The ministers hesitated to force a showdown with the popular firebrand by arresting him on his outlawry. Wilkes quickly presented himself as a candidate for the Commons in the general election which began in March. Defeated for a seat from the City of London, he entered the contest for Middlesex, and with the aid of Temple and other influential patrons he was returned at the head of the poll. At that, he himself forced the issue with the ministers by surrendering to his outlawry before Mansfield in the Court of King's Bench. On June 8, 1768, Mansfield reversed his outlawry on a technicality, and ten days later Wilkes was sentenced to a fine of £1,000 and twenty-two months in prison for having published the *North Briton* No. 45 and the "Essay on Woman."3

The King, meanwhile, was intent on Wilkes's being expelled from the Commons.4 The ministers, despite the opposition of Bedford's and Bute's followers among them, decided that no action should be taken during the short session of Parliament which met in May and June, since Wilkes's case was still in court. But they realized that the question could not be put off indefinitely.5 Indeed, the Parliament was prorogued hurriedly in June in order not to have to take up the Wilkes question.6

When the Parliament reassembled in the autumn, however, Wilkes thrust himself upon them. He did not content himself with presenting the Commons a petition for redress of the punishments imposed in 1764. He also wrote and published a libelous statement concerning Lord Weymouth, one of the Secretaries of State. The ministers did not wait this time for action in the law courts. They introduced a motion in the Commons that the paper be declared a libel.

Grenville at this point declined to constitute himself Wilkes' champion. To have done so would have been inconsistent not only with his conduct as minister but with his opinion of Wilkes. But he did take up arms in behalf of constitutional law and liberty. "We ought not prematurely to vote anything a libel which might be tried and proved so at Common Law," he advised the House. There was now no privilege of Parliament to cover such actions. The House of Commons, furthermore, was not the place to take up the charge, since the libel was on a member not of the Commons but of the Lords. The ministerial majority, however, were not so enamoured of legal niceties. Wilkes' publication was declared a libel by 239 to 136.[7]

The vote was only preparatory to the larger measure, the expulsion of Wilkes, which came on the following day, February 3, 1769. When North, who was now managing the Commons in the place of Conway, had the evidence read, Lord Barrington[8] moved Wilkes' expulsion on four counts: his libel of Weymouth; his publication of the North Briton No. 45; his publication of the "Essay on Woman" and the other "impious libels" of 1764; and his imprisonment. Seconded by Rigby, the motion touched off a fierce debate which lasted until three in the morning. In the course of it, the ministers were tendered much good advice. Burke advised them to let Wilkes drop into obscurity. "Disappoint him," he said; "cease to persecute him and he dies in a moment." Other speakers, such as Thomas Pitt, pointed out that it was the function of the Commons to interpret, not to thwart, the will of the electorate.

The speech of the evening, however, was made by Grenville.[9] Carefully disclaiming any connection with either the ministry or the opposition, he announced that his conscience compelled him to stand up against the expulsion of the man he had formerly attacked. No doubt he rationalized his position to himself as he did to the House. He was not changing his opinions "with levity and inconsistency...as may best suit my situation;" he would not "palliate this man's offenses," but neither would he "inveigh against him in bitter terms." He took his stand not for Wilkes but for justice, and thus he reconciled his position with Temple's support of Wilkes.[10]

Having made his situation and his motives plain, at least to his own satisfaction, Grenville proceeded to rip the ministers' case to shreds. Barrington's motion, first of all, was illegal, as it combined four separate causes for the same action. "Is it not evident," he asked, "that by this unworthy artifice Mr. Wilkes may be expelled, although three parts in four of those who expel him should have declared against his expulsion upon every one of the articles contained in the charge?" Elaborating on this truth, he then proceeded to show that no one of the charges was sufficient to warrant Wilkes' expulsion. It was no business of the Commons to punish a libel on a member of the other House, even though the lower House had pronounced it a libel. Imprisonment had never been deemed a disqualification for a seat. And to expel Wilkes for the crimes for which he was already serving sentence was to violate the sacred principle that no man can be punished twice for the same offense.

Turning from the legal aspect of the question, Grenville concluded by examining the expediency of expulsion. Entirely aside from the question of popular opinion on the action, the dignity of Parliament and the rights of electors would be endangered.

In the present disposition of the county of Middlesex, you cannot entertain a doubt but that Mr. Wilkes will be re-elected after his expulsion. You will then probably think yourselves under a necessity of expelling him again, and he will as certainly be again re-elected. What steps can the House then take to put an end to a disgraceful contest in which their justice is arraigned and their authority essentially compromised? You cannot, by the rules of the House, rescind the vote for excluding Mr. Wilkes, in the same session in which it has passed, and I know but two other methods which you can pursue. They...are both almost equally exceptionable. You may refuse to issue a new writ, and by that means deprive the freeholders of choosing any other representative.... If you do not adopt this proceeding, the only other alternative will be to bring into this House...a man chosen by a few voters only, in contradiction to the declared sense of a great majority of the freeholders on the face of the poll.... I believe there is no example of such a proceeding, and...the attempt to forfeit the freeholders' votes in this manner will be highly alarming and dangerous.[11]

Had the ministers heeded this warning from Grenville they would have saved themselves much embarrassment and anxiety, for seldom has any prediction been more literally fulfilled. That Grenville's words carried some weight with the Commons is shown by the diminution of the majority, who carried the motion for expulsion in a full house by only eighty-two votes, far below their usual margin.

The accuracy of Grenville's prediction was now demonstrated, as Wilkes proceeded to draw the ministers further and further into confrontation with the county of Middlesex. On February 16 he was re-chosen for Middlesex without opposition. The following day, the ministers carried a motion not only that he should be expelled again, but that he should be ineligible to sit in that parliament.[12] Wilkes' re-election in March met with the same fate. The Commons, having pushed the matter to a contest, could not retreat. Grenville regretted the situation aloud in the House. "I thought the expulsion an act of great injustice and imprudence," he told the Members. "I said this very consequence would result from it." Yet, while he affirmed that he would always "resist the expulsion of any man unless I hear better reasons given than any I have heard given for the expulsion of Mr. Wilkes," he approved re-expulsion lest the punitive powers of the House be reduced to an idle sham. "The House has come to a resolution that the gentleman is inadmissible," he said; "in this session, therefore, he cannot take his seat amongst us."[13]

With Wilkes' fourth election for Middlesex, April 13, 1769, the constitutional issue was brought sharply into focus. The ministry had persuaded one of its supporters, Henry Lawes Luttrell, to stand against Wilkes.[14] He gained only 296 votes in the poll against Wilkes' 1,143, but when the Commons had again expelled Wilkes, George Onslow introduced a resolution that Luttrell "ought to have been returned" for Middlesex, since Wilkes was incapable of being elected. The motion was fraught with the gravest constitutional implications. If the House could, merely by its own resolution, declare one man ineligible and another elected contrary to the sentiment of the great majority of the electors, what could the House not do? It might, without the concurrence of either the Lords or the King, override the law, saddle constituents with whomever it chose as members, elected or not, and exercise an unbridled despotism. Grenville sprang heatedly to the attack. To declare Wilkes ineligible and Luttrell elected was to make law by resolution of the House of Commons, he asserted. "The law of the land, an act of Parliament, is to be the guide of every man in the kingdom.... The man who will contend that a resolution of the House of Commons is the law of the land is a most violent enemy of his country!"

Grenville's earnestness in this question was attested by the heat with which he spoke. In the midst of his argument, he was forced to sit down in a fit of coughing and spitting up blood. Before the debate was over, however, he was again on his feet. His words rang through the chamber. "The declaration of this day is that you have defeated the right of voting," he cried. "What you are doing is unjust, unparliamentary, illegal. I again prophesy that the freeholders of Middlesex will not quietly acquiesce under this kind of election: that they will, in some shape or form--I hope properly, for I am an enemy to mobs--assert their rights." The warning did not fall upon deaf ears, but the ministers' majority held, though by only a margin of fifty-four.[15]

Once again Grenville's prophesy was to be fulfilled, not only in Middlesex but over the whole country. Mobs there were, both in Middlesex and in the City, but more significantly, a movement was soon on foot in many counties, cities, and boroughs to express the popular indignation through petition to the Crown for a dissolution of the Parliament and a new general election. Before the Parliament met again in the autumn, the ministers would have ample reason to wish they had heeded Grenville's advice.

iii.

Meanwhile, simultaneously with the development of the Middlesex election controversy, the American colonies brought themselves back to center stage in the Parliamentary drama with their resistance to Charles Townshend's taxes of 1767. True to Grenville's prediction, they paid little attention to the distinctions they had formerly drawn between internal and external taxes. Massachusetts took the lead in the resistance, but she was closely followed by the other colonies. Non-importation agreements, binding all colonists to boycott English manufactures and particularly those on which duties were levied, spread from colony to colony. The assembly in Boston, meanwhile, issued a circular letter to the other colonial assemblies from Newfoundland to Trinidad, declaring the new taxes unconstitutional and inviting them to join the agitation for their repeal.

When the Massachusetts assembly ignored a demand from London to rescind its proceedings, it was dissolved by the Grafton government in the summer of 1768. Resolutions by the Virginia House of Burgesses soon brought dissolution upon it as well, and then during the autumn the same action occurred in Maryland, Georgia, North Carolina, and New York. Yet the measures accomplished little, for the new assemblies which were elected were much of the same mind as the old.

Decisive action was clearly necessary. Either the Parliamentary right of taxation had to be asserted and established at once—a project which would entail troops, expense, and probably bloodshed—or the right had to be given up entirely. No middle course would do; for Parliament to continue to assert the right while it failed to enforce the tax and crush the resistance would not only bring the legislature into contempt but also encourage further resistance.

Grenville expressed his ideas on the subject during the summer of 1768 in a series of letters to William Knox.[16] He was ready, he said, "to suggest temperate measures as long as they were practicable." "Whatever blame there is," he asserted, "is owing to those in England who have weakly or wickedly misled the subjects in America, and not to the colonists themselves, who have done no more than any other people would have done to whom an immunity from taxes had been holden forth and who had been encouraged as they have been." Yet he would not advocate giving up the right of taxation. "If Great Britain, under any circumstances, gives up her right of taxation, she gives up her right of sovereignty, which is inseparable from it in all ages and in all countries." "To such a surrender I can never be a party," he declared, "as I think it the highest species of treason against the constitution and the sovereign authority of this kingdom to deprive it of one-fourth part of its subjects."

Still, he would not be intransigent if the ministers decided that relinquishment of the right was the best way out of the dilemma. Although he could not "approve the plan," he could "submitt to it, and having done my duty to the utmost...I shall wait the event till experience has given conviction one way or the other." Certainly there should be no further taxes. "I own," he told Knox, "that in my opinion the disputes between us and our colonies are already of so very serious a nature that I would on no account open a door to any farther uneasiness."17

In the autumn, Lord Chatham recovered his heath sufficiently to consider politics again, but he did not resume direction of the ministry. Instead, disapproving of the policies Grafton and his colleagues had pursued in his absence, he went up to town and resigned the Privy Seal on October 14. Shelburne followed shortly by resigning as Secretary of State on October 19. Grafton, undismayed, put the Earl of Rochford18 in Shelburne's place and bravely faced the new session.

Grenville did not know what to expect as the opening of Parliament neared. It was, he said, "to use the expression of Milton...'confusion worse confounded.' I wish but cannot say I expect to find it otherwise." The prospect offered no charm. "I am too old to find pleasure in fishing in troubled waters & in a storm. I shall arrive therefore to be a melancholy spectator of the ruin of the King & kingdom...." There was little anyone could do, he said, until the ministers recognized the danger they were running. "In the mean time I follow Voltaire's advice in Candide & say with him, 'Cependant cultivez toujours votre jardin.'"19

When the Parliament met, however, the ministers elected to follow a course which was certain to lead to the "farther uneasiness" which Grenville feared. They neither repealed the duties nor took measures to enforce them. Instead they contented themselves with minatory resolutions and addresses to the King. On December 15, 1768, Lord Hillsborough introduced in the Lords some eight resolutions condemning the actions of the Massachusetts assembly and the disorderly conduct of the citizens of Boston. Bedford followed him, moving an address to the King approving the dissolution of the colonial assemblies and asking that a statute of the reign of Henry VIII be revived to bring colonists accused of treason to England for trial.20

In the Lords, the measures met with little opposition or debate. Temple declared that they were completely worthless and railed at the ministers' "paper war with the colonies," but he found no support except from

Richmond, who "rather cavilled at the resolutions than stated any particular objection." Once he had delivered his sentiments, Temple left the
House without waiting for a vote.21

When the measures came before the Commons, however, the debate
was more lively. Burke and Dowdeswell attacked Bedford's proposal for
reviving the anachronous treason law as both "most cruel to the
Americans and most injurious to ourselves." Grenville reluctantly gave
his assent to the resolutions and address in their final form, for fear that
he might be guilty of countenancing rebellion. But he was bitterly contemptuous of the ministers, who he said would "hold out angry words on
the one hand and give no remedy on the other." "Such a line of conduct,"
he cried, "is not only odious and contemptible, but destructive. Do not let
us stand shiffle-shuffle between two measures! Do not let us make use of
big words and then suffer ourselves to be laughed at." Either repeal the
taxes or enforce them, he told the House; do not attempt to take a pusil-
lanimous stand on empty words. "Suit your words to your actions, and
your actions to your words. You are absolutely doing nothing."22

Yet the ministers still steered the middle course. The resolutions were
passed, but the taxes remained without any attempt either to enforce or to
repeal them. In February, Grenville again urged the House to take some
action. "If you mean to give up the proposition that you have a right to
tax America, do it like men," he insisted; "if you do not mean to give it
up, take some proper measures to shew your intention. But do not stand
hesitating between both! If you do, you will plunge both countries into
confusion."23

As the session of 1769 slipped away and still the ministers took no
action, men outside the government decided to force the issue. On April
19, Thomas Pownall24 introduced a motion for the repeal of Townshend's
American taxes. Lord North would not be hurried; pleading that it was
too close to the end of the session for a question of such moment to be
given proper consideration, he moved that action on the matter be postponed until the 1770 session. Grenville took the ministers to task both for
their lack of policy and for their delay. "If you are ready to repeal this act,
why keep it in force a single hour?" he asked. "You ought not to do so
from anger or ill-humour." He would not pass his judgment on whether
they should repeal the act, however, until he heard of "some system,"
until the ministers declared a policy either for the right or against it. "How
far do you intend to go on repealing it bit by bit, from compulsion? How
long do you mean to pursue this shuffling, double-dealing line of
action?" North gave his answer in the vote on his motion: at least until

the following session.25

Having been pressed this far, the ministers met on May 1 to decide what should be done about Townshend's duties. All were agreed that relief should be given by repeal, but they were not agreed on the extent of repeal. Grafton was in favor of total repeal of the duties in the 1770 session, and he was supported by Conway, Camden, and Granby. The majority of the Cabinet Council, however, felt that some token duty should remain to assert Parliament's right of taxation. Gower, Weymouth, Rochfort, North, and Hillsborough outvoted Grafton and his supporters, and the decision was made to repeal the duties on paper, glass, paint, and lead, but to retain the duty on tea.26 Thus Grenville's advice was rejected, and the middle course which he had deprecated and warned against was the one chosen. The concessions proposed would not conciliate the colonies while the tea duty remained, and it would be a continual incitement to resistance and rebellion. Would Grafton's divided ministry be able to pilot the program through the Parliament?

iv.

There was no organized opposition in the sessions of 1768 and 1769 such as had faced Chatham in 1766-67. Rockingham and his followers generally acted together, and so did Grenville's on those issues on which he chose to oppose. Frequently the two groups fought side by side against North and Conway. But there was no liaison between them. The Middlesex election affair in 1769 gave them opportunity to unite on a common principle, and the sentiments Grenville was now expressing concerning America were not offensive to the Marquis. The situation seemed ripe for an agreement. Indeed, there was some communication on the strategy for the Wilkes campaign, as when Dowdeswell kept Grenville informed of the debate after he left the House on February 28 and suggested, "Mr. Dowdeswell has satisfied Lord Rockingham and his friends in the House of Lords in this matter, and if Mr. Grenville is of the same opinion he wishes he would hold the same language to his friends there."27 But such arrangements were essentially *ad hoc*. The rumor was in March, Lord Buckinghamshire reported, that "an alliance, offensive and defensive, had been concluded between you and Lord Rockingham, through the mediation of the Earl of Chatham."28

It was no surprise to anyone, therefore, that the two parties actually achieved a rapprochement when the session was over. On May 8, after the debates over declaring Luttrell elected, Dowdeswell proposed a meeting of the two groups the following day at the Thatched House Tavern. Seventy-two of the opposition in the Commons, headed by Burke, Dowdeswell, and Grenville, met together in convivial company. A formidable list of twenty-two toasts were drunk, beginning with "the King and the constitution; the rights of electors; the law of the land," on down to "the peers who are friends to the liberties of the Commons," and "to our next happy meeting." "The whole meeting," wrote Temple, "appeared to be that of brothers, united in one great constitutional cause. The minority is at least two hundred, or two hundred and twenty."[29]

How much of the initiative in the Grenville group came from Grenville himself and how much from Temple? One suspects that Temple was the driving force. Grenville told William Knox in the spring of 1770 that he "hated being in opposition, but had been dragged into it by Lord Temple, who imputed his indisposition to take a part to his keeping up old resentments, which God knew, he said, he was the farthest man in the world from entertaining."[30] This, however, was immediately after the death of Mrs. Grenville in December, 1769. Whether he was unenthusiastic about joining Rockingham in May, 1769, is uncertain.

If Grenville was moderate about opposition, Temple was not. After his break with Chatham in July, 1766, he had begun a virulent campaign of propaganda against the new First Minister. Soon after Chatham took office, Cotes and Almon produced several pamphlets revealing the details of private conversations between the brothers-in-law which were very damaging to Chatham's popularity and reputation.[31] Doubtless much of the abuse which appeared against Chatham in the correspondence columns of the daily newspapers was inspired by Temple. Then in May, 1767, Temple and his cohorts began collecting the best items of propaganda from the various print media, which Almon then published in a monthly magazine called the *Political Register*.[32]

Through this medium, the essence of the propaganda produced about town could be disseminated in easily accessible form throughout the country. In the magazine appeared letters, essays, "impartial reviews" of the latest books and pamphlets, cartoons, and all the accoutrements which the experience of a long life in politics had taught Temple. The Earl, of course, stayed always in the background, but his prestige, influence, and wealth were there to back his agents in case the ministers attempted the sort of suppression which Grenville's ministry had resorted to in 1763-1764. What was more, the ministers recognized that influence and feared to force the issue with it.[33]

In the summer of 1768, however, Almon had a narrow escape with the government, and in July he turned the management of the magazine over to Henry Beevor, a partisan less well known on the political scene and less connected with Temple. The relationship of the Grenville family with the organ appears to have waned with this change. Throughout 1769 and 1770 the magazine pursued the issue of the Middlesex election with relish, its sentiments coinciding generally with those of Grenville and Temple. But by the time of Grenville's death in 1770, it was beginning to swing away to the left, becoming an organ of the radicalism of Wilkes and Horne Tooke. Deprived of Temple's patronage and protection, it rapidly sank into obscurity.34

Meanwhile, in January, 1769, the celebrated letters of Junius began making their appearance, presenting the ideas of the Grenvilles in bold, scurrilous language. It matters little whether, as W. J. Smith asserted in the *Grenville Papers,* the letters were written by Temple himself or whether they were the products of an associate or associates. The important fact is that they took up the propaganda campaign at the point where Almon left off, and that they continued to appear as long as Temple retained an active interest in politics.35

Propaganda was not the only medium through which Temple expressed his discontent with the ministers. With the prorogation of the Parliament, May 9, the movement for petitioning the Crown for a dissolution rapidly gained support and momentum. Among the most enthusiastic supporters of the movement was Temple. The campaign was mainly a matter for individual, personal solicitation rather than propaganda. As autumn approached, Temple was employed in directing the solicitation of signatures to the petition in the county of Buckingham. By mid-October, he could report that "our petition goes on here to our hearts' content."36

In all this agitation and activity, Grenville was largely a bystander, though a very interested one. When Temple was asked by Rockingham's friends whether or not Grenville approved of the petitioning campaign, he replied that he was "commissioned by him to declare that he did; but that he imagined he could do them more effectual service in another place [i.e., the Commons] by not being a party to the petition."37 Thus Grenville, in spite of the agreement with Rockingham, kept himself formally unconnected and preserved his disinterested status. When the new session opened, he would once again be able to be above the fray in the role of elder statesman.

In the midst of this scene of political agitation and planning, Chatham reappeared on the stage of active politics. Temple had made a personal reconciliation with the great Earl soon after his resignation from office, making visits to Hayes on November 25 and December 5, and it was reported that Grenville dined with his sister and brother-in-law at Hayes on November 28.[38] From that time on, Temple set about to win Chatham over to the program he and Grenville had set out on. His letters to Lady Chatham contained broad hints that Chatham might regain his popularity and his prestige by joining his brothers. He had heard it said in town, he informed his sister in January, "that if the King would call for the assistance of a certain *triumvirate* the whole [agitation against the ministers] would stop in the twinkling of an eye and rage be converted into joy and approbation."[39] In March came another broad hint: "You will find by our friend the Gazeteer that I have been sent for to town in order to concert with Lord Chatham on a plan of administration."[40]

The overtures of Temple for reconciliation were not to be disappointed. Chatham had tried to "go it alone" in 1766-67, with his brothers-in-law in opposition; the attempt was a miserable failure. Probably that failure was a factor in bringing on his depression. He had no notion now of re-entering politics apart from his brothers. Before the Parliamentary fight over Wilkes' expulsion was over, Chatham had agreed to support Temple and Grenville. A long conversation between Chatham and Temple ended "most fraternally and amiably, so that I have nothing left to wish on that score."[41] Shortly thereafter, Temple was telling his close friends that Chatham "was strongly against the measure of expelling Mr. Wilkes,"[42] and by July Chatham had decided to support the program of petitions.[43]

Having warned the King, in a sudden appearance at court, July 7, that he might feel himself obliged to oppose his ministers,[44] Chatham set the seal on the new political arrangement in a visit to Stowe, beginning July 30, followed by several days' stay at Wotton. "So all that family are once more reconciled," wrote Lady Mary Coke, "and as they are now some way advanced in life, I think they had better quarrel no more."[45] From that time until the end of Grenville's life, relations among all parts of the family remained on the most cordial footing.

v.

The Parliament did not meet for the winter session until January 9, 1770. Its assembling found Grenville even less inclined to engage in headlong opposition than he had been the previous session. As he expressed it, both his health and his spirits were gone. For, in addition to his own declining vigor, he was oppressed by the recent death of his wife, Elizabeth.

She had never been in robust health since shortly after their marriage, when she had her first bilious attack. Many and frequent were the occasions on which she was obliged to retire to Bath or the seashore to "take the waters."[46] At length in the summer of 1766 the attacks began to be more severe. In May, 1768, she was so ill at Wotton that Grenville was obliged to rush down from London with their physician, Sir William Duncan, one of the most renowned surgeons in the realm. Those attending her feared she would not live to see their arrival.[47]

"I had the comfort to find Mrs. Grenville last night much better," Grenville wrote the next day to Whately, "tho' she had had some pains in the day which had threatened her with a return of the fit.... I should wish if I could to keep Sir Wm Duncan here for a day longer, but the state of some of his patients in town whom he left on such short notice makes that impossible."[48]

Elizabeth reported on May 18, "I have the pleasure to tell you with my own hand my Dearest Love that I past [sic] yesterday without pain or sickness & much more comfortably than my appearance would give hopes for most exceedingly yellow I am indeed."[49]

She remained jaundiced, with occasional crises which kept Grenville from attending to business. Her final illness began shortly after Chatham and his family visited Wotton in August, 1769. Elizabeth looked "terribly," reported Lady Mary Coke, "very yellow indeed, and seldom a day free from pain."[50] In October, the illness was "in some respects considerably abated,"[51] but improvement was only temporary. At length, Temple informed his sister on December 5 of the sad news. "The dreadful blow was struck this morning a little after 5 o'clock," he wrote. "She died at last, easy, after having suffered most excruciating torments for many days. No words can surpass in expression the true account of her magnanimity, sense, and dignity."[52]

"My brother bears this shock and incredible agony of heart with a firmness and moderation beyond my hopes," wrote Temple the following day; and two weeks later: "My brother left us on Monday.... I hear he bore his return to Wotton better than was expected."[53] Yet Grenville felt the loss keenly. "Time will necessarily soften the first emotions after so severe a stroke," he wrote to Lady Chatham three weeks after Elizabeth's death, "but the painful consequences must remain if not increase." He expressed no bitterness. "I acknowledge with gratitude the divine goodness which gave to me that happiness which I enjoyed in so unusual a degree for above 20 years. Religion, wisdom, and every duty call for my submission when it is His pleasure to deprive me of it. I try to obey the call even in the moment when I feel it most bitterly."[54]

When the Parliament convened in January, Grenville had not much zest for plunging into the heat of political battle. His brothers and the Rockinghams, having come to a working agreement during the autumn to oppose on the issue of the Middlesex election,[55] opened a savage attack in the House of Lords.[56] In the Commons, however, Grenville was apathetic. He supported Dowdeswell's motion that the address of thanks be amended to call the King's attention to the "unhappy discontents" which were prompting the petitioning campaign, but the correspondent who reported the debate for *Gentleman's Magazine'* thought so little of his speech that he simply wrote: "Mr. George Grenville spoke in favor of the amendment."[57]

It was in vain that Burke had pointed out that Grenville brought Temple and Chatham "all the following that they possess[ed]," or that Rockingham had spoken of Grenville as "the best for us...among the three brothers" and anticipated that he would "be of service...in the House of Commons."[58] Grenville was worn out and ill; he had no mind to be used by Rockingham in opposition. "I am no longer capable of serving the public," he told his friend William Knox with a deep sigh; "my health and spirits are gone." His one interest was the great constitutional issue on which he and his brothers had embarked. "The only thing I have any intention of doing," he told Knox, "is to endeavor to give some check to the abominable prostitution of the House of Commons in elections by voting in whoever has the support of the Minister, which must end in the ruin of public liberty if it be not checked."[59]

Meanwhile, Chatham, Temple, and Rockingham in the Lords brought Grafton's government down with a crash. Immediately Chatham appeared in opposition, Camden joined him; although he refused to resign the Great Seal, he was swiftly dismissed. Grafton then persuaded Charles Yorke to accept the woolsack, but his triumph was short-lived. Torn between his desire to be Lord Chancellor and the wishes of his brothers and friends in opposition, Yorke died three days after his acceptance, a victim of his own contending emotions.[60] At this unexpected blow, Grafton gave up the ghost of administration and resigned, January 27, 1770, since he was able to find no suitable successor to Yorke.[61] But the King, undaunted by the opposition, persuaded Lord North to undertake the Treasury and the nominal headship of a ministry which George III himself really directed.[62] North was to hold the office for twelve years, to the sorrow both of his country and of himself.

During the first Parliamentary session of North's ministry, although he spoke often in debate, Grenville took a prominent part in only two questions: the partial repeal of Charles Townshend's American duties and the reform of trying contested Commons elections. North brought on the first issue on March 5. In accordance with the decisions of the Cabinet Council the preceding May, in which he had voted with the majority, North brought in a motion that all the Townshend duties except that on tea be repealed. Once again Grenville entered his plea for consistent ministerial policy toward America. "Do you intend to execute it?" he asked, referring to the tea duty. "It is impossible! And yet you do nothing but throw out angry expressions, and heap distress on the country." He could not give his assent to the bill, he told the House; it would serve neither to enforce British authority in America nor to conciliate the colonies. The ministers, said he, were "responsible to God and their consciences, to their King and their country, for the plan they shall hereafter adopt; for, up to his hour, I think they have formed none."[63]

Grenville made one more pronouncement on the subject of America. Rising and facing North across the House at the close of his last session in the Parliament, May 9, Grenville delivered this solemn warning to the minister:

I owe it to myself...the last time I may have the opportunity, to enter my protest...if next summer I find no plan settled upon. I shall tell the noble Lord, be he seated on that bench or where I now am, that he will be responsible to the country, and criminal in the highest degree. To his neglect the King may owe the loss of America; a loss which, to his mind, would be an affliction as severe as that felt by another sovereign of this country, who in her last illness exclaimed, 'When I am dead you will find Calais written on my heart.'[64]

Prophetic words! And once again, a prediction of George Grenville was to be fulfilled to the letter, although he would not live to see it.

Meanwhile, Grenville had introduced in the Commons the measure for which he is most justly remembered with respect, the act which he had consented to remain in the Commons to carry through. On February 28 he suggested to the House the idea of a bill to regulate controverted elections in the Commons. He wished, he said, to arraign no one—no individual, no administration past or present. "If there is any blame, it will fall upon us all." He proceeded to lay the ground for the bill, to establish

machinery for referring contested elections to a select committee authorized to hear evidence under oath. It was absurd, he asserted, for contested elections to be tried "by a judicature of between five and six hundred
persons," bound by no sort of oath. It was completely unknown to this
constitution." He therefore wished "simply to collect the sense of the
House as to whether they think the present situation is a desirable one,"
and if they thought not, to ask leave to present "a plan to remedy the
existing evils." He was not so young or inexperienced, he said, as to draw
his "notions of reform from Harrington's *Oceana.*" He simply meant to
return the House to the "known, established principles of the constitution," for the existing system of trying elections was "not the original
mode of judicature practiced here."[65]

Although the measure obviously grew out of the ministers' expulsion
of Wilkes and the declaration that Luttrell was elected, there were few
even in the government to oppose Grenville's proposal. Rigby and the
Bedfords were hostile, and North avowed his dislike of the measure. Yet
the conscience of the House was touched, and the majority of the body
was with Grenville. When he introduced his resolution, March 7, it was
debated thoroughly. But in the end it was agreed to without dissent, and
Grenville was placed in charge of a committee of ten to prepare and bring
in the final bill.[66]

North opposed the bill when it was considered in committee, March
21, and again on March 30. When he called a division, he was beaten by
185 to 123.[67] Thereafter, North bowed to the breeze and gave up further
opposition; to have continued would have given the opposition the very
triumph it was seeking. The bill passed its third reading, April 2, without
opposition,[68] and its course through the Lords was so smooth that Temple
informed Chatham there was no need for him to come down to the House
to support it.[69]

Thus Grenville took a major step in correcting one of the most flagrant
abuses in the eighteenth-century Parliament. The act did not settle every
problem of controverted elections, of course; it had continually to be
revised and amended. But the great step had been taken; election controversies would no longer be settled by the brute force of a majority. Some
of the measures of Grenville's career had been unfortunate; some might
even have been considered "entirely wrong," as Pitt once said.[70] But concerning his final act in the Parliamentary session of 1770 few could
complain.

vi.

The session of 1770 brought Grenville's political career to a close. When the King met his Parliament again, Grenville would lie dead. His fatal malady, indeed, scarcely awaited the prorogation of the Parliament, May 19, to lay hold on him. Only days after, Grenville was under such an "indisposition" that Whately was "most solicitous" for his heath.71 His condition refused to improve as the summer progressed. In late June and July he was able to visit his brother Henry at Eastbury, where his brother-in-law, Lord Thomond, wrote to him clearing up details of the estate of his brother, Lord Egremont, and Mrs. Grenville. The estate owed Grenville £10,000 from Elizabeth's marriage settlement.72 This was money, Grenville wrote back, "which was intended for a happier purpose, if it had pleased God that I had dyed first." It would now be "divided amongst all or some of my children, In such shares as I shall direct." The tone of his letter implied that the division would not be long in coming.73

He was well enough in early September for Lord and Lady Chatham to spend a few days with him at Wotton, but then the disease closed in for its final siege. For a time in late September, he was so ill that his closest friends forbore writing to him, for fear that the least disturbance "would be a burthen."74

Then for a few weeks there was a rally. His physician in Buckinghamshire, Dr. Ashe, reported that he could see "a daily amendment" in his condition.75 Grenville even talked of attending the Parliament when it met on November 13. His recovery, however, was not complete enough to withstand the journey by coach to London. Temple met him on the way to town from Wotton, October 21, to put himself under the care of Sir William Duncan.76 "He looks shockingly," Temple wrote to Lady Chatham, "and I should be indeed alarmed did I not place great confidence in that [the skill] of the doctor."77 Soon after his arrival at his house in Bolton Street, Piccadilly, Grenville had a serious relapse. He never again rose from his bed. "He soon fell into a desperate state," wrote Horace Walpole, "followed by a delirium that lasted to his death, which happened the very morning the Parliament met."78

As the time for the opening of the Parliament came on, Grenville's personal and political friends were gravely concerned. Temple, Lyttelton, and Lady Chatham gathered in Bolton Street to keep watch at his bedside. When Rockingham pressed them to concert with him on opposition strategy, Temple and Lyttelton sent their excuses. "The state of my brother's illness has been so alarming for many days past," wrote Temple, November 12, "that I have not been able to wait upon your Lordship as I should otherwise most certainly have done.... The situation of my brother is now grown almost totally desperate." Lyttelton wrote in the same sad vein: "Poor Mr. Grenville's present state makes it impossible for me to attend to any public business. May your Lordship's health be so good as to supply to the nation (if it can be supplied) the want of his assistance in this perilous time."[79]

It was a weary vigil. Chatham, himself in bed at Hayes with a severe fit of gout, was as anxious as the rest. "For God's sake send me a word as soon as possible," he wrote his lady. He was concerned, moreover, for all the "sad assembly" in Bolton Street. "My fears also go to Poor Lord Temple, whose nerves are ill fitted for such scenes."[80]

Lord George (Sackville) Germain expressed the feeling of Grenville's political following during this last illness: "His natural or political death would be the greatest misfortune to his friends and a real loss to the country.... If any accident should happen to him, it will require very serious consideration what part we are then to take." And again, two days later: "If poor Mr. Grenville dies, what is to be the object of opposition? I hope not to make Lord Chatham minister. If it is, you cannot suppose I shall be very sanguine in such a cause."[81] Thus political clouds gathered 'round Grenville's bedside.

The long vigil came to an end at seven o'clock in the morning. November 13, only a few hours before the King went down to the House of Lords to address the Parliament at its opening.[82] The *London Chronicle* reported in its issue of November 15-17, after an autopsy had been done, that his was "the most extraordinary case ever met with of the kind." Walpole later wrote: "His body being opened, his case appeared most singularly uncommon, his ribs were carious or quite worn away, and his skull as thin as paper. This extraordinary malady was imputed to a disorder in his blood, which had penetrated to the blood-vessels of his bones, and had corroded them."[84]

The author presented all the available evidence on Grenville's health to a forensic pathologist, Dr. Robert E. Zipf, Jr. of Nash General Hospital, Rocky Mount, N.C., who made the following comments concerning the cause of Grenville's death:

> I think you have probably described two different disease processes in your letter. At the age of 30 he probably had an infection or re-infection of tuberculosis from which he recovered after spending some time in the

more balmy climates of France and Italy. Most Northern European adults of the 18th century are thought to have had at least one bout of tuberculosis. Many cases were asymptomatic or only mildly debilitating.

After more than 25 years of apparent good health, he developed a rapidly progressive fatal illness which leads me to consider a differential diagnosis of four diseases: (1) recurrent tuberculosis; (2) multiple myeloma; (3) leukemia; and (4) rickets. The description that this was a "singularly uncommon" case with "carious ribs," "skull as thin as paper," with "disorder in his blood, which had penetrated the blood vessels of his bones and corroded them" is most consistent with multiple myeloma. Multiple myeloma is a malignancy of the plasma cells arising in the bone marrow and involving the bones primarily. The plasma cells penetrate the bone marrow and their rapid proliferation produces wide-spread corrosion and thinning of the bones. It occurs after 40 or 50 years of age. Survival after diagnosis is usually for a year or two with pneumonia and easy bleeding, which may explain the episodes of coughing and spitting up blood.

Leukemia has some similar characteristics but does not produce the widespread thinning and corrosion of bone. Recurrent tuberculosis also has some similar characteristics and can produce bone corrosion but it is generally localized to an area such as the spine and not wide-spread. Rickets also produces thinning and softening of the bones but this usually occurs in younger people and is not a rapidly fatal illness. Also, myeloma was an "uncommon" disease whereas tuberculosis and rickets were common diseases in the 18th century.

I could be more certain of this diagnosis if I could examine his remains. If you can arrange this I will be happy to accompany you to London. The best time to go would be during a week with a full moon. If you will bring the oil lamp I will bring the shovel. Better yet, if you can get permission for an exhumation, we won't need the oil lamp.[85]

Since the family denied the author access to Grenville's banking records, he decided that an exhumation was out of the question!

The day following Grenville's death, Chatham made the painful journey to town to pay his respects.[86] Then Temple set off for Buckinghamshire with the body to lay it in its final resting place.[87] In the little stone church of the Wotton parish, sheltered by towering cedars, Grenville was laid to rest among the remains of his ancestors. An eloquent eulogy by Lyttelton graced his tomb, a tribute to his friendship and "manly sense." Burke spoke another epitaph before the House of Commons: "He took public business not as a duty which he was to fulfill, but as a pleasure which he was to enjoy.... Undoubtedly Mr. Grenville was a first-rate figure in this country."[88]

Once Grenville was dead, the clouds which had shrouded the political scene in the minds of his followers soon disappeared. They had fought mainly for their leader and not for his program. One of Bute's followers observed that they might be expected to accede to government soon, for they had "never embarked with great cordiality" on opposition.[89] When their leader disappeared from the scene, they sought a new master. And as Burke observed, they were Grenville's followers, not Temple's. With Grenville's death, they acceded almost en masse to North's government. Wedderburne became Attorney-General, and Whately took a seat at the Board of Trade. Lord Suffolk, who had fought beside Temple in the Lords on many an issue, was given the Privy Seal and shortly became a Secretary of State. The rest of the old Grenville band either melted into the governmental majority on the back benches or trooped off after Chatham. The government's supporters could expect calmer times in the Parliament. "I am glad the present session is not likely to be troublesome," wrote one; "Mr. Grenville's death will perhaps make it less so."[90]

Temple took little interest in politics after Grenville's death. Within a few months, he retired to the rural life he loved, rarely leaving the comforts of Stowe to go up to London and the House of Lords during the remaining nine years of his life. He left the field to younger men. A new day was coming, however, when once again Pitts and Grenvilles would dominate the political scene.

NOTES

CHAPTER XVI

[1] Rockingham resented Grenville's conduct in the opening days of the 1768 session, for example, when Grenville, having first opposed the ministers on a new bill to limit East India Company dividends, "kept away in the House of Commons" in the later stages of the debate. Rockingham to Newcastle, January 27, 1768, Newcastle MSS., Add. MSS. 32988, f. 81.

[2] By January, 1768, North, Conway, Granby, Strange, Hervey, and Nugent (now Viscount Clare) had gone over to Grafton's ministry. Grenville's kin and friends such as Whately remained firm. There were some additions. Alexander Wedderburn had abandoned Bute for Grenville in 1766, and Lord George Sackville (afterward Germain, 1770, and Viscount Sackville, 1782) joined the group in December, 1766. Sackville to Irwin, December 9, 1766, H.M.C., *Stopford-Sackville MSS.,* I, 117.

[3] Howell, *State Trials,* XIX, 1109-1124; Lecky, *History,* III, 139-142.

[4] George III to North, April 25, 1768, Fortescue, *Papers of George III,* II, 21.

[5] Newcastle to Rockingham, May 16, 1768; Rockingham to Newcastle, May 17, 1768, Newcastle MSS., Add. MSS. 32989, ff. 71, 83; Walpole, *George III,* II, 21.

[6] Bradshaw to Grafton, May 31, 1768, Grafton, *Autobiography,* p. 210.

[7] Harris to Hardwicke, February 3, 1769, Hardwicke MSS., Add. MSS. 35608, ff. 334-335; Cavendish, *Debates,* I, 139-151.

[8] William Wildman Barrington, Viscount Barrington in the Irish peerage and M.P. for Plymouth (1717-1793).

[9] Temple and many others regarded the speech as the greatest of Grenville's career to that time: "My brother made what was universally deemed the best speech he ever made, against expulsion." Temple to Lady Chatham, February 4, 1768, *Pitt Correspondence,* III, 350.

[10] Some men were willing to attribute Grenville's action wholly to Temple's influence. "It would astonish me that G[eorge] G[renville] should be one of that minority," wrote one member of the Commons, "if I did not recollect his late reconciliation and now perfect intimacy with Lord Temple." Dedgwick to Weston, February 4, 1769, H.M.C., *Reports on the Manuscripts of the Earl of Eglinton et. al.,* London, 1885, p. 412.

[11] Cavendish, *Debates,* I, 151-185.

[12] Temple to Lady Chatham, February 16, 1769, Chatham MSS., 62, f. 155; Cavendish, *Debates,* I, 227-237.

[13] Cavendish, *Debates,* I, 345-355; Harris to Hardwicke, March 17, 1769,

Hardwicke MSS., Add. MSS. 35608, f. 348.

[14] Luttrell (1743-1821) was M.P. for Bossiney, but accepted the Stewardship of the Chiltern Hundreds (i.e., resigned) to run against Wilkes.

[15] Cavendish, *Debates*, I, 366-386.

[16] Grenville was advising Knox, who at this time was writing the most famous of the pamphlets which he produced for Grenville, *The Present State of the Nation*, which he published October 15, 1768. Knox to Grenville, October 15, 1768, Grenville MSS., Add. MSS. 42086, f. 149.

[17] Grenville to Knox, June 27, July 15, 1768, H.M.C., *Report on Manuscripts in Various Collections*, 8 vols., London, Dublin, and Hereford, 1901-1914, VI, 95-97.

[18] William Zuylestein, Earl of Rochford (1717-1781), a veteran diplomat.

[19] Grenville to the Earl of Suffolk, October 22, 1768, Stowe MSS. 7, 11.

[20] *Parl. Hist.*, XVI, 476-480.

[21] *Parl. Hist.*, XVI, 476,

[22] Cavendish, *Debates*, I, 191-207.

[23] Cavendish, *Debates*, I, 217.

[24] Former Governor of Massachusetts (1722-1805).

[25] Cavendish, *Debates*, I, 391-401; *Parl. Hist.*, XVI, 610-622.

[26] Grafton, *Autobiography*, pp. 229-233.

[27] Dowdeswell to Grenville, February 28, 1769, *Grenville Papers*, IV, 411-412.

[28] Buckinghamshire to Grenville, March 20, 1979, *Grenville Papers*, IV, 412-413.

[29] Temple to Lady Chatham, May 10, 1769, *Pitt Correspondence*, III, 359-361.

[30] Knox, *Extra Official State Papers*, II, 41.

[31] *An Enquiry into the Conduct of a late Rt. Hon. Commoner*, London, 1766; *An Examination of the Principles and Boasted Disinteredness of a late Rt. Hon. Gentleman*, London, 1766; etc.

[32] *The Political Register and Impartial Review of New Books*, 11 vols., London, 1767-1772. See Robert R. Rea, "The Impact of Party Journalism in the *Political Register*," *The Historian*, XVII (1954), pp. 1-17.

[33] When Grenville once complained during a November, 1767 debate that he was being "wounded by libels," Conway answered him that Almon abused him "once a month for being avaricious," but that "he always bought the pamphlet— the only hurt he did to the printer." Walpole, *George III*, III, 115.

[34] Rea, "Party Journalism," *The Historian*, XVII, 15-16. Almon continued to be an instrument of Temple's pamphlet propaganda after his connection with the *Political Register* was severed.

[35] *Grenville Papers*, III, xiii-ccxxviii; *The Letters of Junius*, edited by C. W. Everett, London, 1927. Many of Junius' early letters were printed in the *Political*

Register. There is an enormous literature on the letters of Junius and their authorship. The volume of the material prevents specific citation here.

[36] Temple to Lady Chatham, October 19, 1769, Chatham MSS., 62, f. 170.

[37] Temple to Lady Chatham, September 17, 1769, Chatham MSS., 52, f. 168.

[38] Temple to Lady Chatham, n.d. (c. November 27, 1768), Chatham MSS., 62, f. 143; Hardwicke to Yorke, November 28, 1768, Hardwicke MSS., Add. MSS. 35362, f. 235; Grenville's diary, *Grenville Papers,* IV, 403-406.

[39] January 24, 1769, Chatham MSS., 62, 147.

[40] Temple to Lady Chatham, March 28, 1769, Chatham MSS., 62, f. 161.

[41] Temple to Lady Chatham, n.d., Chatham MSS., 62, 149.

[42] Almon to Wilkes, n.d., Wilkes MSS., Add. MSS. 30870, f. 107.

[43] "Lord Chatham told Trecothick the other day that the people must have satisfaction for the vote respecting the Middlesex Election. This is *de science certaine.*" Lloyd to Grenville, July 25, 1769, Murray MSS.

[44] Grafton, *Autobiography,* p. 237; Chatham to Temple, July 7, 1769, *Grenville Papers,* IV, 426-428.

[45] *The Letters and Journals of Lady Mary Coke,* edited by James A. Home, 4 vols., Edinburgh, 1889-1896, III, 127.

[46] Grenville's correspondence is literally filled with references to Mrs. Grenville's frequent illnesses. Murray MSS., Stowe MSS., Grenville MSS. These references have largely been deleted from the published correspondence.

[47] Coke, *Journals,* II, 269; Whately to Grenville, May 19, 1768, Murray MSS.

[48] Grenville to Whately, May 19, 1768, Stowe MSS. 7, letterbook II.

[49] Elizabeth Grenville to George Grenville, May 18, 1768, Stowe MSS., box 7.

[50] Coke, *Journals,* III, 107.

[51] Grenville to Lady Chatham, October 12, 1769, Chatham MSS., 34, f. 40.

[52] Chatham MSS., 62, f. 175.

[53] To Lady Chatham, December 6, 21, 1769, Chatham MSS., 62, ff. 177, 179.

[54] Grenville to Lady Chatham, December 28, 1769, Murray MSS.

[55] Burke and Rockingham were reluctant to join with Chatham, whom they had so cordially opposed two years before; consistency was always Rockingham's creed. Temple, however, brought them to agree to a narrow union solely on the Middlesex election issue. Once again, Grenville remained aloof from the negotiations. See Burke to Rockingham, September 12, October 9, 29, November 6, 1769, *Correspondence of the Right Honourable Edmund Burke,* edited by Charles William Fitzwilliam, fifth Earl Fitzwilliam, and Sir Richand Bourke, 4 vols., London, 1844, I, 191-197, 201-214; Rockingham to Dowdeswell, September 19, 1769, *Rockingham Memoirs,* II, 104-106; Whately to Grenville, September 7, 1769, *Grenville Papers,* IV, 440-452.

[56] *Parl. Hist.,* XVI, 644-668; Walpole, *George III,* IV, 34-36.

[57] *Parl. Hist.,* XVI, 668-728.

[58] Burke to Rockingham, October 29, 1769, *Burke Correspondence,* I, 202-203; Rockingham to Burke, October__, 1769, Rockingham MSS., 1, f. 685.

[59] Knox, *Extra Official State Papers,* II, 41-42.

[60] The story of Yorke's death, written from the Hardwicke MSS., is graphically told in Winstanley, *Chatham and the Opposition,* pp. 296-315. See also Basil Williams, "The Eclipse of the Yorkes," *Royal Historical Society Transactions,* Third Series, II, 146-149.

[61] Grafton, *Autobiography,* pp. 249-250.

[62] George III to North, January 23, 1770, Fortescue, *Papers of George III,* II, 126.

[63] Cavendish, *Debates,* I, 483-500.

[64] Cavendish, *Debates,* II, 36.

[65] Cavendish, *Debates,* I, 476-479.

[66] *Commons Journals,* XXXII, 760; Cavendish, *Debates,* I, 476-514.

[67] *Parl. Hist.,* XVI, 907-923; *Commons Journals,* XXXII, 846.

[68] "My brother's bill is this day passed in the House of Commons, the court having given up the design of opposing it on the third reading, which was fully intended, as it was said, yesterday." Temple to Chatham, April 2, 1770, *Pitt Correspondence,* III, 439.

[69] Temple to Lady Chatham, April 3, 1770, Chatham MSS., 62, f. 196. See also Whately to Grenville, April 10, 1770, *Grenville Papers,* IV, 515-516; *Parl. Hist.,* XVI, 924.

[70] See above, p. 257.

[71] Whatley to Grenville, May 28, 1770, Murray MSS.

[72] Thomond to Grenville, June 30, 1770, Stowe MSS., box 18.

[73] Grenville to Thomond, July 2, 1770, Stowe MSS., box 8.

[74] Whately to Grenville, June 8, October 4, 1770; Grenville to Thomas Pitt, July 29, 1770; Lloyd to Grenville, October 2, 1770, Murray MSS.; Grenville to Lady Chatham, September 11, 1770, Chatham MSS. 34, f. 60.

[75] Lyttelton to Grenville, October 8, 1770, Murray MSS.

[76] Walpole, *George III,* IV, 125.

[77] October 21, 1770, Chatham MSS., 62, f. 207.

[78] Walpole, *George III,* IV, 125,

[79] Temple to Rockingham, Lyttelton to Rockingham, November 12, 1770, Rockingham MSS., 1, ff. 754-755.

[80] Chatham to Lady Chatham, n.d. (two letters), Chatham MSS., 5, ff. 245, 247.

[81] Sackville to Irwin, October 23, 25, 1770, H.M.C., *Stopford-Sackville MSS.,* I, 131-132.

[82] *London Chronicle,* November 10-13, 1770.

[83] *London Chronicle,* November 15-17, 1770.

[84] Walpole, *George III,* IV, 125.

[85] Letter to the author, March 15, 1991.

[86] Chatham to Calcraft, November 13, 1770, *Pitt Correspondence,* III, 586.

[87] *London Chronicle,* November 13-15, 1770.

[88] *The Speeches of the Right Honourable Edmund Burke in the House of Commons,* 4 vols., London, 1816, I, 205.

[89] Harcourt to Jenkinson, November 20, 1770, Liverpool MSS., Add. MSS. 38206, f. 308.

[90] N. Wetherell to Jenkinson, November 20, 1770, Liverpool MSS., Add. MSS. 38206, f. 306-307.

Richard Grenville-Temple, 2nd Earl Temple

CONCLUSIONS

i.

In any oligarchic society, the influence of family connection in politics is certain to be great. The wealth and the cohesion which great aristocratic families can employ give them an advantage in a political struggle which at least some are sure to profit from. Probably recent historians of eighteenth-century British politics have overplayed the "family connexion" interpretation which this generalization suggests. Family was only one of the factors which served as a basis for political organization and success. Personality counted for much; the mysterious combination of abilities which made one a good "Commons man" and led others to tie their fortunes to him defies explanation on the basis of family. Men were driven to seek the respect of their fellows by obtaining high position and to form alliances for that purpose no matter what their antecedents or who their relatives.

Nevertheless, the Grenville family prior to the autumn of 1761 offers an almost ideal illustration of the "family connexion" principle in operation. The Grenvilles were one of the many families which grew to political prominence out of the squirarchy in the eighteenth century. Having vegetated on the Buckinghamshire soil for centuries, they began a sudden but persistent advance in the second decade of the eighteenth century after their union with the Temples of Stowe. By ability and ambition, by fortunate marriages, by skillful investment, by using influence with the ministers to gain prestige, peerages, and further influence, by enthusiastic cultivation of adherents to their political train, the family rose steadily to the top of British politics in the 1740's and 1750's.

In the vanguard of this family corps was George Grenville. Ability, ambition, and industry in office contributed to his advancement, of course, but the operative factor in Grenville's climb to high office was his connection with a family political following. The King was obliged to have ministers who could manage the House of Commons. If the Grenville group was to be managed—and since it contained such a firebrand as William Pitt, affairs went much more smoothly if it were managed—its leaders had to be given office and kept satisfied by reasonably steady promotion.

The decisive step in Grenville's rise to the Treasury, however, was his kicking from under him the family ladder on which he had climbed and his attaching himself to the coattails of George III's favorite, Bute. Grenville rationalized the decision by blaming it on Pitt's mistreatment of him. But the chief motive must have been a conviction that he could go farther with Bute than with his family, who were going out of office.

When Bute decided to retire from office in the spring of 1763, he and the King were forced to choose Grenville as his successor almost in spite of themselves. He was virtually the only man available who could serve their purposes. He had ability and experience in finance. But more important, he was unconnected with a "party" in the Commons, having been renounced by his family; his presence in the ministry weakened his family in opposition; and he knew how to manage the majority which Bute and the King could provide him. There seems to have been little expectation that Grenville would be a tool in their hands; his behavior in regard to the peacemaking had indicated he might be intractable. Therefore, Grenville was given the chief office but not the full direction of the ministry. The King constituted Grenville, Halifax, and Egremont a "commission" to hold the headship of the government.

The death of Egremont gave Grenville the headship of the ministry solely because George III was unable to find anyone else to whom he was willing to open his closet. Pitt refused to take office without his "connections," and the King chose to let Grenville take the whole leadership of his government rather than submit to dictation from factions. Yet the coalition which Grenville formed of his own adherents and Bedford's "Bloomsbury gang" soon became as much of a connection as Pitt's. As the tie solidified, the King's resentment solidified against it. That resentment was finally the factor which brought about the dismissal of the Grenville ministry.

ii.

George III's intent of picking his own advisers and presiding over them personally, independent of the factional and family connections in the Parliament, came more or less into conflict with every First Minister he had before the American Revolution except Bute. Grenville's ideas of the prerogatives of the First Minister came violently into conflict with that intent of George III. As the conflict between them developed, the King, unable to replace Grenville by anyone more suitable, first took flight from his problem by going temporarily insane. When he recovered his sanity, he attempted to solve the problem by calling in a coalition of Pitt and the Newcastle-Rockingham group. The attempt failed, but the King at least succeeded in ridding himself of the irritating presence of Bedford and Grenville by submitting himself to his uncle, Cumberland, and the Newcastle-Rockingham faction. The struggle between the King and the factions in opposition continued throughout the period before the American Revolution, although in 1770 the King finally found a minister to his liking in Lord North.

Grenville's dismissal in July, 1765, is a significant commentary on the point to which "responsible cabinet government," as Bagehot described it, had developed in England at this date. Grenville and his colleagues in the spring of 1765 had as complete a control of both Houses of Parliament as was seen in Great Britain during the century. Moreover, Grenville behaved more like a modern head of a cabinet than had any previous minister. He insisted, in the face of fervid and emotional opposition from the King, that he should have the power to select and dismiss all of his colleagues in the government. He insisted, moreover, that no member of the government, no matter how great or trivial his office, should presume to speak to the King on the business of that office without first clearing the matter through him as head of the ministry.

Yet in spite of the facts that the ministers had complete control of the Parliament and that they effectively carried measures which he desired, George III dismissed them on his own initiative and called in other advisers, who could command only a fraction of the Parliament without the help of the King. George's grievance against Grenville and his colleagues was not the manner in which they carried on his business but their personal relationship with him. He would not submit to his ministers' "giving him the law" on any point whatsoever. It was the very fact that Grenville behaved somewhat like the modern head of a cabinet which brought about his dismissal.

It should not be thought, moreover, that George III was singular among the Hanoverians in holding such sentiments. His grandfather was fully as insistent that he should not be dictated to by his ministers. The incident of 1746 will serve as an example. The difference lay not in their sentiments but in their success in implementing them. At what date "responsible cabinet government" was actually achieved in Great Britain is a question for speculation, but it seems evident that it had not been reached in 1765.

iii.

One of the most effective and powerful adjuncts to the organized expression of opinion in politics is the press. This is particularly true in the modern "mass state," but it was true also in the oligarchic society of eighteenth-century Britain. The mass of the populace, of course, had no outlet for articulate expression through election of members to the legislature. Propaganda organs did not exist to line up an electorate, for the mass electorate did not exist. But nevertheless a factional press could stir up mass emotions and mobs (with the aid of skillful personal manipulation) and could give added strength and additional voice to the factionalism within the Parliament.

The financing and promoting of a newspaper or magazine is an expensive and hazardous venture, and therefore one not undertaken with success without a considerable amount of backing and support. This was particularly true in the eighteenth century, when the laws of libel were at best rather indefinite, when propaganda warfare was rough and ready, and when methods of suppressing unwelcome propaganda were likely to be primitive. Thus organs of political opposition, such as the *Craftsman,* the *North Briton,* or the *Political Register,* were seldom undertaken without the support and patronage of some "great man," who could bear the expense involved and whose influence could restrain the government from attempting to suppress it. Few men of the century were more active in backing or more skillful in directing opposition propaganda efforts than was Grenville's elder brother, Lord Temple.

The traditional means of combatting an opposition press was a governmental press, financed by funds from the Treasury and conducted by hireling hacks. Grenville kept up pamphlet propaganda against Temple and the opposition during his whole administration, but he did not attempt to compete with his brother in the newspaper press. Temple was too skillful a general in that sort of battle. Urged on by the King, he set about to silence Temple's organ, the *North Briton,* by legal prosecution, and then to put a muzzle on the press as an instrument of opposition. In the short run he succeeded, but actually Temple outsmarted him. Grenville was successful in ruining Wilkes and in silencing opposition in the press. But Temple, by the simple maneuver of bringing Wilkes's case before a judge friendly to him, succeeded in dramatizing for the mob mind the struggle between the King and the opposition.

The opposition press, as a result of Grenville's program of suppression, was almost completely bottled up during the debates on the first

American taxation bills. Only slowly were new media of propaganda developed and the suppression evaded. The Middlesex election, Wilkes's expulsion, and the complex of issues growing out of that episode dramatized the struggle between the King and the opposition factions still more strongly. Out of the suppression of the *North Briton* and Wilkes finally sprang a whole complicated set of agitations and reforms. Grenville in the initial stages participated in them, having turned to march with Temple in the fray. His bill for the reform of trials of contested elections was a moderate and constructive measure in the midst of a fever which brought forth all sorts of radical societies and reforms. The issues in the movement were quickly seized on and manipulated by the same factional forces which had stirred up the original noise. It might almost be said that Grenville's suppression of the press led directly to the unleashing of radicalism in Great Britain.

iv.

The writings of Americans on the origins and development of the struggle between Great Britain and the colonies have largely isolated the American issues from the political milieu of which they were intimately a part. The great point which strikes one in a study of the development of the issues in Britain is the fact that those issues were never considered separately on their own merits. Rather than being isolated from the factional struggles of the time, they were almost wholly submerged in them.

The preoccupation of politicians with their own factional controversies is nowhere more evident than in the decision to tax America and in the preparation of the acts. Grenville and his colleagues in the ministry were not motivated in taxing America by a belief that the colonies should bear a fair share of the burden of their defense. They were concerned about balancing the budget and maintaining themselves in power. Hesitant to lay a greater tax burden on their own supporters in the Parliament, and reluctant to give opposing factions new issues by placing additional taxes on them, they turned to America as a neutral ground from which to draw a small fraction of the deficit. The fact that a major part of the burden imposed by the American taxes fell on English merchants of the opposition factions played no small part in the later controversies over the taxes. Moreover, in the drafting of the measures the work was delegated to underlings, while the ministers busied themselves with the everyday questions of politics and administration.

Grenville had no intention or expectation of getting into a controversy over constitutional principle. He was simply trying to find revenue in a postwar situation when everyone desired lower taxes. In his preoccupation with daily problems of administration and politics, he raised a question which ought never to have been raised. In so doing, he brought on a question which every colonial power faces sooner or later: what does one do with ripe colonies? The question was without precedent. Perhaps it would have been beyond the wit of the greatest statesmen of the day to solve the problem satisfactorily.

Yet in the years which followed, many realized what would have to be done to keep the immediate loyalty of the colonies. Even Grenville, it appears, came eventually to realize that the power of taxation and perhaps even that of legislation would have to be given up, or at least not asserted. But in their preoccupation with factional quarrels, none of the politicians of the day had the wit or statesmanship to lead the Parliament in doing what was necessary to save the empire. Rockingham got the Stamp Act repealed because Pitt demanded it and because Rockingham felt Pitt's support necessary to the continuance of his government. He passed the Declaratory Act because he believed, probably correctly, that the Parliamentary factions would not join in repealing the Stamp Act without it.

Thus the American question became another football in the struggle between the Parliamentary factions and the King, both in the Parliament and in the closet. The concatenation of political circumstance governed action, not consistent, thoughtful policy. Alternately giving provocation and encouragement to colonial rebellion, the King, the ministers, and the Parliament continued their bickerings until the colonies were lost. Some politicians were not lacking in understanding. A few realized what needed to be done. But they were divided on other factional questions, and thus they were never able to unite to enact the measures which they knew could save the empire.

v.

As a politician, George Grenville embodied many qualities which were eminently desirable. In an age marked by its political opportunism if not its corruption, he maintained an unsullied reputation for honesty and integrity. Industrious and energetic, capable of great exertion and attention to detail, he was an able administrator in office, high or low. He was never an orator; he appears to have been long-winded and boring in his speeches, especially to those who disagreed with him. But he was an effective and ready debater. He knew, moreover, how to manage men and issues in the House of Commons, even without using the governmental patronage for what George III called "House of Commons jobs." Had the King given him the support which he later gave to Grenville's nephew, the younger William Pitt, Grenville might have had a much longer and more successful administration.

Lacking that support, Grenville as First Minister was, in many respects, a failure. He was wholly lacking in the intuitive sense of drama which his brother-in-law had. Although he could manage a Parliamentary majority (which Pitt could never do), he could neither dramatize himself so as to inspire wide admiration and devotion nor mobilize the emotions of the nation in his support. Preoccupied with the arts of management and the politics of the hour, he allowed himself to be blinded to the broad implications of measures which he introduced. The struggles with the press and with America were the outgrowth of that preoccupation.

Intrinsic faults Grenville had, but the King never really allowed him to use his good points. George III's growth as a politician during the first decade after his accession is one of the most striking aspects of the political history of the time. By 1765 he had not reached his full stature as a politician, but he was able in many ways to impose his own will in administration over that of his ministers. He knew how to play differences among his ministers to his own advantage and to thwart the ministers when their policies disagreed with his ideas. Finally, George III dismissed Grenville on his own whim at the moment when his management of the Parliament was having its greatest success.

Even in opposition Grenville was ineffective. Here, perhaps, his lack of a sense of the dramatic hurt most keenly. Pitt was able to fire an entire opposition with enthusiasm; Grenville could only draw about him a dwindling band of close friends and associates. He could lead in opposition because of his knowledge and talents in Parliamentary warfare, but he could not inspire fervor or real confidence, either in his own following or in the other leaders of the opposition.

Grenville was at his best in the last role he played in politics, that of elder statesman. Here there were satisfactions and even triumphs. His opposition to Wilkes's expulsion, while it was not successful in preventing expulsion, was a major stroke in introducing the struggle for freedom of election. His bill for the trial of contested elections put an end to one of the most flagrant abuses of the "unreformed" House of Commons. His final stand on America, while it had little effect, at least gave evidence of an understanding which many of his fellows were unable or unwilling to emulate.

Grenville had many abilities, but he had significant limitations which, in the critical time in which he served the Crown, loomed particularly large. As it was, he climbed to the top of Disraeli's "greasy pole," no small accomplishment in itself. But he seemed to display more statesmanship after ambition ceased to goad him so strongly than when he held the position of the King's First Minister.

SELECTED BIBLIOGRAPHY

Manuscripts

The correspondence of George Grenville is scattered about in various repositories in Great Britain and the United States. Grenville was a meticulous man; he apparently kept and dated almost every letter he ever received. Unfortunately a great mass—probably the bulk—of his papers perished in the fire which consumed Wotton Hall in 1820, but still a large number of letters was preserved at the estate at Stowe. The second Duke of Buckingham sold most of these to John Murray, the London publisher, in 1848, and the latter engaged W. J. Smith, the librarian at Stowe, to select a portion of the papers for publication. The selection appeared in four volumes in 1852-1853 as *The Grenville Papers*. Yet much remains of the collection which Smith did not publish.

The main body of the manuscripts purchased by Murray remains in the possession of Sir John Murray, the present publisher and editor. His collection includes the portion of the correspondence published in the second volume and the first half of the third of the *Grenville Papers,* from which many passages were deleted by Smith without markings, and a great number of letters, dating from the late 1720's to the end of Grenville's life, which Smith apparently did not have access to. Some are informative on Grenville's education; some throw light on family matters between the Grenvilles, Pitts, and Lytteltons which had a strong bearing on the political story of the time; a few throw additional light on the passage of the American taxation bills; and many are letters from Thomas Whately and Charles Lloyd which throw new light on Grenville's years out of office, 1765-1770.

Other letters, which comprise the last half of volume three and all of volume four of the *Grenville Papers,* and the whole of Grenville's diary (which is printed in Smith) are deposited in the manuscripts collection of the British Library (cited as Grenville MSS.). The collection is uncatalogued as yet. Other portions of the correspondence purchased by Murray are in the Bodleian Library, Oxford; in the William L. Clements Library, Ann Arbor, Michigan; and in the private possession of Mr. Wilmarth S.

Lewis, Farmington, Connecticut. Another valuable collection of papers of Grenville and Temple is the Stowe collection in the Henry L. Huntington Library, San Marino, California (cited as Stowe MSS.).

With the collections in the British Library Additional Manuscripts other than the Grenville MSS. researchers in the field are familiar. The Newcastle MSS. and the Hardwicke MSS. were of incalculable value throughout the period of Grenville's career. The Liverpool MSS. throw much light on Grenville's financial measures and especially the American taxes. The Wilkes MSS. and the Wilkes Trial Papers contain much valuable information on the struggle with the opposition press and on the Middlesex election, as well as Wilkes's early connections with the Grenville family. The Astle collection, the Buckinghamshire papers, Bute's correspondence, and the collection of papers on proceedings in Parliament helped to fill in the political story.

Of the manuscripts at the Public Record Office, London, the Chatham MSS. and the Treasury Papers were of the greatest value. Chatham's papers illuminate much of the political and personal connection between the Grenvilles and William Pitt in addition to providing much information on Grenville's actions themselves. The Treasury Papers, with interesting sidelights in the Board of Trade Papers, tell much of the story of Grenville's financial difficulties and his taxation of America in 1763-1765. The manuscripts of the first Earl of Egremont, opened to the public in 1947, also provided some valuable information.

The manuscripts of the second Marquis of Rockingham, deposited among the Wentworth-Woodhouse Muniments in the Sheffield City Library, were chiefly useful in tracing the course of the opposition after 1765, but there is also valuable information on the politics and propaganda warfare of the period from Newcastle's resignation in 1762 until Grenville's dismissal.

Printed Materials

An Account of the Proceedings against John Wilkes, Esq., from his Commitment in April, 1763 to his Outlawry. London, 1768.

Adolphus, John. *The History of England from the Accession to the Decease of King George the Third.* 8 vols, London, 1840-1845.

Albemarle, George Thomas Keppel, Earl of. *Memoirs of the Marquis of Rockingham.* 2 vols. London, 1852.

[Almon, John]. *An Examination of the Principles and Boasted Disinterestedness of a late Rt. Hon. Gentleman.* London, 1766.

————. *Biographical, Literary, and Political Anecdotes of the Most Eminent Persons of the Present Age.* 3 vols. London, 1797.

————. *The Correspondence of the Late John Wilkes, with his Friends.* 5 vols. London, 1805.

————. *The History of the Late Minority.* London, 1766.

Alumni Oxonienses, 1715-1886. 3 vols. London, 1888.

Alvord, Clarence Walworth. *The Mississippi Valley in British Politics.* 2 vols. Cleveland, 1917.

Annual Register, The. London, 1758-1770.

Archives of Maryland. Baltimore, 1883 ff.

Auditor, The. 1762-1763.

Austen-Leigh, Richard Arthur, editor. *Eton College Lists, 1678-1790.* Eton, 1907.

Ayling, Stanley E. *The Elder Pitt.* New York, 1976.

————. *George the Third.* New York, 1972.

Bartlett, John R., editor. *Records of the Colony of Rhode Island and Providence Plantations.* 10 vols. Providence, 1856-1865.

Bateson, Mary, editor. *A Narrative of the Changes in the Ministry, 1765-1767, told by the Duke of Newcastle in a Series of Letters to John White, M.P.* (Camden Society Publications, New Series, vol. 59). London, 1898.

Beer, George Louis. *British Colonial Policy, 1754-1765.* New York, 1933.

Bence-Jones, Mark. *Clive of India.* London, 1974.

Bleackley, Horace. *Life of John Wilkes.* London, 1917.

Briton, The. 1762-1763.

Brooke, John. *The Chatham Administration of 1766-68.* London, 1956.

————. *King George III,* London, 1972.

Brown, Peter Douglas. *The Chathamites.* New Have, 1967.

Browning, Reed. *The Duke of Newcastle.* London, 1975.

Burke, Edmund. *The Speeches of the Right Honourable Edmund Burke in the House of Commons and the Westminster Hall.* 4 vols. London, 1816.

Calendar of Home Office Papers, 1760-1765. London, 1878.

Calendar of the Inner Temple Records. 5 vols. London, 1896-1936.

Cavendish, Sir Henry. *Debates of the House of Commons during the Parliament of 1768.* Edited by J. Wright. 2 vols. London, 1841.

Chesterfield, Philip, Earl of. *The Letters of Philip Dormer Stanhope, fourth Earl of Chesterfield.* Edited by Bonamy Dobrée. 6 vols. London, 1932.

Christie, Ian R. *Crisis of Empire: Great Britain and the American Colonies, 1754-83.* New York, 1966.

Climenson, Emily Jane. *Elizabeth Montagu, the Queen of the Bluestockings, Her Correspondence from 1720 to 1760.* New York, 1906.

Cokayne, George Edward. *The Complete Peerage of England, Scotland, Ireland, Great Britain, and the United Kingdom.* 13 vols. London, 1910-1940.

Collections of the Connecticut Historical Society. Hartford, 1860 to date.

Collections of the Massachusetts Historical Society. Boston, 1792 to date.

Collins, Arthur. *Peerage of England: Genealogical, Biographical, and Historical.* 6 vols. London, 1812.

Corbett, Sir Julian. *England in the Seven Years' War.* 2 vols. London, 1918.

[Cotes, Humphrey, and John Almon]. *An Enquiry into the Conduct of a Late Rt. Hon. Commoner.* London, 1766.

Coxe, William. *Memoirs of Horatio, Lord Walpole.* 2 vols. London, 1820.

———. *Memoirs of the Administration of the Right Honourable Henry Pelham.* 2 vols. London, 1829

———. *Memoirs of the Life and Administration of Sir Robert Walpole, Earl of Orford.* 3 vols. London, 1798.

Dickerson, Oliver M. *The Navigation Acts and the American Revolution.* Philadelphia, 1951.

Dickens, Lilian, and Mary Stanton. *An Eighteenth-Century Correspondence.* London, 1910.

Dickinson, H. T. *Bolingbroke.* London, 1970.

———. *Walpole and the Whig Supremacy.* London, 1973.

"Documents on the Debates on the Declaratory Act and the Repeal of the Stamp Act," *American Historical Review,* vol. XVII (1912), pp. 563-586.

Dodington, George Bubb. *The Diary of the Late George Bubb Dodington, Baron of Melcombe Regis, from March 8, 1749, to February 6, 1761.* London, 1785.

Dorn, Walter L. "Frederick the Great and Lord Bute," *The Journal of Modern History,* vol. I (1929), pp. 529-560.

Ellis, Henry. *Original Letters Illustrative of English History.* 4 vols. London, 1827.

Ericson, Fred J. "The Contemporary British Opposition to the Stamp Act," *Papers of the Michigan Academy of Science, Arts, and Letters,* vol. XXIX (1929), pp. 489-505.

Evans, Florence M. Grier. *The Principal Secretary of State; A Survey of the Office from 1558 to 1680.* Manchester, 1923.

Eyck, Erich. *Pitt versus Fox, Father and Son.* London, 1950.

Feiling, Keith Grahame. *The Second Tory Party, 1714-1832.* London, 1938.

Fitzmaurice, Edmond George Petty-Fitzmaurice, first Baron. *Life of William, Earl of Shelburne, afterwards First Marquis of Lansdowne.* 2 vols. London, 1912.

Fitzwilliam, Charles William Wentworth Fitzwilliam, fifth Earl, and Sir Richard Bourke, editors. *Correspondence of the Right Honourable Edmund Burke.* 4 vols. London, 1844.

Foord, Archibald S. *His Majesty's Opposition.* London, 1964.

Fortescue, Sir John. *The Correspondence of King George the Third from 1760 to December, 1783.* 6 vols. London, 1927-1928.

Gazetteer and London Daily Advertiser. 1764-1765.

Gentleman's Magazine. 1731-1770.

Glover, Richard. *Memoirs of A Celebrated Literary and Political Character.* London, 1813.

Grafton, Augustus, third Duke of. *Autobiography and Political Correspondence of Augustus Henry, Third Duke of Grafton, K. G.* Edited by Sir William R. Anson. London, 1898.

Guttmacher, Manfred S. *America's Last King: An Interpretation of the Madness of George III.* New York, 1941.

Guttridge, George Herbert. *English Whiggism and the American Revolution.* Berkeley, 1942.

Harris, George. *Life of Lord Hardwicke.* 3 vols. London, 1847.

Haydn, Joseph. *The Book of Dignities.* London, 1894.

Henderson, Alfred James. *London and the National Government, 1721-1742.* Durham, 1945.

Historical Manuscripts Commission:

Diary of the First Earl of Egmont (Viscount Percival). 3 vols. London, 1920-1923.

The Manuscripts of his Grace the Duke of Rutland, K. G. 4 vols. London, 1888-1904.

The Manuscripts of the Duke of Beaufort, K. G., the Earl of Donoughmore, and Others. London, 1891.

Report on Manuscripts in Various Collections. 8 vols. London, Dublin, and Hereford, 1901-1914.

Report on the Manuscripts of Mrs. Stopford-Sackville of Drayton House, Northamptonshire. 2 vols. London, 1904-1910.

Report on the Manuscripts of the Earl of Denbigh. Part V. London, 1911.

Reports on the Manuscripts of the Earl of Eglinton et. al. London, 1885.

Report on the Manuscripts of the Marquess of Lothian Preserved at Blickling Hall, Norfolk. London, 1905.

Historical Register, The. 25 vols. London, 1714-1738.

Home, James A., editor. *The Letters and Journals of Lady Mary Coke.* 4 vols. Edinburgh, 1889-1896.

Howell, Thomas B. *A Complete Collection of State Trials and Proceedings for High Treason and Other Crimes and Misdemeanors from the Earliest Period to the Present Time.* 34 vols. London, 1809-1828.

Hughes, Edward. "The English Stamp Duties, 1664-1764," *English Historical Review,* vol. CCXXII (1941), pp. 234-264.

Humphreys, Robin Arthur. "Lord Shelburne and the Proclamation of 1763," *English Historical Review,* vol. XLIX (1934), pp. 241-264.

Hunt, William. *The History of England from the Accession of George III to the Close of Pitt's First Administration, 1760-1801.* (Political History of England series, vol. X.) London, 1905.

Ilchester, Giles Stephen Holland Fox-Strangeways, sixth Earl of. *Henry Fox, First Lord Holland, His Family and Relations.* 2 vols. London, 1920.

———. *Letters to Henry Fox.* London, 1915.

Ilchester, Mary Eleanor Anne, Countess of, and Lord Stavordale, editors. *The Life and Letters of Lady Sarah Lennox, 1745-1826.* 2 vols. London, 1902.

Imlach, Gladys M. "Earl Temple and the Ministry of 1765," *English Historical Review,* XXX (1915), pp. 317-321.

Jesse, J. Heneage. *Memoires of Celebrated Etonians.* 2 vols. London, 1875.

The Journals of the House of Commons.

The Journals of the House of Lords.

Jucker, Ninetta S. *The Jenkinson Papers, 1760-1766.* London, 1949.

Junius. *The Letters of Junius.* Edited by C. W. Everett. London, 1927.

Knox, William. *Extra Official State Papers.* 2 vols. London, 1789.

———. *The Present State of the Nation.* London, 1768.

Langford, Peter. *The First Rockingham Administration, 1765-66.* London, 1973.

Laprade, William Thomas. *Public Opinion and Politics in Eighteenth Century England to the Fall of Walpole.* New York, 1936.

———. "The Stamp Act in British Politics," *American Historical Review,* vol. XXXV (1930), pp. 735-757.

Lawson, Philip. *George Grenville, a Political Life.* Oxford, 1984.

———. *The Excise Crisis: Politics and Society in the Age of Walpole.* Oxford, 1975.

Leadham, Israel Saunders. *The History of England from the Accession of Anne to the Death of George II, 1702-1760.* (Political History of England series, vol. XI). London, 1909.

Lecky, William Edward Hartpole. *A History of England in the Eighteenth Century.* Second Edition. 9 vols. New York, 1888.

Lipscomb, George. *The History and Antiquities of the County of Buckingham.* 4 vols. London, 1847.

Lloyd's Evening Post. 1760-1766.

London Chronicle, The. 1760-1770.

London Evening Post. 1762-1765.

London Gazette. 1763.

London Magazine. 1732-1770.

Lucas, Reginald. *Lord North, Second Earl of Guilford, K. G., 1732-1792.* 2 vols. London, 1913.

McCulloh, Henry. *Miscellaneous Representation Relative to Our Concerns in America Submitted (in 1761) to the Earl of Bute.* Edited by William A. Shaw. London, 1905.

Melville, Lewis. *Lady Suffolk and Her Circle.* London, 1924.

Members of Parliament. A return to two orders of the House of Commons, dated 4 May, 1876, and 9 March, 1877. 2 parts. London, 1878-1891.

Monitor, The. 1762-1763.

Morgan, Edmund S. "Colonial Ideas of Parliamentary Power, 1764-1766," *William and Mary Quarterly,* Third Series, vol. V (1948), pp. 311-341.

———. "The postponement of the Stamp Act," *William and Mary Quarterly,* Third Series, vol. VII (1950), pp. 353-392.

——— and Helen M. Morgan. *The Stamp Act Crisis: Prologue to Revolution.* Chapel Hill, 1953.

Namier, Sir Lewis Bernstein. "Charles Garth, Agent for South Carolina," *English Historical Review,* vol. LIV (1939), pp. 632-653.

———. *England in the Age of the American Revolution.* London, 1930.

———. *The Structure of Politics at the Accession of George III.* 2 vols. London, 1927.

——— and John Brooke. *Charles Townshend.* London, 1964.

———, eds. *The History of Parliament: The House of Commons 1754-90.* 3 vols. London, 1964.

Newman, A. N. "Leicester House Politics, 1748-51," *English Historical Review,* October 1962.

Nobbe, George. *The North Briton: a Study in Political Propaganda.* New York, 1939.

Norris, J. *Shelburne and Reform.* London, 1963

The North Briton. 1762-1763.

Oldfield, Thomas Hinton Burley. *The Representative History of Great Britain and Ireland: being a History of the House of Commons and of the Counties, Cities, and Boroughs of the United Kingdom, from the Earliest Period.* 6 vols. London, 1816.

Opposition More Necessary than Ever. London, 1742.

Owen, J. B. *The Rise of the Pelhams.* New York, 1971.

Papers of the New Haven Colony Historical Society. 9 vols. New Haven, 1865-1918.

Parliamentary History of England from the Earliest Period to the Year 1803. 36 vols. London, 1806-1820.

Pennsylvania Archives. Harrisburg, 1852 to date.

Phillimore, Robert Joseph. *Memoirs and Correspondence of George, Lord Lyttelton, from 1734 to 1773.* 2 vols. London, 1845.

Plumb, John H. *Sir Robert Walpole.* 2 vols., London, 1956-60.

Political Register and Impartial Review of New Books, The. 11 vols. London, 1767-1772.

Postgate, Paymond William. *The Devil Wilkes.* New York, 1929.

Public Advertiser, The. 1760-1766.

Public Ledger, The. 1765.

Public Records of the Colony of Connecticut. 15 vols. Hartford, 1850-1890.

Rea, Robert R. "The Impact of Party Journalism in the Political Register," *The Historian,* vol. XVII (1954), pp. 1-17.

Really, Charles Bechdolt. *The Early Opposition to Sir Robert Walpole.* Philadelphia, 1931.

Riker, Thad W. *Henry Fox, First Lord Holland.* 2 vols. Oxford, 1911.

Ritcheson, Charles R. *British Polticis and the American Revolution.* Norman, Oklahoma, 1954.

———. "The Preparation of the Stamp Act," *William and Mary Quarterly,* Third Series, vol. X (1953), pp. 543-559.

Robertson, John Mackinnon. *Bolingbroke and Walpole,* New York, 1919.

Rosebery, Archibald Philip Primrose, fifth Earl of. *Lord Chatham: His Early Life and Connections.* New York, 1910.

Rudé, George F. E. *Wilkes and Liberty.* London, 1963.

Russell, Lord John, editor. *Correspondence of John, Fourth Duke of Bedford.* 3 vols. London, 1842-1846.

St. James's Chronicle. 1760-1766.

The Scots Magazine. 1739-1766.

Sedgwick, Romney, editor. *Letters from George III to Lord Bute, 1756-1766.* London, 1939.

Sellers, Charles G., Jr. "Private Profits and British Colonial Policy: The Speculations of Henry McCulloh," *William and Mary Quarterly,* Third Series, vol. VIII (1951), pp. 535-551.

Smith, William James, editor. *The Grenville Papers, being the Correspondence of Richard Grenville Earl Temple, K. G., and the Right Hon. George Grenville, their Friends and Contemporaries.* 4 vols. London, 1852-1853.

Stanhope, Philip Henry Stanhope, fifth Earl. *History of England from the Peace of Utrecht to the Peace of Versailles, 1713-1783.* 7 vols. London, 1853.

Stephen, Sir Leslie, and Sir Sidney Lee, editors. *Dictionary of National Biography.* London, 1917 to date.

Stuart-Wortley, Emmeline Charlotte Elizabeth. *A Prime Minister and his Son.* London, 1925.

Sutherland, Lucy Stuart. "Edmund Burke and the First Rockingham Ministry," *English Historical Review,* vol. XLVII (1932), pp. 46-72.

———. *The East India Company in Eighteenth-Century Politics.* Oxford, 1952.

Taylor, William Stanhope, and John Henry Pringle, editors. *Correspondence of William Pitt, Earl of Chatham.* 4 vols. London, 1838-1840.

Temperley, Harold W. V. "The Causes of the War of Jenkins' Ear, 1739," *Transactions of the Royal Historical Society,* Third Series, vol. III (1909), pp. 197-236.

Thomas, Peter D. G. *The House of Commons in the Eighteenth Century.* London, 1973.

———. *British Politics and the Stamp Act Crisis.* Oxford, 1975.

Tomlinson, John, ed. *Additional Grenville Papers, 1763-1765.* Manchester, 1962.

Torrens, William M. *History of Cabinets from the Union with Scotland to the Acquisition of Canada and Bengal.* 2 vols. London, 1894.

Treloar, William Purdie. *Wilkes and the City.* London, 1917.

Tunstall, Brian. *William Pitt, Earl of Chatham.* London, 1938.

Victoria History of the County of Buckingham, The. 4 vols. London, 1927.

Waldegrave, James Waldegrave, first Earl. *Memoirs from 1754 to 1758.* London, 1821.

Walpole, Horace. *The Letters of Horace Walpole, Fourth Earl of Orford.* Edited by Mrs. Paget Toynbee. 16 vols. London, 1903-1905.

———. *Memoirs of the Last Ten Years of the Reign of George the Second.* 2 vols. London, 1822.

———. *Memoirs of the Reign of King George the Third.* 4 vols. London, 1844.

Watson, John Steven. *The Reign of George III.* Oxford, 1960.

Westminster Journal and London Political Miscellany. 1762-1765.

[Whately, Thomas]. *The Regulations Lately Made Concerning the Colonies, and the Taxes Imposed Upon Them Considered.* London, 1765.

Wiggin, Louis M. *The Faction of Cousins: a Political Account of the Grenvilles, 1733-1763.* New Haven, 1958.

Wilkes, John, and Charles Churchill. *The North Briton.* 4 vols. London, 1772.

Williams, Basil. *Carteret and Newcastle: A Contrast in Contemporaries.* Cambridge, 1943.

———. *The Life of William Pitt, Earl of Chatham.* 2 vols. London, 1914.

———. *The Whig Supremacy, 1714-1760.* (Oxford History of England series.) Oxford, 1939.

Winstanley, Denys Arthur. "George III and His First Cabinet," *English Historical Review,* vol. XVII (1902), pp. 678-691.

———. *Lord Chatham and the Whig Opposition.* Cambridge, 1912.

———. *Personal and Party Government; A Chapter in the Political History of the Early Reign of George III, 1760-1766.* Cambridge, 1910.

Wyndham, Maud, editor. *Chronicles of the Eighteenth Century.* 2 vols. London, 1924.

Yorke, Philip Chesney. *The Life and Correspondence of Philip Yorke, Earl of Hardwicke, Lord High Chancellor of Great Britain.* 3 vols. Cambridge, 1913.

INDEX

References to George Grenville in the sub-entries are abbreviated "GG."